Praise for
GOLDEN YEARS

"Are you now, or will you someday be, retirement age? Then treat yourself to *Golden Years*. Learned and lively, it's a fascinating story filled with surprises about the varied ways Americans have experienced—and altered—the meaning of aging over the last century."

—Nancy MacLean, author of *Democracy in Chains*

"As America ages, the numbers of us who need attentive care will only grow. Overstretched family members and severely undervalued care workers shoulder this immense responsibility with little to no public support. In *Golden Years*, James Chappel expertly uncovers the historical roots of this crisis of care while also offering a powerful vision for aging that is more secure and dignified for all."

—Ai-jen Poo, president, National Domestic Workers Alliance

"Today, there are more Americans aged sixty and older than under age eighteen. What kind of future do they face? Chappel's balanced discussion of the advances we've made and the ones we failed to make is a must-read for any age."

—Stephanie Coontz, author of *The Way We Never Were*

"Aging in America is often depicted as a looming disaster, with terms like 'silver tsunami' and dire warnings from officials that we must work longer and harder to balance budgets. *Golden Years* challenges us to look at history and see that aging doesn't have to be this way. Aging is a collective and social experience, and our aging needs require social solutions: not-for-profit, safe, and regulated nursing homes; well-paid home health aides; and decent pensions and housing. These goals are within our nation's reach."

—Teresa Ghilarducci, author of *Work, Retire, Repeat*

"Who deserves to retire, and under what conditions? What should this retirement require of others? Going beyond cliches about Social Security as the 'third rail of American politics,' Florida, and nursing homes, *Golden Years* illuminates how the struggle to define old age has proven central to the meaning of citizenship and inclusion in America, touching every aspect of our common life."

—Gabriel Winant, author of *The Next Shift*

GOLDEN YEARS

Also by James Chappel

*Catholic Modern: The Challenge of Totalitarianism
and the Remaking of the Church*

GOLDEN YEARS

YEARS

How **AMERICANS INVENTED** *and* **REINVENTED OLD AGE**

JAMES CHAPPEL

BASIC BOOKS
New York

Basic Books
Hachette Book Group
1290 Avenue of the Americas, New York, NY 10104
www.basicbooks.com

Printed in the United States of America

First Edition: November 2024

Published by Basic Books, an imprint of Hachette Book Group, Inc. The Basic Books name and logo is a registered trademark of the Hachette Book Group.

The Hachette Speakers Bureau provides a wide range of authors for speaking events. To find out more, go to hachettespeakersbureau.com or email HachetteSpeakers@hbgusa.com.

Basic books may be purchased in bulk for business, educational, or promotional use. For more information, please contact your local bookseller or the Hachette Book Group Special Markets Department at special.markets@hbgusa.com.

The publisher is not responsible for websites (or their content) that are not owned by the publisher.

Print book interior design by Bart Dawson.

Library of Congress Cataloging-in-Publication Data
Names: Chappel, James, 1983– author.
Title: Golden years : how Americans invented and reinvented old age / James Chappel.
Description: First edition. | New York, NY : Basic Books, [2024] | Includes bibliographical references and index. |
Identifiers: LCCN 2024007956 | ISBN 9781541619524 (hardcover) | ISBN 9781541619517 (ebook)
Subjects: LCSH: Old age—United States. | Retirement—United States. | Aging—Social aspects—United States. | Older people—United States—Social conditions.
Classification: LCC HQ1064.U5 C427 2024 | DDC 305.26—dc23/eng/20240327
LC record available at https://lccn.loc.gov/2024007956

ISBNs: 9781541619524 (hardcover), 9781541619517 (ebook)

LSC-C

Printing 1, 2024

CONTENTS

A CAROUSEL OF PROGRESS

When I was a kid, I frequently found myself at Walt Disney's Magic Kingdom, one of many perils of growing up in Central Florida. For whatever reason, I always insisted on going to an attraction at Tomorrowland called the Carousel of Progress. My family and I would file into a dark auditorium, taking our seats before a stage featuring an animatronic family inside their house. Eventually, the family creaked to life. The first act was set around 1900, and the robotic patriarch crowed about all the technological wonders of the age. Then the exhibit rotated, and the same family appeared again, a few decades later, enthusing about a new set of innovations. This happened four or five times, until the action ended in a tech-utopian future.

In retrospect, it's curious that I was so infatuated with this so-called ride, the tedium of which can be confirmed on YouTube. Like so much at Disney World, its pleasures were less corporeal than emotional. It assured us that in the future, as in the past, the happy family would be sitting around the den, chuckling and singing and celebrating

Christmas. The Carousel was, as its name implied, circular, and the real point it made was that nothing fundamental would change at all. This was comforting to a child around 1990 because so many visions of the future just then were jarring and unsettling. I certainly didn't want to be burned up because of holes in the ozone layer or dissolved by acid rain. I wanted to imagine a future in which I'd live in a home very much like my own, but with more advanced technology.

While there were children in the Carousel's imagined future, I was more interested in the older people on display. After all, in the future I would be old. This explains, I think, the canny decision by the designers of the Carousel to include older people in every stage of the ride: it allowed viewers to see how they as individuals would experience the glittering future to come. The grandparents were always present, and always included, and always enjoying the fruits of progress (it's Grandma, in the last scene, who has strapped on the virtual reality goggles). This was the most deeply comforting part of a deeply comforting ride. In the American future to come, the viewer was told, there will be a place for you, however old you might be. You are not going to age out of the great American experiment.

While I didn't know it at the time, the ride was itself a historical relic. It opened in 1964, mere months before the passage of Medicare. It belonged to an era when newly dubbed "senior citizens" were claiming their part in the national project, really for the first time. The ride was just one of many, infinitely many, places where a coherent and attractive vision of "old age" was created in the middle decades of the twentieth century. Beginning with the 1935 passage of the Social Security Act, Americans were sold an *idea* of old age: what it was, and what it was for. The core idea was simple. Older people, while distinct in capacities and purpose from younger ones, had a meaningful place in the world. They ought to be valued and respected, and they deserved security and dignity even if they were no longer participating in the waged labor force. Older people, in short, belonged on the Carousel.

This idea was overwhelmingly successful. Older Americans organized, found allies, and became perhaps the most powerful interest group in twentieth-century America. Spending on the elderly since the 1940s has become a mammoth portion of the federal budget. All told, about a third of federal dollars are spent on income security and health care for older citizens. Those programs aren't perfect, but their effect has been remarkable nonetheless. Older Americans today are far more economically secure than they were a century ago. Poverty rates for the elderly have plummeted. They are healthier too. While it's true that life expectancy for some groups is trending downward, this is because of increased mortality in the young and middle-aged. Once Americans make it to age sixty-five, they are likely to have fifteen or twenty good years left. After all, older Americans are the only ones with guaranteed, government-sponsored health care. All of this cashes out into the most important currency: happiness. Polls statistically show that older Americans report higher senses of subjective well-being than younger ones.[1]

This is a book about how the dream of the "golden years," against the odds, became a reality for millions of Americans. It's about where the ideology of the Carousel came from, and how it was put into practice. But it's also a book about the limitations of the Carousel and the world that made it. For many people, the promised security remained a theme-park fantasy. The ride tells the story of American history from the perspective of a white, middle-class family with a couple of kids and two able-bodied grandparents. Many older people, and probably a majority, don't fit this mold. Older women living alone are especially prone to poverty and isolation (when the ride appeared, about a quarter of older women lived alone, and the number has gone up since). People of color have had limited access to Social Security, private pensions, and the various other mechanisms that the white middle classes used to fund their dignified retirements. Likewise, Social Security and Medicare were designed to pay for the lives of healthy people with short-term hospital needs, not people with chronic disabilities, many of whom required expensive long-term care. Millions of families today are bankrupting themselves, emotionally and financially, in their attempts to navigate the long-term-care "system," if that word is even appropriate. The aging of the American population, and especially the explosion in the population of those age eighty-plus, necessitates vast amounts of care labor. That labor has fallen through the cracks and is mainly done by women who are either unpaid, as family members, or poorly paid, as home health aides or nursing home employees. "Other countries have social safety nets," the sociologist Jessica Calarco has pointed out. "The U.S. has women."[2]

This book, then, is about the dream represented by the Carousel, and the limits of that dream. And it's a book, too, about the fate of that dream. Ironically for a ride in Tomorrowland, the Carousel was already out-of-date when I visited. It was one of the oldest exhibits in the park, and the family members' jerky movements were low tech when compared with the other marvels of Magic Kingdom. The mid-century ideology of the senior citizen was, by century's end, slipping away, and the future for older Americans was not looking as bright. Old age eventually came to seem less like a marker of our progress and more like a personal and national burden. Social Security was in constant threat of being cut, and the retirement age was raised. The headlines about Medicare were about fraud and austerity, not about improved health outcomes. With the birth of IRAs and 401(k)s, retirement security became an individual responsibility, rather than one that individuals shared with their employers and the government. This is the world in which we still live. The dream of the golden years seems to be slipping away as the optimism of the Carousel has given way to a generalized anxiety about insufficient retirement savings and unaffordable housing.

One can imagine a world in which, after 1964, the American discussion of old age became more diverse and more inclusive. That isn't quite what happened; instead, it started to be ignored. From the 1920s to the 1970s, old age was a perennial issue in national politics. Since then, no major legislation has been passed, beyond some insufficient reforms to the preexisting system. The crisis in long-term care, the mounting cost of health care, labor protections for caregivers in one of the fastest-growing segments of the economy: all of these are, by any measure, among the most pressing issues facing the body politic. And yet, in election cycle after election cycle, they are neglected. The status of Social Security is emblematic. It is widely known that the system needs to be reformed, and fast. If nothing is done, somewhere around 2033 the system will have used all its reserve funds. This would not mean an implosion of the program, but it would mean steep cuts in benefits (about 25 percent), a catastrophic outcome for the millions of Americans who rely on Social Security to stay out of poverty. It is certainly possible to fix. Doing so would not even be all that difficult, and the bills have already been written. The longer we wait, the more challenging the task will be. And yet, year after year nothing is done.[3]

The myth of the powerful old-age lobby obscures the fact that population aging is not discussed nearly enough in our politics. Two of the greatest disasters to befall twenty-first-century America were Hurricane Katrina and COVID-19. Each of them created important and meaningful conversations about climate change, infrastructure, racial equity, and more. What few discussed was that each of them was an issue primarily for older people. A full 70 percent of those who died in Katrina were over the age of seventy. Likewise, mortality rates for older Americans were so much higher during the coronavirus pandemic that some deemed it a genocide for the elderly. More than half of those killed by COVID-19 in the first three years of the pandemic were over seventy-five; three-quarters were over sixty-five. There were important conversations to be had about demographic aging as it relates to natural disasters and pandemic preparedness, two issues that have defined the first quarter of the twenty-first century and will almost certainly define the rest of it too. Those conversations did not happen.[4]

This book is an attempt to understand how we got here and where we might go. We will try to understand why a particular vision of old age was constructed in the twentieth century, and why it fell apart, and what might come to replace it. The book is not exactly entering a crowded field. There are hundreds of books about the history of childhood and since 2008 an entire journal dedicated to the field. The history of aging, in contrast, has always been a niche concern, despite the fact that there are nearly as many older people in America (people over sixty-five) as young ones (under eighteen). You could easily fit all the books ever written on the subject onto one bookshelf. And even among those, few have attempted, as this book does, to take the story of American aging from the advent of Social Security to the near present.

While I will always include information on changing demographic and social realities, my main interest is in evolving *ideas* about old age, as produced by gerontologists and policymakers and screenwriters. I want to understand the stories we are told about old age, which shape the stories we are able to tell ourselves—about our own aging, and that of our loved ones, and that of our society. Old age is well suited for such an approach. Aging is itself a temporal process, and old age is always something we are racing toward, as individuals and as a nation. Discussions of old age, as with the Carousel, tend to focus on the future—on the imagined world down the line, when we will ourselves be old or older, or when an imagined demographic wave of Americans gets old and bankrupts the government. And so those discussions, however full of facts and figures they might be, are inevitably infused with fears, myths, and dreams.

As a shorthand, this book will often refer to the "old-age movement" as its topic of study. That movement was never unified, and the term has never referred to just one organization. I mean that phrase, instead, to refer to the constellation of artists, intellectuals, policymakers, caregivers, and activists who have struggled to define old age— who have, in other words, tried to answer the many questions posed by America's aging population. Old age in modern America was not something worked out independently by millions of older people. It was a political, social, and cultural project, made and remade by people in specific institutional and political contexts.

Many stewards of that project are well-known: American presidents, famous scientists, and the like. Their stories are important, but they aren't enough. Most people, when sorting out their expectations for old age, didn't read long books about it or listen to politicians' speeches. Perhaps they heard a sermon on the radio, or maybe they turned on *The Golden Girls*, a popular 1980s TV show about older women, while they ate dinner. Maybe they idly paged through an issue of *Modern Maturity*, the magazine put out by the AARP (now called *AARP: The Magazine*, and for decades the most widely circulating periodical in the country). In this book, I'll try to take these kinds of cultural products just as seriously as I do the more austere policy and medical journals. Because in fact they are all related to one another. Policymakers, just like the rest of us, are impacted by the cultural expectations they imbibe from the world around them. Moreover, those who produce pop culture, whether consciously or not, are responding to the policy and medical environments of their time.

Crucial as they are, those sources are not enough. A book that brought together policymakers and popular culture would still leave out the experiences and labor of millions of people. It would be a book about Hollywood, the Mayo Clinic, and Washington, DC, and it would be a book largely about white men (even *The Golden Girls* was mainly written by men). The inclusion of women is especially crucial for our story because women make up the majority of older people. There are roughly 125 women over age sixty-five for every 100 men, and the imbalance increases in the older age bracket (almost two-thirds of Americans over eighty-five are women). And moreover, women make up the majority of people of all ages who do the labor of caring for older people, whether as nurses, home health aides, or unpaid family members. According to one 2018 study, a full 80 percent of workers in the senior care industry are women; moreover, about three-quarters of unpaid, informal caregivers are women too. In this book, we'll spend time with some of these women who have labored behind closed doors. And we'll spend time with the women who started the first senior centers, set up the first home health care programs, created Meals on Wheels, and allowed millions to die with dignity in hospice.[5]

The story of American aging can only be told by including people of color, who were marginalized in the mainstream discussion of twentieth-century aging (though they will not be in this book). To be sure, for much of that period the vast proportion of the older population *was* white, both because Black Americans died so young and because the Hispanic and Asian immigrants ushered in by the Immigration and Nationality Act of 1965 were not yet old. But both of those factors are starting to change as Black life expectancy climbs and as the population of nonwhite immigrants ages. As of 2020, about a quarter of the sixty-five-plus population was a racial or ethnic minority, and that number is only going to increase. In this book, we will especially explore activism by older and formerly enslaved people, along with gerontologists and activists in the 1970s who tried to bring the energy and insights of Black Power into this sphere.[6]

Women of color, at the intersection of these categories, are crucial to the story of aging in America. Time and again in this book, they will emerge as sharp critics of the American age regime, and also as prophets of a better one. They played this role precisely because they were disenfranchised by the system that, for other communities, worked so well. Black women are more than twice as likely as white women to live in poverty. And far more than white women, they have to confront challenges of gentrification, food insecurity, and family insecurity brought on by mass incarceration. Moreover, they are disproportionately affected by labor issues in the caring professions. Black women make up about 7 percent of the US labor force, but they constitute 30 percent of the home health care field.[7]

The making of American old age was a collective project. As with any collective project, some people had more power than others, and many were excluded altogether. But without studying as many of the actors as possible, we can't fully understand how that project worked, who was excluded and why, and how the project might be extended in our own time.

The book, divided into three parts, is organized around the shifting vocabulary that has been used to describe the portion of the population that is above sixty-five (or thereabouts; as we'll see, the age barrier has shifted over time). Part I (Chapters 1 and 2) covers the period from 1900 to 1940, when the sixty-five-plus population was known as "the aged." In these years, for the first time, older Americans began to organize and to press for aid in the form of state-delivered pensions. The questions, though, were who would receive them and how they would be paid for. Some thought that the formerly enslaved should be prioritized, and that pensions should be a form of reparations. Others thought that pensions should go to everyone over sixty, and that they should be equal for all, regardless of race or gender or previous occupation. Both of those models were championed by large social movements, and each sought to use old-age policy to radically remake the American economy. The model that triumphed as Social Security took a different approach. It provided pensions to workers in specific waged sectors of the American economy: workers who were mainly men and mainly white. Benefits payments would not be equal for all but would be based on the size of the recipient's contributions into the system. Old-age pensions would therefore reproduce, rather than challenge, the hierarchies of race and gender that governed the labor market itself. The Social Security program is one of the great wonders of the American state, and it is our greatest poverty-reduction program. Millions of older Americans would be in poverty without it. All the same, its triumph required the suppression of more progressive and egalitarian visions of what American aging might be.

Part II (Chapters 3–6) covers the middle decades of the century, when the sixty-five-plus population, tired of the disparaging term "the aged," preferred to be known as "senior citizens." Chapter 3 shows that senior citizens, far more than before, were living by themselves, apart from their children, and were retiring from their jobs. Together with allies in the trade union movement and both political parties, they organized to push for new programs to make that kind of independent, retired life possible. The greatest accomplishment of this period was Medicare, but it was far from alone. By the 1970s, as Chapter 4 explores, "retirement" emerged as a genuine phase of life, with its own infrastructure that in many ways mirrored the schools and childcare centers that were increasingly structuring the lives of the youth. Nearly every institution we associate with contemporary aging belongs to this period: most prominently, retirement communities, senior centers, and nursing homes.

At the same time, the old-age movement was backing itself into a corner. As American political life in general became more polyphonic and boisterous, the old-age movement continued to focus on the same population of able-bodied white couples. Older people with disabilities were left to fend for themselves, as Medicare did almost nothing for them. Older people of color, who had their own distinct needs, labored unsuccessfully to create a more diverse old-age movement. Chapter 5 focuses on a network of Black gerontologists and activists, allied with nursing home administrators and groups of the elderly poor, who tried to pioneer an antiracist form of aging. They sought more than just "color-blind" applications of Medicare and Social Security; those programs were, by the 1970s, reasonably good on that score. They sought instead new kinds of policies and institutions that would recognize the specific realities and challenges confronting older Black people, who had faced a lifetime of discrimination and disenfranchisement. One of the leaders of this movement was a Black sociologist named Jacquelyne Jackson. Together with allies at the National Caucus on the Black Aged, she organized protests, made documentaries, lobbied Congress, and published reams of scholarly research. For all their efforts, they were ignored, and by the end of the 1970s their movement had run out of steam, at least for the time being.

That failure represented a deeper reluctance in the old-age movement to adapt to the changing political climate of the 1970s, as Chapter 6 shows. The movement was not diversifying, and it was dependent on institutions, like trade unions and the Democratic Party, that were about to enter a crisis themselves. When the economic and political challenges of the 1970s hit, the old-age movement was damaged. Americans became ever more distrustful of the Social Security system. Nursing homes and Medicare, once the vanguard of a new aging future, came to seem instead like cesspools of fraud, waste, and even abuse. Politicians and activists on both the Left and the Right failed to develop coherent and legislatively actionable programs for what aging could be in a deindustrializing, politically polarized America.

When the policy environment that had created the "senior citizen" came under strain, the term itself fell into disuse. It has been in free fall since the 1970s and has been replaced by "older people" and its variants, like "older adults" and "older Americans" (the terms I use in this book, which is itself a product of its time). That moniker is more ambiguous, as befits a new era when older people have been intent to prove that they are, in essence, just like younger ones. For decades, the central idea had been that "the aged" or "senior citizens" were a distinct identity group with distinct needs, and that those needs should be met by the state. The term "older people" does not do that work. It is hard to advocate for the rights and needs of older people; it is not even clear who they are. It certainly did not designate the sixty-five-plus population, and in practice it was used to refer to anyone over fifty-five, or even fifty.

In Part III (Chapters 7–10), the book no longer chronicles an organized old-age movement seeking to influence state policy, but a loosely organized interest group that is working, with the help of private industry, to improve its quality of life and to combat negative stereotypes about older people. Chapter 7 discusses the political life of the older person, represented above all by the AARP. Founded in 1958, this organization was, in the first two decades of its existence, one aging group among many. After the 1970s it skyrocketed in influence and power. If previous old-age movements had advocated for more aggressive policies, the AARP was focused overwhelmingly on the battle against ageism, a new term and concept that denoted cultural and economic discrimination against the elderly. The AARP distanced itself in every way possible from the idea that the sixty-five-plus population was a specific group with specific needs. It kept moving the age of eligibility downward, until eventually anyone over fifty could qualify for full membership. It also removed the very idea of retirement from its name. "AARP" long stood for "American Association of Retired People" but is now known simply as AARP—an acronym that stands for nothing.

The AARP was more devoted to selling seniors products from the private sector than it was to pressuring the government into action. Older people in the 1980s were asked to be entrepreneurial and to provide from their own initiative what the government would not or could not. Chapters 8 through 10 use *The Golden Girls*, a smash-hit sitcom, to explore this new, entrepreneurial reality. Chapter 8 focuses on women, sexuality, and health. The television show is obsessed with these themes: the protagonists are sexually active and health conscious (they go on diets, take aerobics classes, and so on). Although Medicare still existed in the eighties, of course, the emphasis of the show, and of the culture in general, was on health as an individual responsibility rather than as a public good. Chapter 9 traces this same sensibility into the world of retirement financing. Just as the TV show's characters were responsible for their own health, they were responsible for their own finances. Social Security was supposed to provide for retirement security, but in the 1980s many people didn't trust that they would ever see it. IRAs, 401(k)s, and financial planners entered the scene, as did the whole new mantra of "retirement savings" that we know so well today.

The emphasis in this period was on increasing freedom and opportunity for older people who could afford to take advantage of them. Public policy hardly changed at all. Its limitations and exclusions were not addressed, especially when it came to people with long-term disabilities, a group that was beginning to be called the "frail." Thanks to public health interventions and antismoking campaigns in the 1960s and 1970s, the 1980s saw a spike in the number of eighty-plus individuals, and therefore a spike in the number of people in need of long-term care. As we will see in Chapter 10, this created a genuine crisis of care, one that threatened to bankrupt millions of American families. Many activists had ideas for how that crisis might be resolved: through an alliance of older people and caregivers to create a stable and well-funded system of long-term care that would work for seniors and those who cared for them. Nothing of the sort happened. In practice, the crisis of care was handled in more fragmented ways. For some, this involved assisted-living facilities and home health aides, paid for out of pocket. For most, though, it involved some combination of Medicaid-funded nursing care and unpaid labor by family members—normally, by female relatives.

Older people have accrued new freedoms in the past few decades, to be sure, but there is a darker side to that story too. When it comes to health care expenses, retirement financing, housing costs, and especially long-term care, many older Americans are in trouble, and if present trends continue, the next generation of older Americans will have it even worse. In part, this is because of recent shifts in the US economy, and in the American state's increasing reluctance to fulfill basic tasks of social welfare. But in part, too, it can be explained by the long history of the old-age movement. That movement, while benefitting many millions of seniors of every skin color and gender and sexuality, had always been premised first and foremost on the needs of one class of people: middle-class, married, white couples. The movement had succeeded by creating a bubble of protection around that specific group. Those who fell outside it, perhaps because they had disabilities or were divorced or widowed or queer, benefited from the movement's success, but they never had access to true security. In an ideal world, the bubble of protection would have been expanded in the past fifty years, and many have tried to make it do so. While they have had some success, the tendency has been instead to shrink it. As wages continue to stagnate and Social Security teeters toward crisis, the economic precarity of older Americans is becoming ever more acute, engulfing even those families that found representation on the Carousel.

I don't end the book there, though, because all in all this story is not a tragedy. The situation in the early twenty-first century is, for most older people, immeasurably better than it was a century ago. This is true for men and women, for white people and people of color, for able-bodied people and those with disabilities. Every chapter of this book features men and women who worked themselves to the bone to improve the lives of older Americans, and who were, in the main, successful. And this story is not a tragedy because it's not over yet. As we'll see in the book's Conclusion, activists and politicians are rising to the challenge of our new era, striving to imagine a new form of old age that is appropriate for the twenty-first century: one that is at home with more diversity, more disability, and less carbon.

These issues are important—incalculably so. The number of older people is going to keep growing for the appreciable future; soon there will be more Americans over sixty-five than under eighteen. The United States, the prototypical nation of striving youth, is now a nation of older people. What should that new nation look like? It is certainly possible that we will as a society continue to blunder along as we have done for the past few decades, relying on the heroic labor of unpaid and underpaid people, working with creaky government systems that are in desperate need of reform. This situation would be fine for many older people, maybe even most of them, but for millions of others—people with disabilities, the rural poor, and many more—it would very much *not* be fine.[8]

That, I propose, is not good enough. We all, as Americans and as human beings, deserve a dignified old age. My own aging, however comfortable, is not truly dignified if it is not shared. To return to where we started: one of the pernicious elements of the Carousel of Progress is that it only showed one family. Aging, it suggests, is something that we will deal with at the domestic level, behind closed doors and with curtains drawn. It is indisputably true that there is something private about aging. What could be more intimate? At the same time, though, every part of the aging process—how many years we have, what we think we should do with them, what we have the *capacity* to do with them—is shaped by history. That's another way of saying that it's shaped by our common world. As individuals, and as a nation, we are all getting older. We will be making decisions together about how to shape the gray future. And in doing so, it might help to understand a good deal more about the gray past.

PART I

THE AGED

(1900–1940)

CHAPTER 1

WHO GETS TO GET OLD?

O n a hot Sunday morning in 1922, a seventy-seven-year-old man with a long, gray mustache stepped out of his hotel in Lawrence, Kansas. He was troubled. A few decades earlier he had sold his considerable property, abandoned his wife and children, and embarked on a journey across the country. He seems to have had serious alcohol problems, and his tattered suitcase was full of medicines and apocalyptic religious tracts he had picked up along the way. He seemed like a man who had spent most of his life unwilling to make commitments. On this morning, at least, he was in a different mood. Wearing his best suit, he walked to a nearby park and drank a glass full of strychnine. His body was discovered by a gardener later that day.

The story of Hugh Boyle is about many things: it is about land, family, religion, and substance abuse. This is how it was reported in the newspaper of the tiny town of Lawrence. And yet it is not how most Americans learned the story. A few weeks later, a notice appeared in the newsletter of the Fraternal Order of Eagles, one of the biggest such orders in the country. For hundreds of thousands of readers, Boyle's story was much simpler. Excising the more sordid and human elements, the article described a man who had succumbed to poverty and who "needed an old-age pension."[1]

A pension would not have saved Boyle. He had burned through more than $60,000, a fortune in those days. And yet by the early 1920s this seemed to many people the obvious way to interpret his story. Americans were warming to a new theory of industrial society: one in which the elderly were great victims, forced into poverty by the machine age; one in which they were condemned to penury and, for some, eventually suicide if the state did not step in with a pension. This theory, while historically dubious, proved to be enormously powerful, and it helped to build support for the Social Security Act of 1935. After all, such a massive state intervention in a particular community is only possible if policymakers and voters believe that the targeted group is in some way *worthy*—that is, if it has been harmed for reasons beyond its own control.

Boyle is not, himself, of great historical importance. We are beginning with him, though, because his particular tragedy was turned into a widely circulated story about aging in America. Those stories, which impact both social policy and our own experience of our lives, are the true subject of this book. In the early decades of the twentieth century, and really for the first time, Americans of all stripes were thinking about older people, and how they were suffering, and how they might be helped. In the nineteenth century, there had been very little reflection on older people as a specific group with specific needs, and there were no advocacy groups for older people as such. In the early twentieth century, this began to change as older people started to organize and to find advocates for the first time. They did so under the banner of "the aged" or sometimes "the aged and infirm." This term was purposely stigmatizing. Indeed, the whole point was to show that the sixty-five-plus population, as a group, needed help. Hugh Boyle certainly did.[2]

But who *were* the aged? Which kinds of older people deserved attention, study, and eventually money? The Fraternal Order of Eagles had an answer. A social organization with hundreds of thousands of members, including several US presidents, it was the group that put old-age poverty, and old-age pensions, onto the political map. In the view of its members, the state should offer pensions to impoverished men who could not find stable employment in an industrial economy. Those men were suffering because the heartless, modern factories had no place for older people, who were thrown onto the scrap heap. They were, in other words, innocent. That vision put white men like Boyle at the center. It presumed that women would be helped through their husbands' pensions, and it didn't consider nonwhite older people at all (the Eagles were, after all, an all-male, whites-only organization).

The Eagles' efforts were right at home in the Progressive Era. Reformers and politicians across the country were hard at work addressing the injustices of industrial society, passing laws against child labor and in favor of workplace safety and sanitation. For the most part, though, they did so without questioning the hierarchies of race and gender that structured America at the time. This was, of course, the world of Jim Crow legislation too. The Eagles' campaign bore some similarities to child welfare campaigns of the same era. Those efforts, in order to build support and sympathy, had generated an image of the innocent, virtuous child in need of protection by the state. Inevitably, that child was white, and white children were granted a kind of purity and innocence that never accrued to Black ones, who were believed to be, in essence, young adults, with all the vice and culpability that implied. The deserving aged person, like the deserving child, was primarily depicted and understood by political elites as white and virtuous—a canny political move to be sure, but one that drew attention to certain populations and problems over others.[3]

All the same, this was never the only idea in play. It was the dominant understanding for the people who mattered in crafting old-age policy—the sociologists, the experts, the politicians—but it always competed with different, more diverse accounts of who the American aged were and what they deserved. Sometimes those divergent accounts were ignored, and sometimes they were suppressed. The Fraternal Order of Eagles was not actually the first social movement to advocate for the aged. The order's predecessor was the less famous Ex-Slave Mutual Relief, Bounty, and Pension Association, led by a widowed, formerly enslaved woman named Callie House. (Henceforth I will refer to it simply as the Ex-Slave Pension Association.) Founded in 1896, it called for old-age pensions long before the Eagles did. Its members were indifferent, though, to the plight of men like Boyle, who from their perspective were far from the neediest of the aged. Their focus was squarely on the formerly enslaved, who by that time were of course elderly. They reasoned that since they had performed so much uncompensated labor and had entered such a discriminatory labor market after emancipation, formerly enslaved people surely deserved compensation from the state. Old-age policy should be, therefore, a form of reparations.

For both the Eagles and the Ex-Slave Pension Association, old-age pensions were to be available to those who had labored in the past. Also at stake in this confrontation, then, was what sorts of labor would count as true labor from the perspective of the state. The Eagles focused on industrial, waged labor: the kind that wore out the bodies of white male workers, forcing them into poverty. They did include agricultural labor, although they didn't talk about it much, but many other kinds were implicitly excluded—specifically, almost every kind of work done by women. Housework and domestic work, for instance, were not understood by the Eagles to be genuine labor. The Ex-Slave Pension Association, by contrast, was led by a washerwoman. The movement was capacious in its understanding of labor, and designed its legislation in a way that would have helped women like her. After all, they were seeking remuneration for the labor of the formerly enslaved, the paradigmatic form of unpaid labor.[4]

Neither of these movements was successful in the traditional sense, and neither went very far legislatively. While a few states did pass old-age pension laws sponsored by the Eagles, they were in practice small, serving hundreds rather than millions of older people. The Ex-Slave Pension Association fared worse: although its legislation was introduced in Congress, it was never passed, and its legal campaign to recoup government taxes on slave-produced cotton failed as well. The important question for this period was not which approach would inspire sweeping legislation, as neither did, but which would get to define the problem of "the aged" for American policymakers, politicians, scholars, and experts. When political elites turned to the question of aging, would they be wondering about urban, wage-earning white men, mainly working in industry? Or would they be thinking about rural Black farmers and domestics, and those economic sectors that were not part of the formal, waged economy?

The 1910s and 1920s are crucial to the history of old age in the United States, not because important legislation was passed, but because this question was answered—and answered so decisively that it would set the terms of the old-age movement for decades to come. What happened ultimately is that the Ex-Slave Pension Association was suppressed, with its leader thrown into jail. The association's approach, rooted in racial justice and in recognition of the many kinds of meaningful labor, represents the great "path not taken" in the history of American aging. Its defeat allowed the Eagles an open field to define "the aged": who they were and what kinds of labor made them deserving of aid. And for them, wage-earning men, mainly white and mainly in cities, were the aged group that mattered. It's not only that women and people of color were ignored—it's rather worse than that. Their work was instead romanticized. It was coded as domestic and familial, taking place outside the marketplace and thus not deserving of labor protections or benefits. This was true even when the work was done for wages. Black women were far more likely than white women to be performing waged work, and the majority of that work was in domestic service (the 1930 census showed more than one million Black women in that category). That work did not, in the Eagles' estimation, entitle them to a pension because it was not truly work—at least, not the sort that mattered. Older Black women especially were understood not as workers participating in a market economy, but as "mammies," reprising the kinds of supposedly caring labor, done for love and not for money, they had performed in the days of slavery.[5]

We'll return to this ideological conflict, but first it's important to understand something about the social history of American aging before it was transformed by Social Security in 1935. The Eagles tended to tell a decline-and-fall narrative about American aging. Once upon a time, the story went, older people were venerated and cared for in intergenerational homes. Alas, with the advent of modern industry, this tableau dissolved. Families splintered apart as children moved away for work, and older people were threatened with desperate poverty because modern factory labor was incompatible with their declining bodies. State-delivered pensions, therefore, would serve to alleviate one of the sad and unintended consequences of industrial development. This story proved very useful to the Eagles and their followers, including the architects of Social Security. It is, though, largely false. Since it is still accepted by so many people today, we should take a moment and dispense with some of the most persistent myths embedded in that narrative.

The first myth is that older people in the past were venerated because there were so few of them. This is based on a misunderstanding of life expectancy statistics. While it's true that life expectancy hovered around forty years, this doesn't mean that a wave of people were dying at age forty. It means that many were dying in infancy, skewing the numbers. In 1850, according to the US Census, about 4 percent of the white population and about 3.5 percent of the enslaved population were over sixty. While there are about four times as many older people today, proportionally speaking, it's not as though an older person was a rare sight. In fact, once people made it past childhood, they had a decent shot of making it to old age. A thirty-year-old in 1850 could expect, on average, to live about thirty more years.[6]

The second myth is that households in the past were intergenerational. This one, too, has a grain of truth. Older Americans for the most part remained ensconced with their children. Before the Civil War, more than 60 percent of older Americans lived with at least one adult child. This made economic sense in a world where the bulk of the labor force worked in agriculture. Older people could still do some farm labor, and in any case they tended to be the landowners. Children, in turn, would stick around in the hope of inheritance. There are two caveats, however. The first, of course, is that one in three older people did *not* live with children. And the second is that, even if intergenerational living was common from the perspective of older people, it was not all that common from the perspective of younger ones. Nineteenth-century Americans had more children than their successors, and they didn't live as long. There were, in other words, fewer older relatives to go around, and more grown children to choose from. Only about one in ten households in 1880 included older kin.[7]

The third myth is that older people with disabilities were cared for in the bosom of the family. The truth is that middle-aged Americans today do vastly more caring labor for older relatives than was ever done in the past. The reason is simple: not many people lived to the age when they would need that sort of care or need it for very long. In 1850, less than one hundred thousand Americans counted by the census were over the age of eighty, or less than one-half of 1 percent of the population (a proportion that has increased tenfold). In a world like this, very few middle-aged women were caring for their parents. As late as 1900, the majority of fifty-year-old Americans did not have a living parent at all—and the vast majority of sixty-year-olds, more than 90 percent, did not.[8]

The fourth myth is that older people were harmed by industrialization because their bodies could not handle the strains of factory labor.

To evaluate the truth of this assumption, let's look at the economic status of older Americans in the 1920s, a moment when America had industrialized but when older people did not yet have access to Social Security. Older men, at least, were generally still at work in this period. Per the 1930 census, 70 percent of men and 11 percent of women age sixty-five to sixty-nine were in the official workforce, compared with 94 percent of men and 23 percent of women in their later thirties. That workforce, of course, looked very different from today's. A full half of workers were engaged in either agriculture or manufacturing. The rest were split among white-collar work, clerical work, and domestic service. Older people could be found in all those spaces. People over sixty-five made up 5 percent of the US population. More than 7 percent of the agricultural workforce, however, was over sixty-five. Five percent of domestic workers were over sixty-five, and 3.6 percent of the manufacturing workforce.[9]

Not only were older Americans working, but they were handling the shift to an industrial society reasonably well. Some were even beginning to retire. Although they did not have access to Social Security or an infrastructure of retirement, many of them (both rural and urban) were voluntarily leaving the workforce before death. According to one calculation, about 20 percent of fifty-five-year-old men in the workforce around 1900 would, at some point before their death, do so. Some were already receiving state support. About a third of older men in 1900 received some kind of pension from the federal or state government, and many older women received one, too, as survivor benefits. Beyond that, many had access to other sources of money, from savings to proceeds from property sales to income transfers from their children. Others could dangle the promise of testamentary rights in exchange for companionship and care from family members or friends. Retirement in this period, though, was unequally available, and white industrial workers were better served than many. Older Black Americans, and especially Black women, were more likely than their white counterparts to be in the workforce. A full one-third of Black women in their late sixties were in the workforce, mostly in domestic service. And 88 percent of Black men in that age group were working, mainly in agriculture.[10]

The experience of aging before Social Security was so diverse that it's challenging to present just one picture—so instead I'll provide four. In rural areas, where most older people still lived, many of them would stay in their homes with one of their children. Many others would sell their property and move to nearby small towns, where they would rely on a combination of family support and odd jobs to make a living. Their lives might resemble the anonymous farmer's wife in her early sixties who wrote about her life on a Pennsylvania dairy farm for a woman's magazine in 1920. After thirty years of farming, she and her husband sold their property and moved into a nearby house—one, she proudly reported, that had running water and a piano. They lived with two of their daughters and, in her words, "retired with enough saved up and invested to provide for us in comfort and plenty the rest of our lives." (It's clear that in this case, as in many instances of intergenerational coresidence, the older couple remained the heads of the family.)[11]

Many older people in urban areas were immigrants, and in the absence of widespread pension legislation they typically continued working at their jobs for as long as they could. Urban areas were more closely studied than rural ones. A pioneering sociologist named Mabel Nassau looked at older people in New York City around World War I. A typical profile in Nassau's study depicted a seventy-five-year-old Italian woman who spoke little English. She lived with her children and their families in an apartment building, and she sewed clothes to contribute a small bit of income. The arrangement was that she would work as long as possible and then be cared for by her family.[12]

Both the farmer's wife and the seamstress were relatively privileged; at least they had living family members and able bodies. Many older people, like many younger people, did not have the familial, physical, or financial resources to provide for themselves. Today, such a person would likely be in a Medicaid-funded nursing home. In the 1920s, there was no such thing as Medicaid, and no such thing as a nursing home. What there was, in most places, was the almshouse: a catch-all institution in which impoverished or disabled older people would coexist with other populations, of whatever age, without a place to go. Conditions were often atrocious, as numerous state commissions found. While some were humanitarian catastrophes, in even the better-appointed ones, a Pennsylvania study found, most of the residents were "sullen" and "depressed," with nothing to do except nurse "grievances and discontent."[13]

Many older people, of course, were not white, and the story for them was even further removed from the "decline and fall" mythology of the Eagles. Before the Civil War, most Black people were enslaved, and older enslaved people endured atrocious conditions. Sometimes they were separated from family and sent to live alone in a cabin in the woods, awaiting death while scraping together some kind of survival. Sometimes they were sold, although they did not command much of a price (before being auctioned, their skin would be oiled up to make them appear younger, and their gray hairs would be plucked). Frederick Douglass, one of the great abolitionists, included a discussion of "my poor old grandmother" in his classic 1847 narrative. In his telling, after a lifetime of enslaved labor she was simply cast into the woods to fend for herself and die "in perfect loneliness."[14]

In the era between abolition and Social Security, the older Black population was made up almost entirely of people who had been born into slavery. The popular memory cleaves to those ambitious younger people who sought "the warmth of other suns" up North. But most Black Americans, and especially older ones, stayed put in the rural South. And for them, the situation was very hard, as demonstrated by the famous interviews with formerly enslaved men and women conducted by the federal government in the 1930s. Whereas the point of the interviews was to collect reminiscences about slavery, the interviewees were, of course, very old, and the grim realities of their aging can be spotted in the margins of the text. Consider an interview with Andrew Boone, who resided near Raleigh, North Carolina. He was living in an old tobacco barn without water or electricity, and he was unemployed. The government would not hire him "cause dey said I wus too ole to work." He went on, "I ain't got any check from the ole age pension an' I have nothin' to eat." Or the one with Clara Jones, a formerly enslaved woman in rural North Carolina who at some point in the 1920s was struck blind and was no longer able to work. She lived with her forty-year-old son, a Baptist minister with heart disease and no congregation. They had no running water and were on the brink of starvation.[15]

In sum, the experience of aging before Social Security was wildly diverse and far removed from the Eagles' narrative, according to which older people in the preindustrial era were ensconced in familial warmth, only to be cast shivering into the streets with the advent of the modern economy. The diversity of experience had political ramifications. Because older people had so little in common, they did not (yet) form a coherent interest group. In this book, we are most interested in the ideas and expectations that people have held about "old age" as a stage of life. And in the pre–Social Security era, it is only a slight exaggeration to say that such a thing did not exist. There was no organization for older people, and no magazine for them. The older people just mentioned were not inhabiting a stage of life they would call old age. The very idea presumes that we can divide a human life into three temporal boxes: one for education that we call youth, one for work and child-rearing that we call adulthood, and one for retirement that we call old age. Before 1900, it was uncommon to think in terms of three stages and more common to divide life into decades. In the 1850 census, there was no designation for old age as such, and no importance given to sixty-five as an age barrier. There was simply a count of how many people were in each age bracket (this many in their sixties, that many in their seventies, etc.). In popular culture, this classification system took the image of life as a staircase, with each decade representing a step: a person would ascend to a peak around middle age and then decline toward death.

One reason that old-age policy became more important in the early twentieth century is that age in general was starting to matter more. Before 1900, many people did not even *know* their age. In a world without compulsory schooling or pension policies or child-labor laws or even standardized birth certificates, one's age was not all that important. In the early twentieth century, though, this began to change. The American state, like its counterparts elsewhere, began to get more involved in the creation of what is sometimes called a "normative life course": a pathway from birth to death, with social norms and state institutions available at each step of the way. Age-based policies were becoming increasingly common, on both the front and the back ends of life. On the front end, they took the form of education; on the back end, of pensions or some other kind of retirement financing.[16]

Pensions in general received less attention than did schooling, just as older people received less attention than younger ones. Older people were not a serious object of legislative or scientific concern in the nineteenth century, in either Europe or America. This was the great era of social investigation and sociological inquiry, when social workers and scientists and reformers were swarming through cities and towns studying public health, suicide, poverty, and more. They were not, however, studying older people. Few realized that lifespans were about to explode, and that population aging would be a major component of modernization. Karl Marx thought that capitalism was shortening lifespans. The most important nineteenth-century American thinker to address old age was the psychologist and neurologist George Miller Beard. He was not interested, though, in family patterns or old-age poverty; he cared about when geniuses like Socrates or da Vinci did their most important work, which had no implications whatsoever for public policy—or for the vast majority of us who are, alas, not geniuses.[17]

There was therefore little discussion before the 1930s about old age as we think of it today: something that happens to all individuals in similar ways, and which requires special kinds of public policies to help people once they reach a certain age. Instead, numerous discussions took place about specific groups of older people, some of which eventually led to the creation of a genuine national discourse and policy around aging. In Germany, for instance, the initial focus was on industrial workers. While that same topic would eventually dominate the American discussion, that is not where it began. In the US, crucially, the discussion of old-age pensions began with Civil War veterans, who benefited from America's first federal system of pensions. For most of its existence, that pension system applied only to those who were unable to work because of disability, whether caused directly by the war or not. In 1906, though, the system was changed to allow old age itself to qualify a veteran for a pension. The resulting system was massive, similar in size to the systems for older people that were being created in Europe at the same time. By 1910, almost one in five older Americans was receiving a pension benefit from the system.[18]

America's first pension system, then, was not aimed at older people as a group. It was aimed at a particular kind of older person who, it was believed, morally deserved the pension for his exemplary service to the nation. In the early twentieth century, though, Civil War veterans were dying off. The debate after 1900 was about which other population of older people was most deserving of pensions—which one, in other words, was a worthy successor to Civil War veterans. One might expect that socialists or trade unions would lead the way. And indeed, the Socialist Party, inspired by the European example, called in their 1912 platform for old-age pensions. That was far, though, from a headline demand; it was almost an aside in a long list of goals, and it was not one that the party prioritized. Trade unions were surprisingly ambivalent about government-delivered pensions. Organized labor, in short, was not yet at the vanguard of old-age politics. The real energy lay elsewhere.[19]

As mentioned earlier in the chapter, there were two mass movements for pensions before 1930, targeting two different groups of needy older people: the Fraternal Order of Eagles, which took the position that aging industrial workers were the most obvious candidates for pensions, and the Ex-Slave Pension Association, which promoted the idea that the formerly enslaved should have pride of place. Both were explicit about the connection to the Civil War and to veterans' pensions. The Eagles often referred to older men as "veterans of labor," drawing an implicit connection between aging workers and aging soldiers. The Ex-Slave Pension Association made a subtly different argument. "If the saviors of a nation are entitled to the aid of the government," wrote one of its advocates, "surely the wards of the nation are worthy of practical assistance." In other words, if the government was paying out money to the soldiers, Black and white, who had delivered America from slavery, then surely it ought to also pay out to those who were delivered and who had labored for so long without pay.[20]

Even before abolition, writers like Frederick Douglass had been drawing attention to the desperate conditions of older enslaved people. And after abolition, Black activists worked hard to draw attention to the desperation of those who had been raised in a slave society and were thrust into a new world, without education or property, and often with bodies broken by their enslavement. Harriet Tubman and Sojourner Truth, two of the crusading abolitionists of the era, were concerned with old age from this perspective. Truth wanted the government to give land to, and construct old-age homes for, formerly enslaved people. Tubman had to collect funds from abolitionists to care for her own aging parents. After the end of the Civil War, she turned to this issue in earnest, and she created a home for aged African Americans in New York (she was one of many to do so: W. E. B. Du Bois referred to these homes as the "most characteristic Negro charity").[21]

Although forgotten today, there was a vibrant movement in support of pensions for formerly enslaved people. The idea was introduced to Congress in 1890, following a pressure campaign led by a white Democrat from a slave-owning family named Walter Vaughan. His Freedmen's Pension Bill, as he called it, was presented as "a measure of recognition of the inhumanity practiced by the government in the holding, for a century, of men and women as slaves in defiance of human right." The idea was that legal emancipation was not true emancipation, because the enslaved were being released into penury. Vaughan proposed that a large pension be paid to those who were at least seventy years old. The legislation was a radical piece of work. For one thing, it recognized the labor of enslaved women, promising equal benefits "to male and female alike." And for another, the bill recognized the rights and responsibilities of caregivers, stipulating that in the case of severe disability, family caregivers themselves would be designated "pensioners upon the bounty of the United States." One formerly enslaved person wrote to Vaughan to say that he was liberated "when quite young," so wanted nothing from the government. "But justice should be done to the older ones, at least, who were turned loose at an old age, without education, homes or money, and broken down in health." "The news of such a measure," he continued, "has spread among [the formerly enslaved] like wildfire."[22]

Many formerly enslaved people loved the idea of pensions but were distrustful of Vaughan personally. Eventually, they took over leadership of the movement themselves, notably in the Ex-Slave Pension Association. Callie House was the most dynamic of several formerly enslaved leaders of what one historian has called "the largest grassroots movement of African Americans to have existed." Precise numbers are hard to come by; the organization itself claimed to have six hundred thousand members, while the government estimated that membership was about half that. In any case, it was exceptionally large.[23]

The Ex-Slave Pension Association never intended to become a model for a universal policy that would provide benefits to all older people. Even so, it represents a path not taken for the old-age pension movement as it sought to grow from its origins in Civil War pensions. Its advocates put forth a model of old-age policy that would not discriminate between men and women, and that was designed specifically to reward unwaged labor. Indeed, one of the association's surviving songs, presumably sung at club meetings across the South, began, "Our women nursed young masters, upon their honest breasts!" It went on to detail the various kinds of labor that had been done without compensation by the formerly enslaved, before ending with "Our times went on and we unpaid, and now we're asking gold." After all, by promising pensions to men and women alike, House and her collaborators were insisting that there was no important difference between work in the fields, oriented toward the market, and work in the home, oriented toward familial care and domestic work. Their proposal was much broader than the programs for Civil War pensions, which went almost entirely to men. Perhaps, if the pension movement for the formerly enslaved had succeeded, it might have built the basis for a very different sort of old-age policy than the one that was in fact built.[24]

Nonetheless, the movement was suppressed. From the start, it was hounded by accusations that it was swindling gullible formerly enslaved people out of their money. The Bureau of Pensions and the US Postal Service claimed that House and her associates were making unfounded promises to their supporters, and that they were using the funds to pay their own salaries rather than to advocate for the bill. In retrospect, historians have determined that these charges were largely false. Nonetheless, House was a target, perhaps because, as one government official complained, she "seems to think that the negroes have the right to do what they please in this country." Callie House served a year in prison after having been convicted of mail fraud in Nashville by an all-white, all-male jury in 1917. She returned to her life as a laundress, and while the Ex-Slave Pension Association struggled on in some places, its momentum had been sapped.[25]

One of many obstacles faced by House and her organization was the widespread belief that old age for the enslaved and the formerly enslaved was a beautiful thing. In the same years that her movement was growing, another group of thinkers and writers was arguing that rural slave societies provided a positive model for successful aging, in contrast to the supposedly heartless and brutal realities of old age in industrial cities. A version of this theory, which used the status of the elderly to critique industrialization, had been circulating among European conservatives since the mid-nineteenth century. In America, that kind of traditionalist conservatism found its happiest home in the South. Empirical reality notwithstanding, the nobility of aging in a slave society became unquestioned in Southern letters, both before and after the Civil War. Southern writers were keen on comparing the aging of the enslaved with that of the supposedly "free" workers of the North. The pioneer here may be John Calhoun, who devoted space to this theme in a famous 1837 speech on the Senate floor. Compare, he suggested, the poor workers in the North or in Europe with "the sick, and the old and infirm slave" who is "under the kind superintending care of his master and mistress." James Shannon, the second president of the University of Missouri, released a notorious proslavery pamphlet in 1855 that made the same point. "In decrepitude from sickness or old age, the slave can say, 'I have all things and abound.' . . . Not so the poor hireling, who is wholly dependent on his daily labor for his daily bread. In sickness or old age, and often at other times, his only prospect is starvation."[26]

This argument was a particular obsession of George Fitzhugh, a Virginia attorney and one of the leading intellectuals of the South. His *Sociology for the South, or the Failure of a Free Society* (1854) was the first American book to use the word "sociology" in its title. Southern societies, Fitzhugh explained, are bound by morals and custom, rather than simply by monetary exchange. This allows more room for human frailty, as the dependent are not destroyed by the pitiless market. "What a glorious thing to man is slavery," Fitzhugh enthused, "when want, misfortune, old age, debility and sickness overtake him." "Old age," he wrote elsewhere in the book, "is certain to overtake" the free laborer, finding him "without the means of subsistence." In one purple passage, he imagined that he could faintly hear, in the North, the cries of "aged parents too old to work," locked in a cellar to die.[27]

This discussion of aging in slave societies was the most well-developed one available about older people in an industrial age—and a corollary was that industrial workers in the North were the ones who needed help. Rural older people, even Black ones, were presumed to be fine because they had access to supposedly caring, traditional societies. Following abolition, even though slavery itself had disappeared, Southern writers continued to insist that older Black people, both before and after abolition, had an admirable social position. They appeared in Southern writing as figures of nostalgia and remnants of a nobler age. The famous Uncle Remus stories (published in 1881), to take one example, featured a kindly old man spinning folktales. Uncle Tom himself, protagonist of *Uncle Tom's Cabin*, began to be portrayed as an old man at this time (in the novel he is middle-aged). Remus and Uncle Tom became almost indistinguishable in the popular iconography of the period, and sometimes even reversed roles. "Old Aunt Jemima" also participated in this emergent form of nostalgia.[28]

In the very same years that the Ex-Slave Pension Association was organizing the rural poor in the South, the social-scientific study of aging began—and it ignored that population entirely, preferring to focus, as Fitzhugh and the other writers would have appreciated, on the supposedly grim position of the elderly in the urban North. The very first study of "old age dependency," which appeared in 1912, based its accounting of the extent and nature of old-age poverty on the state of Massachusetts alone. The rationale given was that, although much of the country did not yet look like industrial Massachusetts, the nation was headed that way. The fact that the author could use as the basis for a national study a state that at the time was 99 percent white and 93 percent urban was typical of this early generation of scholarship. He made no mention of the Black or rural elderly, and in fact repeated the myth that aging white workers had it considerably worse than the formerly enslaved.[29]

A decade later, the next important book on American aging appeared. Abraham Epstein was no racist; he was a Russian Jewish sociologist who had cut his teeth with a sympathetic study of Black communities in Pittsburgh. But by the time he turned to old age, the contours of the discussion had been set (for a brief period, he actually worked for the Eagles). *Facing Old Age* (1922) was based on a detailed and sophisticated study that focused on older people residing in Pennsylvania almshouses. But in some important ways, it was similar to its 1912 predecessor. *Facing Old Age* was more scientific, but not more representative. Pennsylvania, like Massachusetts, was a very white state: about 3 percent of the population was Black. And even if he didn't mention slavery, Epstein shared the sense that aging had been somehow better in preindustrial settings. He began the book with a bizarre and unsourced anecdote about China and the exaggerated respect older people had there.[30]

Books like these were important in policy circles, to be sure. But the movement for pensions for the formerly enslaved was a mass movement, and it would need to be answered by another one. The energy was provided by the Fraternal Order of Eagles. It was a huge organization, with about half a million members, concentrated in the West and Midwest. Right around the time that Callie House was being imprisoned, the Eagles began their grassroots movement for old-age pensions.

The Eagles' platform belonged to the conservative, nativist, and antisocialist mood of the United States during and after World War I. This was the era of the Red Scare, when anything that smacked of socialism was pilloried as foreign and un-American. And it was the era, too, of the revived Ku Klux Klan, when movements like House's had no chance of propagating in the open, much less of succeeding legislatively. While the Fraternal Order of Eagles had historically been a rather progressive organization, its leaders knew which way the wind was blowing. "There is no room," the order's president thundered in 1921, "for the red flag of anarchy, or the black flag of treason." He went on to praise federal efforts to expel socialist immigrants—or, in his more colorful language, "for taking those human reptiles and throwing them back on the dung heap from whence they came."[31]

It was in this conservative moment that the Eagles began agitating for old-age pensions. Whereas their competitors hoped for large payments to be provided to any formerly enslaved person by the federal government, the Eagles saw that as too radical, both socially and economically. They envisioned instead small payments, based on state-level legislation, provided to small groups of impoverished seniors. And whereas the ex-slave pensions were designed to recognize unwaged labor in the fields and in domestic service, the Eagles focused overwhelmingly on the needs of aging industrial workers. Their plan was based on Civil War pensions as a model, but in a different way because the Eagles interpreted that war differently. In their view, Civil War soldiers were getting pensions because they had labored for the nation, so anyone who was a "veteran" of industrial service ought to get one too. Frank Hering, leader of the organization and former football coach at Notre Dame, declared himself in favor of pensions for "age-disabled veterans in our Country's industrial army." Aging workers deserved pensions because industrialization was challenging for them, just as it was challenging for workers all over the world. Slavery, from this perspective, had nothing to do with it, nor did the specific contours of American history.[32]

The Eagles were crystal clear about whom they were trying to help with their old-age pension legislation. Hering insisted that "swift-speeding modern machinery" was to blame for the premature superannuation of the older worker. "They are not idlers," he went on. "They are simply victims of an economic system." This focus was so intense that it led to cognitive dissonance. In 1922, the Eagles' journal published an article titled, simply, "Who Are the Aged?" It included demographic information that clearly demonstrated that most older people were women, many of whom lived in the South. And yet, in the article's qualitative delineation of the "four groups" of the aged, that fact was ignored. The four groups were, first, those who were independently wealthy; second, those who received government pensions (mainly Civil War veterans); third, "wage earners" who live "near the poverty line"; and fourth, people with disabilities. It was a typology designed for white men, and it is unclear where women or sharecroppers would even be located in this schema.[33]

The Eagles were, in the end, committed to serving their own members, defined in their constitution as "male members of the Caucasian race of sound body and health." It should be no surprise that the Eagles did not go out of their way to envision pensions for the formerly enslaved, given the movement's deep-seated racism. Their journal advertised minstrel shows, and when Black men petitioned to be admitted as members, they were denied. Whenever the Eagles presented an image to represent worthy old age, it was of a well-dressed white gentleman, perhaps with a dutiful wife in tow. Hering was even clearer when he had to be, as when he prepared a report on old-age pensions at the behest of the governor of Indiana. "It is," he assured his readers, "the native-born, white citizen who goes to the poorhouse." Legislation to empty the poorhouse of elderly citizens would not be wasted, in other words; it would be for the benefit of "Americans of the purest gender."[34]

This all matters because it was really through the Eagles that the issue of old-age pensions first entered the political mainstream. Hering encouraged each chapter of the Eagles to create an Old-Age Pension League, designed to pressure local and state officials toward pension legislation. In Milwaukee, for instance, which had a population of around four hundred thousand, the four thousand Eagles were able to enroll ten thousand into the league. They did so through a multi-pronged campaign of speaker series, pamphlet distribution, and dramatic productions. They even rented a theater hall and put on a play about the ravages of old age, which was followed by an address about the need for pensions and an appeal to join the pension league.[35]

It wasn't that Callie House and formerly enslaved women like her were ignored by the Eagles, or by American culture more generally. That might have been expected. Demographically speaking, the group was a small one. But perhaps because they had been pushing so hard for compensation, they were not ignored at all, and they became something of a cultural sensation. House had been trying to draw attention to the plight of older, formerly enslaved people in need of just compensation for their years of labor. What happened instead was that the same people were reimagined as the paradigmatic providers of unpaid care labor. In other words, just as older white men were being imagined as impoverished and unemployed through no fault of their own, older people of color were imagined as happy laborers whose sturdy bodies could keep them laboring into old age—and who, therefore, had no need for a pension.[36]

At just that moment, the "mammy" became an inescapable stock character in American culture: the kindly enslaved caregiver who raised white children in the master's house. Even though the reality of such a life was horrifying, involving a great deal of drudgery and sexual violence, the mammy was heavily romanticized in the early twentieth century. For instance, Woodrow Wilson, a Southerner in the White House, dedicated the Confederate Memorial at Arlington National Cemetery in 1914. The memorial featured as one of its two Black characters an elderly "mammy" caring for the children of a noble Confederate soldier. *Birth of a Nation* (1915), the blockbuster film about the early Ku Klux Klan, featured a sixty-six-year-old actress in blackface playing the "mammy" role, remaining devoted to her white supremacist family even after the abolition of slavery.[37]

Many popular songs about mammy figures were performed in vaudeville acts and musicals. It got to the point where in 1922 a satirical magazine published an article called "Getting Tired of Mammy." "It's mammy this, and mammy that," the author complained. "Let's have a song of dad." The most famous of such tunes is probably "My Mammy," written by three white songwriters and first performed in 1918 (it was included in *The Jazz Singer*, released in 1927 and one of the first "talkies"). The song, from the point of view of an older man of uncertain race, waxes nostalgic for the "mammy" from "Alabammy" who had cared for the singer in his early days. For our purposes, the crucial element of the song, and of "mammy" culture more generally, is that the mammy, despite her age and life experience, is not in need of care. The singer is not going to Alabammy to care for his mammy, but to *receive* care from her. "I'm your little baby!" the singer intones, reminding Mammy and listener alike that her work of caring was not at an end.[38]

When the Fraternal Order of Eagles considered Black aging, which it did infrequently, they did so in just this way. In 1922, at the height of their pension campaign, their journal published a short story titled "The Municipal Report." In it, a Southern gentleman visits Nashville and meets "a stalwart Negro, older than the pyramids," wearing a Confederate jacket that had been repaired for him by "some surviving 'black mammy.'" Uncle Caesar was a formerly enslaved man who spent his time caring for the daughter of his former master, who was then about fifty years of age. The woman would only accept aid from Caesar, who contributed to her upkeep from his own meager earnings as a coachman. A cartoon reprinted in the journal showed Uncle Caesar, hunched but dignified, handing a dollar bill to the smiling daughter of the man who had once owned him. In the world of this short story, formerly enslaved men and women were praiseworthy insofar as they continued to provide dutiful caretaking service. This vision was part and parcel of the Eagles' campaign for pensions, which was explicitly aimed at white Americans. And it could not have clashed more explicitly with the vision of Callie House and her Ex-Slave Pension Association. House would have lamented the working conditions of Uncle Caesar and called for him to receive a federal pension.[39]

The history of old age in twentieth-century America would have looked very different had Callie House and her movement been more successful. The Ex-Slave Pension Association *could* have inaugurated a century-long conversation about how the state might support marginalized communities, especially those whose members had worked outside the traditional labor market. It could have started a conversation about how old-age policy could redress the injustices of American society, rather than reproducing them. But that is not what happened.

The Ex-Slave Pension Association was suppressed, leaving the Fraternal Order of Eagles to define the conversation about American aging.

Perhaps it could not have been any other way. The Eagles were a richer and more powerful organization than the Ex-Slave Pension Association. And their program was more in step with the mainstream of American politics, which in the early twentieth century was more concerned with industrialization than with racial justice. In the 1920s, their notion of old-age pensions, focused on industrial workers in the North and Midwest, circulated among hundreds of thousands of Eagles, leading social scientists, and, increasingly, politicians. It had not yet gained much traction as actual policy, but that would soon change. In 1935, just a decade after the events we've been describing in this chapter, Social Security became the law of the land. By that point, the Eagles were no longer the only game in town, and many other movements had taken up the cause. Still, they were honored as pioneers; Franklin Roosevelt said as much when he joined the organization. And when the legislation was signed, a leader of the Eagles stood proudly behind Roosevelt. They were even presented with one of the pens used to sign the act. That legislation has been magnificently successful and has lifted many millions out of poverty. Yet it was a creature of its time. Even though many formerly enslaved people were still alive, none of them were arrayed behind Roosevelt. Social Security was not for them.

CHAPTER 2

SOCIAL SECURITY AND ITS LIMITS

In November 1939, a woman named Ida Fuller retired from her job as a legal secretary in a small town in Vermont. She was unmarried and had no children. She was therefore the kind of person who would, at most times in American history, have had a challenging time in old age. She might have had to rely on charity or even enter an almshouse. Fuller, though, knew that for the last few years, she had been paying for something called "Social Security." She didn't know much about the program, and had voted against Franklin Roosevelt, the president who made it possible. All the same, she stepped into a government office to inquire. She didn't expect anything to come of her query, but she was in luck. As it happens, that was the very day that the first application forms for the new program had arrived. She filled them out. Just two months later, a check arrived in her mailbox with the auspicious number 00-000-001. Miss Ida Fuller thus entered the history books as the nation's first recipient of Social Security.[1]

Fuller was one of many millions of people whose lives were shaped by Social Security, which was the grandest expansion of the welfare state in American history. It has played an incalculable role in shaping the American economy and the life course of American citizens. Social Security has also been the greatest poverty-reduction program in American history. According to the Center on Budget and Policy Priorities, in 2022 the program kept 21.7 million Americans above the poverty line, most of whom were over age sixty-five. The program also helps people with disabilities and some other target groups. It is largely thanks to Social Security and its many amendments, of which Medicare is one, that old age in America is as good as it is.[2]

Social Security hasn't just made old age better. The program was in many ways responsible for the *invention* of old age in this country. Before 1935, there was very little sense that "old age" was a coherent stage of life, with its own institutions and benefits. "Youth" was certainly understood that way, as a time for state-sponsored education, but old age was not. Not many older people were retiring, and few of the institutions that we associate with modern aging existed yet (retirement communities, senior centers, nursing homes, and so on). Social Security created, for the first time, a legitimate expectation that Americans could look forward to ten or fifteen years of comfortable life on the far side of the labor market. It created, in other words, a broadly shared idea of what old age could be.[3]

Social Security is a form of social insurance funded not through general tax revenues but through taxes paid by workers and employers. The level of benefits an individual receives is determined by the amount that was paid in under their name. Richer people, therefore, receive higher benefits than poorer ones. Politically, this proved to be a masterstroke. Proponents of Social Security were able to argue that it was revenue neutral. It did not involve the general taxation system at all, and the government could purport to be guarding taxpayers' money in order to pay it back to them later. Supporters could argue, too, that it was not a form of welfare, because benefits are based on contributions rather than on need. All things considered, Social Security is modestly progressive, in the sense that it redistributes some income from the higher-earning half of the population to the lower-earning half. That was not, though, an advertised feature of the program, which was sold as an effort to bring economic security to the industrial working class.[4]

All of these facts are familiar, and in essence the program operates the same way today as it did when Fuller received her check. The program is so large and such an impregnable part of our political landscape that one can easily forget how strange it appeared at first, and how many alternatives to it were in play when it was passed. In fact, no social or political movement was clamoring for the kind of social insurance that Social Security promised. The Ex-Slave Pension Association, which was dormant by the 1930s, had sought large payments to formerly enslaved men and women. The Fraternal Order of Eagles had sought state-level welfare programs for impoverished older people. And during the Great Depression, massive social movements had been pushing for old-age pensions. Most importantly, the grassroots Townsend movement gathered millions of older Americans across the country in support of a plan that would give large pensions to all American citizens over sixty, irrespective of their race or gender or what kind of work they had done before retirement. The Townsend Plan, like most other pension schemes of the era, relied on general tax revenues rather than special taxes deducted from some workers' paychecks. And the Townsend Plan, like the Ex-Slave Pension Association and unlike Social Security, had expressly egalitarian goals. Its advocates sought to provide a dignified life to the vast majority of older Americans, regardless of what kind of labor they had done and how much they had earned doing it.

If the Townsend movement was in some ways a spiritual successor to the Ex-Slave Pension Association, Social Security was directly indebted to the Fraternal Order of Eagles and its more conservative and exclusive account of American aging. "All social welfare laws," the historian Edward Berkowitz has observed, "reflect the conventional wisdom of the era of their founding." Social Security was no different, and in that time and place the conventional wisdom had been guided above all by the Eagles. Social Security's advocates argued, as the Eagles had, that industrial civilization was uniquely challenging for older people, who could not keep up with the modern factory and became unemployed through no fault of their own. It was thus up to the state to step in and provide pensions. Many people and many kinds of labor were excluded from the legislation. Agricultural and domestic labor, both paid and unpaid, was not included, and therefore most Black Americans were excluded altogether, and most women received benefits only through their husbands. The popular image of the aged—and the one enshrined in Social Security—remained male, white, and urban.[5]

Even though the legislation was heir to a broad and culturally conservative conversation about aging, it remains astonishing that it was ever passed. When Franklin D. Roosevelt assumed the presidency in 1933, the nation was in turmoil. One in four American workers was unemployed, the economy was disastrously contracting, and food riots were starting to break out in American cities. Roosevelt and his team had a mandate to remake the economy, but few would have guessed that he would turn old-age security, which had an unclear relationship to the overwhelming issue of unemployment, into one of his top priorities. The issue, after all, had hardly come up in the election. In his lengthy speech accepting the Democratic nomination for president, Roosevelt talked about tariffs and farm relief and welfare relief and federal employment programs. In fact, he talked about most all of the commitments that would mark the New Deal—all, that is, except the elderly, who weren't spared a word. And in his inaugural address he mentioned banking, credit, the rural crisis, and unemployment as facets of his plan for the nation to recover the values of hard work and interdependence. Again, nothing at all was said about the elderly or about old-age pensions.[6]

The administration's commitment to old-age pensions is all the more curious because there was very little evidence available in the 1930s to suggest that older people as a group were hit very hard by the Depression. As the first report of Roosevelt's Committee on

Economic Security admitted in the lead-up to the legislation, "No even reasonably complete data are available regarding the means of support of aged persons." When that data was compiled, as it was a few years later by researchers at the new Social Security Board, it demonstrated that older people were faring reasonably well, at least when compared with other age brackets. The married elderly, the study concluded, are "economically among the most favored segment of the population." Children were far more disadvantaged than older people. "No matter how analyzed," the author concluded, "the data indicate that dependent minors are the neediest group in the population as a whole."[7]

Roosevelt, however, had experience with old-age pensions. He was a member of the Eagles, and when he joined he praised them for their commitment to the old-age pension movement. Partially in response to their agitation, he had signed a pension bill for the state of New York in the spring of 1930. "New social conditions," he explained, "bring new ideas of social responsibility." "Poverty in old age," specifically, was normally a "mere by-product of modern industrial life," leading older persons to become "dependent." The bill, like other state-level plans of the era, didn't do much. Basically, it released funds to local welfare offices to provide as relief to New Yorkers with disabilities over the age of seventy.[8]

This tradition only flowered into Social Security once Roosevelt became president and was forced to contend with a variety of insurgent campaigns, on both the Right and the Left, that were hoping to remake American politics. Crucially, many of the movements promised old-age pensions. The populist Huey Long, a perpetual thorn in Roosevelt's side, wanted to give pensions of thirty dollars per month to anyone over sixty. Upton Sinclair, as part of his 1934 campaign to become governor of California, promised even more: fifty dollars a month, again to people over sixty. The trade unions supported the Lundeen Bill, which folded old-age pensions into a broader welfare program that would use general taxation revenues to provide benefits to older people, the unemployed, the sick, and new mothers.[9]

Insurgent political movements had for decades called for old-age pensions, following the European example, as one of a laundry list of demands. The true novelty of the era was the appearance of organizations dedicated *solely* to old-age pensions. The National Old Age Pension Association, based in Oklahoma, was the first of these, beginning to operate in August 1932. Many more would follow. But without a doubt, the one that mattered most was known as the Townsend movement. After the Ex-Slave Pension Association and the Fraternal Order of Eagles, it was the third mass movement in American history to devote itself to the cause of old-age pensions.[10]

The plan was conceived of by a physician named Francis Townsend. The story, perhaps apocryphal, goes that he was looking out the window of his Southern California home in 1933 when he was moved to action by the sight of three older women picking through his trash for food. This, he reported, sparked the idea for the proposal that would sweep the country. The simple plan was first laid out in a letter from Dr. Townsend to his local newspaper. He had a background in socialist politics, and he shared with many observers at the time the notion that the automated economy of the future would require many fewer workers. The workers lost in the Depression, Townsend argued, weren't coming back—unless, that is, the government stepped in to prime the pump by giving purchasing power to millions of Americans. The fairest way to do this, Townsend reasoned, was to tax every transaction in the country at a rate of 2 percent, and use the proceeds to distribute $200 per month to every American over sixty. If *someone* was going to be spared work, it may as well be older people who had already done a lot of it. He proposed a truly astronomical sum, necessary to confront the gravity of the problem as he understood it: $200 in the 1930s equals almost $5,000 in 2024 dollars (and that's per person per month, not per household). And what's more, older Americans would have to spend it. The plan wouldn't work if they just hoarded it, so a condition of receiving the money would be that they had to get rid of it all, every thirty days.[11]

This sounds like a crackpot scheme—and maybe it was. But it was a popular one. While largely forgotten today, Townsend led one of the most active social movements in the first half of the twentieth century. Townsend Clubs sprang up everywhere in America, most prominently in the West and Midwest. At the height of its influence, in 1936, about two million Americans belonged to Townsend Clubs, and even more signaled their support for the plan. The demographics of the movement are hard to ascertain, but it was certainly more diverse than the Eagles before it. Unlike the Eagles, the movement included many women. And unlike the Eagles, the vision of the Townsendites was explicitly universalist, and was thus attractive to many people of color. Across the country, Black Townsend Clubs were set up, some of which had hundreds of members. "The Negro people will benefit more from this Plan than any other class of people," explained one Black newspaper in Nebraska. "It will be," for the Black American, "his day of opportunity for full and abundant life, such as he has never known."[12]

The scheme's popularity isn't hard to fathom. Townsend wasn't just promising miserly, means-tested pensions to keep older people out of poverty. Important as such pensions might have been, they weren't exactly stirring. He was promising a *new way of life* for older people, and he was offering them a chance to participate in the salvation of the American economy. He was offering that way of life to all American citizens in equal portion, regardless of what kind of work they had done. And he was doing it with style. With the help of a local real estate agent named Robert Clements, Townsend turned his movement into a market juggernaut, complete with memorabilia and a flashy newsletter. Townsend himself became the charming face of the movement, linking in his person a folksy, down-home appeal with seemingly modern and irrefutable economic knowledge.

The Townsend movement harnessed utopian energies to homespun values. Consider the Townsend Club in Holcombe, Wisconsin, a small town of less than a thousand people about fifty miles north of Eau Claire. On a November evening, dozens of people gathered at the town hall for the Townsend Club meeting. They sang "America the Beautiful" and recited the Pledge of Allegiance before reading about the progress of the Townsend Plan in Congress. They then pledged allegiance to the Townsend Plan itself before settling in for the entertainment portion of the evening. A fifty-nine-year-old housewife led a "Kitchen Band," whose members played music with kitchen utensils. After some political theater dramatizing the plan, the townsfolk socialized and danced while an orchestra played. This slice of Americana, played out regularly in more than ten thousand chartered clubs across the country, convinced Americans that payments from the state to the elderly were not a form of welfare, but were a demand of justice and economic good sense. The Black Townsend Clubs, it should be said, had a similar atmosphere. In Stockton, California, one of them put on a Townsendite play in 1936.[13]

Congressmen and Roosevelt administration officials were inundated with literally millions of letters demanding that Congress pass the Townsend Act. Nonetheless, it failed. As a matter of legislative history, it impacted some provisions of Social Security, and it goaded the Roosevelt administration to focus on old-age pensions. That, though, was not Townsend's goal. He wanted to pass the Townsend Plan or something like it. Even the more pragmatic version of the proposal that actually made it to Congress, known as the McGroarty Bill, didn't come close to passing. This is mainly because, even as amended, the bill would have been massively expensive, and many experts thought the scheme of taxation and forced spending was harebrained. Moreover, the Townsendites were politically inexperienced and had little constituency beyond their mostly elderly club members. Conservative business interests balked at the vast taxation; labor and the Left supported the Lundeen Bill and were more interested in unemployment compensation than in old-age pensions.[14]

Roosevelt's objection to the Townsend Plan was not only fiscal; it was also moral. The Townsend Plan, after all, was not merely a piece of social policy. It was an argument about what the purpose of old age ought to be, and about what the nation owed to its older citizens. It might even be argued that Townsend and his movement were the first group in American history to conceive of a vision for modern aging—one that sought to fundamentally rethink the place of the elderly in an industrial society.

The question about the *meaning* of old age in modern societies had not excited much discussion before. In the nineteenth century, when the topic was discussed at all, it was answered as it had been for centuries: through religion, perhaps, or ethics. Most of the discourse around old age was religious or didactic in nature, and not so far removed from discussions dating back to antiquity. The presumption was that "old age" was not a long phase of life that began at sixty-five, but a short one that was marked by disability and decline. When the *Journal of the American Medical Association* published an article titled "The Needs and Rights of the Old," as it did in 1897, the emphasis was on how to keep from becoming old. And once one did become old, as inevitably happened at different times for each person, the advice given by the physician was moral, based on Cicero and the Bible. Basically, older people were to seek contemplation and tranquility. Even in the 1920s, when the Fraternal Order of Eagles was spearheading state-level conversations about old-age pensions, the organization was circumspect about what, precisely, older people were supposed to do with themselves once they received the pension money.[15]

Townsend had a new answer: "Youth for Work," his slogan went, and "Age for Leisure." *Leisure.* This was a novel idea, at least in the sense that Townsend meant it. Dating back to antiquity, many had argued that older people ought to pursue cultivated leisure, understood in terms of contemplation, instruction, and religious practice. Townsend didn't care about that. He wanted older people to spend money and to have fun doing it; he envisioned older people driving cars and hitting the town. Some critics argued, practically enough, that older people couldn't possibly spend so much. Local Townsend Clubs were laboring to prove that they could. One enterprising club in Washington gave

$200 to a sixty-three-year-old man, and the national press watched with interest as the man and his wife scurried around the town buying fancy haircuts and clothes.[16]

Townsend proposed a democratic culture of leisure for the aged—an idea that in the past century has had enormous influence but at the time was a surprising one. It's hard to know precisely where he got his inspiration, but the seed had probably been planted decades earlier. Before he was famous, and before he even moved to California, Townsend had been a small-town socialist back home in the Midwest. And like millions of other Americans, Townsend had been infatuated with the utopian visions of Edward Bellamy, whose *Looking Backward* (1888) was one of the best-selling and most influential books of its era. The novel was about a man from Bellamy's day who supposedly fell asleep and woke up in the year 2000. In the future, he imagined, everyone would have access to higher education, simply by the addition of more compulsory grades to the normal curriculum. Everyone would go to school up to the age of twenty-one, an unimaginable luxury at the time. And at the other end of the spectrum, everyone would cease working at the age of forty-five in order to embark on a life of leisure. The truly revolutionary part of Bellamy's vision was the sort of democratic leisure he had in mind. He knew that some people would be drawn to science or art, but not most of them. For them, "the last half of life" would be chiefly a period of "enjoyment" to be spent traveling, relaxing, and pursuing "every imaginable form of recreation."[17]

Townsend's basic impulse was the same as Bellamy's. Even if he placed the age barrier at sixty rather than forty-five, he believed in a state-sponsored division of the life course into three component parts, structured by the fact that, due to technological automation, the economy only needed the labor of those between twenty and sixty years old. Townsend called those the "productive years of life." Before twenty, he presumed that people would be in the life stage called "youth," defined as a "period of education and preparation for life's work." And after sixty, they would enter a new phase called "old age," dedicated to "leisure and buying power in declining years." Townsend imagined a hedonistic old age, in which enormous appetites for style and consumption could be harnessed in ways that would benefit the nation as a whole.[18]

Townsend was a utopian, and he was unabashedly political in his case for what old age ought to be. He had a vision and a way to pay for it. Its folksy veneer hid an astonishing radicalism. What struck contemporaries most was the gargantuan size of the benefits. But what's most striking a century out is its egalitarianism. Townsend wanted to pay the same benefits to men and women and to citizens of any race. He did want to exclude noncitizens and those with criminal records, but the breadth is striking nonetheless. He also imagined a uniform benefit payment that would be unrelated to work history, paid for by a massive new tax that would be collected at the point of consumption rather than through payroll deductions. Like Callie House before him, Townsend was uninterested in the precise nature of the labor that recipients had performed, whether it was waged or unwaged, in the home or the factory or the fields.

Townsend's polar opposite in almost every way was the person who would actually play the leading role in the creation of old-age policy: Frances Perkins. While committed to noble ideals, Perkins was no utopian and no dreamer. She had already spent decades involved with concrete proposals to improve the lives of America's working people. When Roosevelt passed his old-age law in New York, Perkins was serving as his industrial commissioner. And when Roosevelt became president, he invited Perkins to serve as his secretary of labor, a position she held for a full twelve years and from which she played a massive role in extending the federal government's capacity to regulate the economy and improve conditions for workers. Working with great speed and Roosevelt's blessing, Perkins put together an all-star team of economists and intellectuals to imagine what economic security might look like in Depression-era America, and how the government might provide it. With the exception of Perkins, these were experts without much connection to social movements or trade unions. As the biographies and memoirs of the major players indicate, they were broadly antagonistic to the significant social movements that *were* pressing for pensions, most notably the Townsendites.[19]

When Perkins and Roosevelt thought about old-age security, they did not, like Townsend, imagine a political program funded by sales taxes that would hand out millions of dollars to older people. They were not steeped in utopian literature but in the more humdrum and realistic discussions of the experts on social insurance and their allies in organizations like the Eagles. From that perspective, the goal was not to use old-age policy to solve larger economic problems, but rather to address, in as focused a way as possible, the specific problems faced by impoverished older people. And in their view, the issue that mattered was "dependence," symbolized above all by the almshouse. That key word, "dependence," was crucial to their thinking. Lee Welling Squier and Abraham Epstein, who wrote the first two major books on old-age pensions, included it in the very titles of their books as the problem they were meant to solve. Dependency is clearly related to poverty, but it is not quite the same thing. Dependency implies a *relationship*, as when one person is dependent on someone else. As the sociologist John Lewis Gillin pointed out in 1921, not all kinds of dependency are problematic. A child, for instance, is dependent on his parents, just as a housewife might be dependent, economically speaking, on her husband. Relations like this, in his view, "create no social problem." But "abnormal" dependency results in "abnormal social relationships" and does create social problems. Gillin imagines here a pauper in a poorhouse, or children whose parents refuse to care for them.[20]

If an older person was forced to rely on charity or welfare, this was clearly the wrong kind of dependency. From the Eagles onward, pension advocates had been thinking about just this situation when they designed small, means-tested programs to help the indigent elderly scrape by without being institutionalized in an almshouse. They did not want to give old-age assistance to *everyone*. If that happened, it was thought, pensions would upset the moral and economic fabric of the nation by encouraging grown children to abandon their parents. It was, in other words, still considered a natural and "normal" kind of dependency for adult children to care for their parents. In 1910, a Massachusetts commission argued that pensions would "take away, in part, the filial obligation for the support of aged parents, which is a main bond of family solidarity." This position remained common well into the 1920s. "There is something pathetic" about the pension movement, an observer argued in 1929. It harms the family and public morals to relieve the youth of "the obligation of piety" toward "their elders."[21]

The successful move of national pension advocates in the 1930s was to claim that, in modern economies, it was abnormal for aged people to be forced to rely on their children, and that this was in principle not very different from being forced to rely on charity. Even though precise data was lacking, it was at least reasonable to assume, and backed up by anecdote, that unemployed older people were putting strain on their children's families, hard hit as they already were by unemployment. This in turn created resentment and familial strife. From this perspective, old-age pensions weren't destructive to the family; they allowed the family to thrive by removing the specter of privation and allowing older people to play their approved roles as benevolent overseers of family life. A speaker at a 1930 conference on old-age security made this case explicitly. Imagine a scenario, he offered, where a son or daughter, "at a real sacrifice," offers a home to "some aged relative." Then unemployment strikes. Even if they still house the relative, "how can they prevent the economic burden involved from influencing the relationships existing between all the members of the household?" The older relative could not possibly command "the respect due to experience and age," which harmed her own standing in the family as well as the moral fiber of the children.[22]

This line of thinking, which allowed Social Security to appear as a good thing for families, was taken up by Frances Perkins and her team. According to the report of the Committee on Economic Security—the body that Roosevelt put together to study the issue, and which Perkins stacked with advocates for social insurance—"dependence is normal" for children but not for older people. Whereas in the past, grown children may have borne the cost of supporting their aging parents, the Depression made it impossible for many families to do so. And given the fact that younger people were losing their savings and older people were increasingly exiting the workforce, it was unlikely that the earlier system would ever return. The committee was acutely aware of both the economic and the psychological costs of dependency. "Dependency," they insisted, was "enormously expensive not only in the cost of actual assistance" but also in "the psychological results of the loss of self-respect and the constant fear of insecurity."[23]

The provisions of Social Security make sense once we understand the maintenance of independence as its goal (a goal, to reiterate, that was quite foreign to the Ex-Slave Pension Association and to the Townsend movement, both of which were stalking larger quarry). The bill, as it pertains to the elderly, can be broken into two parts. The first part was known as Old-Age Assistance (OAA), an altered version of which exists today as Supplemental Security Income, or SSI. This part of the bill was *not* a form of social insurance but a form of means-tested welfare, meaning that it was targeted directly at the impoverished elderly. It was the component of the bill that was most similar to the one the Eagles had long championed, and which was most directly designed to keep the poorest elderly out of the almshouse. OAA was massively utilized: by 1940, a full quarter of Americans over sixty-five received some sort of OAA benefit. Because it was administered by the states, the level and availability of benefits varied enormously. In the West, payments were extraordinarily high, mainly because masses of the nonwhite poor could be excluded as noncitizens. In the South, older Black people were eligible, and indeed were disproportionate users of OAA: in 1937–1938, about 14 percent of OAA benefits went to Black seniors, who made up 7 percent of the aged population. The program was designed for the poor, and thus these expenditures had a major impact on health outcomes and longevity: the benefits allowed the impoverished elderly to afford an extra doctor's visit or an extra month of heat. At the level of the household, social workers reported that a small benefit like this could do a great deal to make elders feel more welcome in the household and less like a burden.[24]

The other part of the bill, and the one that we colloquially call "Social Security," was known as old-age insurance (OAI). An entirely different animal, it was based on the premise that retired older Americans, in order to maintain independence from their children and from charity, would need variable amounts of resources depending on the income and lifestyle they were used to. OAI, as passed into law in 1935, worked more or less the same way it does today. Salaried workers make contributions to Social Security from each paycheck, and employers contribute as well. Taxable income was capped at a certain limit, originally $3,000 per year. Upon retirement, then set at age sixty-five, the worker begins to receive monthly checks from the government. Those payments would be indexed to the size of the contributions, ensuring that wealthier people would receive larger Social Security checks.

This system was more complicated than the Townsend Plan and less radical in its implications. The Townsend movement, like the Ex-Slave Pension Association before it, would have used old-age policy to attack and redress some of the most insidious injustices of American society. Social Security, in contrast, tried to ensure that the hierarchies of the labor market would be maintained after retirement. It should not be a surprise, then, that the Social Security Act disappointed most everyone who cared about old-age assistance. Townsend and his movement thought that Social Security was far too meager a program. So did Upton Sinclair. Even the sociologist and author Abraham Epstein, probably the most respected expert on social insurance in the country, was unhappy with the legislation, which he considered a confusing rush job that had failed to take the European experience enough into account.[25]

The racial inequities of the system were apparent from the start. Millions of Black workers were frozen out of Social Security because they worked either in agriculture or in domestic service. Some believe this was an explicit bargain made by the Roosevelt administration, which needed the support of racist Southern senators to get the bill over the finish line; however, there is not much evidence for a transparently cynical ploy like this. It would be more accurate to say that because the architects of Social Security were heir to longer discussions of how "old age" ought to be understood as a social problem, they were simply not thinking about race. Because they were laser focused on industrial workers, they devoted little attention to the rural and domestic spaces where most people of color were working.[26]

Gender came up more explicitly than race in legislative discussions, partly because networks of female reformers exercised a great deal of sway over these issues at the time. Those reformers, though, were of a different stamp from the feminists of a later generation. They tended to agree that women were best served by accessing benefits through their husband, rather than through subjecting themselves to the misery and misogyny of the labor market. Nonetheless, it is still the case that the proceedings were male-dominated, and that some ugly clichés framed the discussion. "A single woman," the chairman of the advisory council explained, "can adjust herself to a lower budget on account of the fact that she is used to doing her own housework whereas the single man has to go out to a restaurant." Unpaid care labor was invisible to the Social Security system, whose framers presumed that women could best be cared for by receiving benefits through their husbands. And when women *did* work, they often worked in intermittent or underpaid roles that resulted in small benefits. If they were married, they often received no benefits at all as an individual, but rather an "allowance" through their husbands. "In many cases," one analyst concluded, "the working wife receives a retirement benefit no larger than the nonworking wife may receive as a dependent." Likewise, the system incentivized against a scenario where both partners worked for lower salaries: the family's benefits would be larger if the husband earned one high salary than if both partners worked for lower ones, even if total family earnings were the same.[27]

As even this modest foray into the details of the program show, Social Security was complicated, and it was greeted with befuddlement by many people—especially those who were required to start paying the taxes several years before benefits were scheduled to begin. They understood the Townsend Plan and maybe even supported it. For all its deficits, it was at least easy to comprehend, and it was propagated for years by all sorts of media outlets. Social Security was different. Even the legislators in Congress didn't show much understanding. Rather than proceeding through the labor committees, which had deep experience with industrial issues, the bill entered the floor by way of the veteran politicos of the Ways and Means Committees, who were less prepared to understand the minutiae of the legislation.[28]

Regular Americans, of course, did not devote weeks to studying the bill, so their grasp was even more limited. In the early years, thousands of applications had to be redone because of errors; newspapers printed guides to understanding all the intricacies of who would be covered and who would not, alongside columns by syndicated writers complaining about the "needless" complexity and "useless red tape" of the system. An author in the *Washington Post* derided "the utter complexity" of the bill, which in his view created "a most remarkable disinterest in the whole subject." Polls from the period consistently showed that Americans were uninformed about whether they were eligible for Social Security when they aged, and about what precisely their payroll tax deductions were being used for.[29]

Old-age policy did not *have* to be this way. In some countries, simpler systems, funded by general tax revenues, were used, and in more egalitarian ways. By contrast, Social Security was not designed to treat older people equally, or even to alleviate poverty among all older people. It was designed to help the industrial working class weather their old age without becoming dependent. It was thus heir to a long American discussion about aging and the economy, and it was built on discriminatory understanding of who the aged were and what kinds of labor counted.

Those limitations should not distract us from the truly gargantuan accomplishment of the legislation, which probably could not have been any more progressive than it was, given the congressional constraints the Roosevelt administration faced. However small-bore it might seem when compared with the Townsend Plan, Social Security as enacted represented an enormous expansion of the state, and an enormous promise from the state to its citizens. Over the years, this commitment has often been underestimated. As President Ronald Reagan's Social Security commissioner put it, using a metaphor that has become ubiquitous, Social Security was meant to be "one part of a three-legged economic stool"—in other words, it was intended to supplement private savings and employer pensions. Under the surface the message was that Americans ought not to expect too much from Social Security, which was not meant to do more than top up the funds acquired through personal industry. There is a grain of truth to this thesis, which has been repeated endlessly in the last few decades. Transparently, Social Security was not designed to provide the no-strings-attached largesse of the Townsend Plan. While the New Deal as a whole owed its power and plausibility to the existence of widespread, and often insurgent, social movements, its reforms were not especially radical. They were designed mainly to save capitalism from its excesses while leaving hierarchies of class, gender, and race more or less intact.[30]

And yet every indication is that Perkins and Roosevelt sought a kind of old-age insurance that would provide more than a floor. After all, that floor was provided by old-age *assistance*, the welfare portion of the bill. Old-age *insurance* was supposed to provide something different: the possibility for true independence for America's elderly. Whenever Roosevelt discussed his legislation's purpose, he expressed quite lofty ambitions. As early as 1931, dissatisfied with the meager support provided by his state bill, he was calling for a form of contributory social insurance that would assure older Americans "not merely of a roof over head and enough food to keep body and soul together, but also enough income to maintain life during the balance of their days in accordance with the American standard of living." The head of his Committee on Economic Security explained that Social Security would be, for older Americans, "sufficient to provide for their needs." The primary expert on old-age issues that the committee relied on, the labor lawyer Barbara Nachtrieb Armstrong, was of the same opinion: she sought "respectable old-age security," and she didn't write a word about the need for state-sponsored pensions to be supplemented with savings (in fact, she criticized those who beat the drum of "self-reliance" while ignoring the real hazards of aging).[31]

Two years after the bill's passage, the committee put out a book explaining its work and the new legislation. In it, they affirmed that Social Security was designed to provide a "modest retirement income." They clearly did not think it would be lavish, but they also thought it would do more than keep older people above the poverty line. And they did not think of it as a supplement to other forms of income. In the 1930s, few Americans were covered by private pensions, and not many even had bank accounts. There was certainly no such thing as an IRA or a 401(k). Social Security, designed for the industrial working class, was supposed to provide enough money for dignified independence.[32]

If one great value of Social Security was its relative generosity, another was its capacity for evolution. In the first four decades of its existence, the Social Security Administration (SSA) had just six chief executives—and one of them, the well-regarded Arthur Altmeyer, ran the agency for sixteen crucial years (1937–1953). Americans trusted the SSA and wanted its leaders to improve the system. In 1943, a poll indicated that more than three-fourths of respondents wanted to expand Social Security to uncovered occupations. And this soon happened. By the 1950s, farmworkers and domestic workers were folded into the system, which largely resolved the issue of Black participation. From the 1940s to the 1970s, benefits were consistently increased, a trend that reached its apogee in the presidency of Richard Nixon, when they were at last indexed to inflation. Those reforms have not addressed every injustice in the system, of course, but they have shown that Social Security can be a living, evolving piece of legislation.[33]

The most famous amendment to Social Security was passed in 1965: Medicare. That legislation emerged from a separate conceptual universe. For all their differences, the Ex-Slave Pension Association, the Townsend movement, and Social Security addressed the same population: "the aged." And they tried to address the problems of the aged in the same way: by providing money. After World War II, the whole tenor of the conversation changed. As Social Security checks started to flow out by the million, and older Americans became increasingly prosperous, they began to fight for more than just income support. They wanted full participation in the life of the nation. They would need health, and they would need things to do: senior centers, golf courses, and more. And they didn't want to be called "the aged" anymore either. That term was stigmatizing by design. They wanted a name that would signal their desire to belong to the American experiment in the fullest sense. The aged were no more. Now they were senior citizens.

PART II

SENIOR

CITIZENS

(1940–1975)

CHAPTER 3

MEDICARE AND THE INDEPENDENT SENIOR CITIZEN

On July 1, 1966, the American medical system changed forever—as did the American experience of aging. For on that date, hospitals opened their doors to patients who were on Medicare. The date had been looming for some time. Physicians and hospital administrators were worried that a crush of patients would overwhelm them; patients were concerned that doctors were going to boycott the new system (as many had threatened to do). All in all, though, the day went off without a hitch as seniors entered the brave new world of paperwork and hospital care that would do so much to define the experience of American aging.[1]

Medicare was greeted with somewhat less fanfare than Social Security. The first recipient of Social Security, Ida Fuller, was captured in a famous photograph, holding her check and beaming. Journalists kept tabs on her for decades. The first recipient of Medicare was a woman in Tennessee named Lillian Avery, who was chosen because a communications director from Blue Cross lived nearby. The photograph is less inspiring: a confused-seeming woman is signing paperwork with her husband's help while a jovial hospital administrator looks on. The world lost touch with her, and when an effort was made to find relatives a half century later for a Medicare commemoration, nobody turned up. Few foresaw just how big Medicare would be. It was actually passed as an amendment to Social Security, and in 1968 traditional Social Security was costing three times what Medicare did. But over the years the ratio has shifted, and in 2022 the costs were roughly the same. Within a few decades, Medicare will likely be worth more to the average beneficiary than Social Security.[2]

Like Social Security before it, Medicare emerged as a moderate and compromised piece of legislation once more radical ideals had failed. At the same moment in the late 1940s that many countries were opting for some variant of government-provided health care, the American effort to do the same collapsed, thanks in part to strident opposition from the American Medical Association (AMA). This led to the strange situation that has defined health care in the United States ever since: most Americans, if they have insurance coverage at all, get it through their employer rather than through the state. That coverage, then as now, included dependents like spouses and children, but not older parents, who in the post–Social Security era were no longer considered dependents in that way. Older people, therefore, were excluded from the postwar system of American health care. Medicare emerged as a way to include them.

Just as Social Security responded to a broader cultural conversation about "the aged," Medicare responded to a similar conversation about the "senior citizen." "The aged" was falling away as a term of art. It seemed too stigmatizing and old-fashioned for an era when older people were trying to improve their image and participate more fully in all the trappings of American citizenship. The term "senior citizen" hardly existed before 1940. But by 1960, there were senior citizens' councils, senior citizens' clubs, and senior citizens' housing; in 1963,

President John F. Kennedy inaugurated Senior Citizens Month; by the later 1960s, we arrived finally at the all-important "senior citizen's discount." And by 1975, surveys showed that "senior citizen" was by far the appellation preferred by older people themselves.[3]

Google has digitized millions of pages of English-language books and periodicals, and it has a tool that allows you to track the popularity of words and phrases over time. In 1945, "senior citizens" outstripped "the aged and infirm" for the first time. And a decade later, it overtook the more colloquial names for older people. Around 1955, "senior citizen" became more common than "oldster," and "senior citizens," in the plural, became more common than "old folks." The popularity of "senior citizen" itself exploded, its usage increasing more than 2,000 percent in frequency between 1945 and 1965.[4]

More than its predecessor, "senior citizen" was a term that older Americans positively identified with and that had a positive valence. Senior Citizens Month, for instance, was not a month of mourning for the desperate plight of the American aged (the idea of an "Aged Month" is inconceivable). It was instead a celebration of everything that seniors could do for America. President Lyndon Johnson made this clear in his proclamation of the month in 1964. He declared the theme to be "Opportunities for Older Americans." He wanted all Americans to ensure that seniors had "a real chance to enjoy health, love, and a life of dignity," and that their "skill and wisdom" could be shared with younger age cohorts. The month's suggested activities were designed to celebrate seniors: the government recommended that local communities give awards to seniors, including "Mr. and Mrs. Senior Citizen," and that they host a "hobby show" in which local seniors could display their handicrafts in the lobby of a department store.[5]

"Senior citizen" was not much more inclusive as an identity category than "the aged" had been, and in some ways it was less so. The National Council of Senior Citizens, an advocacy group that played an important role in the passage of Medicare, and *Senior Citizen* magazine were dominated by white, urban men. Trade unions played an outsized role in senior citizen advocacy, and they were most concerned with the status of white, ex-industrial workers. Older people with disabilities were in many ways excluded from senior citizenship, just as their long-term-care needs were unmet by Medicare. "The aged," as a term, had been inclusive of people with disabilities and was often extended as "the aged and infirm." After all, the whole point of advocacy for the aged had been that older people were differently abled than younger ones, which is why they deserved different benefits. The "senior citizen" as an identity category had a different logic. The ideal senior citizen was supposed to be active in the community, adding "life to years" instead of simply "years to life" (to use a phrase that was becoming common). New ideals of aging involved independence, service, and vitality—noble values, to be sure, but ones that tended to exclude and stigmatize those who, for whatever reason, could not achieve them.

This neglect extended beyond older people with disabilities and to their caretakers. The American discussion of age tended to isolate the older person, focusing on that person's welfare and health without paying much attention to the welfare and health of those who cared for her. Organized labor played a large role in the construction of old-age policy, but the laborers most directly concerned with the issue, like nurses and other hospital staff, were not involved. Care workers were rarely organized labor, and private non-profit hospitals were, in 1947, excluded from the 1935 National Labor Relations Act. Medicare was, in its essence, a plan to use government funds to support extant hospitals. Labor relations inside those hospitals went unaddressed. At this crucial moment in the history of American medicine, when care work was becoming an ever-larger sector of the economy, it could have become a well-regulated and well-compensated profession, one that was aligned with the political activism of the older people the workers cared for. That did not happen.[6]

The purpose of Medicare was to pay the medical expenses of older Americans who were briefly dependent because of an acute illness and then return them to sturdy independence by granting them access to the technological wonders of modern medicine and modern hospital care. So before returning to the topic of Medicare, which we'll do at the end of the chapter, let's take a tour through the life and times of the senior citizen between 1945 and 1965, exploring what independence meant for that group, why it seemed so important to so many people, and what the consequences were for those who were, because of poverty or disability, "dependent." Medicare can then emerge as a response to the needs of the senior citizen as understood in the decade before its passage—just as Social Security served the needs of the aged as articulated in the 1920s.

Independence for older people had been a goal in the Social Security era, too, but at that time it referred strictly to economic independence. The postwar invocation of independence was more robust: senior citizens, more than the aged before them, were supposed to live independently of their children, and to have full and fulfilling lives apart from them, socializing with others in their own age cohort. In the 1930s, this kind of independence would have made little sense. Older people in that era, born around the time of the Civil War, were used to intergenerational living. Older people in the 1960s had, in the aggregate, very different life experiences. They had grown up in a rapidly industrializing America, with electricity and appliances and automobiles. Millions had moved out of tenements or farmhouses and into the suburbs.

Independence after World War II was not just an ideal, in other words. It was, for many, a reality. This was most obviously true when it came to housing and employment. Older people increasingly lived apart from their children. They still tended to live nearby and to be involved in their children's lives, both emotionally and financially, even if that relationship was more about pitching in money for furniture than sharing income to purchase food and housing. Nonetheless, the trend toward independent housing was undeniable. This was, after all, the age of the great housing boom, when millions of Americans streamed into new homes in the suburbs, and when the tidy, single-family home became the emblem of the American dream. And those new households were not intergenerational. In 1930, more than 40 percent of older white people lived with their grown children, while in 1960, fewer than 20 percent did so. Older Black Americans were more likely to live with their children, but not by much: about a quarter of them lived with their children in 1960. This separation from their children's houses was mirrored by a separation between older people and their employers. Between 1950 and 1960, the percentage of men over sixty-five in the labor force declined from 46 percent to 33 percent—a number that continued to fall. This statistical decline was broadly shared: the vast majority of older women were not working, and older Black men were actually less likely than older white ones to be in the labor force.[7]

Independence in housing was a by-product of independence in finances. Social Security was beginning to transform the meaning of aging in the United States. In 1950, fewer than 3 million Americans were receiving Social Security checks; by 1960, the number had risen to more than 14 million. Put differently, in 1950, only 16 percent of older people were receiving old-age insurance payments from Social Security, while in 1960, a full 64 percent were. Social Security benefits were going up, too, which allowed senior citizens to partake in the general economic expansion of the period. Many older people could also rely on defined-benefit pensions, the traditional sort of pension that the employer controls and that pays out as long as the beneficiary is alive. That idea itself was not novel. Some firms had been offering defined-benefit pensions for decades. As World War II came to a close, a full 6.4 million workers were covered by private pensions of this sort. That is a lot of workers, but still a small slice of the labor force. After the war, though, pensions became a top-level demand of trade unions for the first time. This was an era of union strength and collective bargaining. And thanks to a series of court decisions and IRS regulations, fringe benefits could be negotiated by collective-bargaining agreements. This meant, in other words, that trade unions could do more than just haggle over wages and working conditions. They could now bargain over benefits like health care and pensions—and they did. Nonunionized workforces often followed suit. Within just three decades, the number of workers covered by employer-sponsored pensions more than quintupled to 33 million as defined-benefit pensions became something that broad swaths of the middle class could rely on for the first (and last) time.[8]

These benefits were unequally shared, to be sure. The median income for an older white married couple was almost double that of an older nonwhite married couple. In part, this was because of Social Security's design. The issue was not primarily that Black Americans weren't receiving Social Security benefits; most of them were. The issue was the *level* of benefits, which were indexed to a racially inequitable labor market. Retired white workers received, on average, seventy-five dollars per month, compared with fifty-nine dollars for nonwhite ones. That discrepancy, while large, can't explain the entire income gap. Another important piece of the puzzle concerned the private pension system, which was even more racially unequal than Social Security. White workers in this period were more than twice as likely as Black ones to be covered by private pensions. It should be little surprise, then, that a different system was disproportionately utilized by older Black Americans: the welfare program that was still known as Old-Age Assistance.[9]

Senior independence was, for many, a reality—and it was a cultural mandate for all. There was a pull factor here, as many older people desired independence. And there was a push factor, too, as they were being, in many ways, exiled from the post–World War II American family. At least in part, this was due to the new understanding of family life that became hegemonic in the nervous early decades of the Cold War. Communism was understood to be both a foreign threat and a domestic one. So just as political elites worried about the balance of powers abroad, they worried about the moral strength of the nation back home. And the traditional family—the sturdy churchgoing family with a well-paid father and a stay-at-home mother—appeared to them as the true bedrock of American strength.

Crucially for our story, that family was defined quite narrowly. The definition of "family" itself was in flux in those years, and increasingly it was used to refer strictly to the two-generational unit living under one roof. The model of the reproductive, heteronormative, and nuclear family that emerged at the time was powerful enough to authorize the policing and disenfranchisement of those who fell afoul of it. This attitude reached its apogee with the Moynihan Report of 1965, which blamed the challenges of Black life in the United States on the supposed pathologies of Black family life. Likewise, queer Americans were oppressed mercilessly in this period, their divergent sexual practices coming to seem like an antechamber to communism.[10]

Older Americans had little place in the anticommunist family, which was strictly for working-age parents and their children. Suburban homes were not designed for intergenerational families, and, to take the other paradigmatic space of Cold War domesticity, bomb shelters weren't either. Bomb shelters were designed for nuclear families, not for extended kinship networks. Sometimes lip service was paid to the wisdom of the elders. One of the government's civil defense campaigns of the 1950s was called Grandma's Pantry. As one Atlanta journalist put it, in the old days "grandma could meet nearly any emergency," helping neighbors in need with "her well-stocked larder." Such a sensibility, she went on, "may prove a lifesaver in this atomic age." The aura of the grandmother, though, did not require any actual grandmothers; this was very much a production of the civil defense establishment and its nutrition experts. As such, most of the items required for the modern pantry would be, in the journalist's words, "much different from the bulk raw products grandma stores."[11]

Fictive grandmothers might be deployed in the name of military preparedness, but it was hard to see how real ones could be. As the idea of the family became increasingly two-generational, it became unclear whether older people even *had* a family. "Are the last fifty years of life," one scholar wondered, "considered as ex-family?" As a 1951 textbook on family life put it, "the middle-class family in America is small," in that "the ideal is to have a separate household for each marriage pair and their children." Elderly people simply vanish from the story. That much was common, but this particular textbook went above and beyond. In the introduction, the authors explain that the individual went through five phases, of which grandparenthood is the last. They promise to devote a lengthy section to each phase—but they simply don't. Old age is almost entirely ignored, except to warn against the "psychological" dependence of older people on their children's families.[12]

The nuclear family enjoyed a great deal of prestige in the social scientific thought of the era. Talcott Parsons, an important social theorist, presumed as a matter of course "the reduction of the importance in our society of kinship units other than the nuclear family." That family was no longer a political or economic unit but a pedagogical and psychological one, tasked with "the care of infants, household maintenance, and individual tension management." Larger households with complex kinship networks were viewed as less modern and less advanced, associated with immigrant communities or the Third World rather than with the squeaky-clean suburbs that would win the Cold War. David Riesman, perhaps the most influential social scientist of postwar America, made the same case. His magnum opus, *The Lonely Crowd* (1950), sold more than a million copies. Old age plays a pivotal role in the narrative structure of the book, which is essentially about America's transition to a land bereft of tradition. In the olden days, Riesman argued, elders and ancestors played a huge role in embodying the "tradition" that was indispensable to primitive societies. But in modern societies they relinquished that role entirely. "Grandparents," Riesman concludes, "stand as emblems of how little one can learn from one's elders about the things that matter."[13]

If sociologists preferred to make confident predictions about the increasing irrelevance of the aged, it was psychoanalysts who took it upon themselves to make the moral case that elder interference in the nuclear family could only result in pathology. Freud himself had been skeptical of overinvolved grandparents, as had other early psychoanalysts. This trend was crowned in America in a 1938 article by Hermann Vollmer, a Jewish refugee from Germany then practicing in New York, titled "The Grandmother: A Problem in Child-Rearing." In his view, there was something troubling about the grandmother, who through an attempt to relive her glory years as a mother ended up creating insoluble conflicts between herself, her children, and her grandchildren.[14]

In the postwar period, this idea became more widespread. Across the Cold War West, psychologists were discovering family separation, through either war or divorce, as a foundational trauma. The healthy child, it was believed, could only emerge through healthy relationships with a nurturing mother and a powerful father. Any tampering with this relationship threatened mental illness—tampering of the sort that overeager grandparents could provide. The most developed version of this theory was provided by David Rapaport, a Massachusetts-based clinician and one of the leading psychoanalysts of the era. In 1956, he coined the notion of "grandparent syndrome." Like Vollmer and others, he saw the nuclear family as the ideal scenario for ego development and could only perceive of elder relatives as disruptions to the Oedipal drama. He delivered lurid tales of children overidentifying with grandparents and becoming terrified of death at an early age, or perhaps fantasizing about becoming, like their grandparents, in some way dominant over their parents. They were matched by grandparents who overidentified with grandchildren as a way to stave off their own mortality. All these dynamics were neurotic.[15]

The theory of the isolated elder became the received wisdom for a generation of social workers, who at the time drew on psychology to explain poverty and to convince the government to provide therapeutic, individualized services to the needy. "Our role as case workers," one expert reported, "is to help both the [older] parent and the [adult] child free themselves from a too stifling parent-child relationship." That belief was backed up by studies in social work journals arguing that powerful grandmothers were at fault for all kinds of sexual and psychological neuroses. In one study, mothers and children "underwent intensive psychotherapy" whose main goal was "helping the mothers bring out their feelings of hostility and resentment toward the grandmothers." In 1958, the assistant director of Jewish Community Services of Long Island worried that changes in American life "have tended to eliminate the grandparent from the home." "The emergence of the nuclear family" in the place of the "extended family," he went on, led to a new situation of "kinship loyalty only to spouse and children."[16]

This combination of neglect and suspicion of older relatives can be found in the era's popular culture too. Sitcoms from the 1950s and early 1960s like *Ozzie and Harriet, The Donna Reed Show*, and *Bewitched* tended not to feature "grandparent" figures at all: the drama was entirely about the two-generational, nuclear family. When older characters did appear, they were more likely to cause problems than they were to transmit homespun wisdom. Sometimes they provided comic relief, as with Lucy's scatterbrained mother in *I Love Lucy*. At others, they were meant as a genuine foil to the family, as with Endora in *Bewitched*, a literal witch who detested her daughter's decision to marry a mortal. Interestingly, in both these cases the elder characters comedically butchered the names of their sons-in-law, signaling an inability or lack of desire to bless the union.

Many films of the era featured older protagonists who had challenging relationships with the younger generation or with their own children. This was true of melodramas like *Sunset Boulevard* (1950) and *All That Heaven Allows* (1955); it was memorably the case in horror films like *Psycho* (1960) and *Whatever Happened to Baby Jane?* (1962). In their own ways, all these films are about the dangerous, or even murderous, consequences that can arise if older women do not properly detach themselves and continue meddling in the affairs of the young (in the case of *Psycho*, meddling from beyond the grave!).[17]

These representations exemplified what older people should *not* do, and they coincided with a broad discussion of what older people were supposed to do with themselves once they left their grown children alone. To imagine a positive, modern ideal for senior citizens required a great deal of cultural work, and this work was done in almost every imaginable forum in postwar America. Never before had aging been such an obsession in the cultural and political conversation as it was in the postwar decades—and maybe it has never been since. One scholar complained about the "seemingly countless symposia on the aged." Conferences and workshops and institutes poured endless time and attention into the aging American, asking about her hobbies, health, sexual activity, labor capacity, and more.[18]

Much of this happened on the federal level. In 1950, the White House hosted its first National Conference on Aging, followed by several conferences of state councils on aging in the 1950s and capped off by the 1961 White House Conference on Aging. (They have continued happening in most decades since then.) The National Institutes of Health (NIH) made aging into a major priority after World War II, culminating in the foundation of the National Institute on Aging in 1974. The NIH sponsored five regional centers for aging research. One of them, at my home institution of Duke University, still exists today and has contributed to the research of this very book.

One of the NIH's many endeavors in this field was an Inter-University Training Institute in Social Gerontology, based at the University of Michigan. That word, "gerontology," was something of a key word for this period of aging research. If "geriatrics" refers to a medical specialty, "gerontology" is more capacious. Gerontologists are concerned with older people's health and bodies, but also with their social surroundings. It is an interdisciplinary initiative, involving sociologists and psychologists as much as physicians.

Although the word had been used before, only after World War II did it name a major research paradigm. Previous research into aging had taken one of two tracks: geriatricians researched pathological health processes in older people, while social reformers tackled old-age poverty. Gerontology did something different, defined above all by the *Journal of Gerontology*. The cover of the first issue, published in 1946, featured a motto promising "to add life to years, not just years to life." This particular phrase, which can be sporadically found in the 1930s, became ubiquitous in the 1940s and 1950s, when it was used by government commissions, public health experts, and more. And while "life" was not defined, the clear implication was that gerontologists were concerned with helping older people to craft lives that were vibrant, meaningful, and independent.

The opening editorial was penned by a social scientist named Lawrence Frank. Frank was not a clinician, nor was he linked to a university; he was a social scientist tied to the phalanx of nonprofit institutions that did so much to fund research in this period. Research into aging before World War II had been a fly-by-night affair, performed largely at the whim of state-level commissions that were concerned about almshouses and old-age indigence. Now, much larger sums of money were in play, and they were meant to fund more holistic studies of the American aging experience. Frank himself had recently served as vice president of the Josiah Macy Jr. Foundation, which provided the grant to start the magazine; both the Rockefeller and Ford Foundations were funding gerontological research as well.[19]

In the editorial, Frank's major concern was to show that old age could still be a time of healthy, vigorous activity. True, some people developed disabilities—but not everyone, and not even most people. Time, he explained, is a process that affects everyone in different ways. He analogized human beings to food: some foods age slowly and gracefully, like wine, and others don't, like cheese. He wanted to understand why, if human beings are so similar to one another in most respects, they age so differently. His proposal was that the "degenerative changes" we often associate with age might not be part of "normal aging" at all: perhaps they are related to physiological or psychic trauma, or other "slings and arrows of outrageous fortune."[20]

Frank and other gerontologists were committed to severing the link between old age and ill health. Getting old did not have to mean getting sick, they insisted. In the words of Frederick C. Swartz, chair of the National Committee on Aging, "Geriatrics can no longer be considered a field of medicine, since there are no diseases of old age." Previous studies had focused on the sick or the impoverished and had helped to create the image that older people were, in general, sick or impoverished. After World War II, the research strategy changed, and the image of older people with it. A few years after Frank's editorial, researchers at Duke launched an influential study of "normal aging." The study was very much in the mainstream of gerontology at the time, and an interdisciplinary group of scholars in Kansas City was doing the same. These studies were aimed at a rather strict demarcation between normal aging, which we might think of as successful or healthy aging, and the process of degeneration or decay that was known as unsuccessful or pathological aging.[21]

This ideal of active, normal aging could be found in popular culture too. Such depictions often sent the older protagonist on a voyage, allowing the author to sidestep the thorny question of how older people could be dignified and active while also respecting their children's authority. The most famous example, of course, is *The Old Man and the Sea* (1952), Ernest Hemingway's novella about an aging fisherman's noble struggle with a marlin. The story, which reached millions of readers through its publication in *Life* magazine, is a complex meditation on life, death, and mortality. But at the most superficial level, it is about a very active older man who shows considerable ingenuity and energy (the same can be said of the 1958 film version, starring Spencer Tracy). Readers interested in a more feminine hero pursuing similar adventures could read *Dear Mad'm*, which came out a few years later. It was the memoir of an eighty-year-old woman who was told by a nurse, somewhat to her surprise, that she had "young legs." Like her friends, she had always thought that "everything is over for a woman of eighty." But now, with her young legs, she "determined to embark on an adventure" by living alone in a cabin in the mountains. The book is a charming account of her adventures in the woods—the friends she made, the animals she encountered, and her eventual decision to stay in a beautiful place where she found a sort of chosen family in the new friends she made there.[22]

All of this led to the creation of what one sociologist in 1965 called a "group consciousness among the aging." Older people increasingly began to identify less as members of their multigenerational family and more as members of a new age cohort. All around the country, senior citizens' associations and clubs were being formed as both advocacy organizations and social opportunities. Let's take Baltimore as an example. In that city, as elsewhere in the country, there had been few if any group activities open to seniors qua seniors before World War II. But by 1960 there were more than forty, many set up by the city's Department of Recreation. Religious groups were active, too, giving older residents the chance to participate in senior citizens' camping trips and fellowship retreats. These clubs, which cropped up around the nation, were unlike the Townsend groups of the 1930s: they did not have an explicit social agenda but were designed to give older people an opportunity to socialize with other older people.[23]

This new group identity appeared in the world of periodicals, which did a great deal in postwar America to create and promote group identities. Before the 1950s, there was not really a journal or magazine for older people; even the Townsend movement's journal, like the movement itself, was designed to appeal to all ages. But by the 1960s, older people could take their pick of many. One of the first, titled simply *Senior Citizen*, started to appear in 1955. The magazine devoted itself to the creation of active aging as an ideal: it featured tips on travel and health aimed at older people, for instance. It was also a conduit for the popularization of gerontological ideas, which were reviewed in the magazine. An early article instructed readers how to "stay young while growing old." The article rehearsed Lawrence Frank's notion that aging happens at "different rates" in different people. "The important thing," it prescribed, "is for the individual to seek an outlet for recreating and refreshing himself frequently."[24]

This campaign for old-age recreation was not, though, a belated victory of the Townsendite idea that older people should be lavish consumer spenders. Old age at the time was imagined in somewhat spartan terms that often involved new kinds of small-scale living spaces. A 1955 issue of *Senior Citizen* recommended that seniors set up a "clubhouse" where older people could live together. Each person would have a small room, furnished by themselves; the house would feature a small workshop and a large yard for shuffleboard and checkers. And even in those spaces, the land could be productive, through gardening. The characteristic activity of senior citizens wasn't golf, but service; service to the country, after all, is what citizenship was all about. As President Dwight Eisenhower wrote in his 1956 memo convening the first Federal Council on Aging, "The great majority of older persons are capable of continuing their self-sufficiency and usefulness to the community if given the opportunity. Our task is to help in assuring that these opportunities are provided."[25]

And there were numerous new opportunities to do so, many of which were summarized in a government pamphlet that appeared in 1966 in honor of Senior Citizens Month. The whole tenor of the pamphlet was that older people needed useful activity, including "opportunity for employment with no discriminatory personnel practices because of age." For those who did not wish to work, the pamphlet offered other ideas. They could volunteer, for instance, with the Peace Corps, an organization normally associated with youth but which was intergenerational and was celebrated as such, including in magazines for older people. Or they could work with VISTA, President Kennedy's domestic version of the Peace Corps (and which would soon become AmeriCorps). They could work with Operation Green Thumb, which employed retired farmers to beautify highways in rural areas. Or they could work with the Service Corps of Retired Executives (SCORE), an organization designed to help, in the pamphlet's words, "retired executives provide management assistance to small business."[26]

Scientists and policymakers in the 1950s were interested in social solutions to social problems, and aging was a social problem par excellence, occurring as it did at a massive scale and irrespective of people's individual intentions. Few at the time recommended individual strategies of prevention, fitness, or memory care. Even dementia was thought to be social in nature, the result of insufficiently engaging surroundings. "A physician," one expert reported, "can take the stand that since society is primarily responsible for the elderly patient's problem, society should take the lead in relieving his unhappiness." "Aging," explained another at the University of Chicago, is "a sociological phenomenon," and the biological and psychological changes accompanying age, while real, only make sense when related to "the societal frame of reference within which they are measured." The Saginaw County Medical Society put out a statement saying that there were no such things as "problems of aging." Thus, they encouraged "greater attention to the social, vocational, and economic factors which are so vital to good health among older people."[27]

In the space of a generation, the image of the older American changed dramatically: from the hunched-over "aged" with one foot in the almshouse to the independent "senior citizen," who belonged to senior clubs, participated in service projects tailored to them, and deserved social support in their quest for independence. For the first time, a recognizably distinct senior culture emerged, allowing older Americans an age-based identity that was, crucially, separate from the identities of their children and their families. This is how seniors became citizens.

From one perspective, these changes represented an unalloyed victory for older people, who now had access to a coherent and attractive vision of old age, one shared by policymakers and intellectuals who believed that social and political reform was necessary to make that vision happen. Senior citizenship, like all kinds of citizenship, came with enormous advantages. But senior citizenship was not open to everyone. Remember, this was still the era of Jim Crow, when millions of Black Americans were disenfranchised. And it was the era of the Red Scare, when wide swaths of political opinion were deemed treasonous. Citizenship was by no means open to all in postwar America. It was limited in many ways to those deemed deserving. And senior citizenship was no different.

The primary goal of gerontology in this period was to prove that older people could handle independence—that they could marshal the economic and physical resources to blaze their own trail through later life. To study impoverished, disabled, or otherwise disenfranchised older people would not have been conducive to this effort, so it was seldom done. "America is a middle-class nation," one contribution to a senior magazine argued in 1959, and "there is almost no lower class." While that was certainly not true, you wouldn't guess it from the popular culture of aging. The most obvious "lower class" in 1959, of course, was the Black population, but this was never mentioned in the senior press. It was much more common to find a treacly nostalgia, as when one author in the same magazine swooned about Main Street, U.S.A. at Disneyland, where the visitor could be "whisked back to the colorful era that was America, 1890–1915."[28]

The image of the "independent" senior citizen was largely white. Senior citizens' publications had nothing to say about race and almost never carried images of, or articles by, Black seniors. It was not until 1964, at the high tide of the civil rights movement, that the *Journal of Gerontology* published an article specifically about Black older people and their needs. The first issue of *Senior Citizen* featured nothing on race or any Black writers, but it did celebrate the achievements of "William A. (Uncle Bill) Lundy, 106, one of the three surviving Confederate veterans." Another early issue described "two Negroes" who were at a political meeting, reporting their speech in dialect ("who is dat man?"). The magazine that was doing the most to actually imagine retirement, with guides to hobbies and Florida vacations and so on, was called *Harvest Years*. In the three closing months of 1965, which was perhaps the most important year for civil rights in American history, it featured no articles about Black people or Black aging. Those three issues contained 106 identifiable images of people, most of them showing senior citizens taking classes or doing service projects. Of them, 102 of the people depicted were white; all four of the Black individuals shown were part of a series of articles on service projects (white women teaching "under-privileged" Black youths to read, for instance).[29]

Black researchers and seniors attempted to participate in the broader culture of senior citizenship, with mixed results. A member of the National Urban League, the civil rights organization most clearly committed to the issue, was invited to the 1961 White House Conference on Aging, as were a handful of other Black experts. His confidential report about the event was unenthusiastic. The conference planners, in his view, had "missed the boat as far as racial participation on the program was concerned." Likewise, there were Golden Age clubs for Black seniors, but they faced an uphill battle for acceptance. In 1962, a thirteen-member Golden Age club from St. Louis applied to join the national convention of Golden Age and Senior Citizens Clubs. Of the eighty-two voting delegates, only sixteen were in favor of accepting the group. Moreover, groups from Michigan were only accepted once the Southern delegates made sure that the groups had no Black members. "You have a right to decide who you're going to socialize with," exclaimed a national board member as delegates in Confederate hats cheered her on.[30]

Older people with disabilities were exiled from the new category of the senior citizen too. Disability was of course an issue for older Americans. A study of Old-Age Assistance recipients in Philadelphia in 1950 found that over half had health problems, and that chronic disability was far and away the primary reason that older men were unable to find work. Researchers at Duke found that a majority of older people had some kind of disability, often linked with visual impairment or arthritis; they also found that these disabilities were linked with socio-economic class more than they were with sex or race. In other words, poorer people were more likely to be impaired. And of those older than seventy, more than half experienced enough physical disability that they would likely be kept from low-impact activities like going to church or to clubs. When it came to issues of cognitive impairment, the very definition of "normal" aging was stretched: "only 89 of the 222 could be considered normal," with the rest experiencing some kind of memory loss, neurosis, or even psychosis.[31]

But this reality was seldom considered in the literature or in the public discussions around Medicare. When a gerontological journal published articles about disability, which was rare, authors were careful to distinguish disability from "normal aging" and also to stress the powers of rehabilitation. Likewise, in the lead-up to Medicare there was surprisingly little discussion of long-term care or the whole issue of nursing homes. The easiest place to track these trends is in the proceedings of the White House Conferences on Aging. The director of the first conference (1950) was Clark Tibbitts, a gerontologist who was ubiquitous in the many public-facing ventures of his newly fashionable discipline. In his view, the purpose of gerontology was to help older people enjoy "useful and satisfying participation in the life of the community." And in section after section of the conference, he reported, delegates insisted that older people were not so different from younger ones; they valued friendship, religion, and education, just like anyone else. "Adjustment in old age," in other words, "is merely a continuation of the lifelong adjustment process."[32]

The 1961 White House Conference on Aging, which played a large role in studying and defending the legislation that would become Medicare, continued this trend. The conference's final report emphasized that "a rich and satisfying old age is primarily a personal achievement." It featured a remarkable set of "Rights of Senior Citizens"—and as with many human rights texts, this one essentially gave seniors access to the tools needed to attain individual autonomy. The very first right is "the right to be useful"; the second is a right to work; another promises "the right to live independently." Those might *sound* like obligations, but to clear up any confusion on that front, the bill of seniors' rights was paired with an actual list of obligations, including the obligation to be "self-supporting" as long as possible and the obligation to care for one's own health.[33]

What you *don't* see are delegates emphasizing the disabilities that attend old age—as the topic relates to either older people or those who care for them. Disabilities emerge only as problems to be addressed and minimized to allow a vital and active old age to continue as long as possible. In the section on rehabilitation for the visually impaired, for instance, the delegates could imagine only two solutions. The first was technological or medical: perhaps means might be found to allow people to see again. The second involved personal effort, or what they called "means of self-management as blind individuals." This would require support, to be sure, but the goal would be the restoration of independence. Gerontologists of the era believed in social solutions to the problems of the aged—but not, apparently, when it came to older people with disabilities.[34]

Policymakers were not yet attuned to the challenges of race and disability, but they were quite concerned, as generations of old-age advocates had been, with the troubling specter of old-age poverty. Many seniors, even when taking Social Security into account, lived in poverty. The headline finding of a major study by the Social Security Administration was that in 1963 there were about 5.2 million impoverished older Americans out of 34.6 million impoverished Americans overall; a full one in seven impoverished Americans was over sixty-five. Most of the impoverished seniors were women. And half of the 5 million were living with younger relatives, almost universally because their own incomes were so low. The most marginalized population was older women living alone: only one in four of that group, by the statistician's reckoning, had enough income for a reasonable standard of living.[35]

Many older Americans relied on welfare, specifically, the program that is now known as Supplemental Security Income (SSI) but which was then still called Old-Age Assistance (OAA). About one in five older people received OAA, a form of welfare targeted at the poor, in this period. Older women, especially those who were widowed or unmarried, were the most likely group to need support. Most recipients of OAA were white, but as a proportional matter, nonwhite Americans were more likely to claim the benefit. Indeed, almost half of nonwhite older persons received OAA. In one 1950 study of welfare recipients in a rural Southern county, a full two-thirds were over sixty. Most were Black, most were women, and most were unmarried or widowed. While only 5 percent were bedridden, more than a quarter required significant amounts of care. About half the group lived in dwellings that, in the authors' words, "were below minimum standards for health and decency." One man lived in a shack with an earthen floor, formerly used for storing potatoes, for the last decade of his life. This level of deprivation was remarkable, but many other people in the study were challenged by a lack of indoor plumbing and heat. There was not much for the older folks to do with their time, which "passed slowly."[36]

This persistent poverty had many causes, but one of the major ones was the exponential growth in seniors' medical bills. The American medical system was transforming rapidly in those years, when the basic model we have today was being born. In the 1930s, few Americans had health insurance, but this changed quickly after the war, once trade unions started to negotiate for the benefit in earnest. From 1948 to 1954, just six years, the number of workers covered by union-organized insurance plans jumped from three million to twelve million (and another seventeen million dependents). Older people, though, were left in the lurch; even those who were retiring from union jobs with pensions did not have health care plans that would follow them into retirement (whereas the unions wanted this benefit, employers balked at the cost). Older Americans were thus significantly less well insured than younger ones—and they had more cause to visit physicians too. Congressional hearings from the era featured parades of older people, especially women, who complained that they could not afford to care for their health.[37]

Medical bills, in short, threatened the independence that senior citizens were so anxious to claim. It bears repeating that none of this would have been necessary if Americans had, like many other countries, opted to provide health care to all its citizens. Presidents Franklin Roosevelt and Harry Truman both wanted something like that to happen, but it didn't, thanks largely to the intransigent opposition of the AMA. In place of state-sponsored coverage, insurance arrived for many Americans, as it does now, through their employers, due to the success of collective bargaining for fringe benefits mentioned earlier. Grandma, however, could not be counted as a dependent by her children for insurance purposes, as this would have undercut the entire logic of old-age policy since Social Security.

This conundrum led to the conclusion that perhaps Social Security beneficiaries ought to have help with health care costs—something that the Social Security Administration itself supported as early as 1951, because high medical costs were undercutting the agency's efforts to improve the economic solvency of the aged. Little was possible under the Eisenhower administration, but in the later 1950s an enormous swell of energy grew behind Medicare, as it would eventually be called. Much of that energy came from seniors themselves, who organized under the characteristic name of the National Council for Senior Citizens. Senator John F. Kennedy made it a linchpin of his presidential campaign, and even his opponent in 1960, Richard Nixon, conceded that some kind of government expansion for older people's health care was necessary.

In pressing their case for insurance coverage, senior citizens and their advocates made a canny move. As Roosevelt's team had done in building the case for Social Security, senior citizens' organizations claimed that Medicare was necessary not for their own sake, but for the sake of their children's families. The health of the nuclear family, recall, was the paramount concern of policymakers in this period, and it was that two-generational family, unencumbered by needy and grasping older people, that could provide the moral and economic response to communism.

In 1963, the National Council of Senior Citizens released a video titled *For All the Rest of Your Life.* The film begins with an elder fantasy in which a retired couple moves to the country and devotes themselves to hobbies and housework. The wife's health problems, however, put an end to that dream: they are forced to sell their house and move back in with one of their children. This is portrayed as a tragedy, and indeed at the dinner table the ailing couple sits between the healthy younger parents. "I'd give anything to be back there," the older man says, "standing on our own two feet." "When the big bills hit the retired," explains the narrator, "they hit the whole family." (In one of the dramatized episodes, those bills force a child to drop out of college.) What the producers of the film understood is that it was not enough to display the suffering of impoverished senior citizens. What they had to show was that older Americans, absent government action, constituted a threat to the families of their grown children. This strategy was adopted, too, by John F. Kennedy, who prioritized the issue and gave a speech about it at Madison Square Garden. In it, he painted a picture of a "typical" family in need of help. In that family, a "husband has worked hard all his life" and has "always wanted to pay his own way." He has a fair amount of savings tucked away, but when his wife gets sick and has to go to the hospital, his savings are depleted, and he needs help.[38]

The strategy worked. Medicare became a popular and galvanizing cause. Senior citizens organized in support of it, to be sure, but support didn't come from them alone. Trade unions, concerned with their retirees, fought hard for Medicare. Middle-aged taxpayers, concerned about their future selves and their aging parents, were supporters as well. When the vote finally took place, Medicare passed with bipartisan support. The vast majority of Democrats supported it, of course, and almost half of Republican lawmakers did too.[39]

While there was grassroots support for the principle of the legislation, the details were hashed out in complex bargaining among trade unions, hospital administrators, and the AMA. Britain's National Health Service, for all its flaws, is less complex: the government pays the doctors, owns the hospitals, and sets the prices. In the United States, the government hesitated to become so involved in the health care industry. Medicare did not change this. What it did, essentially, was direct a gusher of money to the preexisting medical system in order to provide (some) health care to a small portion of the population.

The legislation was broken into three parts. Medicare Part A provided acute care, covering hospital visits up to ninety days. This was available to any beneficiary of Social Security over the age of sixty-five, and benefits kicked in after a forty-dollar deductible and a copayment. Part A was funded by a payroll tax. Medicare Part B, a form of voluntary insurance, was designed to help older Americans pay for services not covered in Part A. It covered physician costs after a fifty-dollar deductible and came with a 20 percent copay. It was funded by individual premiums and general government revenues. And finally, Medicaid. In this case, last does imply least, as Medicaid was an afterthought to the negotiations for Medicare. Medicaid was designed to be a means-tested welfare program to provide medical care, including long-term care, for people of any age who could not afford to pay for their own health insurance. Unlike Medicare, Medicaid, like many welfare programs, was designed to be administered by the states rather than by the federal government.

So, to boil that down: Medicare Part A enrolled all older Americans and provided many kinds of acute care; Part B was voluntary and covered *other* kinds of acute care. None of it was free, and all of it involved complex partnerships between the government and private insurance companies. For those who couldn't afford medical insurance, Medicaid emerged as a state-administered welfare program.

Medicare, like Social Security before it, had some very serious limitations—and again, those limitations were a logical extension of the particular shape that the national conversation about old age had taken in the decade before the legislation. For one thing, Medicare and Medicaid together provide nothing like "universal health care" for the elderly. Medicare was not designed to be a poverty-reduction tool, nor did its backers talk about health care as a right. It was designed instead to ensure that older Americans would be able to afford hospital care without bankrupting themselves and their children. Thus, many items were not covered at all. Seniors had no help to pay for prescription drugs, dental coverage, or vision and hearing plans. And of those items that were covered, the deductibles and copays were often considerable. Three decades after Medicare's passage, impoverished seniors were spending more than a third of their family income on medical expenses. Even those with modest incomes, between 125 percent and 200 percent of the poverty line, were paying more than a quarter.[40]

The most consequential decision of all, though, concerned long-term care of the sort needed by older people with disabilities. Medicare, with few exceptions, did not pay for nursing home care, or home health aides, or the many things that older Americans with long-term disabilities needed. Postwar policymakers and gerontologists were interested in getting senior citizens "back on their feet"—that is, interested in the kinds of acute care that could return older people to productive and independent lives. Nursing home care for those with long-term disability was not part of that equation. It was therefore a legislative afterthought, shunted from Medicare to Medicaid, a state-run welfare system that was only for seniors (and people in other age brackets) without resources.

Another constituency that was left out of this settlement was the caregiving labor force. The postwar discussion of aging had so isolated the "senior citizen" that it had become possible to discuss at great length the health problems of aging America without even mentioning the conditions of those who cared for them. The 1961 White House Conference was typical of gerontological discussions, then and since, in that it bemoaned the persistent staff shortages in most every medical field that involved the aged (from geriatricians to social workers to nurses). It was typical, too, in that conference delegates saw the problem as one of marketing and recruitment rather than of labor conditions. The lengthy section on workforce development in the 1961 conference's report has a great deal to say about marketing strategies and about the proper organization of training, but nothing at all to say about wage improvements or any other ways to upgrade the (often very challenging) work conditions of the caregivers.[41]

Still, for all its complexities and limitations, Medicare was a great benefit to Americans of all ages. Over the decades, even the elderly poor have been granted access to an astonishing array of medical technologies. Meanwhile, the legislation has shielded millions of families from the risk of financial ruin from hospital bills. The gains are easiest to show for the richest Americans, who were paying the highest out-of-pocket expenses before the passage of Medicare. And yet, the Medicare package as a whole has been a boon for older Americans of every income. Medicaid especially played a central role in the amazing reduction of old-age poverty.[42]

Medicare, even though it was largely inadvertent, had positive impacts on Black health care too. Before Medicare, health care facilities in both the North and the South were effectively segregated. Hospitals, like schools, could legally be "separate but equal." This was upended with the *Simkins v. Moses Cone* decision in 1963, the medical equivalent of *Brown v. Board of Education*, and the Civil Rights Act of 1964, which prohibited segregation in public spaces. Legal measures like those, though, have limited power to change existing institutions. It was only with the passage of Medicare that the federal government acquired the teeth to actually force hospitals into compliance. And even then, doing so was only possible because an enterprising group of activists and civil servants with the Office of Equal Health Opportunity dedicated themselves to the cause.[43]

Together, Social Security and Medicare transformed the meaning and experience of old age in the United States. In the 1920s, older

Americans for the most part were still working and were still deeply enmeshed in their children's families. For a variety of cultural and economic and political reasons, by the late 1960s this had changed completely. There were many more senior citizens than there had been, and they had access to a lavish array of income supports. Security was not available to everyone, but it was available to many millions of people, and almost every American senior benefited in some way from the new programs. Medicaid and Old-Age Assistance, after all, may have been stigmatizing and underfunded, but they did exist, and they did a great deal to help the most disenfranchised communities.

There was not yet, though, a national infrastructure for retirement. There was not, in other words, a new set of social services and institutional locations in which seniors could actually spend all their free time. If the 1950s and early 1960s created the ideological and financial preconditions for senior retirement, it fell to the later 1960s and the 1970s to create the architectural and institutional infrastructure that could fill it up. And to understand that phenomenon, we should leave behind the gray-suited world of gerontologists and policymakers and enter a different one: more unruly, more creative, more fun. In a word, more Florida.

CHAPTER 4

THE INVENTION OF
RETIREMENT

O n Wednesday nights in the fall of 1975, anyone interested could
attend a free course on retirement planning at Orange Coast
College, a community college outside Los Angeles. It was taught by a
sixty-one-year-old woman named Marjorie Anderson, who had been
studying gerontology and was concerned that people her age didn't
know enough about how wonderful retirement could be—if you
planned for it. Students learned about Social Security and Medicare,
and they learned how to manage nutrition and housing. They learned,
too, how to cultivate a new life for themselves, exploring new interests and hobbies. "Retire to something," she insisted, "rather than from
something."[1]

Anderson and her students were participating in one of the great
innovations of the era: the invention of retirement. Of course, some
people had always "retired," but they did not thenceforth enter a
period of life called "retirement," structured by retirement communities, service agencies, and social insurance policies. Retirement in that
more specific sense only became a reality in the 1960s and 1970s. The

experience of Americans turning sixty-five in 1970 was different in most every way from that of their older relatives. Those who turned sixty-five in 1930 had probably grown up without electricity and had no access to Social Security or even Old-Age Assistance. Those who turned sixty-five in 1950 had probably grown up without a family car and had spent their peak earning years in the Great Depression. While they might be collecting Social Security, they did not have access to Medicare. Those who turned sixty-five in 1970 were entering a new world. They had probably grown up with modern conveniences; they could begin collecting Social Security and accessing Medicare. They had spent their peak earning years in the 1950s and 1960s, when the American economy was growing quickly. They expected something more from their golden years too.

The focus on older people is an unfamiliar vantage point on these decades, which are so often associated with innovative youth cultures, rock and roll, hippies, and student protest. Something just as interesting and important, though, was happening to old age. The two phenomena were in fact related. In the nineteenth century, children and older people were expected to labor. Over the course of the early twentieth century, both of those life stages were gradually shielded from the labor market, at enormous government expense. On the front end of the lifespan, Americans encountered compulsory schooling and laws against child labor; on the back end, they encountered Social Security and Medicare.

In some ways, this period was actually *more* important for older people than for younger ones. In terms of material infrastructure, mass high school attendance had already happened, and mass college attendance was still in the future. In 1970, less than a quarter of Americans over twenty-five had completed a year of college. Retirement, though, was commonplace. In 1950, a full 60 percent of men in their late sixties were still working. That number plummeted to 29 percent by 1980. This was not just the case for white men, either; in fact, the decline was even greater for Black men. The numbers were less dramatic for women. Few women in that period "retired," in the sense of "leaving the waged labor force for good at around age sixty-five." But even if women did not retire in the same way as men, most women in their late sixties were living with a spouse, and their lives would be upended when their husband was forced to, or chose to, retire.[2]

These are astonishing statistics, representing the creation of a new phase of the American life course. The closest comparison does concern education, but not college education. Retirement became a component of most Americans' lives in a way that college never did. The rise of retirement after World War II finds its closest analog with the rise of high school after World War I. In 1920, only 20 percent of US teenagers graduated from high school. Within three decades that figure tripled, and high school became for the first time something that most Americans did and most Americans were expected to do. It entered, as sociologists would put it, the "normative life course." And between 1950 and 1980, the same thing happened with retirement.[3]

High school and retirement are alike in many ways. For one thing, both became something of a legal mandate. While laws about compulsory school attendance had long been on the books, it was not until the early twentieth century that they began to be enforced. Likewise, for many retirees, retirement was less a choice than a necessity, because many firms had compulsory retirement policies that forced workers to leave the job at a certain age. Not every company had mandatory retirement, and of course it did not apply to all kinds of workers. There was no mandatory retirement for domestic workers or farmers. The bleeding edge of the economy, though, was found in large firms with pension plans, and in *those* firms, as one 1960 study concluded, "involuntary retirement policies were decidedly the prevailing practice." Interviews conducted in 1968 with men over sixty-five who were leaving their last job indicated that more than half of them were leaving because their employer insisted on it.[4]

High school and retirement were also alike in that both were unequally available. In 1970, 83 percent of white Americans in their

early twenties had completed high school, compared with just 65 percent of their Black peers of the same age. This dynamic was repeated on
the other end of the life course. Black Americans received lower Social
Security payments because of lifelong wage suppression, and they were
less likely to receive pensions because they were less likely to work in
the kinds of firms that provided them. Middle managers got pensions,
but domestic workers didn't. The golf courses, shuffleboard courts,
and senior centers that provided an institutional setting for retirement
were primarily for white senior citizens. Although legal segregation
was rare, those facilities, like much else in American life, were in practice segregated, and they tended to cluster in white communities. They
were also designed for the able-bodied. People with disabilities, who
had long been an afterthought in the old-age movement, were an afterthought in this respect as well. While retirement communities and
senior centers were designed as bright and welcoming spaces, people
with disabilities were increasingly shunted into highly medicalized,
lightly regulated, and often barbaric institutions called nursing homes.[5]

Old age, again like youth, was being transformed by technology,
and especially by automobiles. Postwar America was built in the service of cars, which became an emblem of freedom and autonomy for
young people across the country. But not just for them! Middle-aged
people were flooding onto roads and highways, leading eventually
to a spike in older drivers as they aged: between 1940 and 1960, the
proportion of licensed drivers over sixty doubled. For them, too, cars
provided access to autonomy, and they were no more willing than
teenagers were to give up their privileges. Public transit options were,
for most older people, few and far between, which created problems for
senior citizens who wanted to have active lives. "The elderly and infirm
who cannot drive," argued one study in 1974, "have great transportation problems." While many agencies tried to provide buses and other
public transport options for the elderly, the default remained that an
older person would need to, in the words of one journalist, "fulfill
his obligation to modern traffic" through education programs. In the

early 1960s, reports started to crop up of family members appealing to judges to remove the licenses of elderly relatives. Even those who could not drive found themselves on the roads. In 1960, forty-five car owners in Lansing, Michigan, as part of Senior Citizens Week, volunteered to take senior citizens on a road trip through the state. And for those who were homebound and could not drive to the market or a restaurant? Food could come to them, in a car: this was the founding era of Meals on Wheels.[6]

The last comparison between high school and retirement I'll broach is that both were, at first, unpopular. High school dropout rates were alarmingly high: as late as 1960, more than a quarter of Americans from sixteen to twenty-four were dropouts. Many younger people didn't want to be in high school, either because they resented it or because they were needed in the workforce to care for their families. The same dynamics appeared at the other end of the lifespan. Many workers were ambivalent or even hostile to the idea of retirement. After all, surprisingly little thought had been given to what was actually supposed to *happen* in retirement—that is, what people were supposed to do all day if they were no longer working or living with their children. Men especially spent their whole lives being taught to find value in their labor, only to be deprived of it at an arbitrary age. In manual trades like steel working and coal mining, as well as white-collar trades like retail sales, studies found that workers got much more from their work than income. They found camaraderie, purpose, and something to fill their days. They were wary of losing those things and had little hope of replacing them in retirement. A sociologist in 1951 asked workers at Inland Steel about their views on retirement. Less than half of workers aged sixty-two to sixty-four wanted to retire, and almost 90 percent believed that there should be no compulsory retirement at sixty-five. More than half thought that retirement was "only for people physically unable to work."[7]

In the 1950s, retirement was often discussed as a problem. *Senior Citizen* published an article by a physician who coined the phrase "retirement neurosis" to describe what happened to the worker after work. He told the story of "a top executive" who retired at a healthy sixty-four. Within two months, he began to "brood" and "developed a profound depression." The author proceeded to give both a medical and an economic argument against forced retirement, which he called "revolting." Gerontologists were also concerned. "Filling leisure time," the chairman of Washington University's committee on gerontology said in 1957, "is one of the biggest problems of retirement." Clark Tibbitts, doyen of American gerontologists, saw the rise of retirement as a "new challenge to American society" because "no other culture has offered the length of life and the amount of free time" now enjoyed by American retirees.[8]

If retirement in the 1950s was posed as a challenge, in the 1960s and 1970s that challenge was met. Retirement became an attractive proposition because the American government, and private industry, too, poured immense amounts of energy and money into it. Within the span of about two decades, a vast new infrastructure for American retirement was created, almost out of thin air. This took a dizzying variety of forms, far more than could be discussed in a single chapter. As a general matter, though, most older and retired Americans found themselves in one of three places: a retirement community, their own home, or a nursing home. In the rest of this chapter, we'll do a tour of American retirement in its golden years, spending time at each of these sites. As we'll see, private developers and public agencies worked hard to provide innovative services, activities, and housing opportunities for the majority of American seniors who were healthy, active, and able to drive. Those developments, available to seniors who lived in retirement communities or in their own homes, excluded older people with disabilities. For them, the nursing home loomed as the only option once they exhausted their ability to live at home. This was not for lack of other ideas—as we'll see, many were trying to come up with alternative options for this population, but their efforts largely failed.

The first stop on our tour will be the retirement community. Before World War II, there had been no such thing as an age-restricted community (ARC), which legally requires its residents to be above a certain age. Its origins belong to the 1950s, when an idealistic Russian immigrant, inspired by Plato's *Republic*, built a community called Youngtown, in Arizona. Youngtown was meant to be something like a utopian commune, organized around communal labor, rather than a leisure paradise. The founder wanted a place where "the elderly can keep busy," funded largely by Social Security. Within three decades, there were thousands of ARCs—first in the Sun Belt and increasingly in other parts of the country—and many of them departed from Youngtown's idealism. And beyond those legal entities, many other forms of congregate living for senior citizens sprang up. The Department of Housing and Urban Development (HUD) built a great deal of housing for seniors, and some communities or neighborhoods simply acted as de facto retirement communities for seniors who, unlike their ancestors, had the means to move.[9]

And the move, by all accounts, was good for them. A bevy of studies showed that communities of this sort tended to be more social and more egalitarian than those in the age-integrated outside world. The sociologist Irving Rosow, based on research in Cleveland, found that older people had better community ties the more age-segregated their housing was. "The number of old people's local friends," he concluded, "varies directly with the proportion of age peers."[10]

Age-restricted communities made sense because they tapped into the novel insight that older people deserved to pursue their own lives separate from their children, and into insights about what they were supposed to do with their time. By the late 1960s, a broad swath of thinkers and observers agreed that leisure was a valid way for older people to spend their time. This new energy led to a smorgasbord of events all over the country. To take just one example out of many thousands, in 1973, a Valentine's Day square dance was held for senior citizens in Queens. It was put on by a conglomeration of local senior citizen organizations, some religious and some secular, some publicly funded and some private. The dance was made possible because there was an infrastructure for senior services *and* a belief that providing leisure activities like dances was something that those organizations ought to do. None of this was true before the 1950s. Essentially, a consumer society for older Americans emerged parallel to, and as an alternative to, the youth-centric consumer culture that we are so familiar with from 1960s and 1970s America.[11]

The new culture of leisure was spearheaded by the ARCs that were coming into being. The primary players here were wealthy California-based developers named Del Webb and Ross Cortese, who founded Sun City and Leisure World, respectively. Both men bridged the world between gerontology and real estate, haunting the halls of universities while bringing to bear their own experience with suburban tract housing and gated communities. By the mid-1980s, about twenty-four hundred communities of this sort had been founded, ranging from developments with a few dozen mobile homes to Sun City, Arizona, with a population of forty-five thousand. The most famous ARC, The Villages in Central Florida, was founded in 1982.[12]

The most influential one, Leisure World Seal Beach, opened its gates outside Los Angeles in April 1962. The main entrance featured a slowly revolving globe, thirty feet in diameter, which, according to its developer, symbolized "the universal significance of the $150 million, 541-acre development." By decade's end, the development, which was restricted to people aged fifty-two and older, had about ten thousand residents, who moved through the complex on large tricycles. They had access to all manner of planned activities and clubs, including bird-watching, crafts, and woodworking. These activities and more were overseen by a full-time recreation coordinator "whose only responsibility," a Los Angeles newspaper reported, "is to guide the residents in activities designed for fun and health." And they were kept safe by a three-member "private police force," headed by a retired detective from the Toronto police department.[13]

Leisure World was rather like a college campus devoted to hedonism. Yet developers were fully aware that they were dealing with an aging population with distinct needs. The housing units—single-story garden apartments—were small, measuring less than a thousand square feet. Doors and sidewalks were extra wide, stairs were replaced by ramps, and electrical outlets were located at waist height. And given that the doors opened just as the nation was debating Medicare, it's no surprise that the developers gave special attention to health needs: Leisure World had its own medical center, directed by the recently retired chief of surgery at a hospital in San Francisco.[14]

Leisure World seems to have been a genuinely fun and inviting place to live. Residents of Los Angeles who flipped on the TV on Veterans Day in 1964 got a taste of goings-on there. George Putnam, one of the great L.A. newsmen, reported on the ten o'clock news that "our cameraman went looking for something different to cover on this Veterans Day," and he found what he was looking for at Leisure World Seal Beach. Former governor of California Goodwin Knight was the keynote speaker at an event that featured, in Putnam's words, "a most unusual parade" of "over 230 flag-bedecked vehicles, truly a Leisure World on wheels." Photos from the event show beaming rows of people, mainly women, who decorated both their bodies and their tricycles with Uncle Sam hats and other bits of Americana. In addition to the parade and the speech, there was, of course, music—provided by a band of women who used kitchen utensils as instruments.[15]

The reporter did not even mention the obvious fact that the older people were having fun without their families. From a historical perspective, though, that was the novelty of the event, and of the age-restricted community in general. For although it had increasingly been a norm for older people to live apart from their children, Leisure World made it mandatory. Children could visit, of course, as a 1971 promotional image made clear. Over a photo of happy grandchildren rushing to embrace their grandparents, the text read, "A Nice Place to Visit . . . A Wonderful Place to Live." The designers of the ad wanted viewers to understand that the cute little grandchildren wouldn't stick around for long. This generational solidarity, and lack of noise, was a selling point for Leisure World residents. One of them wrote to the general sales manager in 1962, explaining that she was a widow who lived a "very lonely" life. "My children were very good to me, but I needed to be with people nearer my own age who could perhaps understand the many problems that people our age face."[16]

The cult of senior leisure, at Leisure World as elsewhere, was aimed specifically at the able-bodied, active older population (note the age cutoff of fifty-two, not sixty-five). Leisure World provided access to acute care but not home health care, and there was no nursing home on the premises. The whole point was that seniors could live a life of activity—even frantic activity, as revealed by a 1977 article in the *Wall Street Journal* about Century Village East, a retirement community near Boca Raton, Florida. On Tuesdays alone, the nine thousand residents had the option of participating in kazoo practice, ceramics, painting, sewing, yoga, swimming, or dancing. More than two hundred classes, lectures, and special events were held each week, mainly in a clubhouse that housed a sixteen-hundred-seat theater, a thirty-four-table billiards room, and more. "We're a summer camp for old folks," reported the head of the recreation staff.[17]

In reality, Leisure World was nothing like a summer camp. There were, in fact, summer camps for seniors, but they weren't like this. Leisure World was really a *suburb* for old folks. It was, after all, the great age of suburban living and planned communities. What Leisure World offered was the opportunity to participate in that particular vision of American prosperity. Ross Cortese, the developer, had built his fortune by pioneering gated communities, or what he called "walled cities." All he did at Leisure World was add yet another layer of segregation and exclusion to his original idea.[18]

And even though some residents traveled around the complex by tricycle, Leisure World as a whole, like the gated communities it mimicked, was only possible because of cars. It was located in a heavily developed and urbanized part of the country—there is no reason why the pioneering retirement communities shouldn't have been urban. Leisure World, though, was not, and its promotional materials emphasized that it was located in a small town with easy access to "all freeways in Southern California." The same pamphlet, from 1961, featured several maps of the surrounding area, drawing attention to the major arteries that were available to each resident. Every unit came with its own carport.[19]

This kind of leisurely, independent, automotive retirement was not open to everyone, and the more luxurious ARCs were expensive. Promotional materials referred to Leisure World as a "country-club city," so it's no surprise that it was overwhelmingly white. A promotional pamphlet from 1969 featured portraits of Leisure World's singing groups (forty-two people), the police force (twelve), and the board of directors (twenty). All were white. In 1974, an anthropologist published a study of an unnamed retirement community outside L.A., which may well have been Leisure World. While the metropolitan area itself was about 18 percent Black and 8 percent Hispanic, the community profiled in the study had zero Black people, and only three who reported any race other than white. Retirement communities in Florida, the other major site for them, were much the same. Some of the ARCs in Florida were set up by trade unions—for instance, the Four Freedoms House in Miami Beach, which was opened by the AFL-CIO in 1963. Such communities would naturally reproduce the race dynamics of the largely white trade unions that created them. The whole notion of "retiring to Florida" was a lily-white phenomenon at that time. In the 1970 census, there were about fifty thousand people in Miami Beach over the age of sixty. Eighty-seven of them were Black.[20]

Leisure World shows us the emergent ideal of old age as a space for fun, suburban living in a setting that replicated the exclusions of race and ability that marked other suburbs at the same moment. Of course, most older Americans didn't live in Leisure World or anywhere like it. But just as American college campuses played an outsized role in crafting a youth culture and politics, communities like Leisure World were central to the cultivation of a new meaning for old age. Leisure World and its competitors received an enormous amount of press—and a visit, in 1964, from a United Nations delegation. Here, a new meaning for retirement was created, and one that could genuinely have appealed to retiring workers across the country. And that vision was translated, in many ways, to the majority of American seniors who lived at home.[21]

Aging at home has always been the dominant model. In the mid-twentieth century, even as senior magazines were full of accounts of older people moving to the Sun Belt, comparatively few of them actually did so. From 1970 to 1974, only 2 percent of older people relocated to a noncontiguous state. Most of them stayed in the same house they'd lived in for years. Florida in 1970 had about a million older people, many of them living some variant of the Leisure World lifestyle. Although Florida's older population had grown enormously, it was still about the same as Ohio's, significantly lower than Pennsylvania's, and less than half the size of New York's.[22]

The meaning of the phrase "aging at home" has changed over time. In the nineteenth century, older Americans also aged at home—but that home was likely to be one they shared with their grown children, and it was likely to be rural. The novelty of the post–World War II period is that older Americans were living in truly their *own* home—not one that they rented or shared with children and various other relatives. They were beneficiaries of a policy largesse toward homeowners that evolved after World War II, when the United States in general became a homeowners' society. In 1940, just a quarter of older people lived in homes they owned, while by 1980 over half did.[23]

Living at home was not always easy. Many seniors' homes, for instance, were falling apart. Older Americans were 50 percent more likely than younger ones to live in "physically deficient" housing, by HUD standards—a reality that especially impacted impoverished senior citizens who nonetheless owned their home (about a third of their dwellings were deficient). Furthermore, many older people could not afford to rent a place of their own, or could not afford to move out of deficient housing. Some assistance was available. Section 202 of the Federal Housing Act of 1959 provided low-interest loans to help construct subsidized rental units for the elderly poor. In its first twenty-five years, Section 202 provided 188,000 units of housing—not much when we consider that more than three million low-income elderly were eligible for housing assistance, and more than a quarter million were on Section 202 waitlists.[24]

Most older people, then, lived in a cold region of the country and in their own home, which was likely to be run-down. This same population retired in droves after World War II. Many did not like what they found; outside their home, there was almost nothing for them to do. It's hard to imagine the paucity of services or opportunities that existed for this population before the 1960s. A sociologist in Chicago interviewed a retired worker in 1949 who was desperate. "Not a damned thing to do all day," he complained. "I'd like you to tell me something: are there any hobbies or old men's clubs or anything like that you know of that I could get into?" In 1949, the interviewer didn't have much to say.[25]

If seniors in the 1930s needed income to keep them out of the almshouse, what they needed in the 1960s were services and activities to keep them out of the nursing home. Money alone was insufficient; it was not poverty that brought older people to institutionalization, but poor health and social isolation. To help keep them healthy and engaged, a generation of talented social workers and welfare officials worked to create a vast new infrastructure of senior activities and services. Almost all of these efforts were local, often accomplished with funding from counties or states, and sometimes with federal assistance provided by the Older Americans Act. Institutionally, much of the coordination took place through the Area Agencies on Aging, or Triple As, which began operating in 1973 (they still exist today).

If the trailblazers of retirement communities and nursing homes were mainly men, it was in social services for older people at home—a space that generated fewer profits and touched more lives—that women predominated. In part, this was because the social work profession, where many new ideas were generated, had long been dominated by women. In part, too, it is probably because women, who as caregivers and housekeepers did not get to "retire" in the way that men did, ended up with new responsibilities as millions of husbands began to spend more time at home. Across the country, women staffed projects large and small to help older people access food, transportation, and all kinds of other services. Margaret Toy was a social worker in Philadelphia who helped found Meals on Wheels in 1954 as an attempt to provide hot lunches to homebound senior citizens. Florence Wald was a nurse who, like Toy, was committed to keeping older people at home as long as possible. She was the American founder of the hospice movement, which aimed to help older people live out their last weeks at home.

The paradigmatic institution that emerged to help older people live successfully at home was the senior center. To discover its origins, we can leave behind the sun-dappled grounds of Leisure World and travel to an unassuming building in Detroit. Here, at 1271 Oakman Boulevard, the United Auto Workers (UAW) ran a senior center. It was open five days a week from nine-thirty to three-thirty and featured a large reception room with magazines, TV, radio, card games, and coffee. It was open not just to UAW retirees but to any interested community members. It offered, in the words of one observer, a "second home" in which senior citizens could reclaim some of the intimacy that their own families could no longer provide. The center hosted monthly birthday parties, which were especially meaningful because, as a researcher reported, "For forty some years, they celebrated everybody's birthday but their own." The center provided artistic outlets, too, adopting singing and drama as ways to engage seniors.[26]

Senior centers had been around since World War II, but they did not truly take off until the 1960s. While they had multiple origin points, the most influential branch of the movement could be found in Detroit. Whereas most senior centers were local affairs, run by charities and churches, here a network of almost a hundred senior centers was founded. Detroit at the time was still the hub of the American auto industry, and it was still at the center of working-class politics. It was also home to an inspiring labor feminist named Olga Madar.[27]

Madar was born to a Czech butcher's family in Pittsburgh in 1915. When she was fifteen, the butcher shop failed, and she and her eleven siblings were uprooted to Detroit. She was a preternatural athlete, playing both basketball and field hockey in high school. After graduation, she embarked on the twin passions that would dominate her long life: sports and labor organizing. She played softball for the Chrysler team during the unionization drives of the 1930s, and all her siblings worked for the auto industry in one way or another. In the early years of Madar's sports career, the teams were used by management as a tool to build worker solidarity with the company. Madar and her peers, though, pioneered a form of sport that brought workers into identification with each other and with their union: "recreation," as she put it, "in which the majority of our people can join and have fun."[28]

In 1941, Madar began work at Ford's Willow Run plant in West Detroit, becoming the recreation director for UAW Local 50. She caught the attention of Walter Reuther and became his loyal supporter. Following Reuther's ascendancy to the presidency of the union in 1946, Madar was appointed director of the recreation department for the UAW, which had well over a million members. During her long tenure, she attempted to turn the union into a one-stop shop for leisure. "It is inconsistent," she wrote in her 1948 annual report, "to fight to work and fight for better living conditions and for more leisure time for our members while disregarding the activities that must fill the leisure hours." And she insisted that leisure would continue to be linked with the political goals of the labor movement. Much of her energy in the early years was consumed by the Fairness in Bowling campaign, which successfully desegregated the sport's bowling leagues.[29]

Unions were concerned about retired workers and the poisoned chalice of limitless leisure. In 1951, Madar and her team began meeting with retirees in Detroit to learn about their needs. Hundreds of workers turned out to planning meetings, and some of them formed a steering committee that worked with Madar's team. They learned that senior citizens needed something to do and places where they could meet up with friends and former coworkers. They hit upon the newfangled idea of the senior center. The first concrete result was the opening in February 1953 of a drop-in center on the east side of Detroit, followed quickly by several more, including the one described above.

The program soon went national as UAW Convention resolutions in both 1957 and 1959 lent support to programming for retired workers. In 1963, the national convention of the AFL-CIO passed a resolution urging all labor bodies to provide "centers for retired workers that can meet their need for education, recreation, and social relationships, as well as for counseling, information, and referral services"; the same resolution recommended "visitation services" for those unable to make it to activity centers. The particular Detroit centers that Madar was directly involved with had a national impact. Anyone who attended a UAW retirement-planning course anywhere in the country received a pamphlet describing the centers and was asked, "Would you like to see a drop-in center program developed in your community?"[30]

By 1968 there were more than ninety UAW-sponsored senior centers operating in the United States and Canada. They were directly in keeping with the socialist doctrine of recreation that Madar had pursued since the 1930s. In 1957, she wrote an article titled "Recreation in the UAW" for the magazine of the AFL-CIO, in which she described the senior centers as part of the labor movement's commitment to democratically planned leisure activities across the life course. Leisure, for her, was never just about "fun." With the help of the centers' coordinator, Elaine Stinson, Madar brought in the Red Cross to give a nine-week session on first aid. It was taught by two women, and twenty-five of the thirty who enrolled earned a certificate. It also gave opportunities for sociability: a seventy-year-old Czech woman took the course, and it was the first activity outside the home she had pursued, other than church, in four years.[31]

The UAW did not act alone; its normal pattern was to partner with other local institutions, public and private, to fund the centers. Whether affiliated with the UAW or not, this model was becoming increasingly ubiquitous in American cities. Remember the lonely and bored Chicago retiree who was interviewed by a sociologist in 1949? In 1957, he could have ventured to Chicago's first senior center, operated out of a massive mansion in downtown; if that one was not convenient, by 1965 Chicago had a dozen more. And they were by all accounts quite popular; this was, after all, a generation of older people that was used to a dense associational life of churches and unions. In Los Angeles, which got its first center in 1960, seniors had to join a lengthy waitlist to even gain access. The first National Directory of Senior Centers, which appeared in 1966, listed 340 of them; just four years later, it recorded 1,200. By 1974, half of senior citizens reported that a senior center was conveniently located for them. About one in five seniors actually visited a center, indicating that a bit fewer than half of seniors who were located close to centers used them. On the one hand, this is an astonishing success for a new form of social space. On the other, it shows the limits of the senior center: far more seniors were regularly going to their traditional sites of sociability, notably churches (77 percent of seniors said they'd been to a place of worship in the past year).[32]

Just as Leisure World impacted senior living for the majority of seniors who didn't live there, senior centers impacted senior living for the majority of seniors who didn't go to them. While churches remained the most important site of sociability for many millions of seniors, they were changing, too, offering more services every year for seniors (including, in many cases, operating senior housing units). In 1975, the North Carolina Council of Churches launched a project called Ministries with the Aging. Under its auspices, clergymen distributed SSI applications to needy parishioners, and a task force was created to address accessibility in church facilities. A few years later, a scholar was curious about what Seventh-Day Adventists in Philadelphia were doing for their older parishioners. He found an astonishing level of energy being devoted to the endeavor. The church offered transport services for older parishioners and worked together with a neighboring community organization that offered more traditional senior services. When the organization needed a new van, the church pitched in to pay for it.[33]

Note the centrality of automobiles to this project. The auto workers' union was a pioneer in developing the model, and across the country vans and buses were purchased to transport seniors to and from the centers. The centers were not common enough, in other words, to provide walkable, neighborhood-level solidarity, which in any case was impossible given the geographic dispersion of their clientele. And yet there were green shoots of a proto-environmentalist style of aging. Guides to senior leisure often discussed hiking, camping, and gardening. Madar herself became head of the UAW's Department of Conservation. In 1968, she wrote an article on "the growing challenge of leisure" for *Free Labour World*, the journal of the International Confederation of Free Trade Unions. She rejected out of hand the idea, central to Leisure World, that leisure should be used for personal cultivation; she viewed this as a bourgeois updating of aristocratic leisure norms. She urged instead a more democratic account of leisure, or what she called "constructive creative leisure." "Leisure," she wrote, "is getting together with our neighbours to make our cities and countries a better environment for living as well as for working." Healthy retirement, she argued, was only possible on a healthy planet.[34]

All these efforts were designed to make life livable, and even pleasurable, for Americans who were aging at home. In the 1930s, almost nothing had been available to that group. By the 1970s, older people could visit senior centers, contract with a home health aide, receive Meals on Wheels, get discounted tickets to local events, receive subsidized transport, and on and on and on. They could even, through hospice programs, expect to receive world-class medical treatment in their homes, and to die in their homes. Together, that network of services, coordinated by Area Agencies on Aging and, at root, mainly by women, constituted a sea change for older Americans.

But it wasn't enough for everyone. "Elderly people least in need of Senior Center services," one observer noted in 1976, "are those who use them most." Just as Leisure World was not an assisted-living facility, senior centers were not rehab facilities. People who were severely ill or had disabilities were not the primary clientele. Eventually, millions of Americans found that they could no longer live at home, even with the help of friends, relatives, church communities, and nonprofits like Meals on Wheels. They found themselves, instead, in another new institution, and one that, unlike the retirement village or the senior center, struck fear into the hearts of many older Americans.[35]

The third and final stop on our tour of postwar American retirement will be the nursing home. The idea of institutionalizing older people with disabilities was not new in the 1960s. But the form of institutionalization was. Since the nineteenth century, the so-called indigent aged had been housed either in almshouses or in mental institutions. State or county medical hospitals had an enormous proportion of older people: in 1950, almost half a percent of older people resided in mental hospitals. Those solutions were increasingly inappropriate. Almshouses had essentially vanished; a stipulation of Social Security was that recipients could not be resident in one, which put almshouses out of business. Likewise, mental hospitals were trying to thin their own ranks as part of a great "deinstitutionalization" campaign in the 1960s. In that decade, as the institutionalization rate for seniors in general was climbing rapidly, the number in mental hospitals declined by a third.[36]

Shutting down almshouses and mental institutions, of course, did not solve the original issue: namely, that many older people had physical and mental disabilities that prevented them from caring for themselves. And the other solutions that were being generated for senior citizens didn't do much for this problem either. Medicare, as we've seen, didn't pay for long-term care, and the retirement communities and senior centers that were revitalizing life for the active elderly were neglecting that community too.

The solution that emerged, of course, was the nursing home. So to end our architectural tour of retirement, let's leave behind the tidy homes of Seal Beach and the lively chatter of Detroit's senior centers to look at one more site: Towers Nursing Home, at 106th Street and Central Park West in New York City. The building was a beautiful one. Built in 1886 as a hospital, it looked basically like a red-brick Victorian mansion. The inside, though, was less immaculate. Refurbished in 1955 as a nursing home, it provided 347 beds. And according to an inspector with the city's Department of Social Services, it was a cesspool.

The home, she reported, had "an abnormally large number of deaths," which so horrified the health department that it quarantined the facility, which was teeming with flies. Even if patients superficially looked clean and healthy, a literal pulling back of the covers revealed something different. Often, those well-combed patients were lying in urine or feces (and the sheets themselves were made of a rough, denim-like material that caused sores). And often, too, the name on the bed did not match the person actually *in* the bed—confusing, to be sure, for the medication nurse, if a nurse was present at all. Residents were often placed in wheelchairs and just left to sit in a hall or lobby all day, without care or oversight. They often lacked undergarments, wore soiled clothes, and were parked amidst piles of dirty laundry.[37]

The nursing home emerged at the same time as the retirement community and the senior center. Thus it was only in the 1960s that nursing homes became a regular part of the American landscape, and places where older Americans might reasonably expect to spend some time. From 1960 to 1970, the number of older Americans in nursing home settings more than doubled, from 388,000 to 795,800. And by 1980, about 5 percent of Americans over the age of sixty-five were in nursing homes—and one in ten over the age of seventy-five. The nursing homes were a specter of boredom and ill treatment that haunted all the services named above. Senior centers and at-home services were designed, in fact, to keep older people *out* of nursing homes. Their advocates explicitly used the fear of nursing homes to defend their own innovations. Even at Leisure World, residents were desperate to stay in their homes as long as possible, living in fear of the unaffiliated nursing homes that sprang up nearby to service those who could no longer keep up with the considerable demands of the Leisure World lifestyle.[38]

All the services for the able-bodied were designed to provide opportunities for cultivation and leisure, opportunities almost completely lacking in the nursing home. One of the most persistent contemporary critiques of nursing homes is that they were, simply, boring. In the early 1970s, a team tried to see how well earned that reputation was. They observed more than a thousand residents in more than forty nursing homes and recorded their daytime activities minute by minute to find out what, in fact, nursing home residents were up to during the day. What they found was shocking. A full 39 percent of the time, residents were doing nothing at all, what the investigators called "null activity," and which included sleeping, sitting alone, or staring into space. Another 17 percent of the time was classified as "passive activity," defined as "a very limited degree of interaction" with the world around them, as when smoking or rocking in a chair. "Thus," they concluded, "56% of the residents' time during the day, from morning to evening, was spent doing nothing." Much of the rest was spent watching television.[39]

Some residents were essentially turned into disabled subjects by nursing home staff. Many spent part of their day physically restrained, sometimes with ropes, in "geri-chairs." Many were chemically restrained by the overutilization of tranquilizing medications. A 1976 government study found that more than half of nursing home residents were prescribed tranquilizers. Another, a decade later, found that the numbers had not changed, despite increasing evidence that the drugs were harmful, overprescribed, and often caused the very problems of confusion and disorientation that they were meant to resolve.[40]

If nursing homes were such dreary places, why did they expand so rapidly in the 1960s and 1970s? It wasn't because families were dumping granny into a home at the first opportunity; if anything, then as now, families waited too long to seek custodial care, exhausting their emotional and financial resources. Instead, nursing homes exploded in popularity for demographic and political reasons. They are most needed by populations in the older age categories: not many sixty-five-year-olds reside in nursing homes, but many eighty-five-year-olds do. And it was that latter category, known sometimes as the "old-old," that grew exponentially in those years. In 1950, there were 576,000 Americans over eighty-five. By 1980, that figure had leapt to 2.3 million, owing mainly to improvements in public health.[41]

This demographic shift, which happened across the developed world, created a demand for long-term-care facilities. Although the need was inevitable, the shape such facilities took was not. Many roads were available for the long-term-care economy, and only one led to Towers Nursing Home.

Many at the time were trying to pave those other roads—and while they largely failed, their efforts are worth recalling. If that effort had one leader in the postwar era, it was Ellen Winston, who climbed the ranks of the welfare apparatus from North Carolina to become the federal government's first commissioner of welfare. Winston was active in the decades between the passage of Social Security and the passage of Medicare, when the long-term-care industry was in limbo. The Social Security Act demolished the old system of almshouses in 1935. And it was not until the late 1960s, after the passage of Medicare and especially Medicaid, that the nursing home became the dominant institutional mechanism in the American system to deal with older people who could no longer live safely at home. In those interim years, Winston was one of many who were trying to keep that from happening.

Winston adopted a twofold approach to deal with the two largest classes of people who would end up in nursing homes. For older people who could stay at home with some help, she proposed the creation of large groups of state-sponsored and licensed housekeepers. "We are just beginning to realize the possibilities of housekeeper services" for the aged, she wrote. "The results in individual contentment are tremendous." In this context, "housekeeper" is a strange term to our ears. According to an educational manual from 1968, it denotes "a worker or aide whose function it is to assist professional health and welfare personnel in maintaining, safeguarding, or improving family life." It was specifically designed as a catch-all role that integrated "a variety of services." Today we would call this person a home health aide.[42]

Housekeepers of this sort had traditionally been provided by local welfare agencies to families with multiple children. After World War II, they settled into their more familiar role as aides to older people, especially those with disabilities. Winston launched a pilot project in North Carolina to prove the efficacy of the approach and the indispensable role of government in providing it. As a pamphlet from her office explained, the purpose of the program was to keep older people in their homes by providing "a little regular help with tasks which they cannot adequately manage alone." This was done by matching female homemakers with older people in need, a process that was completed by a social worker, who remained in close supervision of the entire process. The welfare office's publicly celebrated success stories give a sense of what they were trying to accomplish. Mrs. A., for instance, was an old and poor woman living alone in rural North Carolina. Her estranged son lived nearby, a fact that made neighbors reluctant to help her out. At the start of the process, she was a recluse, uninterested in socializing or leaving the house. The regular visits from the homemaker, however, opened her up emotionally. The homemaker also helped with the shopping. Mrs. A. grew to count the homemaker as a friend, and eventually she left her house to search for her birthplace and ancestral church. The vignette ended with the light falling over Mrs. A., in her old family pew, as she began to sing "familiar hymns," played by the homemaker herself on the church's "old-fashioned organ."[43]

Of course, many people were unable to live at home, even with help from a visiting homemaker. For them Winston labored to create a network of "small foster boarding homes for older people." These private homes were meant to be handpicked for the individual older person with the aid of a social worker, and to provide enough touches of home that the person would be comfortable. The goal was to provide affordable and safe places for older people to live semi-independently, and at prices modest enough that they could be covered by Social Security payments and small contributions from family members. The largest of these were run by churches, but Winston was more interested in smaller homes, the kind of place where the operator "will not accept more residents in her home than she can seat around a large old-fashioned dinner table." By 1958, there were 352 such homes in North Carolina, lodging more than five thousand older people—and, as a fawning profile in *Ladies' Home Journal* indicated, Winston's efforts in this regard were quite popular.[44]

Coordinating among families, social workers, and housing providers to care for older people involved a huge amount of work. At least in theory, Winston and her associates envisioned a personalized touch. One of them recounted a story in which "a very confused old gentleman" entered a boarding home. He was loquacious only on the subjects of his childhood and his love of raising pigs. The home operator found a way to build a pigpen and acquire a pig for him, providing him with both a hobby and a connection to his past.[45]

Winston wasn't opposed to nursing homes. For the most problematic cases, institutionalization was necessary. She was simply trying to diminish their influence and to provide alternatives for desperate families. And she wanted the government to help. On behalf of the

National Council for Homemaker Services, she sent an impassioned letter to the head of the Social Security Administration, imploring him to allow home health aides to be covered by Medicare (something that, she believed, would not require new legislation but only a different interpretation of the extant law). Alas, she failed. Just as Winston was trying to use welfare offices and social workers to keep older people at home, another and more powerful group was building new sites to house them. The future belonged not to Ellen Winston, but to Bernard Bergman, the proprietor of Towers Nursing Homes.[46]

The nursing home industry was a creation of public policy—and without much intention, either, as policy debates tended to have able-bodied families in mind. Two major policy decisions were made that ended up creating spaces like Towers Nursing Home and funneling resources away from Winston's less institutional solutions. The first was that the new long-term-care infrastructure would be part of the medical system (recall that Towers was built on the site of an old hospital). The Hill-Burton Act of 1946 financed hospital construction across the country and ensured that the hospital, for the first time, would become synonymous with American health care. While nursing homes were not originally part of the legislation, 1954 amendments gave federal support for the construction of nursing homes—with the proviso that they be associated with a hospital and be regulated like a hospital. Medicare and Medicaid, in turn, would only fund care in medical-style institutions that were linked with hospitals. Neither home health aides nor mom-and-pop boarding homes were included in the system.[47]

The second major decision made by policymakers specified that nursing homes would be funded by Medicaid rather than by Medicare. There was a sense that long-term care could be extremely expensive and could tank the delicate fiscal balance of Medicare were it included in that program. Long-term care, unlike acute care, was therefore administered by the states as part of a welfare program rather than by the federal government as a universal benefit. This has had incalculable consequences for the industry. Welfare programs administered by states are, in general, less efficient, less generous, and more stigmatized than universal programs administered by the federal government. This was certainly the case with Medicaid. Complaints about poor regulation were rife in the early years of the industry, but nursing home operators were reluctant to make the necessary repairs. And since they were dealing with county or state welfare offices rather than the mighty federal government, nursing home operators generally got their way.[48]

Put differently, public policy pushed older people with disabilities toward institutionalization in poorly regulated nursing homes. Even though nursing home stays were fantastically expensive for the public purse, they were often the only thing individuals could afford. Medicaid, at least, would cover nursing home care. Few families could afford home health aides or other alternatives to institutional care for long. This resulted in a situation where many people who could have lived at home if they'd had a better support system in place ended up in nursing homes. The same study that uncovered the deep tedium of nursing home life also found that nursing home residents were for the most part capable of caring for themselves with only minimal assistance.[49]

All of this worked together to make something like Bernard Bergman's empire possible. Bergman ran a network of proprietary nursing homes, making a fortune on them while delivering substandard care and avoiding enforcement on the lax regulations that did exist. He did so by calling in favors from political officials, and he may have done so with the help of organized crime. The system of nursing home underregulation almost ensured that figures like him would emerge to make a profit.[50]

None of this was a secret—the Bergman story was big news and the subject of congressional hearings. Senator Frank Moss, appalled by the status of nursing homes, embarked on a wide-ranging congressional study of the issue, which was turned into a book. But almost nothing was done. The residents of nursing homes simply didn't have enough sway to influence change. This sort of constituency was capable of creating press outrage but not of mobilizing actual power. As the 1980s dawned, the nursing home industry remained a national disgrace—and a reminder to senior citizens that the promise of a fun, leisure-filled retirement was only theirs until their health ran out.

The nursing home industry was the dark underbelly of the sunnier developments that emerged for older Americans in the 1960s and 1970s. Private developers and municipal agencies worked together to provide activities, services, and housing for America's seniors. That new infrastructure of retirement was designed to service active and healthy seniors—in fact, those services were possible only because they did not take on the challenge and expense of accommodating those in need of long-term care. And for that healthy and active population, this period saw stunning innovation. Remember the sociologist who asked the workers at Inland Steel about retirement in 1951, and learned how reluctant they were? He asked the same question a decade later and found a startling transformation. In 1960, less than a quarter of workers in their early sixties held negative views toward retirement, and more than two-thirds opted to describe retirement as "a reward for a lifetime of work." And a few years later, research in Kansas City revealed that the desire for continued employment, while real, was mainly restricted to the professional classes; many workers looked forward to retirement, and many applied for Social Security so they could retire before age sixty-five, even though that meant reduced retirement benefits.[51]

This shift should be viewed as a signal accomplishment of the American state, and also of the American people. It has been durable. In the early twenty-first century, there are legitimate concerns about the future of retirement. But that anxiety masks the many ways in which the system as designed in the crucial midcentury decades was working as planned. Medicare was providing health care, Social Security was providing financial benefits, and thousands of county offices and nonprofits, organized by Area Agencies on Aging, were providing all kinds of services: busing senior citizens to libraries, organizing meal delivery, and more. An infrastructure for retirement, and an expectation *of* retirement, were set in the 1960s and 1970s, and despite the endless hand-wringing, they have not gone anywhere. In 1980, about 70 percent of men from sixty-five to sixty-nine were retired. That number has crept down somewhat—in 2010 it was closer to 65 percent—but it remains the case that most older people are retired, and the numbers of course are even higher in the older age brackets.[52]

All of that said, the system as designed had a number of issues, some of which would be addressed in future decades and some of which would not. The system was complicated, and it was expensive. It was rigid too. It was not designed to encourage experimentation, but to rivet Americans to a life-course model in which they retired at sixty-five and began collecting benefits. And it was inequitable. As with education at the front end of the life course, retirement at the back end was structured by hierarchies of race, gender, and ability.

My point in detailing these failures isn't to be critical, but to explain why the story didn't end here. We should not imagine retirement as an edifice that was perfectly constructed in the past and that we are tasked with maintaining. We should think of it instead as a serviceable but leaky building, constructed piecemeal from the 1930s to 1970s. It was not compliant with the Americans with Disabilities Act (ADA), and it was built by a platoon of subcontractors, not all of whom were talking to each other or even working off the same plans. The building did its job, but it didn't fit everyone who wanted to be there, and some people were there who didn't want to be. It was also constantly being renovated. The transformation in American aging that took place in just a few decades was astonishingly fast, and there was no reason to believe that it would slow down. Many people had ideas about how to make retirement more equitable and more accessible for the many groups who were left out. The question, though, was whether or not they would be listened to.

CHAPTER 5

BLACK POWER, BLACK AGING

By the 1970s, the senior citizens' movement had succeeded beyond its founders' wildest dreams. Social Security and Medicare had done wonders for older people, and they had been matched at the state and local level by all kinds of new programs and facilities for seniors. There was still work to be done, though: many older people remained in poverty or were disenfranchised in other ways, and the scandal-ridden nursing home industry was in the news every day. There was good reason to believe that this work *would* be done. New social movements were bursting forth from the American grassroots. The civil rights movement was the most famous of them. It was joined by second-wave feminism, the antiwar movement, the gay rights movement, the environmental movement, and more. Older people could easily have joined their ranks, updating their movement and methods for a new political moment.

Old-age advocacy had historically been siloed, focused squarely on the financial and medical needs of able-bodied, middle-class, white families. This strategy had been politically effective, even if it had led to inequitable outcomes. But if the movement was going to survive and thrive in the new political climate of the late 1960s and the 1970s, it would need to evolve, and it would need to serve a broader clientele. Many activists, both old and young, were trying to help the movement do so, providing a more diverse and intersectional account of what it meant to be a senior citizen. An activist group known as the Gray Panthers aimed to link old-age advocacy with other progressive movements, and it led the charge against unsafe nursing homes. In 1977, New York activists founded Senior Action in a Gay Environment, which was devoted to expanding social services for the city's queer older people. More than any other group, though, it was the Black elderly who sought to shake up the American retirement system and make it more responsive to the diversity of America's aging population. This chapter explores their attempts to forge a new account of senior citizenship and to breathe new life into an old-age movement that was struggling to find a reason for being after the passage of Medicare.[1]

Black Power and gerontology might seem like strange bedfellows. They shouldn't, though; the movement for old-age pensions for formerly enslaved people had flourished just a few decades before. In the 1960s and 1970s, this legacy was revived as Black gerontologists with explicit ties to the Black freedom struggle sought to remake old-age policies and institutions in the name of racial justice. They held rallies and marches, and they published incendiary research. They testified in Congress, and they called on the Social Security Administration to provide benefits to Black Americans several years earlier than white ones. After all, even if Black Americans had received equal benefits per month (which they did not because of a lifetime of wage suppression), they still would have enjoyed less benefit from Social Security overall because they did not live as long. Like Callie House before them, activists in this era were trying to use old-age policy to confront and address the most severe inequalities of American life.

In the short run these efforts failed, and by the 1980s they had left little impact on the old-age movement or on social policy. It was a missed opportunity, to be sure. Nonetheless, it is worth telling the story, because the insights from these activists are crucial for the reimagining of old age in the twenty-first century. This is the only chapter in the book that will focus primarily on one person: in this case, a Black sociologist named Jacquelyne Jackson. More than any other figure, she encapsulated the effort to popularize research on Black aging and translate it into policy shifts that would help the Black aged. She spent time with Martin Luther King Jr. before he was a household name; she gave impassioned speeches to bewildered gerontologists and founded the first journal ever devoted to minority aging; she organized protests and she made documentaries. Jackson is narratively useful as a guide through the world of diversity and aging in the civil rights era. But my focus on her is also an attempt to return her to the limelight. If America is going to grapple with the issues surrounding its diverse elder population, we need stories to tell about it. And we need heroes too.[2]

Jacquelyne Jackson was born in Winston-Salem, North Carolina, in 1932. Raised in both North Carolina and Alabama, she was a daughter of the South who left for college in Wisconsin well before the end of Jim Crow. From Wisconsin, she went on to Ohio State University, becoming the first Black woman to earn a doctorate in sociology there. Her dissertation took her back to the South, where she studied civil rights organizations and spent seven weeks doing fieldwork with freedom movements in Alabama.[3]

As of the mid-1960s, there was little reason to believe that Jackson would devote her career to aging. Ethno-gerontology, as the study of minority aging would later be called, was not even a field yet. The most important textbook of the era on old age, prepared by the Social Science Research Council and the Census Bureau in 1958, is simply silent about race, even as it lavishes attention on employment, gender, health, and myriad other variables. When scholars did discuss aging and race, the results were often condescending. One study in *The Gerontologist* pointed out that older Black people were surprisingly likely to commit homicide. Another article in the same journal, the flagship of the discipline, regretted the "invasion" by Black people of inner-city neigh-borhoods in which "older white residents" lived. The author hoped that the older white people would stay put instead of fleeing to the suburbs, which might stave off "complete ghettoization."[4]

Just as the old-age movement had little to say about race, the civil rights movement, at least before 1965, had little to say about old age. Black Americans had so many needs, and were disenfranchised in so many ways, that the movement could not deal with all of them at once. And by any honest reckoning, compared with the needs of younger age cohorts, older Black Americans were comparatively well-off. Social Security and Medicare were, for all their flaws, some of the least racist programs in America, and they did a great deal for older Black people. The poverty rate for Black children and young people was far greater than it was for older ones.

All the same, the nexus between old age and race was a poten-tially explosive one. Black activists had been thinking and organizing around old age since the nineteenth century. The first home for the Black aged was founded in 1864 in Philadelphia by formerly enslaved people, one of whom was named Stephen Smith. The institution sur-vived for a century, eventually becoming the Stephen Smith Home for the Aged. The Ex-Slave Pension Association had organized many for-merly enslaved people—maybe hundreds of thousands—in the early twentieth century. After World War II the mobilization had continued, albeit at a smaller scale. In 1946, for instance, a group of Black old-age advocates in Atlanta formed a Citizens Committee for the Care of the Aged. Responding to the almost total lack of boarding facilities for older Black Georgians, they attempted to create a home specifically for Black seniors on the grounds of an Atlanta hospital.[5]

In the postwar years, activism didn't just require energy; it required knowledge and data. When it came to the older Black population, these things were absent. Before 1960, just a handful of short, scattered publications had *ever* appeared on the topic. This changed above all thanks to the efforts of the National Urban League, one of the nation's oldest and most storied civil rights organizations. Jeweldean Jones, the organization's director for social welfare, tapped Marion Robinson, an experienced social worker, to gather statistics, and Hobart Jackson, the administrator of the Stephen Smith Home for the Aged and a member of the league's Subcommittee on Aging, to serve as coauthor on a more extensive piece of work. Their booklet, which appeared in 1964, was titled *Double Jeopardy: The Older Negro in America Today.* It brought the discussion of Black aging into the civil rights era, arguing that older Black people were uniquely disenfranchised by the system. They were in "double jeopardy" because they suffered the combined indignities of being Black and being old, and those two forms of exclusion interacted with and compounded one another. Black old age, they insisted, should be understood as the capstone to "a whole lifetime of economic and social indignities": "a lifetime of second-class citizenship, a lifetime of watching their children learn the high cost of being a Negro in America."[6]

Jacquelyne Jackson stepped into this long-standing movement, a legacy noted by observers, one of whom called her a "virtual Sojourner Truth of Modern times." In the later 1960s, building on Hobart Jackson's work, Jacquelyne Jackson began to publish prolifically on Black aging from her position at Duke University, where she was the first tenured Black woman at the School of Medicine. (Although they worked together, Hobart Jackson and Jacquelyne Jackson were not related.) It is hard to know what drew her toward elder issues specifically. It seems likely, though, that she encountered, either in her own family or in her fieldwork, people who were "black and female and old and poor," the combination that she would come to call "quadruple jeopardy." She certainly didn't do it to further her career, as her concerns remained professionally marginal.[7]

To many observers, the story about Black aging appeared as a success. Black lifespans had been enormously extended, for one thing. Between 1900 and 1970, the median age of death went up about twenty years for white Americans, and about *forty* years for Black Americans.

As a result, the population of older Black people exploded between 1930 and 1980. In 1930, there were 300,000 older Black people in the United States, representing 3 percent of the Black population. In just half a century, that number shot up to 2.1 million, representing 7.9 percent of the Black population. And most minority seniors were Black at that point: there were about twice as many older Black Americans then as there were Hispanic, Asian American, and Indigenous seniors combined.[8]

The standard of living for older Black Americans had improved, too, thanks largely to social programs. Let's take, as our sample case, households in the later 1970s that were headed by nonwhite older women—widowed women living alone, say, or living with grown children. A full 88 percent of such households were considered impoverished before the provision of state aid. That aid, though, made a huge dent in this poverty level: once Social Security, food stamps, Medicare, Medicaid, and other public programs were included in the calculation, the poverty rate of these households plummeted to 16 percent. This was, it should be said, still quadruple the poverty rate for households headed by white men aged sixty-five-plus, but remarkable progress all the same. (In 1945, according to an analysis in *Demography*, more than 90 percent of households headed by nonwhite older women had been in poverty.)[9]

Jackson and her colleagues pointed out all the ways in which older Black Americans, and especially women, continued to be excluded and left behind. They had comparatively poor health outcomes and shorter lifespans than their white peers. According to the National Center for Health Statistics, the median age of death for white men in 1980 was seventy-four. For Black men, it was sixty-seven. If old age as a matter of social policy began at age sixty-five, then the median white man would enjoy its benefits for nine years, and the median Black man for only two. Comparatively few Black people lived long enough to claim benefits, or at least to claim them for long. Those who lived to their seventies or beyond faced additional obstacles. The older Black population, after all, was still located predominantly in the South, where there was long-standing discrimination in social programs and services. Many

Black Americans were not enrolled in Social Security, either because their employers had not enrolled them or because they themselves sought to avoid enrolling. Living so frequently in poverty, many Black workers were reluctant to voluntarily take a pay cut to cover their contribution. Social Security was only one component of income security for white Americans, who often supplemented it with defined-benefit pensions from their work. It was uncommon, though, for older Black workers to have access to such pensions. More than half of white seniors in the 1970s were covered by some kind of pension plan, compared with just 28 percent of Black men. And 24 percent of nonmarried white women were covered by such a plan, compared with just 7 percent of their Black counterparts.[10]

More granular investigations, pushing behind the national statistics, revealed grim realities. A major study of this topic was conducted in a Southern metro area in 1972, and the racial disparities were stark: 59 percent of white seniors had enough money for daily needs *and* some savings on hand in case of emergency, but only 15 percent of Black residents did. Sixty percent of Black residents had only enough money for daily living, and more than a quarter lived in poverty (compared with less than 10 percent of older white people). What's more, Black families faced serious challenges that often kept them from being a resource for older relatives. Evidence from the 1970s and 1980s suggests that Black seniors were as likely as white peers to receive family support and were quite a bit more likely to *give* family support, likely because of the straitened circumstances of their children (comparatively many of whom were deceased or incarcerated).[11]

Even though social services were not strictly segregated, the systems were set up with white seniors in mind. Social services, as their proponents argued again and again, were designed to stave off institutionalization in nursing homes. But for Black seniors this was hardly an issue, because they were seldom institutionalized in the first place. There were Black old-age homes, but there were not enough of them, and many of those that did exist were closed down after World War II because they could not afford to come up to code. In St. Louis in the early 1960s, there were only ninety-three nursing home beds for Black seniors, compared with more than six thousand for white St. Louisans. A study in Louisiana showed similar, if less shocking, results: in a state that was 32 percent Black, only 12 percent of nursing home beds went to Black residents. Black Americans, with the help of the National Urban League, were less interested in keeping Black seniors *out* of nursing homes than they were in *founding* nursing homes that would accept them and which they could afford.[12]

The low levels of Black institutionalization were not a success story of at-home social services. A study in Kansas, for instance, showed that almost none of the older Black people surveyed even knew about the existence of the county's Council on Aging and its many offered services. America's first senior center was created during World War II and was primarily used by impoverished immigrants. There is no record of any participants of color. And when the seniors wanted to put on a play, they put on a minstrel show—in defiance of the Black workers at the center, who protested. As the centers spread, they were more accessible to white communities than to Black ones. In 1974, twice as many white as Black people reported that a senior center was conveniently located for them to visit. Even those that were visited by a diverse group of seniors played host to racial tensions. After all, someone who was seventy years old in 1974 had been raised in the Jim Crow era. In Tennessee, a major research study conducted in 1966 unsurprisingly found that white visitors to a senior center were prejudiced toward the Black users of the center.[13]

In North Carolina, senior centers responded to a questionnaire from the state's Division of Aging, which wanted to avoid funding segregated facilities. And indeed, the results show that they were not strictly segregated. Nonetheless, between the lines, the racialized life of the centers is apparent (and it was Jacquelyne Jackson's personal belief that senior centers served a "predominantly white" population). At a center in Charlotte, for instance, classes on nutrition attracted an almost all-Black audience, while classes on ceramics were entirely white. In a city that was about one-third Black, the center's premier "social" event had eighty white participants and four Black ones, yet the center director noted that white residents complained that Black people were attending at all. In nearby Fayetteville, the director of senior programming singled out the Black community for critique, noting their "aggressive agitation" stirred up by the Fayetteville Area Poor People's Organization.[14]

Nutrition programs had similar issues. Food delivery is an intimate act. In some places, at least, Meals on Wheels and similar programs tried to do it sensitively by, for instance, serving older Black residents food that had been prepared in a kitchen run by Black dietitians. The end results, despite those sporadic efforts, were dispiriting. "The Black elderly experience," one observer commented in 1975, "is having to get on a bus and travel ten miles across town to a nutrition lunch program because a well-meaning white or black says it is good to 'get out of the ghetto.'" In an early study of Meals on Wheels participants in its first five sites, all of which were urban locales with sizable Black populations, only about 3 percent of program recipients were Black. It's hard to know why; perhaps the parents of the Boy Scouts who often did the deliveries balked at sending their children into Black neighborhoods, or perhaps the program was simply not adequately publicized in those communities. The food may have been an issue as well. It was normally prepared by white or Jewish volunteer organizations and overseen by nutrition experts. In Baltimore, for example, the operation was run by a Jewish organization that provided chopped liver and gefilte fish.[15]

The same was true of hospice, another set of important in-home services that was mainly used by seniors. The early years of the movement were truly heroic in many ways, but the disinterest in racial differences is striking. Both Elisabeth Kübler-Ross and Florence Wald, the pioneers of the movement, dealt with Black elders in their work on grief and death. How could they not? They were exploring cultures of death in Chicago and New Haven, Connecticut. But they were reluctant to confront the issue, and they did not wonder how Black people would feel about having white experts usher them into their death, potentially by withholding lifesaving treatment. It is little surprise, then, that in the first half century of the existence of hospice care, Black Americans tended to be wary of it.[16]

Whereas Black life received the most attention, other ethnic groups had their own legitimate complaints about America's aging services. The National Indian Conference on Aging complained in 1976 that nutrition programs were serving culturally inappropriate foods that were making their seniors sick. In San Antonio, few Hispanic elders were served by the public housing projects that were going up for the elderly. Even for those who had heard of the projects, they were turned off by the high-rise construction and the need to pass through a formal lobby, under the eyes of an observant white doorman, to reach their apartment.[17]

Scholars who focused on these themes wanted not only to interpret the world. They wanted to change it. From the late 1960s to the late 1970s, Jacquelyne Jackson worked indefatigably to find ways to actually improve the lives of Black seniors. She wasn't afraid to make enemies as she did so. A few months after the assassination of Martin Luther King Jr., in October 1968, she rose to deliver a paper at the yearly meeting of the Gerontological Society. The conference took place in Denver, which, like much of the country, was experiencing social unrest at the time. Just a few weeks earlier, a riot had broken out when a white businessman allegedly assaulted a Black youth; just two days before the conference began, a local Black Panther named Lauren Watson had been indicted on various charges related to the riots. And a few days before Jackson's talk, two Black athletes, Tommie Smith and John Carlos, had raised their black-gloved fists at the Mexico City Olympics, a galvanizing moment for the Black Power movement.[18]

Jackson didn't mention these events, but they were clearly on her mind, and her talk can be read as the incursion of Black Power into gerontology—a sort of social-scientific version of a raised fist. Her talk was very much an activist talk, with acerbic asides the likes of which had not been heard before at the Gerontological Society, much less in the staid pages of *The Gerontologist* (which soon published the paper). She raised the issue of segregation in facilities for the aged, an issue, she chided her listeners, that affected both the North and the South. She criticized the urban renewal programs that were decimating the neighborhoods and families of Black seniors. And she criticized, multiple times, the racist attitudes of social workers, who tended to call their Black aged clients "old boys" and "old girls."[19]

We don't know as much as we should about Black aging, she admitted. But we know enough to do something. Jackson had two sets of interventions in mind, both of which she broached in her Denver talk and explored in more detail elsewhere. The first concerned gerontology itself. Jackson was committed to the training of a new generation of Black gerontologists and social workers, and to the revamping of gerontology curricula to teach all students how structural racism was embedded into the very fabric of senior living in America. As she had explained in 1967, the most rigorous studies of Black aging had been conducted by white investigators who had little understanding of their subjects. This could be remedied, she proposed, by more recruitment and training of Black gerontologists. At a conference a few years later, she was more strident. "Racism," she insisted, was "rampant" in both the higher-education system and in the federal agencies responsible for aging programs. Most of the research, training, and services for older Americans were provided by people with "white middle-class-mind-sets," who therefore had "negative and homogenous" views about Black people. The path for Jackson was not to persuade those researchers to be different, but for aged Black people and Black researchers to "eventually gain control over their own lives and destinies."[20]

Jackson's second intervention was grander, reaching out from gerontology to the very heart of American social policy. As she told the audience in Denver, "The minimum age-eligibility for retirement benefits should be racially differentiated to reflect present racial differences in life expectancies." Old-age benefits should not, she insisted, be "colorblind." Because of race disparities in the lifespan, white Americans tended on average to receive benefits for several more years than Black people did. In an equitable system, Black and white people would receive benefits for the same number of years. Ideally, this could be done by helping Black seniors to live longer. That, though, would take decades, if it happened at all. Until that time came, Jackson believed that affirmative action should be enacted for Social Security, and that Black seniors should begin receiving their benefits several years *before* their white counterparts.[21]

A racially differentiated Social Security system was her most explosive proposal, but not her only one. Like many Black activists in that era, Jackson was skeptical of the welfare state, which in her view smacked of white paternalism. "I detest," she explained, those programs "which continue to utilize ineffective and ill-trained social workers as 'agents of God.'" She still saw a place, though, for the state, mainly as a provider of money that Black seniors could spend as they saw fit. She called for "the obliteration of any distinction between Medicaid and Medicare" through the provision of national health insurance for all, including dental and vision insurance. She also wanted the state to subsidize services, like home health aides, that Black seniors determined for themselves that they needed.[22]

As Jackson was working on these issues, she had her eyes set on the 1971 White House Conference on Aging (WHCOA). The 1961 conference had been a central moment in the march to Medicare. And in the very years that Jackson was skewering the gerontological establishment and the civil rights movement was sweeping the land, its successor was being planned. It was not an opportunity that she was prepared to pass up.

She had a partner: Hobart Jackson, coauthor of the *Double Jeopardy* report and someone who, through day-to-day administrative work at a Black home for the aged, knew what it was to be Black and old in America. He was the other firebrand at work in the Gerontological Society, and soon after Jacquelyne Jackson's remarks he delivered some of his own. From the Black perspective, Hobart argued, the Society was "a predominantly white, predominantly middle-class establishment-oriented organization." This wasn't good enough; it needed to be shaken up by a "militant" or a "radical." While Hobart did not present himself as that person, he did remind listeners that the nation was in real crisis, and that gerontologists, like most everyone else, were failing to meet the challenge. He was scathing in his critique of society's—and the Gerontological Society's—neglect of "the old, black, and poor." Progress had been so "negligible," he reported, that many are left "disgusted, frustrated, and even angry."[23]

He was clearly skeptical that the Gerontological Society would become the activist center of his dreams. He soon founded, therefore, the National Caucus on the Black Aged (NCBA), a pressure group that began operating in 1970. The purpose of the caucus, as he told an interviewer, was to advocate for the Black elderly, in his mind the most impoverished and neglected group in the nation. A new group was necessary, he explained, because the gerontological establishment was essentially white, and civil rights groups, for whatever reason, tended to neglect the elderly too.[24]

One of the founding members of the NCBA, inevitably, was Jacquelyne Jackson—and together, the two of them embarked on a crusade to radicalize the 1971 WHCOA. They hit roadblock after roadblock. They had a hard time even gathering data. The Census Bureau did not consider their request to be a priority and told them that it could only provide the numbers they wanted for $15,000, a staggering sum in 1971, when a car could easily be purchased for $3,000. The pair went to the Administration on Aging to ask for the money but were rebuffed there too.[25]

There was reason for optimism, however. The Senate's Committee on Aging was led at the time by a liberal Democrat named Frank Church, who was deeply sympathetic to the two activists and their quest. He contracted with Inabel Lindsay, former dean of the School of Social Work at Howard University, to prepare a report on Black aging for the Senate, which was delivered in the lead-up to the 1971 WHCOA. In that report, she cited Jacquelyne Jackson time and again and provided the Senate with a bibliography, compiled by Jackson, on Black aging. She also recommended that the committee consider an amendment to the Social Security Act along the lines Jackson recommended, one that would provide benefits earlier to "disadvantaged nonwhite minorities."[26]

Lindsay drew special attention to the work of the NCBA as the organization that was doing more than anyone to promote research into Black aging and to propose solutions to help Black seniors. The NCBA was frenetically active before the White House conference. NCBA leaders sent a telegram with a set of "demands" to President Nixon and the commissioner of the Administration on Aging. Some of the demands were for various welfare agencies to prepare, in advance of the conference, detailed plans to address the specific needs of aged Black people—notably, needs for improved housing and a livable income. Some of the demands were more procedural. The NCBA demanded that the Black aged themselves be consulted in the lead-up to the conference and that each state be required to choose a list of delegates that was at least 30 percent Black—the NCBA, that is, was asking for a significant *over*-representation of Black elderly.[27]

The response from the government was, in Hobart Jackson's account, "nice" but noncommittal. While the NCBA considered holding a "counter conference," that plan was eventually rejected. Two things happened instead. First, two weeks before the conference, the NCBA brought eight hundred older and impoverished Black people from twenty states to Washington, DC, to participate in a demonstration designed to, again in Jackson's words, "articulate their *own* needs and problems and to make recommendations for resolving them." That raucous affair was unprecedented. One of the moderators, a seventy-two-year-old woman named Fannie Jefferson, made their purpose clear. "As Blacks," she said, "we were born into America with one strike against us. And now that we're old and poor, we have three strikes against us." Jefferson and the rest put together a list of demands that included a guaranteed income, improvements to Medicare, and an end to the war in Vietnam. The participants tried to carry the demands to the White House but were asked to leave. Most of them did—but Fannie Jefferson didn't, and she was arrested.[28]

Black delegates especially were critical of the conference for, in Hobart Jackson's words, "significant black *underrepresentation*," even when compared with Asian American or Hispanic representatives. Behind the scenes, things were even worse. In addition to the challenges in data collection already mentioned, Jacquelyne Jackson alleged that one delegate from Michigan was "persuaded to absent himself" from the NCBA's session in order to safeguard his scholarship to a gerontology program. Since this delegate was in charge of one of the subcommittees, the special session's final report was incomplete.[29]

Nonetheless, the NCBA led a "special session" at the WHCOA, with Hobart Jackson as chairman and Jacquelyne Jackson as session coordinator. The presiding chairman was Benjamin Mays, the famed civil rights leader who had delivered Martin Luther King Jr.'s eulogy a few years previously. Its recommendations were stunning. Its very first demands, as with the original requests to Nixon, were political, involving not policy handouts but significant Black representation in the committees that would emerge from the conference's work and would help translate its recommendations into policy. Only then did the document enumerate what those policies should be. The "first priority" was "a guaranteed, moderate income for all black aged." That income, as proposed by the delegates at the WHCOA, was actually quite high: $6,000 annually for a single person, or $9,000 for a couple. Delegates agreed with Jacquelyne Jackson that Black men should receive their benefits a full eight years earlier than white men. They also recommended that home care and long-term care be covered by Medicare, and that senior centers, to "be owned and operated by nonprofit indigenous community corporations," should be funded by Medicaid.[30]

As the WHCOA session demonstrates, there was significant energy behind minority aging as a research project and a political project in the early 1970s. Groups of Hispanic and Asian older people held conferences at the 1971 WHCOA too. A few years later, a National Indian Conference on Aging was held in Phoenix, with more than a thousand participants from 171 tribes. Like Jackson, they emphasized the unique ways that seniors in their population were ill served. The issue here was not the legacy of slavery but the legacy of Indian dispossession and law. Delegates complained that, due to the complex legal relationships between tribes and the state, Indian seniors received paltry Social Security benefits; they complained, too, that nursing homes often could not even receive licenses on reservations because of legal uncertainty about who was authorized to license them.[31]

One path forward involved close integration with the federal government and the Administration on Aging to improve service delivery for the minority aged. In that era, many federal agencies genuinely were trying to comply with civil rights ordinances, so this seemed like a reasonable expenditure of resources. As Pennsylvania's secretary of health told Hobart Jackson in 1974, "this year is the first time" that the Department of Health had truly concerned itself with the availability of nursing home beds for "black and other minority communities."[32]

This kind of internal, government-focused advocacy was the path chosen by the National Urban League (NUL), which remained the civil rights organization that was most committed to the minority aged (and one that Hobart Jackson had long been close to). In 1973, amendments to the Older Americans Act included a provision for affirmative action that required contracts and grants to be rewarded to "minority individuals, at least in proportion to their relative number in the planning and service area." The NUL took on the mission of turning that regulation into reality and received a number of large federal grants to give guidance on how to do so. Their vehicle, known as the Minority Aged Services Training Institute (MASTI), hosted dozens of workshops with aging professionals. They prepared, for instance, a report called

Affirmative Action in Aging Programs, which was circulated to agencies on aging across the country. The goal was to improve hiring and training practices at the agencies, in the name of eventually improving services for elderly minorities in need. The NUL also tried to foster agency collaboration with preexisting minority-rights organizations.[33]

It's clear that Jacquelyne Jackson, while peripherally involved, was less than thrilled with this approach. The NCBA remained in alliance with the NUL, which had been working in this space for longer than any extant organization. (Barbara Cowan, who spearheaded the NUL's efforts in aging, served as secretary of the NCBA at the same time.) And Jackson was a consultant on this program, quoted liberally in their grant applications and internal correspondence. But it's clear from both her correspondence and her activities that she thought the NUL's approach of working through the system to slightly improve it was inadequate to the task. In a 1975 letter to its director, she complained about the lack of specificity in the concept of the "minority aged" and also about a feared overlap between MASTI and the NCBA. She complained as well that the NUL was operating too much in the nebulous space of middlemen, doing training for agency executives and neglecting the education of actual, on-the-ground service providers. In a follow-up letter just three days later, she wrote to the NUL to inform them of the creation of yet another organization, called Black Aging, Inc. She had founded this organization together with Hobart Jackson and others to focus *specifically* on the plight of the Black elderly, and she hoped to launch a publication called *Black Aging* devoted to the same theme.[34]

Jackson turned her attention squarely to research and advocacy, choosing two different vehicles to do so. Both of them were relatively low-budget affairs. One was the journal *Black Aging*, which was the first of its kind. Eventually known as the *Journal of Minority Aging*, it was nothing like the glossy *Journal of Gerontology*. An inexpensive, mimeographed publication, it was more a labor of love than a product of the well-heeled gerontological establishment. For a journal that was so important as the founding document for what would become ethno-gerontology, what's striking above all is how bare-bones it was, especially considering that it was edited by a well-published faculty member at an elite university. By decade's end, it was mainly funded by a nonprofit called the North Carolina Senior Citizens Federation (itself founded by a pioneering Black woman named Inez Myles). Nonetheless, the journal published important work about themes that were not yet touched by the mainstream: health care access for older Hispanic Americans in Texas, for instance, and (in an article penned by Jackson herself) mental illness among older Black men and women.[35]

Recognizing that scientific work alone would not move the needle on public opinion, Jackson decided to shift into the realm of aesthetics. She produced a documentary designed to challenge the dominant cultural representation of the Black elderly, a group long stereotyped as representing down-home values and an ethic of care that was supposedly being forgotten in industrial civilization. Ever since the end of slavery, white Americans had consumed a steady stream of folksy tales about, above all, *caring* older Black characters. The life circumstances of those characters, it should be obvious, bore little resemblance to the actual situation of aging Black people. Jackson wanted to change all that—to make an artistic product that would explore older Black communities as they really were.

Her film, titled *Old, Black, and Alive*, explored the life of older Black residents in Macon County, Alabama. Its main town, Tuskegee, had one of the first Black mayors in the country, and that mayor was on the board of Black Aging, Inc. While the county was small and rural, it nonetheless had significant resonance with Black history. It was home to the Tuskegee Institute, a Historically Black College founded in 1881. And the presence of the institute linked the county with two other episodes in Black history, one proud and one disgraceful. The group of Black World War II pilots known as the Tuskegee Airmen trained there. It was also the site of the Tuskegee Syphilis Study, one of the darkest chapters in American medical history, conducted from

1932 to 1972. The Public Health Service and the Communicable Disease Center (as the CDC was then called) enrolled hundreds of Black men with syphilis and withheld lifesaving treatment in the name of science. More than one hundred died. This story became front-page news only in 1972—around the same time that Jackson was planning her documentary.

The documentary explores the resilience of the Black community through profiles of about a dozen older Black people. No white person appears in the entire film. The movie is not about them, and it is not about racism, but it is about the Black community itself. If the movie has a foil, it is not white racists but rather Black viewers who aren't interested in the elderly. Jackson had argued elsewhere that, due to economic progress in younger Black age cohorts, they might rely upon their elders less, and therefore care about them less. The movie begins with a Black child of about ten years old, astride his bike and sharing his basically negative views on seniors. "None of us pay attention to old folks no more," he muses, adding with a smile that they want to censor pornographic films.

The film does not shy away from poverty. We see a retired domestic worker whose ramshackle house has flooded, forcing her to live in a bus on her property. The point of the segment, though, was to celebrate the resilience of the older woman, in defiance of the clear social neglect that she faced. The profiled individuals are truly an impressive bunch: one segment follows an elderly Black physician who uses a government grant to buy a "Health-Mobile," which he drives around the county to offer medical services. We also see an older blind woman being helped into a van by younger Black aides so she can be taken to a nursing home.[36]

Once the action shifts to the nursing home, the film is careful not to fall into the trope of the "social issues" documentary. While one of the residents does complain about conditions, the film is more concerned with celebrating the vitality of its subjects. We are shown, for instance, a half dozen older Black women singing spirituals. One of them breaks down in tears, which the viewer is liable to view as despair. And yet the woman is at pains to assure us that it is not so. She is overwhelmed with gratitude to God for finding what she calls "a new congregation."[37]

The documentary was, in short, a depiction of old age from the perspective of Black Power: these people, Jackson argued, had faced an overwhelming set of obstacles, but they had nonetheless built beautiful and meaningful lives for themselves. They needed a more just social system, absolutely, but they did not need charity, and they did not need pity. For all its beauty, the film, like the *Journal of Minority Aging*, was quite a modest production. Although it was broadcast on public television stations and remained for decades recommended viewing in gerontological programs focused on race, it was not exactly a blockbuster.[38]

The future lay less with Jackson's Black Power filmmaking than with another TV special that had broadcast a few months earlier. *The Autobiography of Miss Jane Pittman* told the fictional story of a 110-year-old woman, tracing her adventure from slavery to the civil rights movement. While based on a novel by a Black writer, the movie itself was written and directed by white professionals. This one was not squirreled away on public television or in libraries; it was broadcast on CBS on a Thursday night in 1974 to more than fifty million people.[39]

Even though Ms. Pittman spent nearly half her life as, technically, "old," neither the film nor the novel it was based on made this a theme. We do not see her developing disabilities or needing health care; we do not see her receiving Social Security checks or wrangling with the welfare office for Old-Age Assistance; we see her neither taking advantage of Medicaid nor struggling with her inability to do so. It is not even clear how she makes a living. The advanced age of the character is a vehicle to cause the viewer to think not about age but about the passage of time and the legacies of slavery. The film invests the older woman with a sort of magical aura of experience and virtue, returning to an earlier mode of representing aged Black people that was familiar from the nineteenth century. Jane Pittman had served as a "mammy," raising the white children on the compound where she lived. In a climactic speech, she compares herself to a dignified old oak tree, arguing that she had seen so much in her life that her voice ought to be respected. By film's end, she turns into a civil rights icon, desegregating a water fountain under the stern gaze of white law enforcement officers.[40]

However progressive its race politics as a whole, when it came to the specific issue of Black aging, the film was a regression to the historical norm. The movie is not at all about the Black elderly as a specific group with a specific lifestyle and specific needs. Jane Pittman's age is erased as a category of analysis. Black old age, instead, is turned into a moral category, as it had been in the nineteenth century.

By any measure, *Miss Jane Pittman* was a greater success than *Old, Black, and Alive*. And moreover, in its wake the long tradition of viewing older Black people as some kind of moral helpers of white protagonists returned in force (the filmmaker Spike Lee memorably referred to such characters as "magical negroes"). In *The Shining* (1980), for instance, a seventy-year-old Black actor portrays Dick Hallorann, who is actually magical and is charged with protecting and aiding Danny Torrance, the young boy living in the doomed Overlook Hotel. Hallorann, the chef at the hotel, leaves the action to summer in Florida for much of the film. As with Jane Pittman a few years earlier, Hallorann's age is unthematized: Why was such an older man still working at all—and in a physically demanding job, no less?

The classic example is *Driving Miss Daisy* (1989), which won Best Picture at the Academy Awards. The movie dramatizes an aging Jewish woman in Atlanta who is cared for by her Black chauffeur (played by Morgan Freeman) as she succumbs to dementia. While the chauffeur character does age, he is not *harmed* by the aging process the way the protagonist is. He remains, as they say, sharp as a tack, and his purpose, like Jane Pittman's before him, is to provide opportunities for moral uplift and racial education to white protagonists. Up to the end of the film, when he is extremely old himself, he is depicted as a caretaker.

The success of these films, so different in philosophy and spirit from Jackson's documentary, signals the eclipse of her radical and intersectional approach to American aging. Aging remained a topic of national conversation, but that conversation reverted to the norm: it was a conversation primarily about white people, and not one that prepared the nation to serve its increasingly diverse older population. Older Black people were culturally depicted as purveyors of wit and wisdom, and not as a disenfranchised population with its own strengths and its own needs. When the issue was studied at all, which was infrequently, it became apparent that seniors of color had disastrous health and financial outcomes when compared with white ones. A 1980 study in diverse San Diego, for instance, found that older Hispanic, Black, and Asian people were all doing very poorly compared with white residents; they had far less money, less access to transportation, and less access to senior services. Despite calls for alarm like this, the plight of minority elders excited little interest outside the small world of welfare providers and social scientists receiving grants from the Administration on Aging.[41]

The Black freedom struggle continued apace, but the needs of seniors were not paramount. MASTI, the NUL's campaign for affirmative action in senior agencies, apparently stopped functioning and receiving grants around 1980. Jesse Jackson's otherwise pioneering campaigns for president of the United States in 1984 and 1988 were not interested in the issue, beyond a boilerplate call to defend Social Security. The NAACP made no special effort here either. The NCBA continued to exist, but it lacked the clout that it once promised to have: the 1981 White House Conference on Aging was far less raucous and hopeful than its 1971 predecessor. The idea to give racial minorities earlier access to Social Security, while taken up by a number of institutions and thinkers in the 1970s, went nowhere, and by the 1980s, Jackson herself had given up on it. Black feminists, for their part, were pioneering in their analysis of intersectionality—but they did so without reference to Jackson, and without theorizing old age as one of the relevant vectors of oppression.[42]

In the twenty-first century, the aging population is becoming more diverse every year. A quarter of seniors of color report that they have been discriminated against by the health system. Likewise, older Americans of color are more likely to experience economically precarious circumstances, compounding their challenges in a twenty-first-century world of spiraling costs in health care and housing. Despite these statistics, the mainstream discussion of aging has yet to come to grips with the diversity of the graying population, and best-selling books on aging in America still presume, as they did a century ago, that race and ethnicity are not important parts of the equation. The contemporary discussion of age, that is, has continued to be defined by postwar efforts to isolate the issue of "old age," rather than by 1960s–1970s efforts to think intersectionally about it.[43]

The point is not that Jacquelyne Jackson failed, but that history presents us with an example of what a more intersectional approach to aging might look like: an alliance of seniors of color, nursing home administrators, and scientists working simultaneously in multiple arenas to draw attention to the needs and contributions of older people of color. Such a thing took determination, and it took imagination too. "Double jeopardy," Jackson insisted, "evokes the notion of 'what might have been' were it not for racial discrimination." And in looking back at her own period, we can wonder what might have been if Jackson and her allies had been taken more seriously. The arc of old-age policy since the 1930s had been toward more expansive and more equitable programs. It was not writ in stone that such a trend would come to an end, and indeed it continued in many other countries. In the United States, though, something happened in the late 1970s—something that made Jacquelyne Jackson's futurist program seem impossible.[44]

CHAPTER 6

THE END OF
THE FUTURE

To think about old age is to think about the future. After all, what is old age, really, other than the future as experienced by the individual? A society's grappling with old age, therefore, is linked to its more general grappling with the future in all its possibilities and dangers. If I believe that the future is going to be dismal, then I am likely to be pessimistic about my own old age, which will of course take place in that dismal age to come. Conversely, if I believe that things are trending in a good direction, then I will likely be optimistic about the process of aging, which will carry me into that brighter future.

The era of the senior citizen, as we've seen in the last few chapters, coincided with a basically optimistic account of where America was headed. Even Jacquelyne Jackson, for all her criticisms of old-age policy and the old-age movement, believed that something better was possible. Old age was swept up in the futurist vogue of an era that sent rockets to the moon and brought unheard-of technology into American homes. In 1961, the stated theme of the White House Conference on Aging was "Aging with a Future." Conference materials were replete with projections about growing old in the decades to come and with the hopeful belief that organized political and community action would make future aging even better. A few years later, the Carousel of Progress opened at the World's Fair. The attraction showed visitors how American aging had gotten better over the decades, and imagined how that progress would continue in the future. In 1968, Nathan Shock, a founding father of gerontology, published an essay in *The Gerontologist* called, simply, "Age with a Future." It was a profoundly optimistic take on the future of aging. He discussed medical advances, cultural acceptance of old age, and ever-expanding benefits from Social Security and Medicare. Amazed by the successes of the past, he saw no reason why they would not continue. Through vast federal expenditures in medicine, technology, and social insurance, old age was becoming something very new, and the future was bright.[1]

Within just a decade, though, the horizons of aging policy had shrunk, and the boundless future had come to an end. Gerontologists and old-age advocates, like many others in America, abandoned Shock's optimism and began preparing for a more austere aging future in which the best that could be hoped for was the protection of past achievements. This constriction had multiple causes, some of which exceeded the world of aging proper. In the decade of Watergate, endless inflation, and grinding economic crisis, the future looked less bright than it once had.

In the specific arena of old-age policy, there was reason for pessimism too. Between 1935 and 1975, astonishing progress occurred in this space. From then on, old-age policy remained stuck. This was, it bears pointing out, a uniquely American phenomenon. Across the world, from Britain to Chile to South Korea, old-age policy continued to evolve. In some places, benefits were cut and workers were automatically enrolled into privately funded pension plans. In others, long-term care was integrated into the welfare state, in recognition of the fact that many more people were living into their eighties and requiring nursing care, either at home or in an institution. In America, none of this happened. Old-age policy fizzled out, and whatever energy there was for innovation passed into private hands. There were some minor changes to Social Security financing in the late 1970s and early 1980s, and the retirement age was gradually raised. Otherwise, Social Security was untouched for decades. As for Medicare, in the 1970s the quest to expand coverage was replaced by the now-familiar quest to restrain costs. Medicare Part C (1997) introduced Medicare Advantage plans, while Part D (2003) introduced a prescription drug benefit. Neither, though, constituted a significant change to the program, which remained in essence the same as it was in 1965.[2]

It wasn't that Congress gave up on aging altogether. The House Select Committee on Aging, chaired by Claude Pepper and Edward Roybal from 1975 to 1993, held many hearings on issues like low-income housing, elder abuse, and home health care. They won at least one large victory: they helped to ensure the survival of Social Security and Medicare, the bedrock of old-age security. They won smaller ones, too, passing legislation to regulate nursing homes and spreading awareness of widespread attempts to defraud older people. Nonetheless, their more ambitious efforts, notably to provide a federal system for long-term-care insurance, went nowhere. Despite their leadership, the well had run dry.[3]

Something happened to the old-age movement in the 1970s from which it has never recovered. This chapter tries to figure out what it was. Our story is bookended by two White House Conferences on Aging, which have always served as convenient sites for understanding the mainstream discussion of old age. The first, in 1971, was an optimistic gathering of experts and everyday people who believed in the power of the government to remake the old-age experience. In popular culture as well, older people in that same year received positive portrayals in the media as fun-loving and rebellious seniors. After 1971, though, things fell apart. The bipartisan consensus around aging broke down, and neither conservatives nor liberals were able to mount a compelling and coherent argument about what the government should *do* about old age. Conservatives devoted themselves to chimerical schemes for Social Security privatization, while liberals essentially gave up on the issue altogether. Meanwhile, in the world of popular culture, the image of the older person collapsed; once an emblem for American success, the senior citizen was now depicted on television as a depressed and abandoned husk. This political and cultural stagnation was the backdrop for the 1981 White House Conference on Aging, organized by the Reagan administration. It was a scandal-filled mess that generated congressional hearings about its own corruption rather than about old-age policy itself.

We'll begin in the heady atmosphere of 1971, when old-age advocates faced a new and exciting question. What was there to say about American aging now that both Social Security and Medicare had passed? What ought the old-age movement push for, if anything? What's striking in retrospect is how optimistic and ambitious the conference proceedings were. In its preparatory documents, a major senior organization asked whether the conference would be "The End of a Beginning?" We have done a lot for seniors, it argued, but that was child's play; it was time to really do something for them, and to truly extend the benefits of the space age to older Americans. If the end of the beginning had come, it was at last time to enter the future.[4]

National engagement in the process was tremendous. The 1971 conference was enthusiastically covered by the media. In preparation, more than six thousand forums were held all over the country, with over half a million participants. The delegates themselves were meant to represent the entire lived experience of aging. Special effort was made to ensure that at least some impoverished older Americans were present, and 20 percent of the thirty-five hundred delegates represented minority groups (about half were Black, while the rest were Asian American, Hispanic, or Native American). Special sessions were held on the needs, respectively, of Black, Asian American, Hispanic, and Native American elders. As we know from the preceding chapter, Black leaders justifiably felt shortchanged by the conference. All the same, their presence indicated a belief in the possibility of federal action. And it was well-founded too: six of the most prominent leaders in the senior rights movement, for instance, signed a statement calling on the WHCOA to pursue politics "that will remove existing inequities ethnic and other minority groups have had to bear."[5]

The conference exemplified a spirit of bipartisan creativity, which had been the hallmark of aging policy since World War II. President Nixon greeted the conference warmly, and in a postconference address to Congress expressed his support for significant expansions to the senior welfare state. Many of the delegates clearly believed that the senior programs that had developed in the past decade would continue to expand. Because aging issues were not directly partisan at the time, and not all the delegates were politicians anyway, many of the recommendations had a charming, back-of-the-envelope quality to them. A delegate from Leisure World Laguna Beach recommended that workers' hours and pay begin descending gradually once they reached the age of fifty-five. An attorney from Milwaukee thought that the Sunday after Thanksgiving should be designated Family Sunday–U.S.A., during which families would reflect on the importance of including grandparents in the family unit.[6]

In Los Angeles, to take one more example, the chairman of the South Central Committee on Aging was a popular Black radio host named Booker Griffin. In the *Los Angeles Times*, he described the wide-ranging process that had led up to the conference, which involved considerable efforts to garner participation from the most disenfranchised seniors across L.A. He went to DC with a list of recommendations in hand that are astonishing in their ambition. On behalf of his community, he recommended a guaranteed annual income for the elderly that would allow them to live a middle-class lifestyle. He recommended an expansion of the food stamp program to cover the nutritional needs of all elderly, and the abolition of property tax for those living on fixed incomes. Perhaps most notably, he recommended an expansion of Medicare so that it would provide more funding for home care and nursing home care.[7]

At the 1971 WHCOA, in short, aging had a future, one that was diverse and experimental and lively. It wasn't just that the WHCOA featured a handful of delegates with radical ideas. The official conference report and its many recommendations promised a veritable utopia for the American elderly. The subcommittees recommended, among other things, a dramatic expansion in Social Security income, the adoption of a national health care plan, and the provision of preretirement counseling for all Americans within five years of retirement.[8]

In popular culture, too, it really did seem as though older people were on the cusp of something new and exciting. In 1971 alone, at least three films appeared that enlisted older Americans explicitly into the counterculture—in other words, into the most exciting and avant-garde elements of the American experiment. Interestingly, all three of them give a twist on the trope of youth rebelling against their parents. The culture of the era has sometimes been oversimplified as generational warfare between young and old. The antagonists of the counterculture, though, were more likely to be middle-aged than old. After all, as we've seen, grandparents and young people had a good deal in common at the time: both age cohorts were disenfranchised in law and culture in order to make way for the all-consuming power of the middle-aged parents. This led to a cultural trope in which old people and young ones made common cause against the middle-aged— the basic plot of all three of these 1971 films (moreover, all three hinge on the fact that the elderly protagonists can drive).

The most famous of the group was *Harold and Maude*, in which a death-obsessed young man is taught how to truly live and accept life by an elderly Holocaust survivor. Maude, the older character, is depicted as fun-loving, carefree, and artistic. In one memorable scene, she careens around the streets in a VW Beetle, the automotive metonym for youth. She exudes a spirit of nonconformity, liberating birds from their cages at the pet store and transplanting city trees to the forest. She embraces her sexuality, has a house filled with erotic art, and belts out Cat Stevens songs. In this movie, it is the older generation—the one that had lived through the trauma of World War II—that can teach the younger how to truly live and, what's more, truly understand the challenges of youth. (Harold's mother does not know what to do with her wayward son.)[9]

In *Bunny O'Hare*, Bette Davis plays a fun-loving elderly woman who resorts to bank robbery. "Enjoy those 'Golden Years,'" promised the movie poster, "with the most profitable pension plan any sweet mother ever devised!" Her children are constantly haranguing her for money—her son to feed a gambling addiction, and her daughter to pay for therapy for her depressed husband. Through a bank error, Bunny loses her home and has nowhere to go. This leads Bunny and a friend to dress as hippies and go on a bank-robbing spree. At the film's end, they decide to head to Mexico and abandon the children to their fate. The film's last line is Bette Davis saying nonchalantly, "Screw 'em!"[10]

And lastly, in *Kotch*, Walter Matthau stars as a genial older person who lives with his children and looks after his grandson. His petty children get tired of him and try to send him to a retirement home. "Old people are a big problem," his daughter-in-law tells his son. "Nationally, it's a staggering problem, but on the local level I've just had it." Kotch refuses the retirement home and finds a new lease on life. He starts to drive again and looks after a troubled teenager, eventually helping to deliver her baby. In the process, Kotch recovers his self-confidence and decides to live on his own in a small but tidy home in Palm Springs. The film ends with him going to "raise hell" with a new friend of his there.[11]

The spirit of optimism and creativity portrayed in these movies would, sadly, prove short-lived. The writing was already on the wall in 1971. In the same year that the WHCOA was grabbing headlines and millions of Americans were watching movies about fun-loving seniors, a more anxious debate was taking place at the Washington headquarters of the American Enterprise Institute (AEI), a conservative think tank. If the WHCOA represented an imagined future of expansion and hope, this other debate foreshadowed the actual future of circular debates and political stagnation that would be the hallmark of aging policy from the mid-1970s onward. On one side was Wilbur Cohen, one of the original architects of Social Security, who argued in favor of the program. On the other was a bold conservative economist named Milton Friedman, who was making a name for himself as a libertarian renegade. While the central question of the WHCOA was something like "How can old age policy be made more equitable and innovative?," the question here was a simpler one: "Should our Social Security system be scrapped entirely?" This was a bold and dangerous question. Social Security represented the most intimate connection that most Americans had with the federal government. It was a *promise*. And if conservatives could convince Americans that this promise was made in bad faith, it would be quite a victory.[12]

This debate forecasted the opposing sides of the old-age policy debate for decades to come. Friedman's skepticism of the program was surprising given Republican politics of the preceding few decades. President Eisenhower had supported Social Security and even expanded it, almost half of Republican congressmen had voted for Medicare, and President Nixon had signed a major expansion of Social Security benefits. But views like Friedman's had long existed outside the mainstream. Throughout the 1950s, articles appeared in small-town newspapers that referred to Social Security as a fraud and a Ponzi scheme. The first standard-bearer of that assessment at the national level was Barry Goldwater, the senator from Arizona and the 1964 GOP presidential candidate. The adviser who had suggested it to him was none other than Friedman himself. In the wake of Goldwater's defeat, Friedman continued to propagate similar views in all sorts of forums. At the time it was still a minority opinion, but Friedman was on to something, and he knew it. After all, Social Security did have some serious weaknesses as legislation—including, notably, the fact that the program was a very complicated one that hid its operations and even its goals from taxpayers.[13]

Friedman was a canny operator, and he exploited those weaknesses for all they were worth. His basic idea, aired in the 1971 debate at the AEI and also in pieces in the New York Times Magazine and Newsweek, was that Social Security was an inefficient mélange of social insurance and welfare, and it accomplished neither of them well. It was ineffective social insurance because people could not expect to get out of it what they paid in. Instead, their contributions were fed into a complex and ever-changing set of government calculations that worked to the advantage of some people and the disadvantage of others (especially, Friedman rightly noted, working women). And it was ineffective as welfare for two reasons. First, the tax system was regressive, because low earners tended to pay a higher proportion of their income in Social Security taxes than high earners due to limits on taxable income. And second, the system delivered large benefits to well-off people who didn't need it, and comparatively meager benefits to those in genuine need. Friedman, presenting himself as a friend to the downtrodden, wanted to disentangle the two parts of Social Security so that each could be done better. Well-off people didn't need the government's help, so they could take care of their own retirement needs. The main elements of Social Security would be rolled back, or "privatized." The poor *did* need the government's help, but Social Security as written wasn't targeting them effectively. By providing more targeted, means-tested welfare, they could be better cared for.[14]

At first glance, there is something intuitive and appealing about such a proposal. But in truth, it is a disastrous and unworkable scheme that would cause great harm to the neediest Americans. Social Security works precisely because it latches help for the poor to a broad middle-class benefit. The type of program proposed by Friedman to replace Social Security, designed explicitly for the neediest and going by the name of "welfare," would be ripe for budget cuts at the earliest opportunity. And moreover, any kind of privatization plan runs into enormous financing challenges. Social Security taxes are not, in fact, invested into an account that the taxpayer will access when older; they are, for the most part, put straight into the pockets of current retirees. Suppose the government were to promise millions of working-age contributors that they could stop contributing to Social Security and begin contributing to individual accounts. What would happen to the millions of retirees who were being funded by those contributions? There is no good answer to this question, and this multitrillion dollar problem has kept the Republican Party from putting together a feasible plan for privatization.[15]

Such niceties have not kept Social Security privatization from enjoying success as a policy idea, if not a policy reality or even a workable legislative proposal. And at the debate in 1971, Friedman was devastating: witty, bright, apparently in total command of his subject. He was confident in part because he was part of a movement involving several other prominent intellectuals. James Buchanan, the originator of public choice theory, was one of the most important thinkers of the American right wing in the late twentieth century. For Buchanan, as for Friedman, Social Security was a ripe target. As he explained at length in his 1966 book, *Public Finance in Democratic Process*, the system only had legitimacy because the public did not understand it. Whereas Friedman focused on it as bad policy, and Buchanan as illusory and misleading, a Harvard economist and future adviser to Ronald Reagan named Martin Feldstein tried to show that it was something even worse: bad for the economy. His controversial and influential paper asked a reasonable question: Since American households can count on Social Security in retirement, how does this affect their level of saving? He concluded that, in the aggregate, private household saving declined by half as a result of Social Security. Social Security, therefore, "substantially reduces the stock of capital and the level of national income." In other words, it hampers economic growth.[16]

At the time of the 1971 debate, the intellectual firepower of these figures didn't much matter, any more than Friedman's commanding debate performance did. Social Security was still popular, was fiscally sound, and was being expanded by a Republican president. This soon changed. Around 1973, the American economy entered a tailspin. The causes are debated, but the effects aren't: grinding unemployment, a slow decline in real wages, reductions in productivity, and a seemingly endless spiral of inflation. The inflationary crisis of the mid-1970s was challenging for the Social Security system, both ideologically and fiscally. The economic depression hurt tax receipts, while payments themselves were shooting up since they were, as of 1972, indexed to inflation.[17]

Amidst this confluence of bad news, previously marginal attacks on Social Security went mainstream. Conservative think tanks led the way. Rita Ricardo-Campbell, a longtime fellow at the conservative Hoover Institution, published a book-length assault on the sustainability of the Social Security system. The founders of the libertarian Cato Institute were obsessed with the issue as well. Murray Rothbard, economist and intellectual guru to the institute, was not far off when he crowed that "the Social Security system, once so sacred in American opinion that it was literally above criticism, is now seen to be as fully in disrepair as libertarian and free-market writers have long warned." His own organization saw to it. Peter Ferrara published a book with Cato in which he rehearsed all the points made by earlier economists, with the added spin that the system was going bankrupt.[18]

National Review and *Human Events*, the two most important periodicals of the right wing in this period, popularized these issues for the many readers who had little interest in book-length economic studies. William Rusher, publisher of *National Review*, reported that Social Security was a "hoax." And his magazine gleefully reported that "Social Security was in pathetic shape, replete with googoo-level deficits and a resulting need for further mammoth taxes." *Human Events*, too, consistently reported on Social Security as a "pyramid club" that was "dead broke." Even *Christianity Today*, the mouthpiece of evangelical Christianity, was in on it; as early as 1972, authors there were complaining about "Insecure Security" and recommending private investment vehicles.[19]

These kinds of ideas began to filter into the public consciousness. *U.S. News & World Report* reached millions of households in 1974 with a lengthy report titled "Social Security: Promising Too Much to Too Many?" The article was unsigned and not explicitly political—it presented itself as a moderate, sensible take. It is striking, then, just how many of the conservative presuppositions about the program it shared, starting from the fact that the system was in deep crisis. The author claimed that "those in the know" were the ones most worried about the program's solvency (almost the opposite was true: those closest to the ground tended to think that modest tinkering would be enough, as indeed it was). Or consider a claim like this: "The sheer size of the system itself—and its growing impact on the economy—is a source of mounting concern." The passive voice here obscures the fact that this was a concern for conservatives; liberals and the framers of the system were not concerned about its size, and even celebrated it.[20]

The message was coming from financial pundits too. In 1979, a financial advisor named Howard Ruff published *How to Prosper During the Coming Bad Years*, which reached number one on the *New York Times* bestseller list. The book aimed squarely at Americans who were worried about inflation and about the safety of their investments. Ruff was convinced that the US economy was no longer delivering for everyday Americans—and that Social Security wouldn't either. He could only claim that the coming years would be "bad" for his readers by showing that they would have no support in old age. He went on, therefore, for pages and pages about the program as a "Ponzi scheme" on the verge of "collapse." Social Security, he concluded, was "the most dishonest, reprehensible, deceitfully unsound scheme ever foisted by government upon a trusting public."[21]

The Republican Party, a longtime supporter of Social Security, began to turn on the program as well. In 1978, a young politician named George W. Bush latched onto Social Security as an issue in his first congressional campaign. As he told an audience at a country club, Social Security didn't just need tinkering; it needed a renovation. "The ideal solution," he explained, "would be for Social Security to be made sound and people given the chance to invest the money the way they feel." The social insurance system, in other words, should be replaced by a set of individual accounts. This idea remained a Republican dream for decades—or at least until 2005, when the same politician, by then US president, expended a huge amount of political capital on a failed effort at Social Security reform.[22]

So although the program itself remained in place, public faith in it was slipping. A 1979 poll reported alarming levels of distrust in the Social Security system. Whereas most people expected to receive benefits of some sort, more than 80 percent lacked full confidence that they would get what they were owed—and 40 percent had "hardly any" confidence in such a thing. Another poll, conducted by the American Council of Life Insurance, found even worse attitudes. Twenty-two percent of respondents reported that they were very confident in the future of the system, with another 41 percent "somewhat" confident. By 1981, only 8 percent were "very confident," and 31 percent somewhat confident. Each category had dropped by more than ten points. A solid majority of respondents were either "not too confident" or "not at all confident" in the system.[23]

When it came to Social Security and its public legitimacy, the success of Friedman and his conservative allies is an important part of the story. But it's not the only part. Friedman's dominating performance at the 1971 AEI debate was only possible because his Democratic opponent, Wilbur Cohen, was so uninspired. Cohen was certainly an expert. He had helped to design the plan, after all, and understood it much better than Friedman. Mastery of policy detail, though, is seldom the way to win a debate. Cohen looked rumpled and irritated as he tried to pick apart Friedman's plans. What's more, he basically accepted the premises of Friedman and the American Enterprise Institute. Social Security, he explained, was compatible with "the capitalistic free enterprise system"; it "reinforces thrift" and "reinforces initiative." With some tweaks, he promised, it could remain solvent.[24]

However reasonable and correct Cohen may have been, he lacked the panache and vision of his competitor, and he was cast in the unenviable position of defending the status quo. It is not Cohen's fault that he was the best defender Social Security had, and that nobody else was available to mount a robust defense of the system. Most leftist intellectuals didn't much care about Social Security—less because it concerned older people than because it was (rightly) understood as a market-conforming piece of legislation that tended to reaffirm the hierarchies of race, gender, and sexuality that they were trying to unwind. The old-age advocates that did exist had moved on to other issues, believing that Social Security was settled law and did not need defending. The most inspired effort to use Social Security in the name of genuine social progress was led by Jacquelyne Jackson and the National Caucus on the Black Aged (NCBA). As we saw, they hoped to introduce principles of racial equity into the program, offering Black recipients earlier benefits to make up for their shorter lifespans. This effort, and others like it, failed to gain traction in the old-age establishment.

Cohen belonged to the heroic generation of Democratic old-age policymaking, and it was a generation without obvious successors. After the economic crisis of the 1970s, Democrats stopped proposing innovative or expansive policy proposals in this space. Between Jimmy Carter and Joe Biden, Democrats did not have an old-age policy worth the name, and certainly nothing to compare with the Right's drive for Social Security privatization. There were occasional efforts to regulate nursing homes or provide more support for long-term care, but they were far from priorities for the party, and those efforts together had a minor impact on the experience of American aging.

Conservatives pushed a particular narrative about Social Security that didn't bear legislative fruit but did have a cultural and political impact. Liberals couldn't even manage that, and they lacked *both* legislative fruit and a coherent vision for old-age policy. Partly this was because the Democratic Party itself was changing. From the Carter presidency onward, the party backed away from the big-government solutions of the New Deal era, seeking more market-friendly and economical solutions to social problems. When it came to aging and many other policy arenas, the era when experts like Wilbur Cohen crafted gargantuan new programs was over. But the party had ambitions in some areas. Bill Clinton, for instance, swept into office in 1992 with an armload of progressive plans. The party's inaction around old-age issues, therefore, remains something of a puzzle.[25]

Just as the relative success of conservative efforts had multiple causes, the relative failure of liberal ones did too. One of them concerns policy expertise. The right-wing assault on Social Security was birthed primarily in think tanks with close relationships to the Republican Party. The Democrats lacked that kind of ecosystem. There were no progressive think tanks to place alongside the Heritage Foundation and the Cato Institute, organizations that were explicitly political and were ruthless in their recommended political strategies (the journal of the Cato Institute recommended a "Leninist strategy" to demolish public support for Social Security). The closest that liberals could come at the time was the Brookings Institution, which prized its objectivity and rationality. Brookings did have a lot to say about Social Security, but it wasn't going to galvanize a movement. Martha Derthick, director of its Governmental Studies program, published a book on Social Security in 1979, but it differed from the missives of the same period that came from conservative organizations. It was essentially a careful study of Social Security's development, emphasizing the power of unelected administrative officials to guide policy change. The book was an impressive study, still admired decades later, but it was not a call for progressive action. If anything, it encouraged liberals to accept some of the conservative critiques of the program and to remain open to reform.[26]

If the think tanks were not pushing a bold aging agenda, what of the vibrant social movements that so often have defined the

Democratic Party's agenda? Why were they unable to push for more aggressive action, as the Townsend movement had done in the past? There were, after all, plenty of organized movements that were advocating for more aggressive old-age policy. The two biggest and most influential at the time were the National Council of Senior Citizens (NCSC), which was allied with the AFL-CIO and the Democratic Party, and the more insurgent Gray Panthers, the most vibrant leftist old-age movement the country had ever seen. To understand why social movements failed to create political energy on the Left around aging, we can follow these two organizations through the 1970s and ask why they were unable to work with each other and with the Democratic Party to come up with a creative and future-oriented vision for American aging.

Let's begin with the NCSC, which was the most likely origin point for a liberal, labor-friendly old-age policy. The group had its origins in 1961 as Senior Citizens for Kennedy and transformed itself into the NCSC during its all-hands-on-deck push for Medicare. Organized labor's support for Medicare was a major factor in its passage, and the NCSC's campaigns were some of the most visible and passionate campaigns of the whole movement. It was a mass organization, with more than two million members in 1968.[27]

To survive and thrive through the 1970s and 1980s, the NCSC would have had to evolve in response to new political and economic realities. The labor movement was in dire straits in these years as the American economy moved toward service-sector jobs, and the industrial sector, the bread and butter of the NCSC, was in terminal decline. The organization certainly could have struck roots into nonunionized sectors, and it could have worked to represent the women and immigrants who increasingly made up the American workforce. It did not do so. The NCSC stuck to its old ways and focused primarily on servicing its own constituency: retired, and mainly white, industrial workers and their spouses. NCSC leadership came almost exclusively from that sector and was primarily based in Washington, DC, and the

Midwest. It also stuck to its origins as a lockstep ally of the Democratic Party. Its head in the later 1970s, a longtime union leader named Nelson Cruikshank, was Jimmy Carter's official counselor on aging. Throughout the 1980s, NCSC leadership continued to pull from the ranks of organized labor, and it remained in every way a creature of the establishment.[28]

The NCSC did good work for community members, but not the kind that garnered headlines or moved the needle on public opinion. The organization partnered with the government to provide benefits for low-income seniors, whether they were members or not. With funding from the Older Americans Act, it ran the AIDES program across the country, which helped to place senior citizens in part-time community-service work (for pay). In 1972, it established a Nursing Home Ombudsman Program, which organized groups of volunteers to visit nursing homes and solve individual problems for residents while also learning about nursing home conditions and pushing for regulatory reform. And with funding from the federal housing authority, the NCSC worked with groups across the country to construct affordable housing units for seniors.[29]

The NCSC, in short, was in the same position as Wilbur Cohen: nobly defending an older consensus as the conditions and audience for that view shrank every year. The NCSC ceded ground, and its membership slowly contracted over the years. It does good work still under the moniker of the Alliance for Retired Americans, as it has been known since 2001. But even its most stalwart defenders would admit that the organization has not had much power to shape the national conversation on aging. They might add, though, that this had never been its only purpose; its goal was to protect the interests of its own members, which it did admirably well. The Gray Panthers, though, were a different story.

The Gray Panthers were an inspiring and insurgent social movement that tried to leverage the issue of old age to help the poor, people with disabilities, and even the environment. It was founded by a woman named Maggie Kuhn. Born in 1905 in Tennessee, she worked as a teacher and for the Young Women's Christian Association before moving on to a job with the Presbyterian church. She in fact represented the church at the 1961 White House Conference on Aging. As 1970 loomed, Kuhn was facing mandatory retirement—a fate that struck her, a radical in a radical era, as an absurd injustice. Located by then in Philadelphia, Kuhn started a discussion group with older people to discuss mandatory retirement and kindred issues. From these humble beginnings, a movement was born.

The Gray Panthers was primarily an organization of retired, middle-class white people, most of them women. These individuals had grown up with second-wave feminism, the National Organization for Women, and the New Left. They were not content to accept socially defined images of old age, especially old age for women, just as they had not been, when younger, content to accept the same constricted definition of middle-aged femininity. They therefore created a different kind of old-age organization. With its street-level organizing, it looked more like Students for a Democratic Society than it did the NCSC, which had powerful establishment contacts. Chapters of the Panthers, called networks, were meant to be bases for organizing, and guidelines from the national organization made it clear that a fair amount of work was required to get one going. All the same, the movement spread quickly. At its peak in 1980, it had about six thousand active members and 122 separate chapters spread across the country, and another sixty thousand regular donors.[30]

The Gray Panthers explicitly aimed to provide a future-oriented vision of old age as a foil to Friedman's capitalist dystopia and the Democratic establishment's ponderous defenses of the status quo. Older people, Kuhn insisted in an interview, ought to be "society's futurists." Unlike individuals working in capitalist industry or training for it, older people were in some sense external to it, and they could therefore "swim against the tide of fierce economic competition." Perhaps out of this energy, "some new knowledge and economic systems might emerge," benefiting everyone. Kuhn had a capacious understanding of what it meant to improve old age. As she explained at the Gray Panthers' first national convention in 1975, she sought a coalition among seniors, people with disabilities, environmentalists, women, and more. Her view, essentially, was that the issues of old age provided an opportunity to create an America that was more caring, just, and peaceful for all.[31]

The name was clearly a riff on the Black Panthers, but this was not just a form of appropriation; the Gray Panthers had a serious commitment to racial justice. Kuhn led a workshop at a conference of the Black-led National Welfare Rights Organization in 1971. She was on the planning committee of the NCBA, and she helped to organize its racial justice–oriented counterprogramming to the 1971 WHCOA. Hobart Jackson, head of the NCBA, was an ally of Kuhn's and wrote for the Gray Panthers' newsletter.

Following in the footsteps of Jacquelyne Jackson's documentary film *Old, Black, and Alive*, the Panthers labored with some success to change the media's negative representation of older people. The Panthers received training from the Council on Interracial Books for Children, which worked to increase racial diversity in children's books. They applied those lessons to the elderly, forming a Media Watch Task Force to address the negative portrayals of aging that were common in popular culture. Panthers across the country were trained in monitoring media and in agitating for better and more senior representation. They lobbied the National Association of Broadcasters to include "age" in the list of identity markers that required "sensitivity." And archival records show that the Panthers were consulted by the producers of a wide variety of TV programs to ensure that they were not offending the senior population.[32]

The Panthers were committed to universal health care and also to a transformative *model* of health care. As we've seen, Medicare was based around acute care and hospital stays. The Gray Panthers wanted to privilege preventative care and long-term care; as they put it in their

1978 *Gray Panther Manual*, they sought a national health *service*, to be distinguished from national health *insurance*. They held a "counter conference" to the American Medical Association Conference in 1973, and the following year, at the same conference, they staged a crafty bit of political theater. Two hundred Gray Panthers, young and old, marched around the convention hall. Then a man representing the "sick AMA" staged his death and was resuscitated by a group of Panthers, who saved him by pulling wads of dollar bills out of his heart. The Panthers' health activism was not all symbolic. In the San Francisco Bay Area, the East Bay Gray Panthers piloted an actual program to show what they had in mind. Working with various local agencies, and showing a canny ability to negotiate bureaucracies, they opened an Over 60 clinic to provide innovative health care to local seniors. They staffed the clinic with elderly volunteers, both to prove cost-efficiency and to provide a model of community engagement and care.[33]

The Gray Panthers, in short, brought the spirit of the sixties into old-age advocacy, and they showed what "left-wing aging" might look like. Maggie Kuhn was something of a celebrity, and she appeared multiple times on *The Tonight Show Starring Johnny Carson*, which had millions of viewers, and even once on *Saturday Night Live* in 1975. She leveraged that celebrity into practical action. "While the Panthers make headlines with their aggressiveness," *U.S. News & World Report* pointed out, "their efforts supplement and, in many instances, parallel the objectives of older and larger organizations." For instance, in 1979 the Gray Panthers won a case in federal court that resulted in a significant change to Medicaid eligibility for nursing home patients in fifteen states. The Over 60 health clinic, for its part, evolved into a chain of community health nonprofits that are still active today.[34]

By the mid-1980s, though, the Panthers were losing their momentum, succumbing to internal conflict, and shedding members. Consider the crucial state of Florida, the new locus of aging politics in America. Kuhn knew that the Panthers would need to succeed in Florida and other Sunbelt locales, so she did a swing through the state in

1980. This had little effect. By 1989, there were only 350 members of the Gray Panthers in the state. "There's a break in the chain," observed the director of Broward County's Area Agency on Aging. The older members were getting, well, old, and were having trouble making it to meetings. And newer retirees—those born twenty years after Kuhn—were not stepping into the breach.[35]

Some of this attrition can be attributed to strategic mistakes by the Panthers. No charismatic leaders emerged to replace Kuhn, who became more of an establishment figure as the years went on. It's likely, though, that the headwinds were too strong. The 1980s were a dismal decade for activist organizations like the Panthers, especially those that were committed to local chapters and mass mobilization. From the 1970s onward, Americans tended to organize into mass advocacy groups linked with DC lobbyists—think, for example, of Mothers Against Drunk Driving, founded in 1980. Organizations like these were often oriented more to the courts than to the streets.[36]

Whatever the cause, the end result was the same. By the 1980s, the Left had manifestly failed to do what the Right had done: create a vision for the future of American aging that brought together intellectuals, activists, and policymakers. Whatever one's politics, this was a disastrous outcome. Social Security privatization emerged as the only coherent vision for major old-age reform, and the only one with a major constituency—but it was both cruel and unworkable. This created a stagnant dynamic in which conservatives could bang the drum of privatization while centrists and liberals were forced to defend policies that had been in place for decades.

The cultural discussion around the aged, unsurprisingly, became more dismal over the course of the 1970s as the culture at large veered toward pessimism and as old-age politics in particular halted its progress. *Limits to Growth*, a gloomy 1972 report that sold millions of copies, set the tone. While the report was only peripherally about aging, a close reading shows how old age was related to the growing pessimism of the era. The authors of the report argued that the expanding lifespan, long considered a hallmark of modern progress, was about to hit a wall. Thanks to pollution, readers could expect lifespans to start going back down.[37]

Gerontology, which had been an optimistic discipline since its 1940s founding, also changed its tune in the 1970s. Robert J. Havighurst, based at the University of Chicago, was one of the leading gerontologists of the age, and his evolving outlook demonstrates the shifting of the tides. In the 1960s, he had partaken in the spirit of optimism pervading the discipline. "Modern American society," he wrote, "is rich enough" to provide "successful living" to all its members of all ages. But in the early 1970s, his attitude changed. He read *Limits to Growth* as well as Robert Heilbroner's fear-mongering *Inquiry into the Human Prospect* (1974), which convinced him that the good days were nearing an end and that older people would have to contend with energy crises and the end of economic growth. Previous plans, he announced, had been based on a set of assumptions about energy and growth that "we now realize will not continue."[38]

Havighurst participated in a 1975 roundtable in *The Gerontologist* about aging and the future. In the previous twenty-five years, of course, old age had been transformed enormously. What's amazing about the symposium is the presumption that the *next* twenty-five years would probably offer nothing of the sort. Bernice Neugarten, a former president of the Gerontological Society and the organizer of the symposium, chided both those who were too grandiose about the future and those who were too dismal. A "more circumscribed approach," she believed, was most reasonable. She presumed slower economic growth, modest technological advancements, and essentially a continuation of the 1975 status quo into the future. The most that could be hoped for, Havighurst opined in his own contribution, was that older people would continue to have "good chances to work out a fairly satisfactory life for themselves."[39]

Most Americans were not reading *The Gerontologist*. But they were reading books. And in 1976, a Pulitzer Prize went to a book called *Why Survive? Being Old in America*, a hard-hitting work whose gloomy take on the topic is telegraphed by the title. The next year, the National Book Award went to Wallace Stegner's *The Spectator Bird*, a fictional take on the same theme. It is a portrait of an unhappily aging man who complains about a society that, in his words, "does not value the old in the slightest" and "isolates them in hospitals and Sunshine Cities." Even those Americans who didn't read books likely read the news—and what they found in those dismal post-Watergate years was discomfiting. When it came to old age, by far the dominant story of the 1970s, aside from the putative crisis in Social Security, was scandal in the nursing home industry. This narrative appeared on TV and in newspapers and in Senate hearings and in muckraking books. The avalanche began with Mary Adelaide Mendelson's 1971 potboiler, *Tender Loving Greed: How the Incredibly Lucrative Nursing Home "Industry" Is Exploiting America's Old People and Defrauding Us All*. Frank Moss, chair of the Senate Committee on Aging, hosted a series of hearings on the subject, in the course of which he gathered dozens of local investigations about fraud and abuse in nursing homes that had been carried out by journalists across the country.[40]

The Social Security Administration came in for bad press too. The agency had for decades symbolized the nation's reliable commitment to senior welfare. In the mid-1970s, that changed. Robert Ball, the stolid administrator who had run the program since 1962, resigned in 1973, and its reputation began to decline. The rest of the decade was a stormy one for the agency, which had four leaders in just seven years. Its main new responsibility in this period was the management of Supplemental Security Income (SSI), and the rollout was a disaster: people were receiving random payments, and often large ones, due to computer mishaps.[41]

On TV, a similarly bleak portrait of aging in America could be found. Television shows in the 1950s and 1960s had not featured many older characters. They were far more concerned with depicting and legitimating the two-generational nuclear family. In the 1970s, this changed, and older characters came to the fore on at least three major sitcoms. *All in the Family* (1971–1979), the most influential of the bunch, used the household of an aging man in Queens to symbolize the drama of 1970s America. Archie and Edith Bunker were in their fifties, and their grown daughter lived with them for economic reasons. *Sanford and Son* (1972–1977), starring Black characters living in Los Angeles, depicted an older man, Fred, living and working with his middle-aged son, Lamont. *Chico and the Man* (1974–1978) had a strikingly similar conceit, featuring an older white man and a younger Latino friend and housemate named Chico. They, too, lived in Los Angeles, and they, too, were in business together (in this case, a garage rather than a salvage shop). All three of these hit shows featured aging parents living with adult children, something that was becoming more demographically common in the 1970s as young adults delayed marriage.[42]

Each series featured depressing accounts of old age and a suspicion of the postwar ideal of "independence" and "retirement" as either financially or psychologically sustainable. In 1973, for instance, *All in the Family* aired an episode called "Edith Finds an Old Man." In it, Archie's wife encounters a runaway from a nursing home and brings him back to the Bunker house. Archie comes home from work, complaining of a rough day and saying he "ain't as young as I used to be" as the old man looms over Edith's shoulder like a specter. The man, named Mr. Quigley, complains that he feels useless in the nursing home, and that he couldn't possibly find an apartment on his Social Security income alone, which does not even bring him to the poverty level. While his mind is still sharp and he is prodigious with mathematics, he had been fired from his job because of his age. "They got all kinds of medicines to keep us living longer and longer," but "now that we're living longer, they don't know what to do with us." His daughter also wants nothing to do with him. Archie is shaken by these events and has a disturbing nightmare about being an old man, rejected by his family and forcibly incarcerated in a nursing home. The idea of the "golden years" can only be a punchline, delivered ironically after a diatribe from Archie's son-in-law about the horrors of aging in America. Mr. Quigley does find an alternative housing arrangement with a love interest, but it's not an entirely happy ending. They can't get married because then she would lose half of her Social Security. The episode ends with Mr. Quigley giving a piece of advice to Archie: "Don't get old."[43]

Episodes from the other shows also cast doubt on the once glittering dream of retirement. *Sanford and Son* had an episode called "Home Sweet Home for the Aged." Lamont Sanford, the titular son, has decided to go on a trip around the world, meaning that he will no longer be able to live with and care for his father, Fred. He decides to put Fred in a retirement home. The home seems quite nice, but Fred is miserable there. The end of the episode, when Lamont changes his mind and rescues Fred from the facility, is portrayed as a reinstatement of proper gender relations and family ties. This plotline, it should be said, became something of a trope. A 1979 episode of *Three's Company* and a 1981 episode of *Taxi* followed the same basic outline. (On *Taxi*, it borders on plagiarism: the episode ends with the same shot as the *Sanford and Son* episode, with the son walking his aged parent out of the retirement home.)[44]

A 1975 episode of *Chico and the Man* tackled a similar theme. Louie, a garbageman and a friend of the titular pair, decides to retire. Chico is nervous about Louie's decision. "When people retire," he muses, "they get older faster," and he tells a story about a friend who was so listless after three days of retirement that he died. Chico is proven right: Louie is miserable without work. He hangs around the garage, bothering everyone, despite being told to "just have fun." In the end, after briefly considering a leisurely Florida retirement, Louie returns to the union hall to get his job back. "That's the spirit that made America great," says Chico.[45]

From 1975 to 1980, few films dealt seriously with the topic of old age, and those that did presented a much darker portrait than had been the norm a few years earlier. The tone was set in 1975 with a strange thriller directed by George Romero, well-known for *Night of the Living Dead* (1968). He was commissioned by a Lutheran charitable organization to produce a film about the challenges of elder life, and specifically about elder abuse in institutional settings. Romero produced a phantasmagoric film, *The Amusement Park*, that depicts old age as a kind of nightmarish time loop, with no escape but death. It follows the misadventures of an older man in a devilish amusement park, where he is robbed, mistreated, and abducted into medical facilities. Like old age, the park is supposed to be a place of leisure and adventure. But in reality, both were sites of exploitation, confusion, and misery.[46]

In 1979, *Going in Style*, starring the legendary George Burns, appeared in thousands of American cinemas. The movie depicts a trio of old men who rob a bank as a way to alleviate the soul-crushing boredom of retirement. The plot is in some ways similar to that of *Bunny O'Hare*, which had come out eight years earlier. But whereas *Bunny* was essentially a comedy about a carefree grandma, *Going in Style* was more of a somber drama. The film begins with the men, already retired, living a life of quiet despair and boredom, antagonizing their children for no reason and squabbling about their bills. They are financially stable, but one of them decides that they need a change, and he convinces his friends to join him in a bank robbery. The job goes off without a hitch, and up to the film's midpoint it feels like another sunny account of fun-loving old age. But soon after the robbery, one of the trio has a heart attack, apparently unable to deal with the stress. The money becomes something of a curse. They didn't rob the bank for any particular reason, so they aren't sure what to do with the proceeds. After various misadventures, one of the remaining two dies in his sleep, also succumbing to exhaustion and excitement. This leads the last one to give away all the money and turn himself in. When a visitor goads him to cooperate with the police, he demurs, explaining that his life in prison wasn't all that bad, considering the tedium and boredom of his usual life. "Inside or out," he concludes, "I'm a prisoner either way."[47]

Going in Style, although it doesn't endorse a particular politics of Social Security, levels criticisms at the system, and at the old-age movement as a whole. In the opening scenes, the tedium of cashing Social Security checks stands in for the tedium of old-age life in general. When George Burns's character is planning the funeral for his first fallen friend, he rejects government help in paying the expenses. "The hell with the Social Security!" he tells the funeral director. In fact, the men set up their own pension system. When they give the money away to someone deserving, they ask him to pay each of them twenty dollars per week for the rest of their lives (setting up, in a sense, a privatized Townsend Plan). The Gray Panthers come in for a subtle drubbing too. When the elderly trio are listening to the radio to hear about their exploit, a representative from the Panthers argues (wrongly) that the silver-haired criminals demonstrate the need for better senior services. Old age is depicted in the movie as *boring*, and it is strongly hinted that the paternalistic attitude of the state is one reason why. It's a movie about malaise, about older people who aren't sure what to do with themselves. It's as though for them, the future has ceased to exist. A reviewer in the *Chicago Tribune* called the portrayal "old age accurately observed."[48]

This was the inauspicious atmosphere in which planning began for the 1981 White House Conference on Aging, the successor to the bold and experimental conference of 1971. The beginnings were hopeful enough. Jimmy Carter named Sadie Alexander, a Black woman and civil rights activist, to be the chairperson. The four deputy chairpersons were each pragmatic and widely respected. Two of them we've met before: Ellen Winston, long-standing representative of the social work and welfare tradition, and Bernice Neugarten, the esteemed gerontologist. They were joined by Arthur Flemming, a longtime government functionary who had chaired the 1971 conference, and Lupe Morales, an advocate for the Hispanic elderly in Los Angeles. The conference promised to be a culmination of the broad trends in aging policy between the New Deal and the Nixon administration, enlivened by the various movements by and for older people of color that had played such a large role in the 1971 conference.[49]

Alas, Jimmy Carter lost the 1980 election by eight million votes. Ronald Reagan swept into office with quite a different attitude, one much more in line with Milton Friedman and the Cato Institute. Reagan had campaigned hard against Medicare back in the 1960s, and his view of old-age policy, as with most domestic policy, was that the government should stay out of it. He was too good a politician to campaign against Social Security. Even though he had long wanted to introduce so-called voluntary features into the system, he also promised during the campaign not to touch benefits. And yet in May 1981, a few months after he was sworn in, his administration released a controversial plan to save the system. Its most notorious provision was a penalty for early retirees, whose benefits would be dramatically cut.[50]

This move was unpopular, and Reagan was rightly concerned that the WHCOA would become a public relations fiasco, with buses of dignified seniors coming to Washington and passing endless resolutions about his perfidy. The administration decided, therefore, to scuttle the leadership team put in place by Carter and create a WHCOA in its own image. Sadie Alexander was replaced by a Republican named Constance Armitage. An art historian with no particular experience in public policy, she was the former head of the National Federation of Republican Women—and a longtime supporter of Reagan and, before him, Barry Goldwater. Most of the deputy chairs were removed and replaced by a new slate that had less obvious connections to old-age policy: an insurance executive, an oil executive, and the president of the San Diego County Federation of Republican Women's Clubs. The administration viewed the conference as a threat that could be politically neutralized and hoped that this new group of leaders would help them do it. It doesn't even seem that Republican planners liked the idea of holding the conference at all. The very first page of the published proceedings declared "growing skepticism on the utility of such conferences in a time of limited resources."[51]

This kind of political manipulation extended to the nuts and bolts of the conference. The session titled "Implications for the Economy" was chaired by an accountant in the life insurance industry who publicly advocated for conservative reforms to the Social Security system. Under his leadership, the conference officially recommended tax cuts and "macroeconomic policies to stop inflation." Likewise, the committee on "economic well-being" was chaired by a former Republican congressman—and it, too, passed an administration-friendly resolution.[52]

The Republican National Committee worked hard, in ways that became scandalous, to ensure these results. Although these allegations remain controversial, it seems that the party tried to ensure that the most important committees were stacked with administration-friendly voices. The ringleader in these efforts was a young lobbyist named Jack Abramoff, who was making his debut in national politics. Decades later, Abramoff would be imprisoned on fraud and conspiracy charges, but his underhanded methods were already evident in 1981. He and his team commissioned a telephone survey that was designed, as leaked documents attest, to determine which delegates were "favorable" and which were "adversaries." That information was then used to stack each session with enough allies to ensure favorable votes. At the conference hotel itself, Abramoff staffed a sort of command center, to which, apparently, one could only be admitted with a special lapel pin shaped like an oil barrel. While Abramoff's suite was doubtless lavish, the delegates were horrified by the inept planning, organization, and facilities at the conference. Reimbursements were delayed, rooms were overcrowded, and the food was subpar. "The conferees," a San Diego delegate complained, were fed "like pigs at a trough." This delegate, who had attended the 1971 conference, despaired at how undemocratic and chaotic the 1981 proceedings were. Carmela Lacayo, director of an advocacy group for Hispanic seniors, colorfully referred to the whole experience as "being stoned to death with marshmallows."[53]

Lacayo and her peers had no real hopes that the conference would serve to launch a new and expansive agenda for American seniors, as the previous two had. Even if the conference had gone smoothly, it would not have changed the political realities of the era. This was the viewpoint expressed by Betty Kozasa, chair of the Asian Pacific Resource Center on Aging and also chair of the Los Angeles City Council on Aging. "Our expectations," she reported soon after the conference, "were muted" and "lower than those delegates who attended the 1961 and 1971 conferences." "We thought," she concluded, "if we could maintain what we had, that would be doing pretty well."[54]

What a gloomy sentence! And yet it is one that encapsulates old-age policymaking in the early 1980s and beyond. For fifty years, the impetus for change had come almost entirely from the government. The construction of a dignified old age had been a public project and one of the top-tier commitments of the American state. Every president from Franklin Roosevelt to Nixon expanded the safety net for American seniors. But with Carter and Reagan, the period of legislative innovation came to a close.

The wind had been taken out of the sails of the state, and as of 2024, whether it will pick back up again remains unclear. The basic political stalemate of 1981 has remained in place. The old-age movement and the experience of aging changed a great deal—but without much involvement from the government. New winds were arising from different places. The captains of the ship would no longer be elected officials or representatives of activist movements, but titans of industry, notably insurance and medicine. They found ways to partner with senior citizens and to market to them, but they bypassed the traditional institutions like trade unions and political parties, and even organized social movements like the Gray Panthers. Another organization was much more suited to this new era. And its name, of course, was the American Association of Retired Persons (AARP).

PART III

OLDER PEOPLE

(1975–2000)

CHAPTER 7

AARP NATION

Since the 1930s, older Americans have been one of the most highly organized segments of the population. The Townsend movement organized millions of older people during the Great Depression, and after World War II trade unions and churches and political parties united senior Americans into all kinds of pressure groups. Many of them were active in advocating for Medicare and in pushing for expansion of senior services during the Johnson and Nixon administrations. As late as 1975, a large number of old-age organizations were vying for dominance. The Gray Panthers got most of the publicity, the NCSC had the most stalwart ties with trade unions and the Democratic Party, and they were joined by a number of smaller groups too. But within a decade, something dramatic happened. One movement emerged victorious and became dominant for far longer than the Townsend movement ever had: the American Association of Retired Persons, or AARP.[1]

The organization had two million members in 1962, seven million in 1975, thirteen million in 1981, and nearly thirty million by the end of the 1980s. The extent of its ascendancy is hard to overestimate. By 1988, only the Roman Catholic Church had more Americans on its rolls. The AARP's group health insurance program was the nation's largest. Its magazine was the largest-circulating periodical in the country. The AARP headquarters had its own ZIP code (20049), and by the late 1980s a full 1.5 percent of the nonprofit third-class mail sent in the country was sent by the AARP.[2]

The AARP was not just bigger than the Townsend movement or the NCSC. It epitomized a new chapter in the history of aging, represented once again by the triumph of a new language. The Townsend movement had fought for the rights of "the aged," who were understood as needy and helpless. The NCSC had fought for "senior citizens," a term that was designed to improve the image of the sixty-five-plus population. The AARP shied away from both those terms, and in fact from any attempt to rigorously define the boundaries of old age. Its founder, Ethel Percy Andrus, had never liked the idea of the senior citizen. The term, she insisted, "does a disservice to all of us. You can't mass older people in a category any more than you can anyone else." That phrase, "older people," was ascendant and would soon supplant "senior citizens" as the term of art. According to Google's digitized sources, "senior citizens" reached its peak as a term in 1978, when it was even more popular than the ubiquitous "old people." It then began a precipitous decline, falling in popularity by 50 percent in the next twenty years.[3]

The AARP's preferred nomenclature took its place and has been the most broadly accepted term since the 1980s: formerly favored terms like "the aged," "the elderly," and "senior citizens" have been rejected as offensive and stigmatizing, both by aging specialists and in popular culture. "Older people" as a term was different from its predecessors—it was less precise, often referring to people as young as fifty, and was therefore less clearly linked with government programs like Social Security and Medicare. While the AARP certainly supported those programs, it saw itself less as a pressure group for those over sixty-five than as a lifestyle organization for those over fifty. If the Townsendites, the NCSC, and the Gray Panthers had all been trying in different ways to goad the government into action, the AARP had a different goal: it primarily sought private-sector solutions to the problems of senior living, and it sought to connect older people with for-profit companies to improve their lives.

The AARP was able to become dominant in part because it was very good at doing that. Older Americans loved its discount club, travel arrangements, and insurance programs. The new era of "older people" did not spell the end of old-age advocacy. It instead signaled a new goal. The problem of "the aged" had been income security; the problem of the "senior citizen" had been health care and meaningful activities for retirement. One path forward for the old-age movement, of course, would have been to deepen its commitment to government-backed security, ensuring that such programs were available to all. That, though, is not the path the movement took. As we have seen, the efforts to push advocates in that direction had faltered. If the old-age movement was going to survive, it would need a new cause.

The AARP was central to defining what that cause would be—what, in other words, the movement for older people would be designed to do. The AARP did care about public policy—primarily the defense of Social Security and Medicare, along with some smaller-bore issues like crackdowns on consumer fraud against older people. But unlike previous aging organizations we've discussed, those were never its primary purpose. From the AARP's perspective, the main issue was that older people were perceived as needy and frail, and often perceived *themselves* as needy and frail, and that these perceptions hampered older people's vast potential for flourishing. The problem to solve for older people, therefore, was prejudice: legal and cultural disenfranchisement by a society that disrespected the old. This came to be called "ageism." That word was coined in 1969 and became central to old-age advocacy within a decade.

Although ageism had not been a priority for old-age advocates before, it was a real problem nonetheless. Mandatory retirement policies, a form of legal ageism, were loathed by many older people, who found them demeaning. They resented the fact that no matter how healthy they felt, many of them were forced to leave their jobs at sixty-five. Older people were discriminated against in public services too. As a damning 1977 report showed, government programs in preventative health, mental health, legal services, and more were geared toward younger clients and were underutilized by the sixty-five-plus population. Likewise, older people truly did have a rough go of it in popular culture in the late 1970s and 1980s. One older woman theorized that comedy writers were in "a rather tight corner" because, due to new sensitivities around race and gender, older people were the only target left. Perhaps the most prominent older person on late-night shows was Aunt Blabby, a loquacious woman portrayed by Johnny Carson. She compared her own body to the economy: both "sagged" and were "hard to get going again." Hallmark, in 1986, began its famous series of "Maxine" greeting cards, featuring a salty older woman making disparaging remarks about her age. "There's an old saying about how great it is to get older," a typical card read. "Too bad I can't remember what it is." *The Simpsons*, which began airing in 1989, uses Grampa Simpson and Montgomery Burns to portray two noxious, if hilarious, stereotypes about the elderly.[4]

Anti-ageism was an attractive cause for the AARP; it was not expensive to fix, and it was congruent with their effort to broaden and loosen the category of "older people." One might argue that the very idea of an old-age organization was ageist. As such, the AARP, in many respects, was not an old-age organization at all. It never tried to organize or represent the sixty-five-plus population. It opened its ranks to anyone above fifty-five, and eventually to anyone over fifty. And that was a completely different group of people. In 1980, there were almost as many Americans in the fifty-five to sixty-five age bracket as there were in the entire sixty-five-plus bracket. Eventually, the group went even further and removed "retirement" from its name altogether. (Today, the official name is AARP, which does not technically stand for anything.) In 1988, 38 percent of members were under sixty-five, and only 54 percent of members classified themselves as "fully retired."[5]

The AARP, in short, heralded a shift in emphasis that engulfed the entire old-age movement—a shift from a politics of security focused on the sixty-five-plus population to a politics of antidiscrimination focused on a fifty-five-plus population. In doing so, it was very much in keeping with the times. In the 1960s and 1970s, and building on the legacy of the Civil Rights Act, all manner of antidiscrimination ordinances were passed. The struggle for social justice and equity was increasingly translated into a legal battle against discrimination. The AARP's crusade against ageism represents the old-age movement's participation in that general trend, which also encompassed the feminist, gay rights, and civil rights movements (political theorists call this the shift toward a "politics of recognition").[6]

The irony is that the struggle against ageism borrowed tactics from those other movements without forging actual alliances with them. While ageism is certainly real and certainly a problem, the discourse of ageism centers the discussion of aging, once again, on white people, and especially on heterosexual and able-bodied white men. The classic cases of ageism involved airline pilots or businessmen forced into early retirement, or perhaps insensitive depictions of older people as out-of-touch geezers. These issues mattered, to be sure. But not to everyone. The challenges faced by the most disenfranchised older people were different, seldom explored through the lens of ageism, and seldom prioritized by the AARP.

This chapter explores the twin rises of ageism as a concept and the AARP as an organization. It begins with the AARP itself, which was founded, along with many other old-age organizations, in the wake of World War II. It then takes a detour into the history of ageism as a concept, including its entanglement with race and its rapid spread across the old-age movement. Lastly, it returns to the AARP to show how the organization, more than any of its competitors, was able to leverage the anti-ageist moment, turning itself into the old-age movement par excellence, a throne it assumed in about 1980 and which, four decades later, it continues to occupy.

Even as the AARP represented a new chapter in the history of old-age advocacy, it was in many ways an inheritor of the older movement. The origin stories of the AARP and the Townsend movement are in fact hauntingly similar. Recall that in the early 1930s Francis Townsend, a retired physician in Long Beach, California, had seen a group of older people rummaging through garbage cans, looking for food. That sight, he claimed, led him to found a sweeping movement for old-age justice that would enroll millions of older Americans. Just a decade later and a few miles down the road, a retired schoolteacher named Ethel Andrus observed a similar sight—in her case, another retired teacher reduced to living in a chicken coop. Andrus claimed that this sorry sight led her to found an organization called the National Retired Teachers Association (NRTA), humble beginnings for what would eventually become the AARP.

Andrus was a different sort of person from Townsend, and she founded a different sort of organization. Townsend, before his movement, had been somewhere between a socialist and a utopian who resided in the Midwest. Andrus was a native Californian and unlike Townsend was already well-known before she founded her organization. From 1917 to 1944, she served as the principal of Abraham Lincoln High School in Los Angeles. She was the first female high school principal in the state and was vocal about her ideas for educational reform. She was especially concerned with prejudice against the educational and physical capacities of female students. Her 1930 dissertation is a remarkable protofeminist manifesto on this theme. Girls, she insisted, should be taught to use their bodies, taught about sex, and given proper vocational training since "economic independence" could be "a weapon for self-defense whereby she has liberated herself from domestic monarchy." She was especially concerned with health and physical education. In a 1935 article, she affirmed her commitment to "healthful living and the acquisition of play activities for leisure time."

"Even for the handicapped," she explained, activities like tennis and golf were useful in forming healthy minds and bodies.[7]

All of this fed into Andrus's decision to found the NRTA and the strategies she adopted once she did so. Like many gerontologists and aging advocates after World War II, she was convinced that older people could aspire to more than dignified poverty, just as she had been convinced that the young girls in her schools could aspire to more than domestic slumber. Older people, Andrus believed, could be active, independent, and self-sufficient. Even more, they could still provide a social service. "While we are still able to function, let us not forget our own mission," she explained. "We owe our country the best we can give her." In her many articles and public addresses, she emphasized again and again that an older person "can be serene of spirit, stout of heart, eager to work and to help. He can grow and learn and want to know." Or as one of her executives put it, the goal of the organization was to defend the "dignity, independence, and purpose" of older people; those who had these traits would be in "the self-sufficient majority."[8]

One thing Andrus knew from her time as a principal and her engagement with retired teachers was that health care was crucial to a flourishing life. She also knew that health care costs were eating an increasing chunk of retired teachers' paychecks. The same year she founded the NRTA, the Truman administration's efforts to create a national health care plan failed, leaving retired teachers in trouble. Individual plans did exist, but they were too expensive for those on a teacher's pension. For these reasons, Andrus started to pound the pavement in search of group health care plans. And that is how she met Leonard Davis, a thirty-one-year-old insurance broker in Poughkeepsie, New York. Davis helped Andrus offer group health plans to retired teachers through Continental Casualty.

Andrus's decision to use the nonprofit NRTA to peddle products for Continental Casualty laid the groundwork for the organization to come. Other old-age organizations were not doing this; they were advocating for government services, not providing private ones. In testimony to Congress during the long lead-up to Medicare, she argued against the idea of enrolling all senior citizens into a government-run health plan. She felt that doing so would violate the dignity and independence of older people, who for religious reasons or any reason at all might prefer not to have health care coverage or might wish to get it from another source (potentially, although she did not emphasize this, from her own organization).[9]

Andrus had hit on something. The idea of a for-profit health insurance program aimed squarely at seniors and vetted by a trusted nonprofit was a sensation—and not just among teachers. Many others wanted in on the action, and in 1958 Andrus and Davis decided to open up the program. The new members weren't teachers, so a new name was needed; hence, the American Association of Retired Persons was born, and the organization as a whole was known by the unwieldy acronym NRTA-AARP. A few years later, Davis, by then fabulously wealthy, formed his own company. Colonial Penn provided a wide range of insurance products, in addition to the classic health care plans, to NRTA-AARP's many members, including life and auto insurance.

As the 1960s dawned, the NRTA-AARP was a strange beast. It was not exactly a political advocacy group, like the NCSC, although its leaders did testify in Congress in support of moderate reforms. And it was not exactly a lifestyle group, like the Golden Age clubs, although it was certainly devoted to propagating a particular leisurely lifestyle for American seniors. The NRTA-AARP was a new kind of organization, devoted to selling its own products and to promoting a generally sunny outlook about aging in America. This was on full display in its pavilion at the 1964 World's Fair, called Dynamic Maturity. As the accompanying pamphlet gushed, "For the first time in the history of World Fairs, an opportunity for people of all ages to learn about retiring dynamically." Throughout, the exhibits "spotlight[ed]" the "philosophy" of the group: "the rejection of isolation, self-pity and inaction; the encouragement of independence, dignity and purpose for a well-rounded retirement life," one devoted both to leisure and to service.[10]

By 1964, the NRTA-AARP was a big organization, but not yet the only game in town. At the time, it had a bit over a million members—less than half as many as the National Council of Senior Citizens. In the early 1970s, the Gray Panthers, with fewer numbers, garnered far more headlines. It was the Panthers, not AARP members, who were appearing on late-night shows. But within about fifteen years, the AARP became the largest aging organization in the country.[11]

The rise of the AARP as an organization mirrored the rise of ageism as a concept—one that became central to old-age advocacy during and after the 1970s, when the traditional goals and strategies of the movement were no longer working (as we saw in the last chapter). The word was coined in 1969 by Robert N. Butler, the first director of the National Institute on Aging. Born in 1927, Butler endured a harsh Depression-era childhood. He was raised in near poverty, primarily by his grandmother. That experience, alongside the general postwar vogue for gerontology, took him into aging studies. Butler, earlier than most researchers, was concerned with the psychology of older people: the way they interpreted their own lives, and the way they were understood by those around them. Among other things, he tried to reinterpret the fact that older people spent a great deal of time dwelling on the past. Rather than viewing the tendency as a dysfunction, Butler wanted his readers to see it as a healthy way to revisit and resolve past conflicts, reintegrating the psyche and preparing for death.[12]

Butler's coinage of "ageism," though, didn't derive from the lab; it came from his intense engagement with the political, cultural, and racial struggles of the late 1960s. In 1968, he was elected as an alternate delegate to the Democratic National Convention in Chicago as a supporter of the antiwar candidate Eugene McCarthy. That convention was a tumultuous one: McCarthy ended up losing the nominating battle to Hubert Humphrey, and violence erupted in the streets. Butler looked on in horror at the rebellious youth and began to think that generational conflict was one of the key issues of the day.

Soon after, Butler saw something in DC that reminded him of the generational anger he'd observed in Chicago. The city had decided to place a new public housing project a block from his home in Chevy Chase. The building, known as Regency House, was meant to provide housing for elderly people of color. The decision led to a public outcry, including at a meeting of the Chevy Chase Citizens Association attended by Butler. It is indicative of his growing political stature that his views on the issue were deemed newsworthy by the *Washington Post*, which dispatched a young reporter named Carl Bernstein to interview him about it (Bernstein was three years away from becoming famous for helping to break the Watergate scandal).

What Butler told Bernstein, and what he would repeat in numerous forums over the years, was that he had witnessed an outburst of "age-ism," defined in this case as simply "not wanting to have all those ugly old people around." He called the community meeting a "middle-aged riot." While the concept of ageism was clearly derived from the notion of "racism," it had a different cause. Racism is rooted in fear of the other, Butler said, while ageism is rooted in fear of one's future self. Many middle-aged people, Butler explained, have not accepted the passage of time and the fact that they, too, will become old one day. Combined with the reality that they were economically supporting the elderly, who were generally depicted as a miserable burden, it should be no surprise that they had discriminatory feelings toward that age group.[13]

Even so, the basic idea of ageism is that older people face types of discrimination that are in principle similar to those faced by people of color. The idea has numerous problems; as Jacquelyne Jackson and others pointed out, the categories are nothing alike. Moreover, the efforts to identify ageism often involved a blindness to other, more powerful dynamics of discrimination. This brings us back to Chevy Chase, Maryland, where the concept of ageism was born.

The inspiration for the housing project came from a HUD directive to local housing authorities, who were tasked with building public housing outside heavily minority communities. The idea was to give impoverished people of color the opportunity to live in more resource-rich environments, in accordance with the Civil Rights Act of 1964. The debate pitted civil rights groups and religious organizations against taxpayers and business organizations, who complained that public funds ought not to be used to change the character of a neighborhood so dramatically. The issue in Chevy Chase was not about age, or at least not primarily. It was about age as inflected by race. If the debate had truly been about age, similar outcries would have erupted elsewhere in the nation when public housing for seniors was constructed in areas where the racial dynamic did not come into play. And that did not happen.[14]

The Chevy Chase incident was a missed opportunity to forge an intersectional account of aging, one that would aim to understand the relations between, in this case, age and race. Imagine how Jacquelyne Jackson and the National Caucus on the Black Aged would have interpreted the same event. But it was not interpreted that way: the *Washington Post* sent reporters to interview Butler, not Jackson. In place of an intersectional approach, old-age advocates tended to rigorously distinguish ageism and racism, and even to make a case for why the former was more important than the latter. "The 1960s were a time of Civil Rights," explained Jack Ossofsky, head of the National Council of Aging and a close friend of Butler's. "I think that the 1980s will be a time for the rights of the aged." In 1973, the *Journal of Gerontology* published a study titled "Ageism Compared to Racism and Sexism." The headline finding was that ageism was at least as important as racism when it came to income and educational equality, and that although racial equality was improving, age equality seemed to be getting worse. Those results were cited by David Hackett Fischer, the first historian of American aging, in his book *Growing Old in America*. Published in 1978, it was organized around the trope of ageism: he wanted to know why older people were culturally disenfranchised and when that had happened. The book had almost nothing to say about race, an omission he explained in the book itself with reference to the 1973 study. "Racism," he explained, "is in retreat; sexism is everywhere on the defense. But 'ageism' is still growing stronger."[15]

Although the fight against anti-ageism served to sideline discussions about race and the concerns of older people of color, it was an attractive and appealing project in its own right for many people. It tapped into a long-standing desire among older Americans for flexibility and creativity in their golden years. Butler believed that the standard life course—education until twenty, work until sixty-five, retirement unto death—was old-fashioned, limiting, and needed to be discarded. Ageism was not just about dirty looks in the street; it was about a whole phalanx of policies and institutions that forced older people into unsatisfying lives. And many agreed with him. Bernice Neugarten and Matilda White Riley, who served as heads of the Gerontological Society of America and the American Sociological Association, respectively, were both critical of the rigid life course. They urged policymakers to jettison arbitrary age restrictions in order to help Americans live more creative and fulfilling lives. And Neugarten called, in 1974, for "an age-irrelevant society in which arbitrary constraints based on chronological age are removed and in which all individuals, whether they are young or old, have opportunities consonant with their needs, desires and abilities."[16]

Ageism was not a concern only for gerontologists like Butler and Neugarten, of course. Sociologists published studies along these lines, arguing that, as one 1980 book put it, "ageism flourishes under the social conditions imposed by industrialization." Fischer took to the *New York Times* to explain what he considered the new "problem" of old age to be. For most of the twentieth century, he wrote, the dilemma of old age had been financial: how are we going to provide pensions and health care for those who have aged out of the workforce? Those issues, he thought, had been largely solved. The more important problems now were cultural. The "cult of youth," he believed, had gotten out of hand, and older people had become the object of "discrimination," most notably but not only through mandatory retirement policies. "Prejudice by age," he went on, "is as unjust as prejudice by sex, race, and religion."[17]

Similar analysis could be found in the sorts of publications that affected actual practice: journals of education, nursing, psychiatry, and so on. Scholars started to poll people, including children, about their attitudes toward the elderly; they conducted quantitative analyses of TV shows and children's books. In 1975, the National Council on Aging released a study it called "by far the most extensive ever conducted to determine the public's attitude towards aging" and its "perception" of getting older. In 1982, *The Gerontologist* published an article by a linguist to help readers root out ageism in their language. The *Journal of Education for Social Work* published a guide to help practitioners grapple with "The Three 'Isms'—Racism, Ageism, Sexism."[18]

Popular culture also got in the game. When Maggie Kuhn, head of the Gray Panthers, appeared on *Saturday Night Live*, she used her time to decry the negative influence of ageism. (As this shows, left-wing advocates were adopting the new language too.) In 1980, *Time* magazine, with a circulation in the millions, published an exposé about ageism, explaining that it worked similarly to racism and affected older people every day in their doctors' offices and places of business. The list could go on; feminist magazines, technology magazines, and Christian magazines like the *Christian Century* took up the cause.[19]

The struggle against ageism had a unifying effect, both for those talking about old age and for those organizing around it. The old-age movement in the 1960s and 1970s had been a bit rancorous because organizations had different styles and agendas. By the end of the 1970s, though, observers recognized a new sense of common purpose. In 1979, more than twenty of the largest groups even came together to form the Leadership Council of Aging Organizations, which would present a common front for the next four decades (at least). From a scattered bunch of squabbling organizations, the movement had become "institutional."[20]

And this allows us, at last, to return to the AARP and to the new shape of old-age advocacy in the anti-ageist era. When Butler was worrying about age discrimination in Chevy Chase, the AARP was still one aging organization among many. But twenty years later, it had risen to dominance, just like Butler's concept of ageism. "If you ask a roomful of seniors if they've heard of the AARP," one observer reported to Congress in 1995, "most will raise their hands." "But ask the same question" about the National Council of Senior Citizens, and "not many hands will shoot up." The AARP certainly could have become marginalized, as many of its competitors did. In the late 1970s, it suffered a bout of scandals and bad press once the public learned that its for-profit insurance partners were guiding the organization and even fleecing their customers. This might have been the end of the road, or at least the end of the organization's growth. But it wasn't, and the AARP bounced back. How did that happen?[21]

For one thing, the AARP was just the kind of mass organization that *did* flourish in the 1970s and 1980s. It had always used a different model from its competitors, and that turned out to be a strength as the ecology for American civil society changed in its favor. "An American Rip Van Winkle who slept from 1960 to the turn of the new millennium would hardly recognize his country's civil life," according to the sociologist Theda Skocpol. Civil society, when Rip began his slumber, was centered around large groups with vibrant local chapters. The Fraternal Order of Eagles and the Townsend movement, for instance, combined national ambitions with everyday sociability (remember the Townsend meetings with their music and dancing). The AARP's competitors continued to follow this model: the NCSC and the Gray Panthers relied on local chapters and newsletters to organize picket lines and other kinds of protest actions. The NCSC grew out of the trade union movement, and the Panthers out of the Presbyterian Church. It is hard to imagine more typical midcentury institutions. But in the later twentieth century, those models fell apart. Trade unions and main-line churches declined as people streamed toward service work and evangelical religion. The landscape of social movements and advocacy shifted as well. The lively organizations of old were replaced by profes- sional nonprofits, aimed more at the courts than at the town hall.[22]

The AARP had always been an advocacy group of this sort: a service-providing nonprofit that operated more through the mail than in the streets or on the soapbox. The AARP was designed less to push an agenda or to organize its constituents than to grow. "Our ideology," one staffer explained, "is 'big.'" Mailboxes across the country were stuffed with mailers from the AARP, which began to target potential members as soon as they turned fifty. Advertisements courting mem-bers showed up in all kinds of publications—even full-page ads in the *Weekly World News*, a mainstay of supermarket checkout lines that featured articles on UFOs and Bigfoot sightings.[23]

The AARP used Gallup to keep track of the concerns and desires of its members—and apparently did a good job, as 90 percent of its mem-bership was retained year over year. Dues were cheap, just five dollars a year. And the association was practical, speaking to the many seniors who wanted consumer discounts and didn't want to waste their golden years marching around in the rain in favor of better housing policy. Services provided by the AARP, it should be said, were getting better; the aforementioned scandal led the association to switch its insurance provider from Colonial Penn to Prudential—and from then on, ven-dors were chosen in open competition without transparent favoritism from the board.[24]

The AARP did offer some opportunities for in-person sociability, but it was of a different sort than previous organizations had offered. People attended the AARP's national conferences for two reasons. First, for the information sessions on topics like stress management and retirement planning. And second, to take advantage of entertain-ment from silver-haired crooners like Tony Bennett. The vast majority of AARP members paid their five dollars, received the magazine, and enjoyed the discounts and services the association peddled. The AARP did not exist primarily to create sociability or organize volunteer efforts. Only 4 percent of members actually joined their local chapter.[25]

This strategy was most effective in the South, and the AARP was extraordinarily effective at appealing to Sunbelt seniors. *Modern Maturity*, its magazine, was always a booster of the South. The sunny and leisurely climes, the conservative politics, and the active spirit of Southern retirees were all a natural fit for the organization's ethos. One article from the magazine turned the myth of Florida on its head. Ponce de León had supposedly sought the fountain of youth. But in present-day Florida, such a thing was no longer necessary, because contemporary seniors had found the fountain of age. Had Ponce de León stayed in Florida longer, the author dreamed, "he soon would have given up the quest for the magic fountain, preferring retirement in its sunny clime to eternal youth elsewhere."[26]

The genius of the AARP was that it was able to marry its own interest to the anti-ageist struggle that was motivating senior citizens and their allies. The Gray Panthers and the NCSC, however much they might have struggled against ageism, only made sense as organizations if older people were considered to be a distinct group with its own specific needs. The Gray Panthers, even if the name was tongue-in-cheek, was primarily for the "gray." And the NCSC was still trying to mobilize retired union members behind old-age benefits and services. They were, in other words, predicated on "ageism" of a sort, as old-age movements had historically been: their whole reason for being relied on a strict demarcation of who counted as "old." Many older people, though, no longer wanted to be mobilized in the name of an age category that they increasingly saw as stigmatized. For them, the struggle against ageism entailed a sunny outlook on aging and a refusal to identify with "old age." Only the AARP was able to ride that wave.

The AARP's entire ethos and business strategy were based on presenting a positive, vibrant ideal of aging. Anything young people can do, you can do too—ideally, by using AARP services! The AARP was the natural outgrowth of postwar gerontology, which had been committed to proving that seniors could have meaningful and independent lives. That was no accident: Ethel Andrus consulted with gerontologists, and her name would soon grace the Andrus Gerontology Center at the University of Southern California.[27]

The AARP's 1984 marketing campaign provides an example of how the organization presented itself to the public. The headline of the full-page ad, which appeared in many magazines, read, "The 50 and Over Do-It-Yourself Kit," and it featured a white, youthful hand holding the AARP membership card for a "Mr. John Doe." Nothing indicated that older people were in crisis or needed help; indeed, every element of the ad copy was designed to show that older people were still active and engaged. The AARP would help them stay that way. For only a few dollars per year, readers learned, they could join twenty-two million other Americans in the organization, which would allow them to make new friends, receive a magazine, sign up for group health insurance, save on prescription drugs, save on car rentals, and even participate in the AARP Investment Program. The ad also listed, as one benefit out of many, that members could "add their voice" to AARP advocacy, but that was defined vaguely; the AARP would participate "wherever and whenever government addresses the concerns of those over 50."[28]

The AARP presented a pleasing image of what it was to be old: older people could continue working, of course, but they could also enjoy the good life. The association was on the ground floor of the explosion in senior travel, for instance. When a *Boston Globe* reporter went to Portugal in the late 1970s, he shared an airplane with an AARP tour group and was amazed at what he saw. More than half the passengers on his flight were "white-haired US senior citizens," "boarding the plane with the eagerness and élan of a Marine Corps rifle company climbing into an assault helicopter." Using a private partner, the AARP offered tours all over the world: everything from a short stay in Florida to a hundred-day deluxe cruise around the world. They provided services that were tailored to the older consumer and were zealous in protecting their reputation as an organization that would care for the traveler's health or take dignified care in case the worst happened. "We get them home," the coordinator of the travel program explained, "dead or alive."[29]

The AARP had a financial services department, aimed squarely at its own members, to help them afford this good life. Members were offered about a half dozen products, including a Ginnie Mae fund, which specialized in mortgage securities, with the option to deposit directly from Social Security. According to the department's director, the AARP funds were designed to be more "service-oriented" than their competitors, and more "attuned to the needs of mature America." Phones were staffed with representatives who were used to dealing with hearing problems and with low levels of financial literacy.[30]

Modern Maturity, the AARP's magazine, brought this new ideal to kitchen tables and waiting rooms across the country. In 1988, it became the largest-circulating periodical in the United States, a title it held for decades. Tens of millions of issues circulated through the country every two months, depicting in words and pictures what aging successfully in America looked like. The magazine differed in every conceivable way from its competitors. The National Council of Senior Citizens had a newsletter called the *Senior Citizen News*. It was a dry affair, reprinting speeches from political dignitaries and trade union leaders. *Senior Citizen*, another early contender, had no pictures and likewise featured long, meandering articles from physicians and gerontologists about how to age most successfully. Compared with publications like those, the glossy *Modern Maturity* was full of fun and pep. To be sure, each issue contained reminders from AARP dignitaries about the importance of doing volunteer work and aging like a dignified American citizen. But the magazine also featured celebrity profiles, travel guides, jokes, and helpful tips that older people might actually use—like ideas about how to clean small apartments.[31]

In its business model and its magazine, the AARP was devoted above all to the creation of a fun, consumerist, and antidiscriminatory ideal of aging. In some ways, this was not a political imagination at all. The idea was that seniors, using AARP services, could attain their desired lifestyle. And the AARP, from its origins, was less politicized than other aging organizations. When it came to Medicare, much to the irritation of other old-age groups, the NRTA-AARP was reticent. It never endorsed political candidates, and unlike similar organizations it did not publish "scorecards" for politicians. It did not create a political action committee. In 1971 the executive director of the NRTA-AARP testified to Congress about amendments to the Older Americans Act of 1965. "Sit-ins, mass demonstrations, picket lines, and civil disorders are not the methods of the older generations," he explained. "We prefer to point to facts" and to "rely upon the good judgment of Congress." It is no wonder that Nixon saw the AARP, unlike other aging organizations, as an ally.[32]

It would be a mistake, however, to view the AARP as apolitical. It was, and is, a massively powerful lobbying group. But it was not political in the same way as more explicitly activist organizations. The AARP, seeking funding and membership above all, has normally raced to the center, and the center in those years was quite conservative. The AARP, for instance, opposed state-level bills that would have limited how much doctors could charge to Medicare patients. It also opposed congressional action to remedy the so-called notch generation. For complex reasons, seniors born from 1916 to 1921 were uniquely disadvantaged by the Social Security system, and many advocates were urging Congress to step in. The AARP, balking at the price tag, opposed this move.[33]

For all its political quietism, the one issue that the AARP was crystal clear about, and the one that united its membership across party lines, was age discrimination, including any policy, in either the public or private sector, that banned people over a certain age from working. Such policies were indeed the legal form of ageism. The Age

Discrimination in Employment Act of 1967 protected applicants age forty and older from being discriminated against in hiring, but it did not touch the still-popular program of mandatory retirement. The AARP not only supported the act; its leader, in congressional testimony, chastised Congress for not enforcing it enough and threatened to throw the association's resources behind legal aid for older Americans whose claims of old-age discrimination were not being pursued.[34]

As the 1970s wore on, age discrimination became ever more front and center in the AARP's legislative work. The organization created an Age Discrimination Project to pursue, as its coordinator argued, "what is becoming, with speed all too deliberate, a civil right—the right to be free from an arbitrary and discriminatory job termination." In 1977, the executive director explained in another congressional testimony that "mandatory retirement practices help to put the stamp of respectability on age discrimination." We have become, she explained, too committed to a restricted image of the life course, creating "educational tracks and career ladders and mandatory retirement—all of which are conveniences for institutions, not for the individual." At the individual level, these structures appear instead as limitations on freedom, rights, and creativity. When Congress was considering the issue of mandatory retirement for airline pilots at the age of sixty, the AARP found within its massive ranks the perfect spokesman: a sixty-four-year-old pilot who had been forcibly made to retire and who happened to have a PhD in gerontology from the University of Chicago. In his testimony, the experienced pilot described how, for him and many of his fellow older pilots, "the door really slammed on the largest and perhaps most important part of my life."[35]

AARP executives even viewed antidiscrimination efforts as the pathway to resolve the Social Security dilemma. In 1982, the executive director of the AARP, Cyril Brickfield, wrote a long letter to Wilbur Cohen, chairman of Save Our Social Security and Milton Friedman's old debating partner, explaining why he and his organization disagreed with Cohen's plan to save Social Security through taxation.

Brickfield advocated for what he called "a long-term solution—aggressive work-promotion strategy for older persons." This meant, specifically, an increase in the early retirement penalty, a phasing out of the earnings limitation for those over sixty-five, and more incentives to delay retirement. Brickfield believed, in other words, that once there was less discrimination against older people, more of them would continue to work, which would help to resolve the fiscal crisis of Social Security.[36]

The struggle against ageism, thanks largely but not entirely to the AARP, was successful. The Age Discrimination Act of 1975 barred age discrimination in any program that received federal funding. And in 1986, with AARP backing, an amendment to the Age Discrimination in Employment Act was passed to ban compulsory retirement in most fields. For many seniors, this was a wonderful thing. Compulsory retirement had never been popular with workers and had always been more of a management prerogative.[37]

Still, as we've seen, the concept of ageism in practice served to distract attention from the neediest older people. The AARP's advocacy was focused on relatively privileged groups, like the pilot just mentioned. The travails of airline pilots had little impact on the much larger groups of older people working in, say, fast food (in fact, fast food restaurants at the same moment were launching campaigns to hire *more* older people). Older people with disabilities, too, were seldom represented in the AARP's anti-ageist activism. The organization was more interested in extending old age downward, drawing people in their late fifties into the ranks, than they were in contemplating the needs of the very old. The AARP in a real sense did not represent the needs of an eighty-year-old person with a long-term disability who was trying to figure out how to use Medicaid to pay for home health care.[38]

It is in the category of race, though, that the limits of ageism as a concept are most apparent. The AARP had very few Black members: in 1984, only about 3 percent of the membership was Black. The Gray Panthers had been stalwart allies of the National Caucus on the Black

Aged—not so the AARP, which remained studiously silent on racial issues. In the spring of 1968, with the nation in turmoil following the assassination of Martin Luther King Jr., *Modern Maturity* labored to present itself as an oasis of calm. "The problems of the day," the editor explained, "sometimes seem overwhelming." "Restless minorities," sadly, "rise in violence to assert their rights." And at the more intimate level, city streets had become too noisy, and there was not enough "parental influence in the rearing of children." But fear not, because where there are problems, there is an opportunity for service, which older people were well positioned to provide. The magazine did not suggest any particular way they might do so, when it came to racial equity at least. It did, though, provide readers a reprint of a booklet from the district attorney of Los Angeles County titled "What to Do in a Riot."[39]

In many ways large and small the AARP signaled its adherence to a fundamentally white vision of what America was and could be. "Remember Patriotism?" chided one article in 1972. "Anyone over 40," it began, "is sometimes dismayed to read today's headlines." It then went on to contrast the aimless youth of the present with the patriotic memories of the author's youth, with churches and apple trees and potluck dinners. Characteristically, there was no effort to imagine that, for Black readers raised in the Jim Crow South, their childhood memories might be a bit different. The AARP magazine hardly even featured pictures of seniors of color (with the exception, as late as 1970, of actors in blackface), much less articles about them. They did print an elegy for Martin Luther King Jr. after his assassination, but it was turned into an anodyne plea to help others—after all, "not everyone in need is Negro." No other article on the subject of race was published for years. When it came, it was a profile of a moderate Black leader, shown socializing with Richard Nixon and quoted time and again about the perils of radicalism among "young blacks."[40]

Surprisingly little changed in the 1980s and 1990s. In 1985, the AARP did found a Minority Affairs Initiative led by a Black woman and former educator named Margaret Dixon. She admitted that "the

AARP has historically been viewed as an organization that was for, and catered to, upper-middle-class white male individuals." Dixon, with a small staff, sought to change that, with uncertain success. The AARP's publications continued to ignore these issues. A 1993 article explained the importance of discussing "diversity," even while acknowledging "the problems it can create." AARP outreach to minority communities had little impact. San Diego, for instance, was right in the heartland of AARP Nation, and the county had thirteen chapters in 1991. None of them, though, was within six miles of the predominantly Black areas of the city. Although this was redressed, what is striking is that it took so long, and that the *Modern Maturity* write-up viewed the new and predominantly Black chapter as a success story. Records from a senior center in Charlotte, about one-third Black at the time, are suggestive. In response to a request from a state agency, the center reported the racial breakdown of its various activities. The AARP meeting had ninety-five white and five Black participants.[41]

As we know from our discussion of Jacquelyne Jackson and her circle, a powerfully antiracist form of old-age politics, scholarship, and even art did exist. The AARP was not the Gray Panthers, and perhaps it's asking too much to expect its members to march across Washington with a flotilla of impoverished people of color, as the Panthers were doing. But even a more anodyne version is imaginable. The AARP could have maintained its positive outlook and moderate politics while, for instance, celebrating elder diversity, or by publishing Spanish-language versions of its magazine, or by following the Gray Panthers' model and publishing a regular feature on Black aging. None of this happened.

The rise of the AARP, therefore, coincided with the retreat and even defeat of more radical or experimental forms of old-age advocacy. The struggle against ageism asked only for older people to be treated like younger ones—a noble goal, perhaps, but not one that was going to change the world. This shift, and its danger, was noted by observers at the time. An administrator at Wisconsin's Department of Health and

Human Services worried in 1982 that what he called "the anti-ageist perspective" had the potential to harm the old-age movement. After all, if older people were just as healthy and capable of working as anyone else, why did they deserve massive outlays of federal funds? As he pointed out, those outlays were predicated on the idea that old age was essentially a period of disability and decline.[42]

The issue is not that the AARP has been uniformly "conservative" in its politics. It has been manifestly successful at protecting Social Security and Medicare from cuts, often against conservative assaults. At certain moments in its history, it has leaned rightward, and at others it has leaned to the left. It has struggled to balance its competing goals of "appealing to all American seniors" and "advocating for all American seniors." It expended considerable capital on a set of bills in the late 1980s that would have provided more assistance for catastrophic health care and long-term care. It was lukewarm, though, on a bill that would have done something to fund home health care. And after much debate, the organization eventually decided to oppose Bill Clinton's health care reform bill.[43]

At the same time, the hegemony of AARP Nation has come at a steep cost. The AARP is not, in the last instance, an organization for older people or a political organization at all. It is fundamentally an organization for late-middle-aged people and active seniors seeking certain kinds of discount programs. When compared with the advocacy of the Townsend movement, the Gray Panthers, or the National Caucus on the Black Aged, it had meager political ambitions. As a result, "old-age issues" have become increasingly restricted, meaning for most people little more than the defense of Social Security and Medicare, alongside a cultural battle to improve the image of the aged. The adventure of old age was increasingly understood to be a private journey rather than a public mission. In AARP Nation, older people were meant to take care of themselves. This required, above all, caring for their own bodies.

CHAPTER 8

AGING BODIES, GOLDEN GIRLS

In the late 1960s, civic agencies began to host competitive events for senior citizens that they called, tongue firmly in cheek, the Senior Olympics. In those early days, the events focused on ceramics demonstrations, cooking classes, and wheelchair rallies—not exactly the stuff of Olympic glory, and more in keeping with the kinds of sedate activities that were recommended to senior citizens after World War II. Over time, as the AARP began its rise and the ideology of the senior citizen declined, the events started to evolve. In 1980 Atlanta hosted its fifth annual Senior Olympics. Still a public affair, it was put on by a community action agency that had been founded as part of Lyndon Johnson's War on Poverty in 1965. It was, though, better publicized and more athletic than its predecessors. Senior runners carried a torch to the Civic Center, kicking off a day of sporting events for Atlantans over sixty, including a marathon walk, relay races, softball- and football-throwing contests, a dance competition, and even an obstacle course.[1]

Over the course of the 1980s, the Senior Olympics truly entered AARP Nation: they went national, they went corporate, and they opened themselves to participants fifty-five and over. The energy came from two St. Louis businessmen—one a real estate developer, and the other a medical products manufacturer—working at the avant-garde of the 1980s economy. Perhaps inspired by the success of the 1984 Olympics in Los Angeles, they hatched a plan the following year to host a national version of the Senior Olympics in St. Louis. They secured dozens of private sponsors, from airlines to department stores. Just two years later the inaugural national games were held at the site of the 1904 St. Louis Olympics. More than one hundred thousand athletes competed in preliminary events in their hometowns, and three thousand of them traveled to St. Louis to compete. When the athletes arrived, they were given a program that featured an advertisement from the AARP on the inside cover, and a welcome note from President Ronald Reagan himself, congratulating the participants for committing to "personal fitness" and a "healthy lifestyle."[2]

Two years later, another and even larger Senior Olympics was held, again in St. Louis. With photographers from *Sports Illustrated* looking on, the attendees prepared, as one of them put it, to "kick some butt." It was a colorful event, and a heartwarming one. A blind woman swam while her seeing-eye dog, Teddy, cheered her on. A seventy-five-year-old nun, wearing her black veil and a T-shirt that said "The Flying Nun," came in sixth in the fifteen-hundred-meter race-walk. Some of the sexual tension of the traditional Olympic village could be found at the Senior Olympics as well. An eighty-six-year-old competitor confided, "I've never seen such good-looking butts and legs in my life." The games were big business. The 1989 event, *Advertising Age* reported, was "a gold-medal event for advertisers targeting the mature market." Six companies, including Pfizer, paid $250,000 apiece to be official sponsors. In supermarkets across America, shoppers strolled by boxes of Bran Flakes that were loudly promoting the Senior Olympics.[3]

The Senior Olympics exemplify the new world of health and fitness that came for older Americans in the 1980s—a world in which, as Reagan explained, older people were meant to take responsibility for their lifestyle, relying on themselves and on private industry rather than on physicians or the government. This was the logical attitude toward older people's health in AARP Nation. After all, if older people were not understood to be intrinsically different from younger ones, there was no reason to exclude them from the vogue for fitness and vitality that swept the nation in the 1980s. Reagan's reference to a "healthy lifestyle," anodyne as it sounds, was in fact rather novel—the usage of that phrase increased by more than 400 percent between 1980 and 1990.[4]

This chapter explores the new culture of old-age health care, and focuses, as much of the discussion did at the time, on women. Even though most older people were women, this fact had long been ignored as policymakers focused on the travails of older men. After all, for much of the twentieth century, the problem to solve was "retirement": the emotional and financial strains that came with leaving the workforce around age sixty-five. This discussion largely excluded women, who had long tended toward intermittent workforce participation as paid labor was interspersed with other roles as housewife and mother. From this perspective, they didn't just retire once, as men did—they retired multiple times, and sometimes retired *out of* child-rearing and *into* the workforce. In the 1980s, older Americans were interested in exploring fun, creative, and flexible forms of aging. In AARP Nation, older people of both genders were encouraged to move in and out of the workforce while maintaining friendships and hobbies. This is something that older women had been doing for decades, and it's no surprise that they entered the cultural spotlight in just these years.[5]

The new prominence of older women was most apparent on television. Historically, older women had been portrayed negatively, as meddlesome neighbors or batty grandmas. In the 1980s, this changed dramatically. *Mama's Family* (1983–1990), for instance, was a sitcom that featured an older widow with a sharp wit who lived with her sister and her adult children. *Murder, She Wrote* (1984–1996) introduced viewers to the adventures of Jessica Fletcher, a retired schoolteacher who wrote novels and solved mysteries, often outsmarting the local authorities as she did so.

Given all these developments, it should be little surprise that the single most important site for the reimagination of old age in the 1980s was a TV series, and that it featured characters in their late fifties who moved into and out of the workforce, and that those characters were women. *The Golden Girls*, an essential piece of NBC's Saturday-night lineup from 1985 to 1992, was a monster hit, with more than twenty million Americans tuning in weekly. The show featured four older women who lived together in a house in Miami. Three of the characters—Blanche, Dorothy, and Rose—were in their fifties, and either widowed or divorced. Rounding out the group was Sophia, Dorothy's mother, an Italian immigrant (and the only character who was clearly in the sixty-five-plus bracket).

The Golden Girls was a comedy, but it was also a serious exploration of what it meant to grow older in modern America. The titular girls faced health scares, AIDS, and financial issues. And there was a sadness at its core. "Our families are gone," Rose laments in the pilot, "and we're alone. And there are too many years left, and I don't know what to do." What *was* Rose supposed to do? How was she supposed to spend her time after years spent child-rearing, when she had decades left to live and the publicly sanctioned ideals of aging, organized around "retirement" and "the senior citizen," were fading away? In the 1980s, answers to this question were found that are still with us today.[6]

In the last three chapters, we will use *The Golden Girls* to explore the brave new world of aging, focusing in this chapter on health and fitness before turning in the final two to retirement financing and the issue of long-term care. The order of the chapters mirrors the level of concern the showrunners, and American culture in general, had for each theme. For as any viewer of the series could attest, the show is obsessed with bodies: with sickness and health, with exercise and breast implants, and above all with sex. It can thus serve as a guide through the rapidly changing cultural and policy environment for old-age health care in Reagan's America. And as with everything in that new world, the show was in some ways genuinely emancipatory. It helped to expand the culturally acceptable ways in which older people, and especially older women, could use and celebrate their bodies. As we've seen time and again in this book, every emancipation involved, at the same time, new kinds of restrictions and exclusions. Precisely because the show placed health back in the hands of the women themselves, it participated in a new, and corrosive, distrust of Medicare and the health care system as a whole. The protagonists of the series receive terrible health care, reflecting a collapse in public trust of the medical system and a continued neglect of geriatrics as a specialty. The response, on TV and in the public sphere, was not to call for better health care. It was to ask older people to take their health into their own hands, securing it through healthy eating and exercise—a lifestyle that might allow them to achieve, in a newly popular phrase, "successful aging." This new paradigm was embraced explicitly by private industry and by austerity-minded politicians, all of whom were trying to restrain medical costs. And that is the great irony of the show, and of the new culture of older health in this era. However liberating the series was in some ways, it was colluding in a new regime of medical austerity and privatization that in the long run has been an obstacle to the flourishing of older Americans.

Let's begin, though, with what was refreshing and empowering about *The Golden Girls* and its attitude toward the health and bodies of older women. A generation of women had grown up in the heyday of second-wave feminism in the 1960s and 1970s, and in the 1980s they were wondering how to lead lives of independence and dignity as they got older. *The Golden Girls*, of course, was not the only vehicle for this exploration. Famous feminists like Simone de Beauvoir and Betty Friedan published books on aging. Meanwhile, older women had organizational clout as never before. In 1980, two older single women founded the Older Women's League, or OWL. They published "Gray Papers" and newsletters about discrimination against older women, and they lobbied to ensure that older women's issues would be granted a prominent place at the 1981 White House Conference on Aging. They also sought to empower older single women, specifically, as political agents and activists. By decade's end, the league had seventeen thousand members in 120 chapters. And it was not just an advocacy group. Like the Gray Panthers, another female-dominated group, OWL provided practical help to older women. In 1986, to take just one example, OWL produced a free pamphlet to help older, recently divorced women figure out how to stay on their husbands' health insurance plans (an opportunity that OWL-supported legislation allowed for, and which was relevant for women not yet eligible for Medicare).[7]

Even in popular culture, *The Golden Girls* was not alone. Viewers of *Murder, She Wrote* watched a retired teacher and widow solve crimes and outwit the local police department. And millions more Americans watched Jessica Tandy, playing a retired teacher, wrestle with race and privilege in *Driving Miss Daisy* (1989), an Academy Award winner for Best Picture. A few years later, Americans flocked to see *Grumpy Old Men* (1993), which featured a vivacious and sexually adventurous older woman at the core of its plot.

The novelty of these depictions is that they gave older women a new cultural script, something other than "retiring, sweet grandma" and "pathetic older woman trying to recapture her youth." Really, *The Golden Girls* was about nothing else than the characters veering between these extremes and finding satisfaction in a more creative, modern role. Consider "Blanche and the Younger Man," a classic episode from the first season of the show. The episode has two plots. The first concerns Blanche and her attempt to date her much younger fitness instructor, who is presented as a lovable hunk. The second concerns a visit from Rose's mother, Alma, who is of course much older and is presented as a stereotypical "old lady" with white hair and old-fashioned clothes.

The first plotline was a warning about trying to act young and deny one's age. Blanche is portrayed as a comic and pathetic figure in her efforts to slim and tone her body for her date. She exercises constantly, injuring herself in the process, while her health and complexion suffer from her decision to subsist entirely on faddish supplements. Although her date does compliment her appearance, it transpires that he is not romantically interested in her at all, seeing her instead as a maternal figure. Even though the younger man turns out to be uncultured and uninteresting to the worldly Blanche, she is still heartbroken.

This plotline is not so different from one that could have appeared thirty years earlier. Older women, the story goes, should not make themselves ridiculous by trying to act younger than they are. But the episode offered a new possibility in its other plotline. Rose presumes that her visiting mother is weak, requiring significant bedrest. She expresses horror when Sophia takes Alma out to the horse tracks to gamble, even though Alma has a wonderful time. The next day, Sophia leaves Alma out alone with her gambling winnings, a bus map, and a Spanish-English dictionary. Rose, again horrified, is seemingly vindicated when she gets a call from the police station saying that Alma was disoriented and confused. At the station, Rose gives her mother a scolding before taking her home. It turns out, though, that Alma had only been apprehended because the police officer, like Rose, believed that Alma was too old to be out alone.

Alma is predictably furious about the ways that she has been infantilized by both her family and the state. "I don't want a cup of tea," she tells her daughter. "I want to go out and have fun!" When they finally confront one another, Rose admits that she was overprotective because of her fear of loss. "Stopping me from living isn't going to stop me from dying," her mother tells her. And in fact, there was a great deal about Alma that her daughter didn't know. Most importantly, after the death of her husband, Alma had had a sexual relationship with a much younger man, a drifter and ex-con who was doing odd jobs at the farmhouse. Their liaison is presented, by Alma and by the show, as a healthy and temporary arrangement.

With these two story lines, the show neatly presents its ideology of old age, which was also, we should remember, the reigning ideology of AARP Nation. Older people should not deny their age, but rather should invest old age with new meanings and possibilities, up to and including intergenerational romantic relationships. Adopting these attitudes would require a jettisoning of most all of the meanings that had accrued to old age in recent decades. Sophia makes this explicit. After watching Rose's pathological relationship with her mother, she discovers a newfound appreciation for her own daughter, Dorothy, who allows her a great deal of freedom. "The one thing you never do," Sophia tells Dorothy, "is treat me like an old lady. You treat me like a human being." To be a "human being," therefore, the Golden Girls and their older viewers were enjoined to slough off their inner "old lady," a phrase that was often used as an insult on the show.[8]

The rejection of "old age" as an identity category was clearly emancipatory for women. The category of "old woman" had always been more demeaning than that of "old man." In 1987, the Boston Women's Health Book Collective, famous for a feminist health guide called *Our Bodies, Ourselves* (1970), released the landmark *Ourselves, Growing Older: Women Aging with Knowledge and Power*. (Activists in OWL had long before called out *Our Bodies, Ourselves* for its neglect of postmenopausal women.) The whole point was that women could grow old with grace and dignity, avoiding the marginalized identity of the "old woman." The authors agreed with Sophia Petrillo that "there is a difference between 'aging' and 'getting old.'" The former is inevitable, but the latter isn't; "getting old" is a "social concept" that women can feel free to reject.[9]

At every turn in the 1980s, older people were rejecting the identity of "old age," which many saw as stigmatizing. A senior center in Chicago promised a "revolution" that would "help retirees come alive." "Self-helpers," it continued, "will discover the fountain of youth and graduate from this world with their boots on." Around the same time, a medical anthropologist interviewed dozens of older people in

California, seeking to understand what kinds of values they associated with old age. To her surprise, she found that they didn't associate much with it at all. "They do not," she wrote, "speak of being old as meaningful in itself." They spoke instead of a continuously developing self, and expressed a strong sense of identification with their younger self—not in the key of nostalgia, but in the sense that they, too, like that younger person, have a certain set of values and identities that will carry them forward in time. Her interview subjects "express a sense of self that is ageless." In fact, she called her book *The Ageless Self.*[10]

Old age, like never before, was supposed to be fun. Much of the energy of *The Golden Girls* comes from the adventurous spirit of the protagonists, which was so far removed from the leisurely lifestyle promised by postwar retirement culture. "Being old was never fun before," one amazed observer remarked in 1990. "Now, it's nothing but fun." If postwar senior activities had been organized around religion, sociability, and service, they were now oriented around exploration, fitness, and pleasure. To list just a few examples, tens of thousands of senior citizens took trips with a program called Elderhostel (now known as Road Scholar), which promised dorm-like living and continuing education for older people. Single older people, like those on *The Golden Girls*, could participate in organized activities to help them meet people and go on dates—something that would have been unheard of a decade or two earlier.[11]

This new ideology of fun, as these examples indicate, offered many opportunities outside the traditional family unit. The Golden Girls, after all, are not a traditional family, even though they appear in that genre—the sitcom—that had been such an important venue for nuclear family ideals. They are clearly "friends," as the show's memorable theme song reminds us. They aren't, though, friends of very long standing: with the exception of Dorothy and her mother, they haven't known each other long. And they aren't just friends either. They see each other through hospital visits and family trauma; they give each other significant financial support. The clear message of the show is that the four older women became something like a family. This was itself a pathbreaking decision by the showrunners. Older women were meant to be keeping house for older men or perhaps for their grown children—not to be boarding with friends and looking for love! And it's not as though the women are living in a tenement, desperate to find a man to whisk them to a new home. They are living in an ideal suburban home, reclaiming that space of nuclear family bliss for a new and more creative family form.

The most transgressive element of the show concerned its attitude to sex. Old-age sexuality had long been rigorously policed, in culture if not in law. It occupied a strange space because it often involved healthy marital sex between committed partners, which is what American culture prized. But American culture also prized reproductive sex, which this was not. This tension led to a taboo against elder sexuality; those who were interested in sex had long been pathologized as dirty old men or desperate old biddies. The famous Kinsey Reports (1948, 1953), based on widespread surveys, did much to structure post–World War II discussions of American sexuality. While its authors broke almost every taboo on the subject, they left this one unexplored. Even while the data showed some surprising facts about sex in old age—notably the continued sexual appetite of older women—that topic was not theorized or discussed at length. Like the culture at large, the authors of the Kinsey Reports were most fascinated by the sexual experiences of younger people.[12]

The tide began to turn in the 1970s, when several pioneering volumes on the topic of elder sexuality were published by gerontologists. Likewise, the various advice books for older people became more sex-positive than ever. In the 1980s, this trend leapt from specialist aging literature into the mainstream. If sexuality had a face and a voice in the 1980s, it belonged to an older woman named Dr. Ruth Westheimer. Dr. Ruth, as she was popularly known, was born to a German Jewish family in 1928 before immigrating to the United States and starting a sex therapy clinic. In 1980, she launched a revolutionary radio program called *Sexually Speaking*, a sex-positive call-in show. The show, and its various televised spinoffs, was massively popular, and she reached millions of people per week. And although Dr. Ruth was sometimes called "Grandma Freud," she did not play up her age for laughs, nor did she present herself as someone who had aged out of sexual desire. She made it clear, in both her advice and in her person, that "we need never give up on sex."[13]

Ourselves, Growing Older included testimony from dozens of women, along with information about masturbation, sex in older lesbian relationships, and guides to physically safe sex for people with disabilities. This kind of sexual advice could even be found in *Modern Maturity*, the AARP's bimonthly magazine. In 1992, when it was the biggest-circulating periodical in the country, it featured a long article by a psychoanalyst titled "Appreciating the Sexual You." The racy article featured explicit discussions of couples sharing their fantasies. All of this would have seemed lascivious if the writer were talking about youth, but of course he was not, as indicated by the recommendation that readers seek medical counsel if they were having physical issues that stood in the way of sexual activity. Once the physical barriers were surmounted, he concluded, old age can give us "a second chance at sexual pleasure and harmony, often a better one than we had in youth."[14]

On the silver screen, too, old-age sexuality became more common in the 1980s and 1990s. In the same year that *The Golden Girls* debuted, *Cocoon*, directed by Ron Howard, won multiple Academy Awards and raked in millions of box office dollars. It's the story of a retirement center in Florida, and it begins with a trio of adventurous older men who are in the habit of trespassing in a nearby mansion to use the pool. That pool, thanks to some visiting extraterrestrial aliens, has restorative properties and gives the men back their health and vitality. That new vivacity was indexed by sexuality. In this case, all three men are given erections by the pool, and they ravish their delighted partners when they get back home.

But it was *The Golden Girls* that truly brought elder sexuality to the mainstream. It was a sexually charged show, and many episodes involved the erotic (mis)adventures of its protagonists. All four of the women, including Sophia, display an interest in sexual fulfillment and even, specifically, orgasm. This is sometimes played for laughs, especially in the case of Blanche. The joke, though, is usually about her promiscuity, and not about her age. The tone was set early in the show's run; the third episode of the series is entitled "Rose the Prude" and concerns Rose Nylund's anxieties about having sex in the wake of her husband's death fifteen years earlier. Charlie had died *while* they were in the act, compounding Rose's trauma and reminding viewers that female sexuality can be a dangerous thing. The other women are shocked by Rose's abstinence, presuming as they do that sexuality is an important part of a happy life. Rose does in fact meet and bed a new man—one who turns out to be an excellent match, both physically and emotionally.[15]

The new celebration of senior sexuality was part and parcel of the cultural shift toward a more creative and less buttoned-up vision of aging—a shift that the AARP helped along but which was being celebrated in many places. This is why so many of the new aging gurus of the 1980s were keen on sexuality among seniors. Consider the case of Ken Dychtwald, who did more than anyone else to bring the spirit of California optimism into the sometimes depressing discussion of old age in America. Born in 1950, Dychtwald was a classic child of the California counterculture. He soon turned his attention to older Californians, wondering how they in particular might be able to better harness their "bodyminds," as he called, in his California way, our unified body and soul. "Before we knew it," he reported later, "we had a breeding ground for highly spirited, highly vigorous, turned-on humans who happened to be 60, 70, or 80 years old." He built this insight into an empire of businesses, publications, and educational series about aging in America. He became something of a celebrity, appearing on *Oprah* and *Good Morning America*; he even graced the cover of *Continental Airlines Magazine*.[16]

In 1989, he used Blanche of *The Golden Girls* as an example of the new approach to elder sexuality in his regular column in the *Chicago Sun-Times*. That same year, he published an influential book called *Age Wave*. The idea of the book was that older Americans can and should abandon everything they think they know about aging. The life course should become entirely flexible. He envisioned a world of serial monogamy in which people could have "different mates for each major stage of life," and in which the staid nuclear family gives way to the more fluid and volitional "matrix" family, bound by choice rather than by law or blood. In this world, older people would have sex with multiple partners. And in this world, "you may never retire, or you may retire several times." And your housing arrangements should evolve too; he envisioned all sorts of cohousing arrangements, not dissimilar from the ones selected by the Golden Girls.[17]

Dychtwald and the Golden Girls were each trying in their own way to imagine more flexible forms of living for American seniors, forms that were less committed to the strict dogmas of family, sexuality, and labor that had governed senior living after World War II. Even homosexuality among older people was embraced with surprising openness. At first, as we might expect, this was a countercultural concern. The earliest celebration of queer aging that I'm aware of was a 1979 special issue of *Sinister Wisdom*, the nation's leading journal for lesbian feminism, on the theme of old age. For three dollars, women across the country could, if they wished, read a remarkable volume of essays, poetry, and photography by and about aging lesbians who were reflecting on themes of sexuality, love, and death from explicitly feminist perspectives. An older woman published an article about her looming death and on being pulled back toward Mother Earth. Readers could also find an interview with a seventy-seven-year-old Black lesbian who celebrated the virtues of female community for older people. In the decade after that volume was released, a surprising number of artists and social scientists turned their attention to the older queer community.

(One scholar suggested "gayging" as a term, which sadly did not catch on.)[18]

The topic did not remain in the avant-garde for long. The AARP article on sexuality mentioned above included a discussion of gay sex. *The Golden Girls* was a pathbreaking show for queer characters on television, and generations of queer Americans have been devoted fans. Gay characters appeared with some frequency on the series. In an Emmy-winning episode from season two, Dorothy's college friend Jean, a lesbian, comes to visit. Jean appears as a warm and engaging character, and one who is accepted by her new friends. Sophia, the oldest of the crew, declares that she would have no problem having a gay son. This is doubtless a message that many gay viewers wished they were hearing from their own parents—especially at the height of the AIDS epidemic, which was explicitly thematized a few years later, when Rose was put at risk because of a blood transfusion. The show criticizes the hysteria around AIDS. Rose uses a fake name for the test because she is aware of the discrimination and fear that attend positive results. Blanche, who gives a paean to safe sex on the episode, reminds both Rose and the audience that AIDS "is not a bad persons' disease, Rose. It is not God punishing people for their sins."[19]

The Golden Girls was in many ways a countercultural show. Among other things, this meant that it was skeptical of the utility of established institutions. For the four women, given their age and ambitions, the most relevant institutions were the ones that provided health care. And strikingly, for a show so committed to health and flourishing, *The Golden Girls* was critical of the medical establishment. Sophia's health is most frequently at issue, and much is made of her justified reluctance to seek treatment. "I hate doctors!" she exclaims at one point. In one episode, she develops a hernia. She is terrified, though, of the hospital, a fear that turns out to be well placed because she gets checked in under the wrong name and abandoned in an elevator. An orderly says that he'll get in touch with patient services, but nobody comes. Two lawyers are sympathetic to her plight until they discover that she is on

Medicare, at which point they abandon her too. Her daughter is the one who finds her—only family, in the world of *The Golden Girls*, can truly be counted on.[20]

Dorothy has her own series of misadventures with the health care system. In the fifth season, a pair of episodes detail her attempts to get doctors to take seriously her months-long battle with fatigue, which is keeping her from work. The first three doctors are indifferent or worse, suggesting that she might have the flu or perhaps be depressed because of the absence of a man in her life. She then goes to a specialist in New York, who tells her again that she's not sick but is just getting old; he recommends that she "go on a cruise" and "change her hair color." This causes Dorothy to break down in tears of despair. Only her friends believe her. "You're not crazy," Rose tells her. "You're sick." Things turn around for Dorothy when she sees a pediatrician who happens to be a personal friend. He sends her at last to the right specialist, who gives her the relatively new diagnosis of chronic fatigue syndrome. "I don't know where you doctors lose your humanity," she tells one of the physicians who had dismissed her. "But you lose it." The episode ends with Dorothy toasting her friends and explaining that they are the only ones who truly care for her.[21]

The show here gives voice to a feminist critique of American health care, which had been virtually absent in the debates around Medicare. The episodes about chronic fatigue syndrome were penned by the showrunner Susan Harris, who had been dismissed in just this way by doctors. While this sort of treatment had been common for decades, if not centuries, older women in the 1980s were speaking out about it more than ever. The health care system, they explained, was staffed by men who did not understand their specific needs, and who offered health care that was so expensive that many of them couldn't access it anyway. *Ourselves, Growing Older,* the sequel to *Our Bodies, Ourselves,* was designed to address just this problem by providing a sort of self-help guide to the aging body. "When we try to get the services we need in this country," its authors wrote, "we face a patchwork quilt of agencies and programs with confusing initials." And "unlike the strong and warm patchwork quilts so beautifully designed and made by women," this one "has many holes and does not cover us when we need it."[22]

Polls showed that health care costs and coverage were a major concern for seniors. Even as older people were constituting ever-greater percentages of the patient population, they were ill served by physicians. "A doctor comes to see me once a month," one eighty-four-year-old woman wrote to the *Los Angeles Times* in 1979. "He spends approximately three to five seconds with me." The year before, a psychiatrist published, under a pseudonym, an influential satire about the era's medical education. Based on the author's real-life experiences at Harvard Medical School, *The House of God* describes an education that led him to devalue older patients. "I had loved old people," the narrator reports. "Now they were no longer old people, they were gomers, and I did not, I could not love them anymore" ("gomer" meant "get out of my emergency room"). Indeed, studies from the time showed that physicians spent relatively less time with older patients than with younger ones, and were often poorly trained in geriatric issues. Stereotypes also abounded about lonely older people treating doctors' visits as social calls and making endless trips to the doctor to air minor complaints.[23]

It was true then, just as it is now, that geriatrics was an underpaid and understaffed discipline, especially in comparison with the number of older people that were in hospitals. Data from the late 1970s showed that, out of 363,000 physicians in the US, about 700 considered geriatrics to be one of their specialties—and just 125, mainly themselves older doctors, considered geriatrics to be their sole interest. And even if they could get a hearing, older people often had a hard time paying for it. Medicare was never designed to pay 100 percent of one's medical costs, and as costs in general went up, so did out-of-pocket expenses. In 1984, the US Congress's House Committee on Aging held an alarming hearing called *Rising Health Care Costs and the Elderly*, at which speaker after speaker detailed the high out-of-pocket costs that seniors were paying for Medicare deductibles, prescription drugs, and long-term care.[24]

The story of medicine in the 1980s was less about improving health outcomes than it was about for-profit hospitals, HMOs, and dramatic cost-cutting measures imposed by the federal government. Physicians themselves appeared less as objective arbiters of medical knowledge than as bureaucrats, or as cogs in a machine they could not control. Instead of trooping down to the family doctor in search of expertise, patients were beginning to act like consumers, interfacing with a medical marketplace dominated less by physicians than by managed-care organizations, insurance companies, and pharmaceutical giants. Dorothy in *The Golden Girls* visits no fewer than five physicians before finding a good fit; the show, therefore, was advocating a new model of medical consumerism.[25]

Nonetheless, the public debate about health care for older people was not about how to improve it—it was about how to limit their access even further. This sensibility made the headlines in 1985 when Governor Richard Lamm of Colorado, a Democrat, said that the elderly had "a duty to die and get out of the way. Let the other society, our kids, build a better life." In the late 1980s, several philosophers and bioethicists began to argue that, given the aging of American society and exploding health care costs, we had no choice but to begin restricting care for older Americans. Policymakers threatened to follow suit.[26]

The Golden Girls, like millions of older Americans, found themselves in a paradoxical place. They were being enjoined to lead lives of carefree leisure, fun, and sex—all of which required health. But they were suspicious of doctors and the medical system, which seemed to provide them with careless and expensive treatment. What's worse, politicians seemed to think that their care was still somehow *too* good and was siphoning resources from more deserving populations. What were they to do? Simple: they were supposed to take care of themselves.

The show was a celebration of self-care as an alternative to physicians' care. When doctors do show up in the series, sometimes their only purpose is to urge the characters to take better care of themselves. In one episode, Sophia has chest pain that she interprets as a heart attack. Blanche calls the doctor, but he can't be reached, and the paramedics can't make it on account of a storm. When a doctor does come eventually, he determines that Sophia is having a gallbladder attack brought on by a day of indulgent eating. "You simply cannot go on eating like that at your age!" he tells her. After he leaves, Rose, Dorothy, and Blanche gather around the table and consider having a dessert. They decide instead to take a walk and burn off the calories from the rich food they'd eaten that day.[27]

Self-care had been a small component of old-age culture before the 1980s. While senior magazines of course included home remedies for corns or ulcers, it was presumed that health was generally an affair for trained physicians. The feminist health movement of the 1970s had envisioned a network of women's health clinics to supplement and supplant the capitalist medical establishment. The Gray Panthers had tried to create similar kinds of clinics specifically designed for older people. In the 1980s, the health advice for older people became more individualistic. In *Ourselves, Growing Older*, for instance, the focus was largely on self-care. "We can prolong our healthy, active years by paying attention to good nutrition," the authors insisted.[28]

The book made sense in a nation that was newly obsessed with fitness, and in which senior citizens in particular were enjoined at every turn to take care of their health. When the Golden Girls took an aerobics class, they were both responding and contributing to this new sensibility. In 1987, PBS began broadcasting a series called *Sit and Be Fit*, which promised to help people with disabilities improve mobility and flexibility from their chairs. The program was begun by a nurse named Mary Ann Wilson, who had specialized in rehabilitation and geriatrics. "The more I worked with older people," she said, "the more confident I became they could realize astonishing benefits from a specially designed exercise routine."[29]

Magazines for seniors also became obsessed with the theme. Traditionally, they had had little to say about health. They featured cultural and political articles alongside nature photography, travelogues, and pious poetry. Even accounts of retirement communities focused on gentle pursuits. A 1969 profile of retirement cities in *Modern Maturity* emphasized billiards, shuffleboard, golf, and churches. In the 1980s, though, senior magazines went mad for fitness. In a typical issue of *50 Plus*, traditional themes like nature, service, or religion were absent. But in "The Right Spa for You," readers could learn all about health spas, "the vacation spot of the 80s" to which older Americans were flocking because of "America's newly raised health consciousness." "The 'fat farm,'" the author explained, "has become the 'fit farm,'" and she urged readers to take "a total plunge into self-improvement" as a way to battle "fogy syndrome." Another article in the issue profiled a well-known health writer who gave tips on losing weight and lowering blood pressure. Interested readers could work on that themselves; the article provided specific targets, and an ad on the back page touted a product that would let readers check their blood pressure right at home. The same themes recurred in *Modern Maturity*, which often featured exercise tips and profiles of active seniors cycling across Europe or trying new sports. Readers of just one issue in April 1988 learned how to renovate their homes to make them safer, how to lower their medical costs through savvy consumer practices, and how to self-administer a health evaluation. The overwhelming message was that the medical landscape was a minefield that older people had to navigate with caution. "The responsibility," one author concluded, "is yours."[30]

In general, this new culture of fitness had much to recommend it. There were many more people in their eighties than ever before in American history. Surely it was for the best that they received gentle propaganda against smoking and in favor of good nutrition. And in the absence of inexpensive rehab options, surely *Sit and Be Fit* and other initiatives like it helped many to remain mobile and active. "I wouldn't be walking around now if it weren't for these exercises," reported one seventy-eight-year-old beneficiary.[31]

At the same time, there was something convenient about self-care from the perspective of insurance companies, hospitals, and pharmaceutical and wellness companies. The evolution of Ken Dychtwald, the countercultural aging expert, was typical. His first encounters with older people, he reported in *Age Wave*, were depressing: "I observed that a lifetime of disregard for personal health led, not to a death sentence, but to chronic disease"—which in turn led to high medical spending and the need for rationing. But it need not be that way! Seniors across the United States, Dychtwald enthused, were embracing "fitness and the active lifestyle." While he may have begun as an anticapitalist dissident, he changed his tune in the 1980s. He explained the shift in a revealing section of his memoir titled "Caught Between the Tao and the Dow." With the help of like-minded physicians and entrepreneurs, he and his wife started a consulting firm devoted to "conscious capitalism." He soon began speaking at investment conferences, and CBS and *Time* magazine hired him to help them understand how to advertise to their aging audience. He specifically sought to leverage the enormous market in senior health care. He established a program called the Alliance for Healthy Aging that would bring together dozens of HMOs and help them learn how to prepare their organizations for the age wave—preparation that included, of course, "patient wellness education."[32]

Dychtwald named two physicians in particular as allies in the cause: James Fries and John Rowe. Together, the pair helped to engineer a sea change in the way that physicians, and even older people themselves, understood aging and health. And for both of them, the message was the same: old age could be a time of wonderful health and productivity if older people were willing to do the hard work of maintaining their bodies.

James Fries was one of the most recognizable and influential physicians of the era. In a pathbreaking 1980 article for the *New England Journal of Medicine*, he pioneered the notion of "compression of morbidity." His goal, he explained in the very first sentence, was to "contradict the conventional anticipation of an ever older, ever more feeble, and ever more expensive-to-care-for populace." Instead, his work showed that there was reason for optimism, because "the average period of diminished physical vigor will decrease." Morbidity, in other words, would be compressed into ever-smaller periods of time at the end of life, so long as American seniors made the right lifestyle choices. If they did—and this is a sentence tailor-made to excite the insurance industry—"the need for medical care in later life will decrease."[33]

Fries was well-known outside medical circles for his coauthorship of *Take Care of Yourself: A Consumer's Guide to Medical Care* (1976). It went through many editions, has sold many millions of copies, and remains in print today. Many of those copies were bought by insurance companies, which sent them to policyholders in the belief that a self-care guide might reduce hospital visits. "You can do more for your health," the first page announced, "than your doctor can." And "you," it went on, "can learn how to cut the high cost of medicine." While most of the book was devoted to short, helpful discussions of athlete's foot and runny noses, the first chapter was about "your habits," because after all, "your health is up to you." The chapter recommended that readers stop smoking, start exercising, and watch their diet. "Make charts," the text advised. "Set goals. Weigh yourself frequently."[34]

Fries provided a medical imprimatur for the same message the Golden Girls got from their doctors: if you take good care of yourself, you won't need me. John Rowe, the other physician mentioned by Dychtwald, had a similar message. Rowe was at Harvard during the Vietnam War and received a deferral to work at a gerontology research center in Baltimore. His task was to explore the effects of age on kidney function, and specifically to understand the rapid deterioration in kidney functioning in otherwise healthy people. Although it was no surprise to find a linkage between high blood pressure and kidney problems, the more interesting finding was that those with elevated blood pressure, even if it wasn't elevated enough to be a problem in and of itself, also had more kidney problems. The upshot was that health and lifestyle improvement, even for those without diagnosable problems, could lead to healthier aging.[35]

This led Rowe to his enormously influential notion of "successful aging." Of course, he was not the first to recognize that some older people were healthier than others. Prior measures for evaluating functional capacity in older people, though, had been rather crude, distinguishing between "normal" and "pathological," or in Fries's case between "vitality" and "morbidity." What Rowe and his team did was introduce a fissure within the category of older people who were not sick or disabled. "Usual" aging referred to the process of slow decline that was normatively common: older people who were not bedridden but were slowly gaining weight, slowing down, and developing minor health problems. That "usual" category was distinguished from "successful aging," which referred to people who were healthy, active, and had relatively little loss of function—the sort of people who might qualify for the Senior Olympics.

Like Fries, Rowe wanted to give the individual responsibility for her own health, implicitly removing it from the medical establishment. As he put it in a best-selling 1998 book, "Successful aging is dependent upon individual choices and behaviors. It can be attained through individual choices and effort." Also like Fries, Rowe was thinking explicitly of the debate about rationing of care for the aged. Rowe didn't deny the need for rationing, but he did deny that old age *by itself* should be a relevant criterion, because many older people were perfectly healthy and many more could become so if they followed his and Fries's regimens. And again like Fries, Rowe was a physician-entrepreneur who eventually developed ties with the insurance industry. In 1988, he was named president of New York's Mount Sinai Medical Center, "one of the most important jobs in health care," as an analyst put it at the time. (It is symbolic that Robert Butler, former head of the National Institute on Aging, served under Rowe as chief of geriatrics at Mount Sinai.) From that post, Rowe was at ground zero for the changes that were rocking American health care in the 1990s, including hospital consolidation as a way to cut costs. His primary achievement was to oversee the contentious merger of the Mount Sinai and NYU medical systems, creating a massive health care system in which Rowe continued to serve as CEO. His effectiveness in this role caught the eye of Aetna, a troubled insurance giant. In 2000, Rowe was tapped to be Aetna's CEO.[36]

Successful aging was big business. In the years since Rowe pioneered the concept, it has become omnipresent in the world of aging, used by municipalities and insurance companies and hospitals alike. When the Golden Girls' doctor told them to watch their diets and take better care of themselves, he was doing more than giving commonsense advice (although he was doing that). He was also introducing them to a new world of health care. Because in a world of potential rationing, they couldn't always count on a physician to be there for them.[37]

So, to sum up the chapter thus far: *The Golden Girls* popularized a new form of old-age flourishing, built around fun, health, and sex. The show's protagonists achieved that goal primarily through individual effort and through the creation of a new family structure built around other older people, rather than by accessing the traditional suite of senior services. This outlook was palatable to seniors themselves because it seemed emancipatory, and to the political and medical establishment because it helped in their efforts to bring down costs. Attentive readers might have noted that we have spent very little time in this chapter with the Social Security Administration, or the Democratic Party, or the American Medical Association, or the other bureaucracies and interest groups that had defined old age for most of the twentieth century up to this point. The world was changing for old-age health as for the old-age movement more generally. Power in the medical field in this period was held less by governments, social movements, and physicians than it was by biotechnology companies, managed-care organizations, and consumers themselves.

Public policy didn't cease changing, but it did evolve in ways that prioritized public-private partnerships. For our purposes, the most important renovations happened to Medicare. The basic structure of Medicare stayed the same as it had since 1965. It remained in essence a way for older people to pay hospital bills without going bankrupt. It was not free, and it did not cover a vast array of things, including prescription drugs and long-term care. But Medicare did change after 1980, in two major ways. In 1997, the creation of Medicare Plus Choice (or Medicare Part C) invited seniors to make a bevy of complicated financial decisions. The basic idea was that since Medicare excluded so many types of medical expenses, and it had no plans to expand, the government might give senior citizens the option to purchase private insurance that would provide those additional services (like vision coverage and hearing aids). These were known as Medicare Advantage plans. "If you're on Medicare, prepare," announced one expert in 1998. "You're approaching the most bewildering few years you'll ever see." And in 2003, Medicare Part D was passed to help older people afford prescription drugs. This, too, was voluntary, and it was contracted out to private insurance companies (most Medicare Advantage plans offered Part D as well).[38]

So public policy, insofar as it changed at all, changed in ways that increased older Americans' reliance on the private sector—and especially on pharmaceutical companies. Here again *The Golden Girls* indexed a growing national concern. In a 1989 episode called "High Anxiety," it was revealed that Rose Nylund was addicted to pain pills. Overmedication had long plagued older people, of course, but the issue had mainly been restricted to those who were institutionalized in nursing homes. The concern was now more widespread, and some evidence indicates that more older people were using and abusing prescription drugs every year. In 1994, an alarming study was published in the *Journal of the American Medical Association* showing that four in five older people were taking at least one prescription drug, and that almost a quarter were taking a drug that, according to an expert panel, should be entirely avoided by that population. A later analysis in the *Journal of Gerontology* showed that between 1988 and 2010, the prescription of harmful drugs decreased. In the same period, though, the median number of prescription drugs taken by adults age sixty-five and over doubled from two to four, while the proportion taking five or more medications tripled from 13 to 39 percent.[39]

This was true of men, too, whose bodies had historically been less prone to medicalization than women's. In the 1980s and 1990s, the aging male body became subject to all kinds of pharmaceutical interventions to replace lost testosterone and lost hair. The condition that was most concerning to millions of men was declining sexual performance. After World War II, impotence was viewed as a psychological problem. But since the 1980s, and thanks to the energetic labors of urologists, it has become medicalized and reclassified as erectile dysfunction (ED). We've seen this dramatized already. In *Cocoon*, the aging protagonists have their virility restored by the aliens' powers, which pointedly heal bodies, not minds. In March 1998, the US Food and Drug Administration approved a new drug created by Pfizer to treat ED: sildenafil citrate, better known as Viagra. Thanks to FDA regulations approved just the year before, it was possible to market drugs directly to consumers. This happened most famously in an ad that featured the GOP senator and recent presidential candidate Bob Dole. In it, Dole explained that he was not suffering from "impotence," which sounded emasculating, but from a medical condition known as ED. Anyone suffering from it, he added, should consult their doctor. The rest is history. Viagra became a cultural and medical phenomenon with few precedents in American history. Within a year of its introduction, more than three million men took the new drug, a figure that doubled by 2003.[40]

Viagra encapsulates the shifting terrain of elder health in the 1980s and 1990s: a major pharmaceutical company, through direct marketing, convinced viewers that their sexual functioning in old age was a problem requiring intervention. The whole process was undergirded by an unstated ideology of aging, according to which impotence was in no way a natural part of aging but rather a pathology that required treatment at about ten dollars per pill. And as with everything canvassed in this chapter, the line between "opportunity" and "mandate" was razor-thin. Many older women, for instance, did not *want* to be pressured into sex by their pharmaceutically enhanced husbands—or, as one older woman wrote to *Modern Maturity* with an unforgettable line, "I'd like to live in a world where sex does not exist!"[41]

In the age of Viagra, older people had to navigate extremely complex health care markets—markets that grew increasingly fragmented as Medicare veered ever further from "universal benefit" to "individualized plan." And older people were not always adept at this kind of financial planning. As one expert has observed, this period saw a "transformation of beneficiaries into empowered but inept consumers." And yet medical costs still didn't go down—in fact, they went up. In 1975, older Americans spent on average $390 per year on health care. In 2016, Medicare beneficiaries spent an average of $5,460 per year on out-of-pocket medical costs, a trebling after adjusting for inflation.[42]

At least in part, this was because more and riskier procedures were being performed on older people. The debate about health care rationing garnered headlines but did not impact policy. Medical anthropologists in the 1990s traced a new kind of "ethical field" as expensive new technologies emerged without much oversight regarding when and how they should be used for older patients. Medical care was now, one 2004 study concluded, "characterized by the difficulty or impossibility of saying 'no' to life-extending interventions." Physicians interviewed in the early 2000s marveled at the kinds of procedures routinely performed on older people that never would have happened a few decades earlier. Octogenarians were the most rapidly growing group of surgical patients, and it became commonplace to do cardiac procedures or kidney transplants on them.[43]

It might seem contradictory, but the twin impulses on display here were two sides of the same coin: a new emphasis on self-care alongside the increasing prevalence of extraordinarily expensive new treatments that were widely perceived as a waste of money. This was the new world of modern medicine as older people experienced it in the 1980s, surely a far cry from the security promised by Medicare. And to what effect? Life expectancy at age sixty-five did creep up between 1980 and 2000, continuing a long trend. According to data from the Social Security Administration, a sixty-five-year-old man in 1980 could expect to live fourteen more years; twenty years later, that number had gone up just shy of two years. For women, the progress was less stark: an increase of about seven months (though they still could expect to live longer than men). But how much healthier were those years? Did we in fact witness what Fries called a "compression of morbidity": an extension of healthy years and a temporal compression of the years of disability and decline? Probably not. Older people live with more chronic health issues than in the past. Of course, this is in itself an indicator of success: more older people have diseases because those diseases have not killed them. Nonetheless, the percentage of people age seventy and up who reported arthritis, diabetes, cancer, or hypertension didn't change much between 1984 and 1995. The compression of morbidity, it's safe to say, has not worked out as Fries had hoped.[44]

All of that said, the era of *The Golden Girls* represented genuine progress on many fronts, and it is a reminder of just how staid and misogynist the cultural and political world of aging had been before the 1980s. Older people in general had more freedom now to play sports, go on adventures, and utilize their bodies however, and with whomever, they pleased. But as with all kinds of freedom in America, there was a catch. They had to be able to afford it.

CHAPTER 9

FROM SECURITY
TO RISK

In 1990, a money manager in Seattle named Paul Merriman had an idea. He wanted to prepare his infant grandson for retirement, so he set him up with an individual retirement account, or IRA. These investment vehicles had been around since 1974, and since 1981 had entered the mainstream as a common form of retirement financing. They were not primarily for infants, of course, but the imperative to save aggressively, and save early, was looming larger every year. You did need a job to get an IRA, but Merriman figured a way around that. He hired the baby as a model to star on the cover of a newsletter he put out. When his subscribers saw that baby, they were looking at America's youngest retirement saver.[1]

While Merriman's example is particularly colorful, the basic spirit behind it is now familiar. Hardly a day goes by without an article being published about the sorry state of Americans' retirement savings and a few more enjoining high schoolers to start pumping money from their minimum-wage jobs into tax-advantaged retirement accounts. It's no wonder that millions of American reach middle age in a state of near panic about their retirement savings. A 2022 poll showed that most Americans believed they would, and I quote, "need to work post-retirement," a nonsensical phrase that indicates just how many of us have given up on the notion of retirement as a life beyond work.[2]

This phenomenon is surprisingly recent, as it requires both the expectation that you should be able to stop working and live in comfort after age sixty-five and the expectation that you will not be able to. The promise of Social Security had been that the state was supposed to provide hard-working Americans with a dignified retirement without their having to rely on private savings. And in the postwar era, the state was expected to provide a network of services, from housing to nutrition, that would give older people all the tools, financial and otherwise, they would need to live with dignity. All of this created the reasonable expectation that Americans should be able to retire in comfort. In the 1970s and 1980s, though, the system fell into disrepute. Headlines about Social Security promised that it was on the brink of insolvency, while those about Medicare were about rationing and fraud. Older people started returning to the workforce, sometimes because they wanted to but often because they had no choice. As health care premiums and housing costs continued to grow, Social Security and private pensions were increasingly inadequate to keep older people solvent. In this sphere, as in so many others, the promise of collective security gave way to the reality of individual anxiety.

The IRA was one of many forms that individualized retirement financing took in the 1980s and 1990s. The shift toward these new vehicles had multiple causes. Some were structural and beyond the control of any one person or institution. At the same time, and as with health care, for-profit institutions and individuals took advantage of those structural conditions and shaped the outcomes. Financiers flooded the marketplace with articles about the unsustainability of pensions and Social Security; they provided self-serving research to Congress about the need for more personal savings and the need for tax incentives to make that happen; they published best-selling books, and even computer programs, designed to guide readers toward their financial products. Meanwhile, a new profession emerged—the financial planner—to both stoke and soothe Americans' retirement anxieties.

For many, retirement insecurity was nothing new, because retirement security had never extended to all Americans. The Social Security Act and the private pensions that emerged after World War II created a bubble of economic security around a set of older people, mainly white men in industrial or white-collar jobs and their spouses. Older women and people of color had always received lower Social Security payments, if they received them at all, and they were less likely to receive generous pensions from their employers. Jacquelyne Jackson and other old-age advocates in the 1970s and 1980s tried to ensure that all older people received the generous benefits that the privileged ones did. That's not what happened. Instead, the precarious conditions that had long afflicted marginalized populations also threatened to engulf the white, male-headed households that had been on the forefront of policymakers' minds. In retirement financing, as in health care, the bubble of security, which once promised to expand in size, started instead to shrink.[3]

The Golden Girls is a useful window onto the financial travails of older citizens in Reagan's America. The show, to recap, depicts a group of four older women, employed sporadically in traditionally female, low-paying jobs. To be specific, the lead characters include an eighty-year-old immigrant woman living with her daughter (a substitute teacher) and two older women with dead husbands who work for nonprofits or in social services. Traditionally, this arrangement would have been fodder for a social worker, not a comedy TV writer. And indeed, social workers' records from the 1930s do paint a dismal portrait of congregate living for older women.[4]

The Golden Girls, though, are defiantly middle-class. They live in an attractive and well-furnished home; they have cars and go on vacations and buy new clothes; they save up money for breast enhancement surgery. The show was not a fantasy—or at least not in this regard. In the 1980s, older Americans in aggregate were doing better than ever. People of their generation (born around 1920) had been at the ground floor of the country's postwar economic expansion. They or their spouses may have enjoyed subsidized education. They may have been able to buy houses with federal mortgage assistance at a time when houses were still affordable to the growing middle class. And in their old age, they could look forward to Social Security, Medicare, and the defined-benefit pensions that had become common after World War II.[5]

The numbers are striking. Between 1980 and 1992, the median income of older Americans, controlling for inflation, increased by 18 percent. Social Security was the largest component of older Americans' income, accounting for 40 percent of the total. The rest was mainly split between asset income and pensions, which in 1992 were being received by almost half of older people. This was the true golden age of pensions—not of the creation of the programs but of their economic impact, because this generation of older people had spent their peak working years in the pension era.[6]

Older people, in general, were not working. Three of the four Golden Girls worked regularly, but this was because they were still relatively young: in their late fifties (about half of women in that age bracket were in the labor force). Sophia, the only main character over sixty-five, worked only rarely, and she was typical of her age bracket too. In the 1980s, as a demographic matter, more people were retired than ever. In 1950, 46 percent of men over sixty-five were in the workforce. By 1985, that number dwindled to a mere 16 percent. And it wasn't that all of these millions were working right up to their sixty-fifth birthday. The real novelty of the period was early retirement. In 1983, according to the General Accounting Office, a full 17 percent of men from the ages of fifty-five to sixty-one were retired and receiving pension benefits—a number that had more than doubled since 1973.[7]

This period was good for older people at the bottom of the economic ladder as well. As late as 1970, older Americans were twice as likely as the general population to live in poverty, but by 1982 they were actually less likely than an average American to be impoverished. This was not only because married white couples were doing better; few of them had been in poverty to begin with. It was unmarried women and people of color who were seeing dramatic gains, even if not enough to constitute genuine security. After World War II, more than two-thirds of households headed by older white women were in poverty. By 1980, that number went down to 22 percent. The trend line for older people of color was similar. After World War II, more than 90 percent of households headed by older nonwhite women were in poverty. Within three decades, that number was cut in half, thanks largely to social insurance and welfare programs. Furthermore, the numbers were trending in the right direction. Poverty rates for older Americans overall declined steadily in the last quarter of the twentieth century, from 25 percent to 17 percent.[8]

And yet, as any viewer could attest, a current of financial danger runs through *The Golden Girls*. Rose Nylund, most pointedly, was in perpetual financial trouble. She had spent decades as a housewife before her husband died, leaving her a small pension, which she struggled to supplement with low-paying jobs. In season five, she runs into real trouble when she gets a letter informing her that her husband's company is going out of business, and that she will no longer collect his pension. She is distraught: "I'm not going to be able to live without that pension!" She needs a better job, so she starts going on interviews, but she fails time and again, with companies telling her that she is too old. "When I was younger," she laments, "I never imagined I'd be worrying about money at this stage in my life." The answer to her prayers comes in the form of a telegenic consumer-interest reporter named Enrique Mas. When she complains to him about her ageist treatment, he is impressed by her passion and hires her as an assistant. "The best part," she explains in the heartwarming conclusion, "is that I get to stay here." The episode ends in a spasm of joy that an aging widow in Miami does not become homeless because a company in Minnesota went bankrupt.[9]

The episode, for all its charm, presents terrible financial guidance to its millions of viewers. The thrust of the story is that Rose is on her own. Nobody suggests reaching out to the government for help. The government, though, would have had a lot to say about a case like this. For one thing, private pensions have been federally insured since 1974; Rose was likely entitled to continue receiving the pension, although she seems unaware of this fact. And for another, age discrimination of the sort that she mentions is illegal and has been since 1967. Even though she works for a reporter—precisely the person who should have known these details—she ends up with no resources aside from her own willingness to work.

"Rose Fights Back" was a highly charged and ideological entry in a set of debates about the financial health of older people in the 1980s. Just as the show propagated a widely shared ideal of health as personal responsibility, it did the same for finances. This was no less important a move, as financial security for seniors was even more foundational to the American welfare regime than health care was. The whole point of the Social Security system had been to save older Americans from penury and to keep them out of the labor market. And yet, in the world of *The Golden Girls*, it is almost as though Social Security doesn't exist. Rose and Blanche would have become eligible for survivor's benefits once they turned sixty, which happened near the end of the show's run, although this is not mentioned. Sophia Petrillo, the oldest of the four, does receive Social Security, but it can't be much; she has nothing to spare for her daughter when she faces bankruptcy in season three. The actress who played Sophia, Estelle Getty, explained in an interview that she had Sophia carry a purse at all times to illustrate the fact that older women are forced to shed so many possessions over the years that they have nothing left that won't fit in a purse. Indeed, when Sophia's room is shown, it is basically empty; an entire episode in 1987 was devoted to Sophia's scheming to find enough money for a television set. The only time Social Security comes up explicitly in the show is in an episode where, due to a computer error, she receives thousands of dollars by accident.[10]

The show, in its depiction of middle-class comfort, accurately depicted the social history of 1980s aging, at least as it was experienced by able-bodied white women. The show also, in its portrayal of looming financial catastrophe, accurately depicted the shifting political and cultural discussion about retirement at the same moment. That conversation presumed on all sides that the good times were coming to an end, and that seniors should no longer count on Social Security. In politics, the name of the game was now "generational equity," which can be understood as the fiscal counterpart to the health care rationing debates we explored in the last chapter. In 1988, the *New Republic*, a highly influential magazine, published a vicious article about greedy old people and the "misdirected sympathy" that many have for them. While not everyone phrased the matter so baldly, a bipartisan consensus was forming that Social Security was in need of saving, and that some combination of privatization, raising the retirement age, and benefits reductions would be needed to keep the system afloat.[11]

Neither liberals nor conservatives were interested in expanding financial benefits for older Americans from the 1970s to the 1990s. On the liberal side, a new generation of younger Democrats, the so-called Atari Democrats, were trying to find more socially beneficial ways to streamline government and leverage the market. Democrats in this vein were loath to actually criticize Social Security, but they were not trying to expand it either. It was a Democratic governor, after all, who made the controversial remark about older people having "a duty to die." And in the late 1990s, Bill Clinton had a series of secret meetings with Newt Gingrich, Republican Speaker of the House, to put together a plan that would have introduced private retirement accounts into the system. Only the outbreak of the Monica Lewinsky scandal kept this from happening by scuttling any desire Republicans had to cooperate with Clinton.[12]

This sensibility was still more pronounced on the Right, where it combined two of the conservative movement's great passions: unraveling the welfare state and attacking Baby Boomers as lazy leeches who had been unwilling to work when they were young and would be just as grasping in their old age. Conservatives created an organization called Americans for Generational Equity, cochaired by a Republican senator named Dave Durenberger. Their attitude was not that old-age benefits ought to be rolled back right away, which would have been political suicide. Rather, they promoted the idea that a great wave of Baby Boomers would wreck the American economy if benefits for senior citizens were not rolled back for them in the future. At the same time, the Cato Institute and other conservative think tanks kept up their steady drumbeat of criticism of old-age programs, and of Social Security specifically as a Ponzi scheme that threatened the health of the republic.[13]

This was not just pundit chatter. Polling indicated that only about half of Americans believed in the solvency of Social Security, and some well-publicized scandals shook their faith in the bureaucracy that made it function (it was no accident that Social Security only entered *The Golden Girls* as part of a bureaucratic error). The message American seniors received was that their retirement was no longer going to be covered by the bottomless coffers of the government. The government would pay some, but it wouldn't be much. Reagan's chosen head of the Social Security Administration made it clear that Social Security was only intended to be a part, and a small part, of a healthy retirement portfolio. "It is so important," she implored, "for today's young worker to begin early to save and plan for retirement."[14]

The AARP devoted itself to protecting Social Security, but even that organization played host to some serious doubts about the matter. In 1992, its magazine provided millions of readers with a lengthy roundtable, going surprisingly deep into the weeds of the legislation. Strikingly, no voice at the table called for an expansion of the system or a more robust safety net; it essentially replayed the same debate that had been hosted at the American Enterprise Institute two decades earlier between Milton Friedman and Wilbur Cohen. On the one hand, a famous economist named Laurence Kotlikoff spoke at length about the solvency crisis in the system and the need to privatize it following the models of Chile and Poland. His opponents in the roundtable countered that the system could be salvaged with some modest reforms, especially ones to encourage later retirement and more labor from older Americans. Two years later, the magazine featured another "debate" between a Republican and a Democratic senator. Again the two shared more than the format presumed: both thought that Social Security was a sound system that needed reform, by either tinkering with contribution rates or raising the retirement age. They differed only in how fast and how radical those changes would need to be ("Social Security is doing just fine" is how the Democratic senator triumphantly ended his contribution).[15]

Even the champions of Social Security saw stagnation as the best possible outcome. But the outlook for private, defined-benefit pensions was worse. Since the 1980s, ever fewer private-sector workers have been covered by these sorts of pensions. Even irrespective of any policy decisions, the economic realities that had undergirded the system were shifting. Widespread, defined-benefit pensions emerged from an era of economic optimism, and specifically optimism about the growth in labor productivity. Pensions made sense in a world where policymakers and employers were hopeful that smaller amounts of labor would be needed each year. This logic simply didn't hold in the 1980s, when American productivity was flatlining. Articles about pensions were no longer about collective-bargaining victories but about massive pension obligations and shortfalls. "Pensions or Productivity?" asked one *New York Times* headline in 1983. Pensions, once viewed as the logical consequence of high productivity, were now viewed as a major cause of the economy's *lagging* productivity insofar as they saddled firms with high costs and, many believed, a complacent workforce.[16]

The Employee Retirement Income Security Act (ERISA), which passed in 1974, also created headwinds for defined-benefit pensions.

As more and more companies offered pensions, more and more people ended up in the situation of Rose Nylund: deprived of benefits from companies that had gone bankrupt. The legislation was designed to address this problem by ensuring that people like Rose would continue to be paid. At the same time, ERISA made defined-benefit pensions less attractive to employers because they were more heavily regulated and required such large reserve funds.[17]

Little surprise, then, that older people eventually started going back to work. The participation of older men in the workforce, which had dropped steadily for decades, bottomed out in the mid-1980s, and in the mid-1990s it began to rise again. The process was accelerated even further in 2000, when President Bill Clinton repealed the retirement earnings test in a bill called the Senior Citizens' Freedom to Work Act (the AARP supported the act, which aligned with its long-standing goal of encouraging older people to labor if they wished). With its passage, Social Security benefits could be claimed upon reaching full retirement age, even by those who were still working. By 2010, men in their later sixties were nearly twice as likely to be working as they had been in 1980. For women, the increase happened sooner and more steadily; participation rates began to rise in the early 1980s, and by 2010 older women were working at rates that approached those of older men.[18]

Much of this work was doubtless undesired and done out of necessity. We should not forget, though, that the ideal of labor flexibility had wide support across the political spectrum, and that many of those who retired in the 1960s and 1970s had done so against their wishes. The Gray Panthers, the most left-wing of the aging groups, had been founded in part in opposition to mandatory retirement, and by the 1980s the Chicago chapter was going so far as to argue that the practice "KILLS people" and allows employers and insurance companies to "reap swollen profits from the unhappiness, even the misery, of the old." More centrist analysts had the same view. Joseph Califano, President Lyndon Johnson's former special assistant for domestic affairs, considered the issue in the *Washington Post* in 1983. He thought the fiscal crisis brought on by old age could only be solved by, in his words, "new kinds of work arrangements that might accommodate greater numbers of older Americans in the work force."[19]

Many of the same figures that we met in the last chapter as apostles for healthy aging were also apostles of elder labor. Robert Butler, head of the National Institute on Aging, was committed to the idea of "productive aging." He held a symposium on the theme in 1987, featuring an address by John Rowe, who was on the cusp of publishing his major essay on successful aging. In his contribution, Rowe went over the evidence to show that many older people were healthier than stereotypes suggested, and that with better exercise and habits they could become even healthier. They could, therefore, work. "Tomorrow's elders," the aging consultant Ken Dychtwald predicted, "will work as long as they are physically able." And they will do so because they "want to." The AARP made the connection between health and finances especially clear. In 1987, the association started hosting "fiscal fitness" workshops for women across the country.[20]

The Golden Girls certainly work out of necessity, but they want to be working too. Many episodes of the show are about the meaning they derive from their work. Rose works as a grief counselor and at several other jobs, Dorothy is a substitute teacher, and Blanche works at an art museum. These jobs get them out of the house, help them feel useful, and provide opportunities for sociability. Even as they approach retirement age, they clearly don't plan on retiring. This is dramatized especially on *The Golden Palace*, the short-lived *Golden Girls* spinoff that aired in 1992 and 1993. The show picked up the story of Blanche, Rose, and Sophia after Dorothy's marriage, which ended the original show. The trio invests in a hotel, only to find that it has no staff. They have no choice but to start doing the work themselves, including eighty-seven-year-old Sophia, and they find that they love it. At the end of the pilot, all three of them sit around a table, raving that the work had given them purpose and a reason to get out of bed. They opt to keep working, even after doing so is no longer financially necessary. In other TV shows about older women, their labor was paramount. In both *Murder, She Wrote* and *Mama's Family*, the supposedly retired female protagonists do all kinds of paid labor—even, in the latter case, at a fast-food restaurant.[21]

In a world where both Social Security and pensions were on the ropes and mandatory retirement was illegal, not much was left of the old idea of "retirement." On *The Golden Girls*, the word normally shows up in reference to Shady Pines Retirement Community, the much loathed place where Sophia spent some time before moving in with her daughter. The show and the spinoff make it clear that none of the girls *want* to retire. Even the usage of the word in the United States began to decline. Peaking in 1979, by 2015 its usage had declined by more than 50 percent. "Retirement communities" began to call themselves something different; from the late 1980s onward, developers opted for some variation of "independent-living communities." Retirement parties became rarer, too, at least in part because so many older workers phased into part-time work.[22]

"Retirement" as a word had at least one remaining use: from the late 1980s onward, articles announcing its end began to appear with some frequency. Even the AARP, which originally designated retired people as its constituency, was suspicious of the idea of retirement. The group had always opposed mandatory retirement, and as we saw in Chapter 7, its leadership believed that senior labor was the key to solving the Social Security crisis. A 1990s president, Eugene Lehrmann, named "work opportunities" as the goal he most sought to pursue in his tenure. "We must," he implored, "encourage and assist more employers to recruit, manage, train, and retrain our increasingly older and more diverse workforce." In 1999, just before the repeal of the retirement earnings test, the organization finally changed its name to remove any reference to retirement.[23]

Several years before its name change, the AARP sent its millions of subscribers a strange but telling article titled "The End of Retirement."

It was essentially a tour of old-age cultures of the Global South. This concept in itself was not so new. Old-age advocates back in the 1920s had looked to non-Western societies as examples of positive aging cultures. The idea had normally been that older people outside the West were properly venerated and respected and were not forced to work for their bread as they were in an industrial economy. In 1993, the non-Western world provided a very different lesson. Now the point was that, unlike the lazy-bones seniors at home, they kept on working! Seniors in other countries, that is, did not expect handouts like their American counterparts, and they recognized that their bodies still had the capacity to labor for the good of their families—and their national economies too.[24]

Working *after* age sixty-five was only one solution offered to the looming crisis in retirement financing. The other was to save and invest *before* age sixty-five. The new culture of old-age labor coincided with a new culture of middle-aged saving. While Americans have always saved, they have not always saved specifically for retirement. In the 1980s, though, they were enjoined to do so at every turn, and from a young age—even, as we saw in the chapter's opening, from infancy. Two new vehicles emerged to help them do so: the IRA and the 401(k). Both were tax advantaged, and both were novelties.

The individual retirement account came first. It was introduced as part of ERISA in 1974. Although the main purpose of the act was to regulate private pensions, it sought as well to help more Americans save for retirement—notably, those who were not covered by a pension plan, and those who were moving between jobs and wanted some way to preserve their pension benefits (the famous "rollover"). To accomplish these goals, the act allowed individuals to create IRAs. At first they were only for those select groups, but in 1982 eligibility expanded so that anyone with paid employment, even if they had a pension plan, could start one.

Meanwhile, in 1978, section 401(k) was added to the tax code. Originally, the provision was designed to formalize an older practice in which employees could opt to defer some of their income, and there-fore some of their taxes, to a later date. It was not a major part of the tax reforms: in the *Journal of Accountancy*'s roundup of the legislation, section 401 hardly merited mention. It was certainly not presumed that the accounts would become important retirement vehicles. A couple of years later, though, a benefits consultant named Ted Benna had an idea: what if section 401 could be used to create retirement accounts, perhaps in a matching scheme with employers? Benna proposed this to a client. They turned it down, but he decided to institute it in his own consulting company, leading to the country's first 401(k) savings plans. It was still unclear if such a plan was legal. Benna happened to be friendly with Drew Lewis, transportation secretary in the Reagan administration. Through Lewis, he was introduced to officials in the Treasury Department, whom he persuaded to interpret section 401 as he did. In the fall of 1981, new regulations were announced, and the 401(k) revolution was born.[25]

Between them, the IRA and the 401(k) remade the landscape of American retirement financing. Unlike traditional, defined-benefit pensions, they were known as "defined-contribution" pensions: employ-ers and individuals could *invest* a certain amount, rather than retirees *receiving* a certain amount. The revolution took place with astonish-ing speed. As early as 1985, the number of employees participating in defined-contribution plans exceeded the number in defined-benefit plans, and the gap has only widened since.[26]

IRAs and 401(k)s have helped millions to save for their retirement and have been a godsend to some categories of employees who were ill served by traditional pensions. But there is no getting around the fact that the system was not designed for them. The defined-contribution revolution happened, as most revolutions do, because powerful people wanted it. Employers loved the plans, especially in a new environment where defined-benefit pensions were a massive financial liability. "A lot of the pressure" to create the plans, a benefits consultant reported in 1982, "is coming from top management." A 401(k) had the potential to save a company a great deal of money. If a firm offered the 401(k), or some kind of matching plan, instead of a traditional defined-benefit pension, it would not have to create a large and closely regulated pension fund, and it would not be on the hook for decades of expenses after a worker retired. Moreover, the amount of the employer contribution to a 401(k) was usually quite small, and most contributions were made by workers themselves. The upshot was that from the late 1970s to late 1980s, the percentage of payroll that firms devoted to pension expenses was cut in half.[27]

Investment firms loved the plans too. IRAs in particular offered the possibility of turning retirement, formerly a public good, into millions of individual consumer relationships, each one turning a profit. When it came to innovative vehicles for retirement savings, the pioneer was Merrill Lynch, and especially the head of its retirement services division, who was named Don Underwood. As soon as IRAs became widely available, he was one of many financial executives who encouraged individuals to open accounts on Wall Street and start engaging in exotic and, for Merrill Lynch at least, profitable investments—everything, in Underwood's words, from "covered call options to limited real estate partnerships, oil and gas royalties partnerships, annuities, and money funds."[28]

It's not only that Merrill Lynch was seeking to claim the new business—of course it was. What's more surprising is how much power Wall Street had in shaping both the narrative about retirement funding and the emerging consensus that Americans were not saving enough. Merrill Lynch in particular conducted a slate of studies to recommend its products. These studies, frequently cited in Congress, were designed to show both that America's low savings rate was a crisis and that IRAs, which were essentially a tax write-off for wealthy savers, were an effective response.[29]

Underwood carried the message to the masses. He began by courting businesses themselves. In the *Harvard Business Review* in 1984, he published an article called "Toward Self-Reliance in Investment

Planning." He repeated the familiar argument that "society will face enormous strains as the baby-boom generation reaches retirement age." The problem, he believed, was that the public had an "entitlement habit." People labored under the delusion that Social Security and private pensions were sustainable, and they did not understand that in the future only "self-reliance" could provide retirement security. "Personal saving toward retirement," he explained, is "a little-understood concept," and it was up to corporations to start hosting preretirement training programs to hype IRAs. Of course, nowhere in the article did Underwood mention that he and his firm stood to benefit enormously from such a program.[30]

He also, together with a writer at *Forbes*, published a retirement guide of his own in 1993, titled *Grow Rich Slowly*. Readers of the book learned that the aging of America was a crisis that could only be resolved through the rediscovery of an ethic of saving. "Your government can't solve all your problems," it instructed, and neither can your employer. But never fear—you can "help yourself." The book predicted that Social Security taxes, by the early twenty-first century, would reach 35 percent (as I write these words in that future, the rate is 6.2 percent). The authors had no hopes for any reform of the system and counseled that the best readers could do was to "reclaim, as much as you can, your own retirement future from the hands of strangers"—or at least to ask the good people at Merrill Lynch, presumably not strangers, to do it for them.[31]

The push for individualized retirement savings came hardest from employers and from Wall Street but not only from there. Americans in the 1980s were subjected to a full court press of advice and marketing that encouraged them to save for retirement. Much of it came from a novel source and a new profession. The notion of a "financial planner" came into vogue in the late 1970s. The father of financial planning was a California-based salesman named Loren Dunton, a founder of both the International Association for Financial Planning and a magazine called the *Financial Planner*. Like many other apostles of flexible aging, he had roots in the counterculture. His first book, published in 1966, was a new-age self-help book that touted the "space age approach to more self-discipline." As he moved toward old-age issues, he continued to believe in grooviness as an ideal. In *The Vintage Years*, a book he published in 1978, Dunton suggested that readers "use the power of your subconscious" to embark on a "self-improvement program" for aging. Much of the material was familiar for the era in that he encouraged "an active life-style" and weight-loss programs; he even praised the emotional and health benefits of "the kind of loving and exciting sex that only mature, experienced people can ever know."[32]

Dunton shared with Underwood a belief that self-reliance was the only path to retirement security. The government, he was sure, could not be trusted. He warned readers against government "handouts," which too often became "a way of life" in which the government sought to "enslave" older Americans. Alongside that moral critique, Dunton reiterated the standard conservative line on Social Security. The program, he wrote in the *New York Times* in 1983, was not "insurance" but rather an unsustainable "welfare subsidy" that would soon bankrupt the nation. The only solution, he insisted, was to severely cut back the Social Security system, perhaps reserving it for only the neediest of the needy, and then giving most people the tools to plan for their own retirement. (This was the argument that Milton Friedman had been making for two decades.) In the same year, he edited a collection of essays, *Your Book of Financial Planning: The Consumer's Guide to a Better Financial Future*. The volume kicked off with an article by a Los Angeles–based financial planner titled "Social Security: It Won't Be Enough," devoted explicitly to debunking "the government's extravagant promise of financial independence for all."[33]

Financial planning as an industry grew in tandem with skepticism toward Social Security and with the general 1980s ethos of self-help as the superior alternative to government bureaucracy. It got to the point where financial planners talked as though Social Security didn't exist at all (echoing the message delivered by *The Golden Girls*). "You have income from two sources," one member of the profession told a reporter in 1987. "Your body working and your property generating income." And since your body is going to give out one day, "you'd better have the property built up" enough to support a comfortable retirement.[34]

The AARP started offering its own investment funds, and its magazine, *Modern Maturity*, offered reams of financial advice, pushing members toward IRAs and complex investment strategies. One 1990 article, "Mastering Your Money: Turn Your Dollars into Star Performers," began by explaining that the reader, like most Americans, probably had not saved enough—but never fear, there were still "options." Readers could take a second job, perhaps by "converting a hobby into an income-producing business." Or they could place a reverse mortgage on their home. All these suggestions, of course, were complicated—as the author recognized, which is why he suggested that readers head to the library or even to a local college to take classes on investing.[35]

In the world of financial advice, as in the world of health care, much of this guidance was targeted at women. *The Golden Girls*, for instance, made it clear that aging women needed to understand their tax situation. Dorothy runs into tax trouble and faces potential jail time in season three because she had let her irresponsible former husband take care of their finances. One 1987 survey revealed that 50 percent of high-salaried women, compared with less than 10 percent of men, were concerned about "outliving their retirement money." As a report in the *CPA Journal* the following year concluded, "Women should manage their income and savings as prudently as possible." An industry emerged to help them do so. Its patron saint was Venita VanCaspel, the "First Lady of Financial Planning." She sold more than a million copies of her books, she hosted TV shows, and she was especially proud of how her advice had helped, in her words, "widows and orphans." *Ms.* magazine recommended a book called *Every Woman's Guide to Financial Planning* as a summer reading pick in 1984; *Ladies' Home Journal* taught women how to navigate their IRAs.[36]

All of this would have been incoherent just twenty years earlier, when the Social Security system was expanding and there was every reason to believe the expansion would continue. But by 1987, it was clear to many that neither the state nor employers were interested in financing retirement. The Social Security system, if it survived at all, would only do enough to keep people out of desperate poverty; employers, meanwhile, might offer matching funds in 401(k)s, but the era of the defined-benefit pension was drawing to a close. When it came to financing retirement, older Americans who wished to stay out of poverty would have to rely on themselves. As Sophia Petrillo once told her daughter, who was feeling despondent about her financial woes, "There's no such thing as security."[37]

If one technological innovation symbolized the period, it would be the worksheets and quizzes, omnipresent in financial magazines and provided for free by investment houses, that helped people understand the gargantuan sums they would need to retire, the puniness of their personal savings, and the financial products that would help them get to where they needed to be. Some of them included a personal risk calculator—a set of questions designed to help readers understand how much risk they were willing to tolerate. The AARP provided one in 1989 entitled "What's Your Risk Factor?" It helped readers understand the different *kinds* of risk in play (due to inflation, the article explained, it was even a risk *not* to invest). What is so remarkable about this tool is that it individualizes the core precept of Social Security. The whole point of that program, as originally designed, had been to help older people *avoid* risk. The avoidance of risk, after all, is a tolerable definition of the word "security." Now, though, older Americans were asked to make precise calculations about how much risk they wished to bear on their own.[38]

The privatization of retirement financing did not do much for people of color, who continued to rely primarily on Social Security for their retirement income. As with defined-benefit pensions before them, defined-contribution pensions worked best for those with steady, well-paying jobs. In many firms, 401(k)s were unavailable to sporadic or part-time workers, who tended to be lower-income or to be people of color. These requirements impacted Hispanic workers the most: about 25 percent of both Black and white workers lacked access to plans, compared with 42 percent of Hispanic ones. It didn't matter much, though, if one had access to a plan. What mattered was whether one chose to participate. Black workers especially were reluctant to do so: 30 percent of those eligible chose to abstain, compared with 16 percent of white workers. Some could not afford to, while others nursed a well-founded skepticism of the financial services industry.[39]

While there are reasons to be worried about the future of retirement security, we should not be too gloomy either. The perpetual panic about retirement savings, stoked by financial institutions that stand to benefit, can obscure how much genuine progress there has been in this arena, even in the past half century. The poverty rate for older Americans fell by about 30 percent between 1980 and 2000. The decline in senior poverty since 1980 has been most marked for seniors of color. In 1980, more than a quarter of Hispanic seniors lived in poverty, and almost 40 percent of Black seniors. Both figures fell, slowly but surely, over succeeding decades; by 2020, both numbers were below 20 percent. These figures are still too high, but they are low compared both with the past and with other age brackets. Older people have long been better off, statistically, than American children, and since 2000, seniors have had lower poverty rates than either children or adults age eighteen to sixty-four.[40]

Some of this decline in poverty, of course, took place because older Americans were working, often out of financial necessity. As depicted in the Oscar-winning film *Nomadland* (2020), older people are indeed working all kinds of jobs in modern America, including, to take an example from the movie, cleaning up our national parks. There can be a tendency to oversell both the novelty and the tragedy of this situation. Labor force participation for older men bottomed out in the 1980s at about 15 percent. Since then, it has indeed crept upward, to 24 percent by 2020. For women, the figures are 9 percent and 15 percent respectively. Those are significant increases, yes, but they represent a return to the 1970s, not to the 1870s. It remains the case that the large majority of Americans over sixty-five are not in the labor force. Moreover, it is often forgotten that many of those who work after sixty-five do so because they want to—and are often able to because of the success of the AARP and its allies in overturning compulsory retirement programs.[41]

The discussion about old-age income security has for decades rested on a set of alarmist assumptions: Americans aren't saving enough! Pensions are disappearing! Grandma is being forced back to work! There is more than a grain of truth in each of these, but together, the cacophony of alarms obscures a more fundamental truth: older people have relatively secure incomes because of Social Security. Social Security is still the bedrock of older people's incomes, especially for the nonrich, which is just what its designers intended. In 2017, middle-class senior households received over half their income from Social Security (the rest came mainly from labor income and retirement accounts). The poorest ones received almost *all* their income from Social Security and SSI, the contemporary version of the Old-Age Assistance that was passed as a component of the Social Security Act in 1935.[42]

One of the great achievements of twentieth-century American domestic policy was the commitment to retirement security as a public good. This was the impulse behind the Social Security Act, but also of all the expansions in that act after World War II, many of which were bipartisan, and one of which, Medicare, is just as important as the original act. The relentless focus on pensions and on individual savings has obscured the fact that retirement security, by and large, still *is* a public good, and that the surest path forward is to reform and expand the Social Security system. For although I've tried to paint a rosier-than-expected portrait of senior income in the past four decades, there is no guarantee that the next four decades will tell the same story, and a good chance that they won't.

The current trajectory, after all, is not a promising one. For one thing, the widespread alarmism about retirement and Social Security is sowing a great deal of anxiety in the American public, which is the polar opposite of the desired value of security. And for another thing, that alarmism is more apposite every year. It is in the nature of retirement policies that the effects take a long time to reveal themselves. Retirees in the 1980s entered the workforce in the 1940s or 1950s and took advantage of the comparatively lavish retirement benefits that were common in those days. Retirees in the 2020s or 2030s, though, will be in a very different situation. They will have spent their working lives in an era when wages stagnated and prices for assets like housing, education, and health care skyrocketed. Even if they have access to a defined-contribution plan like a 401(k), many of them won't have used it, or won't have used it enough. It is even possible that Social Security benefits will be slashed if in fact nothing is done to reform the system before the trust fund dries up sometime in the early 2030s.

The most pernicious aspect of our retirement financing system, though, concerns its interaction with our health care system. That system is set up for basically healthy, middle-class people—people who don't need expensive long-term care, and who have the capacity to put away a little each month into a retirement account, and who can re-enter the workforce if necessary to pay the bills. Again, as at every step in the history of American aging, the needs of people with disabilities, the frail, and the very old have not been part of the conversation. A great deal of the anxiety about retirement income is really an anxiety about retirement health: What will happen to me and my family if I need long-term care? In the body of the frail older person, the weaknesses of the health care system, as depicted in the last chapter, compound with the weaknesses of the retirement financing system, as depicted in this one. Social Security and Medicare, for all their many virtues, do comparatively little for that population. The results have been devastating for older Americans and those who care for them.

CHAPTER 10

ASSISTED LIVING

The Golden Girls was in many ways a realistic look at aging in 1980s America. The women on the show, like many viewers, were worried about their health and about their financial security. The show was admirably forthright about those challenges. Some truths about America, though, could not be turned into comedy. And in at least one major way, the show flinched and proved unable to portray a harsh reality. The issue of long-term care for those age eighty and above was handled abysmally in the United States at the time. Whether they were in nursing homes or cared for by overworked, middle-aged children, the "old-old" faced enormous challenges in Reagan's America. The show was clearly unsure what to do with this topic, and it's the one theme that it could only treat through fantasy.

One of the major characters, Sophia, was in that age category, and she was cared for by her daughter Dorothy. The story itself was common enough. Sophia had lived in a retirement community, but because of poor regulation it had burned down, leading her to move in with her aging daughter. The fact that Sophia was in her eighties, though, was hardly discussed on the show. For one thing, she did not really look or move like a woman in her eighties; in fact, the actress who played her was in her sixties, and was actually younger than Bea Arthur, who played her daughter. And for another, the realities of caring for an aging, immigrant parent are hardly ever dramatized. Sophia is in every sense one of the girls—she goes on adventures, has sex, and trades barbs with the best of them.[1]

This was miles away from the real, and common, experience of women in their fifties caring for parents in their eighties. For a truer account, we can turn to Hope Wolff, a woman Dorothy's age profiled by *Ladies' Home Journal* in 1989. A former medical technician, Hope had been looking forward to a leisurely retirement with her husband. The couple even moved to Florida, chasing the dream of sun-dappled golden years. It was not to be. Her husband's parents, each over ninety, were becoming frail, and they moved into Hope's house. For several years, Hope cared for them, dealing every day with their incontinence and erratic sleep patterns. Eventually, they were forced to hire in-home providers at the cost of $3,500 per month (more than $8,000 per month in 2024 dollars), turning their retirement villa into an ersatz nursing home and devastating their own finances. Once Hope's parents-in-law died, her own father began to suffer from Alzheimer's disease. He, too, moved into their house, and Hope started the cycle again. All of this took an enormous toll on Hope's mental and physical health, as well as on her marriage. "It's a marathon," she told a reporter. "But we do what we have to do."[2]

Hope's story, not Dorothy's and Sophia's, represents the reality of the American system of long-term care as it emerged in the latter decades of the twentieth century. Historically, stories like Hope's were rare, and it was only in her day that, in the words of a researcher in 1985, "long-term parent care" became "a normative experience." The reason was simple. The demographic story of the 1960–1990 period was not the growth of the sixty-five-plus population, which actually grew more slowly that it had in the 1930–1960 period. The real story was the growth of the eighty-five-plus population, which more than doubled, proportionally, in just three decades. Many more middle-aged people, therefore, were in Hope's situation of having surviving parents. In the early 1970s, about a quarter of people in their late fifties had a surviving parent. Less than a decade later, that number had jumped to 40 percent, and it would continue to climb for the rest of the century until eventually most people in that age group had at least one surviving parent. People were surviving diseases that used to kill, and they were enduring long chronic illnesses that were harder to treat and created new challenges of care. At the same time, and thanks to the increase in female labor force participation, there were fewer middle-aged women around to do the necessary care labor.[3]

This coincidence of factors created a genuine crisis of care, one that many observers recognized. The American government could have responded to the new crisis the way that it had responded in the past: through the creation of massive new social programs. It could have created a network of licensed, well-regulated care facilities, staffed with well-trained, well-paid employees. That is not what happened, and instead the problem was swept under the rug. Women like Hope were left to deal with it by themselves. Services did exist, but they were patchy and local; funding for care did exist, but through the welfare system (Medicaid) rather than the social insurance system (Medicare). In addition, the services were difficult to access, requiring huge amounts of knowledge and time to research and complete paperwork for them. Many women didn't bother or were disappointed with the quality of services if they did.

Women like Hope, in short, were abandoned. It's not that nobody recognized the problem or offered a solution; as we'll see, many did. Those solutions, though, went nowhere. Perhaps this was inevitable. As we've seen time and again in this book, older people with disabilities had always been an afterthought to policymakers, who were reluctant to pour resources into a constituency that lacked a voice and lacked political power. Moreover, as we've seen, the discussion of aging in the 1980s was about individualism and entrepreneurialism. The private sector had a number of solutions available, most notably assisted-living facilities, most of which did not accept Medicare or Medicaid. But people who could not afford such a thing had two choices: they could be cared for by family members for free, or they could use their own money, and eventually Medicaid, to pay for a nursing home. Normally, this would happen in that sequence, with the family opting for nursing home care once their own emotional and financial wells had run dry. Family members, typically adult daughters, provided care because there was no other choice, especially given the dismal reputation of nursing homes. And they did it because they were bombarded with propaganda, from the government and from popular culture alike, designed to convince them that it was their duty to care for their parents who had done so much to care for them in their youth.

This chapter will attempt to explain why so little was done to address this problem, and why women like Hope were expected to make such enormous sacrifices. We will begin by showing how the problem of the frail elderly was defined and assessed in the 1980s, and how they were linguistically distinguished from the dominant category of "older people." From there, we will explore why American families did not want to use nursing homes, and what sorts of creative alternatives were emerging to provide a "continuum of care" for that population. Even though those alternatives remained small in scale, they are worth remembering, if only to demonstrate that alternatives to our current system, or nonsystem, did exist. Lastly, we will explain why those alternatives were not taken up—at least, not at scale—and why women like Hope emerged as the solution to a problem that was not of their making.

This book has been attentive to the power of language in naming and defining the older population. As we've seen, the term of art in this period was "older people." That term, though, was seldom used to refer to older people in the eighty-plus age bracket, especially those with disabilities. The whole point of that terminology, as we saw in earlier chapters, was to welcome people in their late fifties into the universe of old age in order to make that category seem younger and more vibrant.

A host of new words and concepts, then, emerged to refer to that population. From the mid-1970s, a distinction began to arise among gerontologists and policymakers between the "young-old" and the "old-old." Since the age barrier of sixty-five was increasingly meaningless, the thinking went that perhaps a new one should be erected around the age of seventy-five—the moment when people's functional abilities began, in the aggregate, to significantly decline.[4]

Perhaps the most common concept used both by experts and by the public to distinguish the old-old from the young-old was frailty. That word had seldom been used to refer to older people before the later 1970s, and never in a clinical sense. But with surprising rapidity, from about 1975 to 1980, the "frail elderly" emerged as a popular concept, providing an identity for individuals age seventy-five-plus that allowed the phrase "older people" to refer in popular parlance to active people in roughly the fifty-five to seventy-five age bracket. The impetus for this new category came from the Federal Council on Aging, which created a task force to study "persons, usually but not always, over the age of 75, who because of the accumulation of various continuing problems often require one or several supportive services in order to cope with daily life." The lead author of the resulting report, a former social worker named Cleonice Tavani, said that "frailty" was chosen as an organizing principle for no special reason beyond "the need for a dramatic term." Nonetheless, it took off, and ever since then, the category of the "frail elderly" has organized social services and research studies.[5]

Just as "frailty" referred primarily to weaknesses of the body, a new vocabulary emerged at the same time to refer to the mind. Alzheimer's disease (AD) had existed as a diagnosis for many years. But for most of the twentieth century, it was rarely discussed because it was only used to diagnose dementia in younger people. Some degree of dementia was thought to be normal in older people, so it didn't require a special diagnosis or name. This began to change in 1976 when a physician named Robert Katzman published an editorial in the *Archives of Neurology* arguing that dementia in older people was decidedly *not* normal and was linked with the same brain abnormalities as dementia in younger ones. (A parallel might be drawn here with impotence. Long presumed to be a part of normal aging, in the 1980s and 1990s it was reclassified as a medical condition.) As this viewpoint became more widely accepted, the number of Alzheimer's diagnoses exploded, as did public discussion of the malady. The cancer researcher Lewis Thomas declared AD to be the "disease of the century," and it was discussed constantly in Congress and in the media, including on television. Americans were consumed with the issue of Alzheimer's, what it was, and how it might be cured.[6]

The new prevalence of frailty and dementia as cultural labels coincided with their increasing prevalence in social reality. As the eighty-plus population increased, so did these two conditions. Dementia, for instance, seems to impact about 5 percent of people in their seventies and more than triple that number of people in their eighties. A government report in 1987 reported that 1.5 million Americans suffered from "severe dementia," requiring continual care, while several million more had mild or moderate dementia. What's more, analyses at the time indicated that the problem would increase exponentially in the near future. That same report estimated that more than 2 million people would require constant care for dementia by the year 2000.[7]

Even if the actual prevalence of frailty and dementia was not increasing, there would still have been a crisis of care in the 1980s. Middle-aged women, who had long performed eldercare without compensation, were every year less available to do it because they were joining the workforce. In 1950, just a quarter of women in the fifty-five to sixty-four age bracket, the prime time for parental caregiving, were in the labor market. By 1990, almost half of them were. At the same moment, hospitals themselves were increasingly reluctant to do the job. Before 1983, Medicare reimbursed a hospital after the discharge of a patient and would pay more for longer hospital stays. While that was no substitute for long-term care, it at least allowed recuperating older people a few days of respite. In that year, though, new regulations were passed to cut costs, so Medicare started paying hospitals in advance, depending on the diagnosis. This incentivized hospitals to discharge patients as soon as possible.[8]

The crisis was also exacerbated by the patterns of retirement that had emerged after World War II. Many social workers had argued for a flexible system that would help older people transition slowly from independent living to the nursing home, with steps along the way in numerous kinds of homestays and care facilities. Those attempts had failed, and the norm of successful aging continued to involve living independently at home for as long as possible. Pressure points emerged where the demands of independent living conflicted with the realities of aging bodies, as with stairs and bathtubs. Cars were a particularly salient flashpoint for many people. This was, after all, the first generation of older people that had spent their entire adulthood in an auto-centric country, and most of them likely lived in places where driving was required. Starting in the 1980s a great deal of concern arose about frail older people and their access to cars. Older Americans felt a strong sense of identity with driving and were reluctant to give it up; families, in turn, found themselves in the awkward position of managing the situation, given unclear state guidelines and uneven access to older-driver training programs.[9]

The glut of frail seniors—who often had dementia, lived in their own homes, and lacked access to transportation—created a thorny problem for policymakers. This population could not be helped much with an income supplement or a short hospital stay. Nursing home care was embedded into the system as the primary publicly financed solution to the eldercare crisis, but it was not a good one. The industry continued to grow, but over time the proportion of older Americans institutionalized in a nursing home leveled off, for a number of interlocking reasons. Nursing homes were expensive—averaging $22,000 per year per resident in 1987, or about triple the average Social Security benefit. They had to be paid for out of pocket until the patient became impoverished enough for Medicaid, the means-tested welfare program, to take over.[10]

Nursing homes were stigmatized, and most older Americans and their families did not want to have recourse to them until the last possible moment. "The mere mention of a nursing home," reported a 1980 article in the *Journal of the American Medical Association*, "is often enough to arouse feelings of terror, frustration, grief or guilt among elderly patients and their families." *Better Homes & Gardens* performed major surveys of its readers in the early 1970s and 1980s, collecting hundreds of thousands of responses, and noticed a stark shift on this topic. In 1972, when asked what the respondent thought she would do when confronted with a frail parent, nursing home placement was the top choice. A decade later, however, and citing both the high cost and miserable conditions of nursing homes, only 10 percent of readers chose nursing homes as their preferred solution. A full 46 percent presumed that their parents could move in with relatives, while 30 percent (fancifully) believed they would opt for "a live-in helper" to move in with their parents. Caregiving daughters, and older people themselves, tended to express horror at the idea of entering a nursing home. "It's a rule of the house," one daughter reported. "We don't talk about going into nursing homes."[11]

The stigma was in many cases well-founded. In 1960, almost half of skilled nursing beds did not meet the fire and health standards then in place. The story through the 1980s stayed the same. Well-meaning federal regulators attempted to implement standards. Nursing home operators, and their formidable lobbying arms, replied that the implementation would be too expensive, they would be forced to close down the homes, and the patients would have nowhere to go. Government agencies in turn responded by loosening the standards, decreeing that "substantial compliance" or some cognate thereof was sufficient. The reduced standards, combined with lax enforcement and inspection procedures, meant that nursing homes remained something of a regulatory Wild West. While efforts were made to beef up nursing home regulations in 1987, the new rules were once again poorly enforced.[12]

High-need patients, like those with dementia, were especially ill served in nursing homes, even though they represented a high proportion of patients. There were no particular standards of care for them, and many methods were downright abusive. This happened not because nursing home employees were cruel, but because the industry required grueling, low-paid work in a poorly regulated environment. The seven-hundred-thousand-person-strong nursing home industry had truly astonishing levels of turnover; one scholar estimated 75 percent per year. When they could be located at all, home health aides, like nursing home staff, were seldom trained in the specific sets of skills necessary to care for people with dementia. The owner of a home health agency in Rochester, New York, lamented the lack of official training before listing the characteristics she informally looked for in assigning staff to Alzheimer's patients. The list, which included an array of physical and emotional skills, revealed just how challenging the job was—and how unlikely anyone with those superhuman qualities would be to stay in low-wage, low-prestige work.[13]

Policymakers and health care professionals agreed with older people themselves that Medicaid-funded nursing homes were an inadequate solution to the crisis in long-term care. And they understood, too, what needed to be done: they needed to create a "continuum of care." This term, which became popular around that time, designated a commitment to providing health care and social service needs that were appropriate to an individual's evolving functional capacity. In other words, a vast spectrum lay between "independent living at home" and "institutionalization in a nursing home." The idea of the continuum of care was to walk seniors along that path with the help of teams of social workers and home health aides, allowing them to retain as much independence as possible at each step.[14]

To be sure, a good deal was done to create this continuum of care, but it varied wildly by state and even by county. There is no reason, in principle, why the federal government could not have deployed its resources to make that continuum of care a reality. In the United Kingdom, long-term care was provided by the government, and it ranged from geriatric day care centers to day hospitals to nursing homes. And many in Washington were pushing for something like that in the United States. One close student of the European scene was Brahna Trager, a consultant to the Senate's Committee on Aging and longtime editor of *Home Health Care Services Quarterly*. She canvassed developments across the Atlantic and pointed out that there, older people were "not being expected to make do with rhetoric." Trager's view was that the seventy-five-plus problem deserved just as expansive and coordinated an effort as the sixty-five-plus problem had. "The best possibility of success for community care systems," she opined, "will be achieved when they are integrated into a single national funding system." She recognized that doing so would be a big political lift because it would require overcoming what she called "the Oedipus complex" of politicians who wanted to open new buildings and launch grand programs rather than simply deliver services to the needy. The solution she sought was nothing so grand, and it didn't even have a name because it would not be just one thing. She wanted funding for a phalanx of services, organized in a new agency that would administer funds, standardize measures of quality and need, and help needy individuals navigate extant services.[15]

Trager was not the only one calling for a federally funded continuum of care, even if she was the most consistent presence at government hearings. The Gray Panthers advocated for similar measures. And some politicians were drawn to ideas like this. In 1988, Congressmen Claude Pepper and Edward Roybal sponsored long-term-care legislation that would have funded home health care for the frail elderly, financed by eliminating the income cap on Medicare taxes. The bill, even with the support of the AARP, nonetheless came up dozens of votes short in the House of Representatives.[16]

It can sometimes seem as though the long-term-care "system" is no system at all and is devoid of logic. But that's not quite true. There were people, in the crucial years when it was being set up, who understood where the system was headed and welcomed it. The touchstone 1978 report on the frail elderly, for instance, shows this. That report was miles away from the similar government reports of the 1960s or the 1930s, which canvassed social need before making a recommendation for sweeping new policies. The political imagination at work in 1978 was, if equally well-intentioned, more limited in scope. The report was essentially a Republican document, produced by a committee set up in the waning days of the Gerald Ford administration. Its primary author, Cleonice Tavani, was a longtime Republican who would go on to lead the Taxpayer's League in Montgomery County, Maryland. She was not a slash-and-burn radical by any means. She was a thoughtful analyst of the needs of the frail elderly, and she believed in state action to support them. But in this report, as in her own published articles, she advocated for incremental, local measures over top-down or statist solutions.[17]

The report foretold the shape of long-term care for decades to come. It proposed a federalist, fragmented approach to the continuum of care, in which federal, state, and local bodies would partner with nonprofits to provide services. The committee recognized the right of older individuals to such a continuum—or at least the right to have access to such a system and to learn about it (a later section clarified that the "universal entitlement" was not to services, but to "case assessment and management"). But the authors pointedly did not think that it should be provided along the lines of social insurance. That is, it should not be folded into Social Security and Medicare. They instead advocated for a complex system of joint federal-state funding combined with individual contributions where possible; federal funds would not be used to launch new programs but to finance those that had already been created by local governments or nonprofits.[18]

The report, which did so much to frame the government's response to the frail elderly, belongs to that moment we traced in Chapter 6: in the midst of the grinding economic crisis of the later

1970s, sweeping visions for the future seemed out of place. The report singled out Brahna Trager, the policy analyst who was pushing hardest for a federally run system, to argue that such a thing was politically unthinkable. "The nation," the authors wrote, "is becoming reluctant to expand use of the social insurance system." The authors didn't even want the Social Security Administration to be involved. The office, they reasoned, had too many duties already, adding that local agencies would have a better understanding of older people's needs in their specific communities.[19]

The vision of the Federal Council on Aging was fulfilled in the two decades after the report's release. Those years saw what one scholar in 1988 called "a second generation of elderly service systems." The first generation had been established by the Older Americans Act of 1965. Under that bill, Area Agencies on Aging (AAAs) were founded across the country and were charged with coordinating services for the noninstitutionalized elderly. These services at first focused on relatively healthy older people, funding things like senior centers, recreational opportunities, and nutrition programs. The programs relied on a bewildering array of funding mechanisms: the Older Americans Act itself, but also other federal agencies, state governments, county welfare offices, and more. In the second generation, the funding complexity remained the same, but given all the pressures we've been discussing, state aging agencies began to focus more on the frail elderly and on home-based care as an alternative to institutionalization.[20]

One of the primary mechanisms for this was the Medicaid Waiver program. Given the expense and unpopularity of nursing homes, the federal government decided to let states experiment with using Medicaid funds to pay for in-home care, so long as that care would not cost more than its institutional alternative. This program began with six participating states in 1982, and by 1997 every state had one—at a total cost of $8 billion, or 14 percent of Medicaid's expenditures on long-term care. What this did was expand Medicaid beyond the delivery of medical care or long-term care in a nursing home. States could provide home-based care, adult day care, and so on. The programs were aimed at a wide array of people with disabilities, but the frail elderly were the predominant target group. Some states used the opportunity more than others. In 1997, Oregon and Vermont devoted more than 40 percent of their Medicaid long-term-care funds to Waiver programs, compared with just 2 percent in Mississippi.[21]

Many of the programs were innovative and tapped into traditions of community care that went back further than the official 1982 launch of the program. For a sense of what they looked like, consider On Lok, one of the earliest and most well-known. The Cantonese name translates as "peaceful abode," and the program served the aging, largely immigrant, and largely Asian population in San Francisco's Chinatown. It was founded by Marie-Louise Ansak, a Swiss-born social worker, and William Gee, a Chinese-born dentist. The pair met on a municipal commission and were both concerned about the health care needs in Chinatown–North Beach. More than half of seniors there were under the poverty line, and many of them were immigrants without family in the area to care for them. Many had dementia and lacked the proper supports to coordinate care from the fragmented and often expensive homemaker and home health services.[22]

Instead of founding yet another nursing home, Ansak and Gee imagined a consolidated suite of services that would help family members shoulder the burden of caring for frail, aging relatives—especially those with dementia. This would include congregate housing, an infirmary, a day care center, and more. (Although the two did not coin the term "continuum of care," they and their agency did a good deal to popularize it.) They began in 1971 with a multipurpose day center, funded with a grant from the federal Administration on Aging. Unlike earlier day centers, this one was aimed at the elderly in poor health, who would otherwise have been institutionalized. From there, from 1972 to 1975, On Lok became more like a "day health service," offering some medical services and funded by a short-term Medicaid grant. From 1974 to 1978, the organization received another grant from the Administration on Aging allowing for home-based services like homemaking and chores and cooking, and from 1978 to 1982 yet another agency gave it a grant to become a Medicare-funded Community Care Organization for Dependent Adults. Finally, On Lok House (which still exists) opened its doors with fifty-four units in 1980. As even this short summary shows, Ansak and Gee had to be politically savvy to keep On Lok running, making trips to Washington and lining up a dizzying collection of grants and funding mechanisms, both state and federal.[23]

The results were remarkable and truly did provide a continuum of care in an impoverished area. Senior centers were integrated with meal delivery services, home health aides, and even end-of-life care. While On Lok did not have an official hospice, it did offer analogous services. One older man had been found dirty and uncared for in a rooming house. He flourished in On Lok's suite of services, and when dying of cancer he opted to remain at On Lok House until his peaceful death, surrounded by On Lok staff.[24]

On Lok also generated employment in its neighborhood. Chinatown had a surfeit of trained medical personnel, many of whom were unemployed (some because their medical training was not recognized in America). Some of them joined On Lok, whose director was committed to providing stable, well-paying jobs. On Lok staffers were given occasional sabbaticals, a clear path for career advancement, and support for continuing education.[25]

Across the country, many more experiments like this transpired. On-the-ground reports run the gamut, as we'd expect. A 1985 newsletter from Chicago's Department on Aging and Disability shows us a chaotic system with warring public agencies and loads of two hundred clients for overworked case managers. Other reports were far more promising. In Connecticut a coordinated care service called Triage sought to provide a one-stop shop for older people in need of services. A conference on the project described a ninety-two-year-old woman who had been tied to a nursing home chair for three weeks to prevent her from falling. With the help of Triage, the woman was moved home. She had a home health aide from a nonprofit in the morning, a meal delivered at noon, an aide from a for-profit agency in the evening, and a monthly nursing visit. She was able to live with these services in place for four years.[26]

Nonetheless, the programs remained small. There was an effort to use the On Lok model as a pilot for a national program called PACE (Program of All-Inclusive Care). By 1999, almost three decades after On Lok's founding, there were about thirty PACE facilities serving six thousand older people. This is impressive, but a drop in the bucket compared with the level of need. The political willpower simply did not exist to expand the programs—or as New Jersey's governor put it in a moment of candor, there was no "constituency for care."[27]

Given the public hostility to nursing homes and the government's reluctance to fund alternatives, private industry rushed into this space. Private-sector investment in long-term care took all manner of forms, most of which were novelties in the 1980s. Some of them were financial. The AARP sold long-term-care insurance, for instance, which allowed people to buy a plan to offset potential nursing home costs. By 1990 more than a million of these policies, which had hardly existed before 1980, had been sold. Meanwhile, in 1989 the first reverse mortgage was issued, insured by the Federal Housing Administration. These were aimed at cash-poor but house-rich seniors who sought to use their house for retirement income. In this scheme, often denounced as predatory, a bank would pay a set amount of money to the senior each month in exchange for equity in their home.[28]

Other innovations were technological. In 1989, a company named LifeCall began airing ads that became instantly iconic and will be remembered by anyone who owned a television. The product was a device, worn around the neck, that you could use to alert neighbors and health care professionals if you were having a medical emergency. Anyone could use the service, but all the actors in the marketing campaign were elderly. One of them was an older white woman lying on the ground with her walker who delivered the immortal line "I've fallen, and I can't get up!"

The largest innovations in housing for frail older people also came from the private sector. "An important new American housing trend is emerging," reported the *Washington Post* in 1989. "Its name is unknown among the general public and little known even within the home-building industry." The author was referring to assisted-living facilities, situated on the continuum somewhere between retirement communities and nursing homes. They offered congregate housing and social opportunities for seniors who could not, or did not wish to, remain in their own homes. These projects grew explosively, meeting as they did a pressing need from a growing demographic.[29]

The concept of assisted living had multiple origin points on both the East and West Coasts. Some early forms did have public funding. But as one AARP analyst pointed out in 1993, "Assisted living has been market driven—that is, developers in the private sector have built programs in response to consumer demand rather than in response to a government mandate or government funding." The key innovators were Paul and Terry Klaassen, who came to the problem after being disgusted by the available options as they sought care for their aging relatives. Paul's grandparents lived in the Netherlands, and he had seen the kinds of senior housing on offer there. There, the state provided en masse the continuum of care that the American state was reluctant to fund. The Klaassens, a married couple, wanted to bring the Dutch model to America as a private venture. So they bought an old, boarded-up home in Oakton, Virginia, and labored for months to make it look like a homey boardinghouse. The experiment was a success. The Klaassens were devout Christians, and in fact had met while performing in a Christian rock band, but the home did not replicate the austere retirement communities run by churches in the past. It was a well-appointed mansion, and the Klaassens sought residents who could pay top dollar (they did not accept Medicaid). Under the brand name Sunrise Assisted Living, Inc., the couple spread the model to hundreds of other sites around the country.[30]

Throughout the late 1980s and 1990s, assisted living became big business, and the market was flooded with private capital. By 1988, a quarter of a million Americans lived in such facilities. To take an example from New Jersey, seniors at Medford Leas Retirement Community could pay $112,000 up front for a two-bedroom unit, and then pay $1,000 per month for the rest of their lives. "In exchange," reported the *Wall Street Journal*, "they get housing, dining-room meals, maid service, sports facilities and endless bridge games. They also are guaranteed whatever medical and nursing care they need." By 2000, more than a million Americans resided in this new architectural-medical experiment.[31]

However much they varied, what united most of these private solutions was their expense. Long-term-care insurance was out of the reach of most seniors; even industry groups admitted that less than half could afford their products. LifeCall was just one of many companies that peddled tech services to older people in the 1980s and 1990s. Many of them, as *Consumer Reports* noted in 1991, were exorbitantly expensive or were simply a scam. The bias toward the wealthy was most apparent in assisted-living facilities. They sought residents who could pay their own way, and while their residents of course had access to Medicare, the nicer facilities did not want to tangle with Medicaid. This was true of new institutions designed for dementia care, too. In 1987 a journal for Alzheimer's care published an interview with Dorothy Kirsten French, the wife of a notable neuroscientist who had died of the disease. She was founding an Alzheimer's residential center in his name, and it had all the humanistic and innovative features for dementia care that were lacking in standard nursing homes. Perhaps readers were excited—until the interview turned to finances. "Unfortunately," French reported, "it will be expensive. People will have to pay the going rate," because "the government has done nothing to help."[32]

Most older Americans could not dream of affording facilities or services like these, a reality that returns us to the dilemma of Hope Wolff, whom we met at the beginning of the chapter. The majority of eldercare, both medical and personal, was undertaken by family members. "The media myth says that America abandons its elderly to nursing homes," commented a task force of the Older Women's League in 1987. "The truth is closer to this: America abandons many of its older women, who are left to care for impaired older relatives entirely on their own."[33]

Of course, women had long been doing this kind of labor. But in the 1980s there was more of it to be done than before, for reasons already described. And thanks to the influence of second-wave feminism, women were less likely to do it in silence. Women's magazines were full of stories of heroic, and grueling, caregiving. Many women even published memoirs about their caregiving experiences; others devoted their careers to studying the issue. So while the labor itself was not new, the extent of it was—and was made more public.[34]

Caregivers in the 1980s tended to be women on the later side of middle age. Many were caring for older relatives, of course, but many were also caring for friends or spouses. They weren't doing it entirely alone. In the absence of a major public commitment, a network of grassroots self-help organizations emerged to help them. Interest was sparked by a "Dear Abby" column in 1980 in which the advice columnist gave her millions of readers information about the Alzheimer's Disease and Related Disorders Association (ADRDA). The association had been founded in that same year as a joint effort by the seven fledgling organizations around the country devoted to the cause. Several of them were shoestring operations run by middle-aged caretakers themselves, like the Minneapolis-based Association for Alzheimer's and Related Diseases, which was led by two women who had been shocked by the lack of information and support available to them as they cared for their husbands with dementia. Over the course of the 1980s, the ADRDA grew into a sizable, national organization that oversaw more than two hundred chapters around the country. The chapters provided assistance that the women in Minneapolis, and millions of others, had been seeking and that the state was not providing, including a toll-free help line and the organization of support groups for caregivers (about sixteen hundred of which were up and running by 1990).[35]

These groups worked wonders for those who could find and attend them, and caregiving memoirs often praised them as the places where the authors had been connected to knowledge and resources. Still, they were too few and too far between. Sixteen hundred groups (roughly one group for every fifteen hundred people with dementia) were not nearly enough given the scale of need. Compare that, for instance, with Al-Anon, a support group for friends and family members of people suffering from alcohol use disorder. That was another vast problem, but one that was better served, at least in this respect. There were more than ten times as many Al-Anon groups in 1990 as there were ADRDA support groups.[36]

Whether they could find a group or not, these women were being asked to perform heroic tasks. Many held outside jobs while caring for multiple generations of dependents. And sometimes they were older people themselves. Miriam Dypold, a sixty-seven-year-old grandmother, spent her days caring for her ninety-year-old mother. This led her to feel, in the words of a journalist profiling her, "more frazzled and tied down than she did during the years when she was raising five children." "This is just the way it is for women of my generation," Dypold said.[37]

The task depleted the time of many middle-aged women. According to the *Ladies' Home Journal*, almost two million women were caring for aged parents in the late 1980s, donating "the equivalent of more than eleven weeks each year," totaling "27 million woman-days of unpaid care every week; on a personal level, they represent hundreds of thousands of unrealized dreams." And it depleted their energy too. Women's stories tended to focus on two things in particular. First, the role of incontinence, which informed the general sense that the relationship was not one of dignity and respect. "My hands," one woman reported with disgust, "began to smell like my father's bowel movements." The other was sleep deprivation, because patients with dementia often experience interrupted sleep. "The last year was devastating," reported an older woman who had cared for her husband. "It became a 24-hour job and I got little sleep because of his restlessness."[38]

All of this had an impact on these women's well-being. It is easy to indulge a fantasy in which women would find a great deal of meaning and satisfaction in caring for aged relatives. And while doubtless there were good days, in the aggregate the task was a depressing one—especially for the caretakers of people with dementia, who might not even recognize their spouses or children. Perhaps one in six caregivers went through economic strain, and one in four went through physical strain. The greatest challenges, though, were emotional and mental. "Caregivers," reported one book in 1985, "routinely report stress-related symptoms, such as anxiety, depression or feelings of fatigue." They are often "angry" and "feel guilty about not doing enough, even though they may spend 24 hours a day with the patient." *Ladies' Home Journal* referred to the "living hell" of Alzheimer's care because caregivers often "have no outside support and no relief from caretaking." "The scourge of Alzheimer's," lamented a journalist in *Woman's Day*, "is that it never stops."[39]

Social isolation and stress in the caregiver, rather than severity of symptoms in the older person, tended to result in nursing home placement. Caregivers could keep older people at home, even those with dementia, for a surprising amount of time if they had the proper support. But they often didn't. One 1986 study found that caregivers expressed "a need for respite services, which they had generally been unable to obtain or afford." "Organized respite services, geriatric day respite, day health programs, chore and companion services for this population are scarce," concurred another study, "and there is decreasing coverage by private insurance and Medicare." Sometimes, of course, families did find the resources. One daughter reported, "We were just lucky the day my mother stumbled on an informed person" who could point them in the right direction. Those stories, though, were uncommon. "The outstanding memory I have," a more typical caregiver said, "is of being abandoned by the institutions I formerly had a great deal of respect for."[40]

Caregivers generally could not rely on home health aides to plug the gaps, and at the end of the decade it was estimated that fully 80 percent of the noninstitutionalized older population with long-term care needs was cared for solely by informal support networks of family and friends. Medicare was still reluctant to pay for home health aides, rendering them unaffordable for many families (through the 1980s, the program's expenditures on home health care were low and not growing). Home health care was, in any case, untrusted and poorly regulated. "Elder abuse" as a term hardly existed before 1980. But by 1990 it was everywhere—on the front pages of tabloids and the subject of many congressional hearings. Even though the perpetrator was almost always a family member, the public outcry often focused on the exploited workforce of home health aides. Sharon Glover, a community college administrator from Minneapolis, had a paraplegic mother who went through numerous different agencies and numerous different aides and had many negative experiences. "There aren't qualified attendants," she told the *Washington Post* in 1987. "And it is an industry that isn't regulated and anything can happen."[41]

Despite the poor reputation and high cost of nursing homes, placement in a nursing facility remained the primary remedy offered to caregivers once their resources and capacities were exhausted. The final decision was often described by adult children as the most painful moment of their lives. And it did not end the cycle of labor. "Nursing-home placement," one 1985 study found, "only shifts the burden families experience, rather than relieving it." Family members often went through a great deal of stress in the process of choosing a facility, organizing finances, and monitoring care. Studies showed, too, that they experienced considerable guilt, especially if there were perceived issues with the quality of care.[42]

History shows that this series of events could have unfolded differently. The crisis of care in the 1980s was, after all, not the first time the American public became consumed by the needs of older people and the stresses they put on younger families. In the 1930s, the Roosevelt administration was concerned that impoverished older people were becoming dependent on their children. Social Security, which as of 2024 costs more than $1 trillion per year, was the result. In the 1960s, policymakers worried that rising medical costs would threaten the independence of senior citizens and once again force them to rely on their children. The result was Medicare, which costs more than $900 billion per year. In the 1980s, a new set of concerns emerged, and a new set of discussions about the dependence of older people on their children. But this time, the solution was different. While the government would eventually spend about $300 billion per year on long-term-care services, most of it would be stigmatized, patchwork care delivered through the state welfare system—rather than care treated as a universal right and delivered through the federal system of social insurance. This time, policymakers wanted to tap the resources of family first, before opening the public coffers. This was often made explicit; the 1978 report on frailty, for instance, presumed that "public policies should enhance existing and encourage additional intergenerational help to the frail elderly." That sentence indicates a sea change in the American logic of old-age policy as it had been developing for decades.[43]

If policymakers in the New Deal era were trying to relieve the family of traditional burdens like eldercare, their successors in the 1980s and 1990s were trying to reverse that effort, placing responsibility back on the family unit. Politicians like Ronald Reagan praised the family precisely because they were asking the family to do and be so very much. The issue of student debt is perhaps the most familiar analog here. In the midcentury, it seemed that education would be a public good, and policymakers envisioned cheap or free tuition at high-quality public universities. Nonetheless, from the 1970s to 1990s, rising tuition costs and legislative decisions led students and families toward student loans. Another obvious example concerns the American attitude toward paid and family leave—an area in which, as with education costs, the American solution differs from that of most of the world. Almost every country in the world offers paid medical leave for new parents or for those who have contracted an illness. In the United States, this never happened. Even the Family and Medical Leave Act of 1993 only mandated unpaid leave, the presumption being that families would have to sort out the financial challenges themselves.[44]

The bipartisan "family values" consensus of the 1980s affected ideas about eldercare too. Those who opted to care for elderly relatives in their own home could receive a tax credit. The critique of nursing homes was also aligned with the broader family culture of the era: nursing homes were positioned as dirty, unsafe places reserved for welfare recipients and unsuitable for dignified older people, who should, by all rights, be cared for by dutiful family members rather than by the welfare system.[45]

The familial consensus was so effective, among other reasons, because it was so readily internalized. In essence, policymakers were leveraging familial affection to solve a policy problem. They were not doing so alone, of course. Caregivers were told at every turn that this kind of long-term care was a natural obligation of grown children, and one that their ancestors had done without complaint. While we know this to be untrue, the story was powerful nonetheless. Women like Wolff took on the duty because, she explained, "I thought that's what you were supposed to do." Many had recourse to the logic of role reversal. "Mom took such good care of me," women told themselves, "and now it's my turn." That notion, however powerful it might have felt to individual people, was also a myth. As activists and scholars were already pointing out in the 1980s, caregiving for children by young parents has almost nothing in common with caring for an ailing parent or spouse with dementia. It is a destructive myth as well, insofar as it infantilizes older people and asks middle-aged women to play, once again, the role of "mother."[46]

Popular culture also promoted the notion that the oldest old were a family responsibility, and nursing home placement was generally portrayed as a tragedy. Dementia was front and center in one uncharacteristically melancholy episode of *The Golden Girls*. "Old Friends" (1987), the first episode of the third season, was watched by almost twenty million Americans. In it, Sophia meets an older man named Alvin on the boardwalk. The two become fast friends. Alvin, however, begins to display some erratic behavior. He seems to forget his wife's name and becomes belligerent with Sophia because he is convinced that she has stolen his seat on the bench. Sophia's daughter, Dorothy, befriends Alvin's daughter and learns the truth: Alvin is suffering from Alzheimer's. His daughter had been taking time off work to care for him, but that arrangement was nearing an end because the daughter was depleting her money. "The family has discussed sending him to New York," Dorothy tells Sophia. "He has a nephew who's a doctor there and can give him special care."[47]

In this episode, Alzheimer's was depicted as a family affair. An ailing patriarch is cared for by a daughter, who leaves the workforce and endangers her own financial health. The "family" decides to send him elsewhere, where another family member, conveniently a physician, can care for him—presumably on his own time, and for free. The notion of hired help or institutional care does not appear in the episode. One senses that the writers recognized that no coherent solution was available, so they invented a physician nephew with oceans of free time.

The "dementia plot" became rather common in 1980s culture, displaying a particular interest, as with *The Golden Girls* episode, in situations where for one reason or another older daughters could not play the role that was assigned to them. Another example was *On Golden Pond* (1981), an Academy Award–winning film starring Henry Fonda and Katharine Hepburn, both of whom were in their seventies. It told the story of an ornery professor named Norman and his wife who were spending time with their daughter and grandson at a lakeside vacation home. The drama concerns Norman's declining faculties. He has trouble recognizing family photos and clearly is in the early stages of dementia. He acts aggressively with neighbors and visitors, and at the movie's end he has a health emergency that nearly kills him. The film was one of the first major representations of dementia on-screen, and it set an important precedent. The problem of aging, by then understood as mental and physical decline, would be handled within the family unit. With the brief exception of an appearance by the mailman, *On Golden Pond* is very much a family picture; nobody outside Norman's family plays a role in the film, or presumably in his care. Norman is estranged from his daughter, leading his wife to do the yeoman's work of caring for him. It seems that he has no official diagnosis for his mental maladies, and therefore no professional support. Even when he has heart troubles, he is unable to reach a doctor and relies on his wife to give him nitroglycerin.

On Golden Pond hits the two beats that would become common in the 1980s: older people were defined above all by their physical and mental health, and lapses in that health, symbolized most clearly by dementia, would be solved within the family unit. This basic plot was reiterated many times throughout the decade. *Do You Remember Love?* (1985), a TV movie, had a remarkably similar plot, again featuring an ailing professor who was cared for by her spouse. And two years later, *The Whales of August* (1987) came out, which like *On Golden Pond* featured titanic film stars at the end of their careers (Lillian Gish and Bette Davis). In this movie, aging sisters go to a vacation house in Maine to enjoy one last summer. One of them is in poorer health than the other— she's blind and becoming increasingly confused—which raises serious questions of care for the other one. As in *On Golden Pond*, the elder daughter is estranged and cannot be relied upon, and an older woman (in this case a sister rather than a wife) is forced to fill the gap.

In all these portrayals, the person with dementia does in fact receive good care without relying on a nursing home. The message was that if families could be creative, solutions could be found—and this message buffeted American women from all directions, including from organized religion. One of the most important elements of 1980s culture was the revitalization of evangelical Christianity. And in those circles, as expressed in *Christianity Today*, heroic eldercare by unpaid women was presented as a new form of the biblical injunction to honor one's parents. If an elderly family member needed help, the editors of that magazine argued, sound finance and biblical morality pointed in the same direction: the family needed to step up, even if that meant reducing their own spending. The most extended meditation on the topic came from William F. May, an expert in medical ethics who would go on to serve on Bill Clinton's health care task force. His lengthy essay mobilized the faithful behind voluntarism and familial care, while even suggesting a cutback in Social Security in the name of needy children.[48]

This cultural pressure was important because American women had to be convinced that the labor of eldercare was something that they should by rights take on as their own. And that, fundamentally, is what happened—and what happens still. The decision to devolve long-term care to American women was at root a policy decision, and one that could have been made differently. It would not have been easy—the issue of long-term care really is a thorny one, and harder to solve than an issue like income security. When it comes to the realities of dementia and frailty, there is no perfect public solution, ready to be implemented with a flourish of the presidential pen. Caring for elderly frail people requires vast amounts of labor—not just money—which means training programs, regulatory scrutiny, and more. All of this is challenging and expensive, and even in relatively lavish welfare states, such as Germany, middle-aged daughters provide a good deal of care. That said, in many other places the situation has not reached the crisis level that it has here because many nations acted earlier and more energetically to provide centralized support to frail older people, including those with dementia, and their caregivers. In the United States, almost nothing has been done. If one reads a caregiving memoir from, say, 2016, it looks depressingly close to one written in 1983.[49]

The situation for long-term care remains bleak. Since 1990, there has been surprisingly little policy movement on this front (though there has been some). It is true today, as it was in 1980, that the catastrophically underdeveloped system for long-term care is the dark underbelly of the relatively developed and successful set of systems and supports for older people who don't have mental or physical disabilities. And yet all is not lost. If this book has shown anything, it's that old-age policies do eventually move with the times, and that the labor of enterprising women is often required to initiate that shift. We can end this chapter where we began. Although the profile in *Ladies' Home Journal* presented Hope Wolff as suffering silently, she was less of a victim than the article suggested. She was in fact an energetic organizer. When the article ran, she was already a member of a group called Adult Children of Aging Parents, a community of caregivers in Boca Raton. Within a few years she was actually in charge of the group. She eventually found an affordable adult-care facility for her father called the Atrium, which marketed itself as less expensive and more dignified than nursing homes. Wolff even appeared in advertisements for the Atrium, declaring to readers of the *Boca Raton News* that she had at last found "peace of mind." Wolff's difficult personal story, it seems, had a satisfactory ending, thanks to a combination of luck, organizing, and private-sector initiative. And if Wolff's story took a positive turn toward its end, then perhaps ours should too.[50]

CONCLUSION

MAKE AMERICA
OLD AGAIN

O ld age, many have said, is like a foreign country: a strange land
with strange ways requiring plenty of advance preparation to
visit and enjoy. The metaphor captures something important about
the experience of aging. Our lives do change a great deal as we reach
our sixties and seventies. Our income changes, our health changes,
our family relationships change. But what the metaphor misses is
that old age is also very much our own country. Aging in the US has
been indelibly shaped by all the promises and pathologies of the great
American experiment. Aging here is more diverse and more experimental than it is in many places, just as it is more chaotic and unequal
and underfunded. In writing this book, I have tried to keep all of this
in mind, writing neither a celebration nor an indictment but a history
of that place called "old age" to which we are all marching, if we are not
already there.

While the failures of American aging policy are important to
examine, they should not distract us from the fact that the struggle
chronicled in this book—the struggle to build a secure old age for

all—has been in many ways successful. Thanks to public health initiatives, there are more older people than ever before. Thanks to Social Security and Medicare, those older people are *far* less impoverished and enjoy *far* better health than was imaginable a century ago. This was a success unequally shared, but it was a success that was shared nonetheless. In the past half century, so often viewed as a dead end for social progress, poverty rates for older Black Americans have continued to fall. Even older people with disabilities, so often neglected in policy discussions, have access to infinitely more services and opportunities than they did a century ago.[1]

As with so much else in this country, the institutional framework of aging is more fragmented than in other places, relying on a confusing network of nonprofits and county-level departments of social services, crowned sometimes with federal funding from the Older Americans Act. The resulting system is imperfect and different in every place, but it does exist. In every town and city across the country, unchronicled social workers and municipal agencies and churches have built an infrastructure for senior living, with senior centers and discounted travel tickets and nutrition programs. A mile from my own home, where I'm writing these words, sits the Durham Center for Senior Life, one of thousands of such centers across the country, all of them produced by the old-age movement as described in this book. Founded in 1949 as a Golden Age Society, it began receiving federal and state funding in the 1960s. This has allowed it to offer an array of services to local seniors: health classes, opportunities for sociability, adult day care, and more.

Some have argued that all of this is too much—that the place called old age has been overdeveloped, sucking too many resources from others who need it more. This is an understandable reaction to the story told in this book. For all the ways in which old-age programs are underfunded, they are incomparably more generous than, say, policies for children. It does not follow, though, that reducing old-age benefits would benefit other marginalized groups. Security is not a scarce resource. The collective project ought to be to make all of us more secure, children and older people alike. "Medicare for All" works, as a slogan and a program, because it promises to expand the security enjoyed by older people to other groups. Indeed, many designers of Medicare hoped this would happen, and in fact for many people it did happen: in 1972, Medicare was expanded to cover people with disabilities and end-stage renal disease.[2]

It benefits *everyone* to provide a secure and dignified old age to anyone who wants it. All of us are either old or becoming old. And in any case, old-age policy doesn't affect older people alone. One of the purposes of Social Security and Medicare was to save *younger* people from being on the hook for their parents' expenses. That scheme has not worked perfectly, but it has worked to an amazing extent: before Social Security, older people scraped by largely through sharing incomes with their children. And while Medicare is an imperfect beast, imagine life without it. How, exactly, would older people afford health insurance? Imagine the insecurity it would bring to young families if older, uninsured relatives were one fall away from gargantuan medical bills.[3]

The point is not just that all of us are aging, but that we are aging into a world where aging will matter more than ever. Sometime in the 2030s, the number of Americans over age sixty-five will surpass those under eighteen. In a real sense, and no matter how well intentioned the slogan might be, the children are not our future. They are our past.

We as a society have failed to understand this fact. The concepts and categories that were developed in American history to govern education, health, labor, and transportation were all premised on the fact that the United States was a young nation. While the successes of old-age policy are innumerable, they were not part of a coherent discussion about how this country would weather the transition to being a much older society. Our architecture and our roads and our education systems have been designed for the young and middle-aged. This will need to change.

If we are going to weather this transition, we will have to remember that aging is not just a corporeal process, but a social and historical one. The medicalization of aging is itself a historical production, and one tracked in this book. Sometime between the 1950s and the 1980s, physicians conquered the public sphere when it came to the public discussion of aging, and they haven't let go. It is still true today that the national conversation on aging is driven by physicians. Many of the books they write, like Atul Gawande's *Being Mortal* (2014) and Louise Aronson's *Elderhood* (2019), are excellent, and I hope you read them. If we are going to really prepare ourselves for the gray future, we will need the perspectives of physicians, absolutely. But not only theirs. We will need engineers, architects, and computer scientists; we will also need novelists, poets, theologians, and even historians. The dominance of medical voices has resulted in the widespread presumption that aging is an individual matter involving primarily individual lifestyles—that in the end, it's up to you to stop smoking, start exercising, and all the rest of it. However good this advice is, it is not the only or best starting place for a serious national conversation about what it means to age in the twenty-first century. It's a return in some ways to the world of a century ago, before aging was taken up as a social cause and when older people were enjoined to seek wisdom and piety.

Many of the problems of aging simply cannot be resolved at the individual level. Civil wars, floods, pandemics, and heatwaves: the bestiary of twenty-first-century living is catastrophic, especially for the aged. It is the bodies of the elderly that crowd the morgues in the wake of pathological outbreaks or environmental disasters. As American policymakers and the American public continue to grapple with the meaning of the COVID-19 pandemic, it is important to remember who was, in fact, lost. More than 75 percent of COVID-19 deaths occurred in the sixty-five-plus population (which at the time constituted only 17 percent of the US population). Nursing homes suffered staggering loss of life. In fourteen states, more than 10 percent of the nursing home population died in the year 2020 alone.[4]

Older people are facing more mundane threats to their security as well. Social Security, unless something drastic is done, will reach a fiscal crisis in the 2030s, leading to a drop in payments that would be devastating to the finances of millions. Even if that does not happen, many seniors are in precarious positions. About one in three older Americans is economically insecure, meaning they are living on less than double the federal poverty level. More than half of older Black and Hispanic people are in that situation. These numbers will likely get worse, as the coming generation of older people is unlikely to have much, if anything, saved for retirement due to the high costs of education and housing in their lifetime.[5]

For reasons tracked in this book, the public discussion in the past half century around aging has been disappointing, as has been political action. From the 1930s to the 1960s, a vast new federal framework for aging was created, along with new ideas and new research programs. In the 1970s and the 1980s, a crisis set in at the policy level, while energy around "successful aging" abounded in the private sector. Since 1990, that dynamic has more or less stayed the same (with a few important shifts, noted below). The public discussion of aging, when it does happen, is depressingly familiar. Many observers take an apocalyptic approach, wringing their hands over the "crisis" of population aging, or spreading fear about the coming "population bomb." The secretary of commerce in 2021 warned that aging would hit the nation "like a ton of bricks." When a front-page editorial about old-age policy is printed, it inevitably calls for older Americans to work longer and harder in order to salvage the fiscal solvency of Social Security and Medicare. Whether or not that is necessary for those particular programs, such an approach is an impoverished and even grotesque response to the crisis of security that threatens to engulf future generations of older Americans. Perhaps even more damningly, it is a form of argument that has been around now for half a century, and it has done nothing for older people, or younger ones, besides force the national conversation onto an endless treadmill of fears and anxieties, divorced from the realities of an aging nation.[6]

Population aging does not have to be a crisis, for us as individuals or for us as a nation. But if we don't prepare for it and find better ways to talk about it and act around it, it will be. It is possible, and even necessary, to imagine population aging as an *opportunity*. Imagine a world in which older people enjoyed opportunities to flourish, and could continue to work if they wanted to, but would not be forced to. A world in which old age was a well-funded period of retirement and health, rather than one of anxiety and fear. Imagine a world in which older people had access to well-trained, well-paid home health aides to help them live at home or with their children until they needed institutionalization in a nursing home. Imagine a world in which nursing homes were not for-profit nightmare factories but safe and regulated spaces stocked with well-trained and well-paid nurses. This world would provide security to millions of older people and to the millions of people who care for them. As Maggie Kuhn, leader of the Gray Panthers, pointed out long ago, such a place would not only be good for older Americans. It would be good for the middle-aged Americans who love them. It would be good for the millions of Americans who are in the caregiving workforce. It would be good for the millions of younger Americans with disabilities who would benefit from improved accessibility. And it would be good for all Americans who are not yet sixty-five but hope to become old one day and might want something to look forward to.

This is a world worth fighting for, and one worth getting old in. And such a world is ours for the taking if we as a society are willing to spend the time and capital to build it. Many people have been working for a century to get us there. We have seen activists linking old age and civil rights; we have seen others fighting for people with disabilities and for nursing home regulation; we have seen others linking old age with ecological issues, seeking more green and nature-friendly kinds of aging. We have seen activists pushing for home health aides, and for stable jobs for care workers; we have seen people and movements goading the federal government into action. The story we've just read is an inspiring one; the tools that we need for a coherent, future-oriented politics of old age are lying right there in our past, ready to be picked up.

In closing, then, I'd like to offer a few lessons from the past that might guide that work, putting them in the context of the ways in which the country we call "old age" has changed since about 1990. The first major lesson is that, even and especially for old-age politics, social movements matter. In my lifetime, social movements have been understood as phenomena of the young. Historically, though, that has not been the case: old-age policy moved when older people mobilized as older people and forced politicians to act. The clearest case of this was in the 1930s, when millions of older Americans mobilized behind Francis Townsend's plan to provide them with generous pensions. That plan did not come to fruition, but it did put the issue of old-age pensions onto the map. The success of the Social Security program itself made older people into a political bloc to be reckoned with; they now had something to fight for, and the time and resources with which to do it. In the 1960s, the passage of Medicare was ensured by the vibrant activity of trade unions and the National Council of Senior Citizens. In the 1970s and 1980s, the Gray Panthers and the National Caucus on the Black Aged asked Americans to think more intersectionally and more radically about old age. The list could go on.[7]

A successful social movement requires some kind of coherent population to mobilize. The second major lesson of the book, therefore, is that progress on old-age politics happens when there is a population of people that identify as "old" and are willing to organize around that identity category. Social Security and Medicare were both born when policymakers and old-age activists had access to an ideal like that. Social Security was designed to help "the aged," understood as impoverished people older than sixty-five; Medicare was designed to help "senior citizens," understood as a sixty-five-plus population with health care needs and without easy access to health insurance. Those terms have fallen away in the past half century, along with the idea that the sixty-five-plus population represents a coherent group of people with shared interests. The new term of art is "older people," a term that is destigmatizing precisely because it does not refer to a specific population at all.

This lexical shift has mirrored a stagnation in the progress of old-age policy. In the era of "older people," American political culture lost its ability to have meaningful conversations about old age. If a pandemic had killed hundreds of thousands of senior citizens in the 1960s, it would have led to an outcry and to legislative action in their name. In the COVID-19 era, this has not happened, and at least one reason is that the identity category of "old age" has fizzled away. Insofar as it has survived, it has been pushed further and further along in the life course. If you're only as old as you feel, then the truly old are those who "feel" old—and that is the sick or frail. In 2018, the AARP published a blog post on ageist language, claiming that the term "elderly" was "not cool." "Let's reserve this word for the over-95 set, please." This was tongue-in-cheek, but it gave voice to a genuinely new sensibility that we've seen growing since the 1980s. As one geriatrician recently wrote, we tend to think of healthy older people as middle-aged, reserving "old" for those who are "ill, disabled, or almost dead." And if we restrict old age as a designation to only the most disenfranchised, it should be little surprise that old age remains a small priority for policymakers.[8]

To state the book's second major lesson in a slightly different way: older people might need to identify once again as old, and to recognize that they do in fact have some important things in common with one another. The third lesson is that this will not happen in the same way as it did in the past, nor should it. Previous articulations of old age as an identity were built upon a set of exclusions, mainly of people of color and people with disabilities. And they were built as well on an outdated and male-centric notion of the life course, linking old age to "retirement" or an exit from the workforce at around the mid-sixties.

This has been true at every step of the old-age movement, from the Fraternal Order of Eagles to the Townsend movement to the National Council of Senior Citizens to the AARP. There have been alternatives, like the Ex-Slave Mutual Relief, Bounty, and Pension Association, but they have been suppressed, ignored, or both.

A revived American identity for older people will have to be more inclusive. The older population of the future, after all, will be more diverse than ever before. The largest change will involve older Hispanic Americans. In 1980, seven hundred thousand of them were counted by the census, constituting 2.5 percent of the sixty-five-plus population. The Hispanic population as a whole, largely made up of recent immigrants, had a median age of twenty-three, more than seven years younger than the median white person. Those young immigrants have, of course, aged and changed the composition of the older American population. By 2019, the proportion of older people that identified as Hispanic Americans increased to 9 percent, and by 2060 it is projected to rise to 21 percent. Any coherent aging policy for the future will have to address this population, which has needs that are distinct from those of both their white and Black peers. In the 1980s and 1990s, when poverty was falling for older Black and white populations, it was *not* for older Hispanics, who were less likely than other populations to be receiving Social Security.[9]

Just as any twenty-first-century old-age movement worth the name will need to be racially diverse, it will need to include older people with disabilities. That population has been expanding rapidly for decades now and will continue to do so. Between 2023 and 2050, the eighty-five-plus population is set to *triple*. In a nation of unprecedented wealth and sophistication, this population is being ignored; in every town, even on every block, frail older people, often with dementia, are struggling to have their needs met. Their savings, and those of their families, are being decimated in an attempt to maintain a dignified life in a society intent on depriving them of one. Every day there are nearly three million Americans who need help with tasks of daily living but are unable to get it. And even beyond those clear-cut cases, many millions of older Americans—almost 40 percent of them—reported in 2020 that they had difficulty walking or climbing stairs. If a new identity for older people is created, it should recognize that older people with disabilities are not a class apart, and certainly not one to be feared.[10]

Furthermore, people with disabilities have been excluded from most policy decisions that have been made about American aging. Advocates have been working for decades to improve the image of older people—to demonstrate that they are more healthy and sexy and fun-loving than they are given credit for. That might be true, but the improving image of aging Americans has come at a cost. It has succeeded primarily by creating a new kind of exclusion: in AARP Nation, healthy people from their mid-fifties to mid-seventies are classed as "older people," or perhaps as the "young-old," while those older than seventy-five are reclassified as the "frail," or the "old-old." Think of how common it is for people to say some version of "When I'm that old, I hope you just shoot me." That horrifying commonplace has academic credentials: Ezekiel Emmanuel, a bioethicist, published an article in *The Atlantic* in 2014 to explain that he would rather die at the age of seventy-five than suffer the indignities of disability and decline.[11]

Caregivers have also been excluded from the old-age movement. Old-age advocates have only rarely associated themselves with the ongoing labor struggles of the home health workers and nurses who have cared for them. The discussion, inside and outside Congress, has more commonly been about elder abuse. While that problem is certainly real, it positions the already exploited caring workforce as a threat rather than an ally. It remains true that family members perform the bulk of the caregiving for the frail elderly, but the home health care industry has been growing rapidly. In the 1950s and 1960s, advocates like Ellen Winston hoped that home health care would be deployed en masse to keep older people from nursing homes. It took half a century, but something like that has in fact happened—perhaps not in the way Winston wanted. She called for well-regulated, state-provided care as part of the state welfare system. What emerged instead were loosely regulated, for-profit enterprises, sometimes paid for out of pocket and sometimes reimbursed by Medicare or Medicaid. From 1990 to 1997, public spending on home health care grew an astounding 20 percent per year, from $5 billion to $18 billion; throughout the twenty-first century, home health care has been one of the largest growth sectors in the entire US economy. Much of this growth was driven by chains, just as it was in the nursing home industry. And as in that industry, too, many of the jobs were low-paying, nonunionized, and held by women of color, many of them immigrants from the Global South. Often these women are paid under the table, thus setting them up not to receive the Social Security benefits they will need when they themselves get old.[12]

Although the long-term-care industry has evolved, the basic facts surrounding how it operates have not changed much since Winston's day. It remains poorly regulated and reliant on low-wage labor without opportunities for career advancement. Partly because the caregiving workforce has been so neglected and underpaid, it is too small. The industry is perpetually short staffed, and sky-high rates of turnover are as much the norm now as they were in 1980. The human costs have been immense, and even deadly. Studies carried out in the wake of COVID-19 have shown that lower-quality nursing homes did indeed have more deaths, because they lacked the technology and staff capacity to regularly test residents and quarantine those who had contracted the disease. Other recent studies have shown that increased immigration is an effective way to improve patient care, implying that anti-immigrant politics, surging in recent years, will negatively impact the care we can provide to our older population.[13]

The mainstream old-age movement has historically sidelined all these voices: people of color, people with disabilities, and their caregivers. This has been politically and morally disadvantageous, and it has also obscured the ways that the categories often overlap with one another. In 2011, an anthropologist interviewed a seventy-eight-year-old Filipina woman in Los Angeles named Letty, who had been doing eldercare work for decades. She was unable to retire because her employers were not paying, as they should have been, into her Social Security. For this reason, she was forced to continue working, in particular by caring for a woman in her nineties even though the work was too demanding for her (she had broken her femur on the job). Letty is precisely the kind of person who is becoming more common in our older population, and she is also the kind of person who has been excluded from the old-age movement.[14]

I offer these lessons less as a blueprint for future action than as a way to celebrate and identify work that is already happening. And it is happening. As I write, interesting and important advocacy is occurring around queer aging, incarcerated aging, immigrant aging, and more. Across the country, nurses and long-term caregivers are organizing into unions. As our diverse nation ages, we are perhaps on the cusp of a new old-age movement that could redefine, for us and our children, what it means to age and age well in the twenty-first century. In closing, and in lieu of an exhaustive exploration of the new landscape of old-age activism, I'd like to draw attention to ways in which the old-age movement is interfacing with two of the most important challenges of the twenty-first century: the crisis of the environment and the crisis of care.

Climate change, like population aging, will be an inescapable backdrop of human activity in the next century. They might seem like separate issues, but they aren't. For one thing, as we've already seen, the bodies of older people are on the front lines of environmental catastrophe. Moreover, as the population ages, a great deal will hinge on how carbon-heavy our response is. In many respects, the solutions thus far have relied on a good deal of carbon—remember the emphasis on senior citizens having access to their own cars and stand-alone homes. At the same time, a green thread has run through this book. Even if not always motivated by environmentalism in the strict sense, many of those dealing with old age have sought to reduce consumption and increase connections to nature. In the 1950 and 1960s, old age was imagined as a spartan period of life. It was often presumed that retirement would involve downsizing, either into trailers or into congregate living. Sometimes even retirement communities adopted green solutions: the Leisure World at Seal Beach was famous for its tricycles. Many seniors were encouraged to garden, both to produce food and to produce beauty. Olga Madar, one of the innovators of the senior center movement and the director of the United Auto Workers' Recreation Department, imagined new forms of leisure that would better the world and the self. "Leisure," she argued in 1968, "is more than the consumption of somebody else's project." Leisure is about creating the world, too—and when it comes to the natural world, preserving it. For her, leisure was something that primarily took place outside, so she encouraged UAW members young and old to use the outdoors, and to go camping, and to protect what she called "our living environment."[15]

In the United States, older people are increasingly engaged with these issues. Bill McKibben, one of America's most prominent climate activists, is pulling on this thread. In 2020, he turned sixty, and he cofounded a movement called Third Act. Older Americans, in his view, bear a great deal of responsibility for the climate crisis given the explosion of carbon emissions in their lifetimes, and they therefore bear a great deal of responsibility for addressing it. Historically speaking, what is interesting about the movement is that it attempts to build an identity for older Americans not around chronological age or biological need, but around historical experience and responsibility. "People over the age of 60," McKibben explains, "may have a deeper sense almost of anyone of how much change has come." Of course, as he is well aware, not everyone in that age bracket bears equal responsibility for the explosion in carbon emissions. All the same, Third Act provides a model for an age-based activism that does not rely on a stigmatizing account of who older people are.[16]

In the future, as in the past, environmentally conscious aging will not come about for environmental reasons alone. Consider the all-important issue of housing. After World War II, a consensus emerged that older people ought not to live together with younger relatives, and that intergenerational living was a lamentable relic of the past. Millions of older Americans ended up on their own, in stand-alone suburban homes. This came at a considerable cost in carbon (to heat and cool those homes, and to drive to and from them). The trend, though, seems to be reversing. Between 1971 and 2021, the percentage of Americans living in households with multiple adult generations more than doubled, from 7 percent to 18 percent. In an era of exploding housing costs and expensive childcare, this kind of household makes sense for millions of families. And indeed, multigenerational households are less likely to be impoverished than single-family ones. Sometimes this arrangement involves multiple generations living under the same roof; it can also involve the construction of aptly named "granny units" (or, more technically, accessory dwelling units, or ADUs). While some ADUs, of course, are being rented out for profit, many others are being used to house aging parents. The end result has the potential to be much more environmentally friendly than the alternative.[17]

Having grandparents close by is one solution to the second crisis I'd like to discuss in closing: the care crisis. Care can be understood capaciously as activities that are required to reproduce and sustain our social life, whether paid or unpaid. The current care crisis encompasses not just eldercare, but also childcare, care for people with disabilities, and even the educational and health care systems as a whole. All those systems have been stretched to the breaking point. The dismal working conditions for teachers, home health aides, and childcare workers have led to staffing shortages and low morale. COVID-19 demonstrated, for all who cared to see, just how precarious the American system of care really is—and how much it continues, in the last instance, to rely on the uncompensated and undervalued labor of women.[18]

Many activists we've met in this book labored to resolve this problem, especially by fighting for older Americans with disabilities. Ellen

Winston ran pilot programs to fund home health aides throughout North Carolina. She also led a national organization for home health workers, lobbying the government to include home health aides in the Medicare program. Brahna Trager called for an integrated federal infrastructure to fund and organize at-home care. Congressmen like Claude Pepper and Edward Roybal tried to make it a reality, and even the AARP backed their legislation. Maggie Kuhn and the Gray Panthers, in the 1970s and 1980s, participated in a struggle to increase the regulatory oversight of nursing homes and to provide better pay and working conditions for nursing home staff. Marie-Louise Ansak and William Gee, the founders of On Lok, leveraged Medicare and Medicaid funds to provide care specifically designed for older migrant communities.

If anyone is carrying their torch today, it is Ai-jen Poo, the founder of Caring Across Generations. Like her predecessors, she is a regular fixture at congressional hearings and is working to design legislation that might prepare our economy for its aging future. At root, Poo is a labor organizer, concerned with the rights and dignity of the millions of Americans who perform the care labor—childcare, eldercare, and more—that makes our world livable. In *The Age of Dignity* (2015), Poo imagined what she calls a Care Grid. The idea is that, using the power of the federal and state governments, a network of well-paid and well-trained home health care workers could fan across the nation, helping older Americans to live at home as long as possible—a situation that is more dignified than nursing homes, and which has the ancillary benefit of providing millions of good jobs.[19]

Both McKibben and Poo know that genuine resolutions to the intertwined problems of aging, climate, and care will require federal action. And this, perhaps, is the fourth major lesson of the book. Grassroots activists and experiments are important, but they will always be insufficient in the absence of aggressive state action. Senior centers and assisted-living facilities and nutrition programs have done a great deal for older Americans, to be sure, but they could only play their role against the backdrop of a Social Security system that provided income security. That system, though, has always been inequitable in some ways, and it is currently nearing a fiscal crisis. A humane response to twenty-first-century aging will almost necessarily involve a reform and expansion of Social Security. The legislation, in fact, has already been drafted: in both the House and the Senate, proposals have languished for years without coming up for a vote and without becoming a legislative priority. Different versions exist, more or less bold in scope, but at their best these bills promise to both repair and expand the system, paying larger benefits and providing credits for caregivers too.

Reason exists, therefore, to be optimistic as we wonder what aging might look like in our own future or in our children's. Despite the challenges of the past few decades, the story of American aging is all in all a hopeful one, and it is not naïve to hope that it might continue to be so. A reform of Social Security, along with more local experiments and vibrant activist movements like McKibben's and Poo's, would not solve every problem that America faces. But it would solve a large one, and it would provide a meaningful and dignified old age to generations of Americans, many of whom struggle to find meaning and dignity in other phases of their life.

That question of meaning and dignity has come up time and again in this book. It does so because old age is at once public and private. Population aging as a phenomenon can only be managed through enormous expenditures and a complicated regulatory apparatus. It will involve the state and the entire organization of our economy. At the same time, aging is also something that happens to each of our bodies and each of our organs in the most intimate of ways. Aging is something for us each to work out in our own lives, with our own families and friends and communities.

If this book has one argument, it's that those two spheres, the political and the personal, are closely linked. Our own aging will of course be shaped by the unique trajectory of our lives: by the bonds we formed or broke, the decisions we made or failed to, the jobs we had or lost.

That much is obvious—we feel it in our bones, and it's one reason why people face old age with such anxiety. What's less obvious is that our personal history is only part of the story and will only accrue meaning in a public context. Our aging will be equally shaped by the *social* apparatus of age, which will provide us or deny us income security, health security, and a set of cultural scripts about what it means to age and to age well in the twenty-first century.

This is why the stories we tell about old age matter so much. There is no "natural" way to age—we have to be taught, by our cultural and political and religious institutions, how to do it well. In closing, then, I'd like to return to my own experiences, which opened this book and which are hiding between the lines of any work of historical scholarship. In the Introduction, I recalled my childhood love of the Carousel of Progress, which presented to me a particular vision of what it meant to age, and how individual family stories would interface with broader national ones. It did this by telling the story of a middle-class, white family, showing how older people could be integrated into a family that remained essentially static even as the world around it changed. In a sense, this book can be read as a long commentary on the vision of the Carousel, which was first unveiled to the public in 1964. There was something powerful but ultimately flawed about the Carousel's vision of what old age could be. However important the work this vision did in its day, it is time now for something new.

My own children have never been to the Carousel; it is for them something so old that it likely would not even tickle their nostalgia. That is probably a good thing, but it's hard to tell which stories will stick with them as they begin to wonder what it means to age in America, and as they watch their parents enter that phase of life. They've had at least one experience, though, that I hope they do remember.

For holidays, in lieu of Disney World, we often go to Topsail Beach, just north of Wilmington, North Carolina. The last time we visited, roped-off nests of turtle eggs were being guarded by volunteers, many of them elderly. To the untrained eye, the volunteers were just sitting there, chatting amiably with each other and with anyone else strolling by. They were, however, doing a job for the Topsail Turtle Project, a nonprofit that is committed to restoring the turtle population in the mid-Atlantic. Their task was a simple one: make sure that nobody trampled the eggs, and should any baby turtles hatch on their watch, make sure the babies safely reached the ocean.

I don't know how struck my children were by the turtle project, but I certainly was, especially as we watched the volunteers man their posts hour after hour and day after day. Imagine: a beach full of volunteers, many but not all of them older than sixty-five, performing a public service simply by sitting, and waiting, and watching. Sentinels watching over the precious life teeming underground, and watching, too, the children laughing on the beach. Almost anyone can sit in a chair and watch for the stirrings of turtle eggs or listen to make sure that nobody disturbs them. All you need is time—the very stuff of old age, the resource that older people for decades have complained they possess too much of. Maybe, as my children grow up, this will be their image of aging. It's more public and more communal than the Carousel, representing both human community and community with other species. This, I think, is an image of aging more appropriate for the gray, hot century to come.

ACKNOWLEDGMENTS

This is a book about care, but it is also a product of care. My name is on the cover, but as any author knows, that's a convenient fiction. A book like this emerges from an institutional ecosystem, full of people who work harder than they have to. It's possible because I had people to educate my children and care for my health. While I cannot thank everyone who performed those kinds of care, I would like to single out the good people at George Watts Montessori School, especially Brittany Rothermel, Amanda Watson, and Sara Zopfi, and everyone else in the Durham Public School system who helped us to weather the pandemic. As is customary in acknowledgments, though, I will focus on a different network of care: the teachers and students and editors who cared enough to make this book possible.

Humanistic research is itself a form of care for our common world. And as with so many kinds of care today, it is under siege, as departments shutter and faculty lines become precarious. I have the extraordinary and undeserved privilege to be at a place, Duke University, that values this kind of work. *Golden Years* emerged from a thriving Department of History and a thriving interdisciplinary conversation about aging. John Martin, Simon Partner, and Sumathi Ramaswamy have been exemplary chairs, helping me find the time and space to research. Malachi Hacohen, fellow director of the Triangle Intellectual History Seminar, has been my model for intellectual probity. Phil Stern texted me through the crisis in the humanities, and with Nicole Barnes

I've shared the joys and sorrows of teaching and learning with young children in tow. Calvin Cheung-Miaw and Cecilia Márquez have been co-instructors, and I've learned as much from them as our students have. Nancy MacLean has been an exemplary senior colleague and stalwart committee partner and has been incredibly generous with her time and knowledge over the years. Ed Balleisen has been a mentor, helping me to summon the courage to tackle a book project far removed, in space if not in spirit, from my first. Jamie Hardy, Craig Kolman, Robin Pridgen, and Julie Talton, among others, have made the department a joy to work in. On the gerontological side of campus, I'm grateful to Harvey Cohen, Lisa Dwyther, Linda George, Deborah Gold, and Heather Whitson for sharing their resources and knowledge. The Josiah Trent Memorial Foundation has provided funding for research assistants. As with any book of historical scholarship, it would not have been possible without the aid of librarians and archivists, dozens of whom helped me with issues large and small. I would like to especially single out Carson Holloway, Kelly Lawton, and Heidi Madden.

Thanks to two children and one pandemic, I have not traveled much in the past few years. I am grateful, then, that I've found such a receptive audience for the work here at Duke, where I've presented at the Trent Center for Bioethics, Humanities and the History of Medicine, the Department of History, the Franklin Humanities Institute, and the Center for the Study of Aging and Human Development. The history department also sponsored a manuscript workshop, and I am deeply grateful to Corinne Field, Nancy MacLean, Gabriel Rosenberg, Robert Self, and Katherine Turk for taking the time to read a full-draft manuscript and give me indispensable feedback.

Teaching, too, is a form of care, a reciprocal one that redounds as much to the teacher's benefit as to the students'. I'm grateful to all the students I've had over the years I spent writing this book. To the extent that this book is at all lucid, it's because I've spent so many hours with you, figuring out how to communicate ideas clearly and cut through the jargon (and to the extent that it's not lucid, it's not your fault). I am especially grateful to my students at the Federal Correctional Complex, Butner, who reminded me what the humanities can mean to people. The most direct contributions have come from the students who have worked for me as research assistants. Erin Greig, Elaijah Lapay, and Melody Gao all worked with me in one memorable summer when this book was truly taking shape (find yourselves in the endnotes!). Brett Adams performed some heroic, late-stage archival research. I also had a team that helped me research the life and times of Jacquelyne Jackson: Madison Butler, Faith Caesar, Della Crawford, Nikhil Gadiraju, and Camille Krejdovsky.

Many institutions outside of Duke lent support too. The team at Basic Books has been a dream to work with. Many thanks to Brian Distelberg for believing in this project from the beginning, and to Kelley Blewster, Alex Cullina, Angela Messina, and Brandon Proia for shepherding it to completion and publicizing the end result. The National Humanities Center provided an idyllic semester for me to think through this project in its earliest stages. I am grateful to Mary Bethel, Richard Fiesta, Paul Merriman, Jack Rowe, Dennis Street, and Rick Zawadski for agreeing to be interviewed. I am grateful as well to organizers and audiences for talks or presentations at the Carolina Labor Seminar, the Columbia Seminar for International History, the National Humanities Center, the Social Science History Association, and the Organization of American Historians' Annual Conference. At a crucial stage in the research, Corinne Field and Nicholas Syrett organized an online miniconference on aging, sponsored by the American Historical Association. Paul Renfro and Carole Haber generously gave feedback on an early version of Chapter 1. Edward Berkowitz lent his enormous expertise to the chapters on Social Security and Medicare. The very first presentation of any of this material was in 2015, at the Mellon Biennial Conference of what was then called ISERP, at Columbia University, where a startling combination of interest and skepticism convinced me that I had to pursue the theme. I am still a Columbia

ACKNOWLEDGMENTS

student at heart, so I can't miss an opportunity to thank Bill McAllister, Samuel Moyn, and Susan Pedersen for their continued example.

This is also a book about family—about what it means, and what it could mean, and the ways that families have been asked to do too much. Some of my interest in these themes is ancestral. My grandfather, the original James Chappel, worked in the pensions department at Gulf Oil. Joanne and Gary Chappel, following a well-worn path described in the book, left the Rust Belt for the Sun Belt and waited in line with me at the Carousel of Progress. Bethany, my wife, has lived with this project almost as much as I have—thank you for everything that you've given to this book, both emotionally and intellectually. And, last but not least, thank you to my children, Oscar and Margot. Even as I've spent my days buried in dusty retirement guides, it's been through them that I've been reminded, every morning at five-thirty, of the glory and the tragedy of getting older. My last book was about Christianity, the religion of the son, and was dedicated to Oscar. This book is much more about daughters and their labors of love. So, Margot: a few hours before I sat down to write these acknowledgments, you told me that you wouldn't read this book because it is too boring and does not have any pictures (for context, you are currently five). I hope, though, that you will one day. There is a lot of your dad in this book, and one of the thrills of growing up is finding pieces of your parents in the things they left behind. The book grew up with you, in a period that I'll always think of as my own golden years. It is for you.

NOTES

INTRODUCTION: A CAROUSEL OF PROGRESS

1. AARP and National Geographic, *Second Half of Life Study* (June 2022), 6, www.aarp.org/content/dam/aarp/research/surveys_statistics/life-leisure/2022/second-half-life-desires-concerns-report.doi.10.26419-2Fres.00538.001.pdf.

2. Renee Stepler, "Smaller Share of Women Aged 65 and Older Are Living Alone," Pew Research Center, February 18, 2016, www.pewresearch.org/social-trends/2016/02/18/smaller-share-of-women-ages-65-and-older-are-living-alone/; Calarco quoted in Anne Helen Peterson, "Other Countries Have Social Safety Nets. The U.S. Has Women," *Culture Study* (November 2020), https://annehelen.substack.com/p/other-countries-have-social-safety.

3. James Chappel, "The Frozen Politics of Social Security," *Boston Review*, February 2023, www.bostonreview.net/articles/the-frozen-politics-of-social-security/. Also see the books reviewed therein.

4. Vincanne Adams et al., "Aging Disaster: Mortality, Vulnerability, and Long-Term Recovery Among Katrina Survivors," *Medical Anthropology* 30 (2011): 247–270; CDC, "Deaths by Select Demographic and Geographic Characteristics," data current as of August 2, 2023, www.cdc.gov/nchs/nvss/vsrr/covid_weekly/index.htm.

5. Administration for Community Living, *2020 Profile of Older Americans* (May 2021), 4, https://acl.gov/sites/default/files/Aging%20and%20Disability%20in%20America/2020ProfileOlderAmericans.Final_.pdf; also see statistics from Argentum, *The Senior Living Employee* (2018), www.argentum.org/wp-content/uploads/2018/05/Senior-Living-Resident-Profile-WhitePaper.pdf.

6. "Over the Past Century," *The Economist* Daily Chart, May 20, 2021, www.economist.com/graphic-detail/2021/05/20/over-the-past-century-african-american-life-expectancy-and-education-levels-have-soared; Administration for Community Living, *2020 Profile of Older Americans*, 7.

7. National Women's Law Center, "Supporting the Economic Security and Health of Older Women of Color," September 2021, https://nwlc.org/resource

/supporting-the-economic-security-and-health-of-older-women-of-color/; Anaïs Goubert, Julie Can, Eileen Appelbaum, "Home Health Care," Center for Economic and Policy Research, October 27, 2021, https://cepr.net/home-health -care-latinx-and-black-women-are-overrepresented-but-all-women-face -heightened-risk-of-poverty/.

8. "Older People Projected to Outnumber Children," US Census Bureau, March 2018, www.census.gov/newsroom/press-releases/2018/cb18-41-population -projections.html.

CHAPTER 1: WHO GETS TO GET OLD?

1. Compare coverage in "Needed an Old-Age Pension," *The Eagle*, September 1922, 31; "Old and Homeless Man Ends His Life," *Lawrence Daily Journal*, July 18, 1922, 1; and "The Aged Suicide Was a Wanderer," *Lawrence Daily Journal-World*, July 20, 1922, 1.

2. This is not to say that Americans were not thinking about longevity at all—only that they were not demarcating "old age" as a particular phase of life deserving of social support. See, above all, Andrew Achenbaum, *Old Age in the New Land: The American Experience Since 1790* (Baltimore, MD: Johns Hopkins University Press, 1978); Thomas Cole, *The Journey of Life: A Cultural History of Aging in America* (New York: Cambridge University Press, 1992).

3. Robin Bernstein, *Racial Innocence: Performing Childhood and Race from Slavery to Civil Rights* (New York: New York University Press, 2011); Shelley Sallee, *The Whiteness of Child Labor Reform in the New South* (Athens: University of Georgia Press, 2004).

4. Lamar Beman, ed., *Selected Articles on Old-Age Pensions* (New York: H. W. Wilson, 1927), 246.

5. Alice Kessler-Harris, *In Pursuit of Equity: Women, Men, and the Quest for Economic Citizenship in Twentieth-Century America* (New York: Oxford University Press, 2001), 43, and chap. 1 more generally on this phenomenon; Jean Collier Brown, *The Negro Woman Worker* (Washington, DC: Government Printing Office, 1938), 2 for 1930 numbers. See also Evelyn Nakano Glenn, *Forced to Care: Coercion and Caregiving in America* (Cambridge, MA: Harvard University Press, 2010).

6. Age data from US Census, 1850, xlii–xliv, www.census.gov/library /publications/1853/dec/1850a.html; life expectancy at thirty from Steven Ruggles, "The Transformation of American Family Structure," *American Historical Review* 99 (1994): 111.

7. Steven Ruggles, "The Decline of Intergenerational Coresidence in the United States, 1850 to 1900," *American Sociological Review* 72 (2007): 964–989; Ruggles, "Transformation," 112.

8. US Census, 1850, xlii–xliv; Peter Uhlenberg, "Mortality Decline in the

Twentieth Century and Supply of Kin Over the Life Course," *The Gerontologist* 36 (1996): 681–685.

9. These statistics about labor participation rates collate the population size of the two age cohorts from US Census, 1930, vol. 2, p. 567, www.census .gov/library/publications/1933/dec/1930a-vol-02-population.html, with the percentage in the workforce of those same groups as reported in US Census, 1930, vol. 4, p. 42, www.census.gov/library/publications/1933/dec/1930a-vol-04 -occupations.html. On different sectors of the economy, and sixty-five-plus participation therein, see US Census, 1930, vol. 5, chap. 4, table 3, www.census .gov/library/publications/1933/dec/1930a-vol-05-occupations.html.

10. Brian Gratton, "The Poverty of Impoverishment Theory: The Economic Well-Being of the Elderly, 1890–1950," *Journal of Economic History* 56 (1996): 39–61; on voluntarily leaving the workforce, Susan Carter and Richard Sutch, "Myth of the Industrial Scrap Heap: A Revisionist View of Turn-of-the Century American Retirement," *Journal of Economic History* 56 (1996): 5–38; on pensions, Brian Gratton and Carole Haber, *Old Age and the Search for Security: An American Social History* (Bloomington: Indiana University Press, 1994), 72; on inheritance, Hendrik Hartog, *Someday This Will All Be Yours: A History of Inheritance and Old Age* (Cambridge, MA: Harvard University Press, 2012); US Census, 1930, vol. 5, chap. 4, table 9.

11. For this account, "Making a Home on a Farm," *Ladies' Home Journal*, September 1920, 132. On this phenomenon more broadly, see Leon Edgar Truesdell, *Farm Population of the United States* (Washington, DC: US Government Printing Office, 1926), 70–74. See also Carole Haber, "Old Age Through the Lens of Family History," in *Handbook of Aging and the Social Sciences*, 6th ed., ed. Robert Binstock et al. (Burlington, MA: Elsevier, 2006), 69–70.

12. Mabel Nassau, *Old Age Poverty in Greenwich Village: A Neighborhood Study* (New York: Fleming H. Revell, 1915), 27–28.

13. Abraham Epstein, *Facing Old Age: A Study of Old Age Dependency in the United States and Old Age Pensions* (New York: Knopf, 1922), 51–58; Gratton and Haber, *Old Age and the Search for Security*, 117–122.

14. Dea Boster, *African American Slavery and Disability: Bodies, Property and Power in the Antebellum South, 1800–1860* (New York: Routledge, 2012), 65–66; Nathaniel Windon, "Superannuated: Old Age on the Antebellum Plantation," *American Quarterly* 71 (2019): 767–787; Leslie Pollard, *Complaint to the Lord: Historical Perspectives on the African American Elderly* (Selinsgrove, PA: Susquehanna University Press, 1996), chap. 1; Savannah Williamson, "The Maintenance of Aged Property: Healthcare and Medicine of Elderly Slaves in the Antebellum Period," *Ageless Arts: The Journal of the Southern Association for the History of Medicine and Science* 1 (2015): 63; Frederick Douglass, *Narrative*

of the Life of Frederick Douglass, an American Slave (Boston: Anti-Slavery Office, 1847), 47–48.

15. *Slave Narratives: Typewritten Records Prepared by the Federal Writers' Project, 1936–1938* (Washington, DC, 1941), vol. 11, part 1, 131; vol. 11, part 2, 28–29.

16. The classic analysis of age consciousness remains Howard Chudacoff, *How Old Are You? Age Consciousness in American Culture* (Princeton, NJ: Princeton University Press, 1992); for an overview of this discussion of the life course, see Martin Kohli, "The Institutionalization of the Lifecourse: Looking Back to Look Ahead," *Research in Human Development* 4 (2007): 253–271.

17. Karl Marx, *Capital*, vol. 1, trans. Ben Fowkes (New York: Penguin, 1976), 376; George M. Beard, *American Nervousness* (New York: Putnam, 1881), 230.

18. Theda Skocpol, *Protecting Soldiers and Mothers: The Political Origins of Social Policy in the United States* (Cambridge, MA: Harvard University Press, 1995), 109, 132.

19. Skocpol, *Protecting Soldiers and Mothers*, 148–150 and chap. 4 for trade unions and social insurance legislation; Theron Schlabach, *Rationality and Welfare: Public Discussion of Poverty and Social Insurance in the United States, 1875–1935* (SSA Report, 1969), chap. 6, www.ssa.gov/history/reports /schlabach6.html; "Socialist Party Platform of 1912," Ohio State University Dept. of History, accessed February 12, 2024, https://ehistory.osu.edu/exhibitions /1912/1912documents/socialis.

20. Walter Raleigh Vaughan, *Vaughan's "Freedmen's Pension Bill"* (Omaha, NE: apparently self-published, 1890), 8, https://babel.hathitrust.org/cgi/pt?id =emu.010002407274&seq=1.

21. Tubman's case reported in James Yerrinton, "The Fourth at Framingham," *The Liberator*, July 8, 1859, 107; Du Bois quoted in Linda Gordon, "Black and White Visions of Welfare: Women's Welfare Activism, 1890–1945," *Journal of American History* 78 (1991): 566. On Tubman and Truth, see Corinne Field, "Old-Age Justice and Black Feminist History: Sojourner Truth and Harriet Tubman's Intersectional Legacies," *Radical History Review* 139 (2021): 137–151.

22. Vaughan, *Vaughan's "Freedmen's Pension Bill,"* 58 (defiance), 39 (details of the bill), 44 (wildfire).

23. Mary Frances Berry, *My Face Is Black Is True: Callie House and the Struggle for Ex-Slave Reparations* (New York: Knopf, 2009), 254 for the quotation. This book is the definitive account of House and her movement.

24. "A Letter by A. Scales and a Song," included in "Constitution and By-Laws of the Ex-Slave Pension Association" (1896), available in a microfilm called *Correspondence and Case Files of the Bureau of Pensions Pertaining to the Ex-Slave Pension Movement* (Washington, DC: National Archives and Records Administration, 2006).

25. Berry, *My Face Is Black Is True*, 124.

26. Marcus G. Harvey, "The Cultural Significance of Old Age in the American South, 1830–1900" (PhD diss., University of Florida, 2001), 35–40; John Calhoun, *The Works of John C. Calhoun*, vol. 2 (New York: D. Appleton, 1855), 632; James Shannon, *An Address Delivered Before the Pro-Slavery Convention of the State of Missouri on Domestic Slavery* (St. Louis: Republican Book and Job Office, 1855), 16.

27. George Fitzhugh, *Sociology for the South: or, the Failure of a Free Society* (Richmond: A. Morris, 1854), 68 (want), 38 (overtake), 243 (cellar). For another example of him making this case, see George Fitzhugh, "Mr. Bancroft's History and the 'Inner Light,'" *De Bow's Review* 29 (1860): 612.

28. Nathaniel Windon, "A Tale of Two Uncles: The Old Age of Uncle Tom and Uncle Remus," *Commonplace: The Journal of Early American Life* 17, no. 2 (Winter 2017), http://commonplace.online/article/a-tale-of-two-uncles/.

29. Lee Welling Squier, *Old Age Dependency in the United States: A Complete Survey* (New York: Macmillan, 1912), 7, 295; for data on Massachusetts's rurality: US Census, 1910, Massachusetts Supplement, p. 571, www2.census.gov /library/publications/decennial/1910/abstract/supplement-ma.pdf; for its racial breakdown as well as Pennsylvania's, see Charles Hall, *Negroes in the United States, 1920–1932* (Washington, DC: Government Printing Office, 1935), 15.

30. Epstein, *Facing Old Age*, 2.

31. "Eagles' President in Patriotic Talk," *Fort Wayne Journal-Gazette*, April 16, 1921, 2.

32. Frank Hering, "Ready, Let's Go!," *The Eagle*, February 1922, 5.

33. Hering, "Ready, Let's Go!"; "Who Are the Aged?," *The Eagle*, July 1922, 7, 24.

34. *Journal of the Proceedings of the Eighth Annual Session of Grand Aerie Fraternal Order of Eagles* (Leavenworth, KS: Dodsworth Book Co., 1906), 401; "The Social Whirl," *The Eagle*, May 1920, 28; *Proceedings of the First Annual Session of the Grand Aerie, Fraternal Order of Eagles* (Seattle: Mensing-Muchmore, 1899), 29, 512–513; *The Eagle*, December 1922, 7; Frank Hering et al., *The Report of the Committee Appointed to Investigate the Question of Old Age Pensions* (Indianapolis, February 1925), 2.

35. "An Old-Age Pension League," *The Eagle*, May 1922, 7–8, 24.

36. US Census, 1930, vol. 2, p. 580.

37. On the myth, see Micki McElya, *Clinging to Mammy: The Faithful Slave in Twentieth-Century America* (Cambridge, MA: Harvard University Press, 2017). On the reality, see Thavolia Glymph, *Out of the House of Bondage: The Transformation of the Plantation Household* (New York: Cambridge University Press, 2008).

38. "Getting Tired of Mammy," *Answers*, April 1, 1922, 1.

39. O. Henry, "A Municipal Report," *The Eagle*, December 1922, 9.

CHAPTER 2: SOCIAL SECURITY AND ITS LIMITS

1. For information on Fuller and her payments, see Wilson Ring, "Meet Ida May Fuller," *Knoxville Sentinel*, February 1, 2015, 33; Ray Bender and Phil O'Brien, "Our First Claimant," *Oasis*, August 1955, 7, www.ssa.gov/history oasis/august1955.pdf.

2. Kathleen Romig, "Social Security Lifts More People Above the Poverty Line Than Any Other Program," Center on Budget and Policy Priorities, last updated January 31, 2024, www.cbpp.org/research/social-security/.

3. On the construction of youth in this era, see Paula Fass, *The Damned and the Beautiful: American Youth in the 1920s* (New York: Oxford University Press, 1977); Sarah Chinn, *Inventing Modern Adolescence: The Children of Immigrants in Turn-of-the-Century America* (New Brunswick, NJ: Rutgers University Press, 2009).

4. Andrew G. Biggs, Mark A. Sarney, and Chrisopher R. Tamborini, *A Progressivity Index for Social Security* (Social Security Office of Retirement and Disability Policy, January 2009), www.ssa.gov/policy/docs/issuepapers/ip2009 -01.html.

5. Edward D. Berkowitz, *Making Social Welfare Policy in America: Three Case Studies Since 1950* (Chicago: University of Chicago Press, 2020), 6.

6. Franklin D. Roosevelt, 1932 DNC Acceptance Speech, www.fdrlibrary .org/documents/356632/390886/1932+DNC+Acceptance+Speech.pdf/066093f1 -bab8-48a8-81b5-65ed8c000f89; Roosevelt's 1933 inaugural address, https:// avalon.law.yale.edu/20th_century/froos1.asp.

7. *Report of the Committee on Economic Security* (January 1935), www.ssa .gov/history/reports/ces5.html; statistician quoted in Brian Gratton, "The Politics of Dependency Estimates: Social Security Board Statistics, 1935–1939," *Journal of Gerontology Series B* 52 (1997): 121.

8. *Old-Age Pensions: Hearings Before the Subcommittee of the Committee on Pensions, US Senate*, February 24, 1931 (Washington, DC: Government Printing Office, 1931), 156; *Public Papers of the Presidents: Franklin D. Roosevelt*, vol. 9 (Washington, DC: Government Printing Office, 1940), 209; the text of the bill is available in *Old-Age Pensions: Hearings Before the Committee on Labor*, House of Representatives, 71st Cong., February 20, 21, and 28, 1930 (Washington, DC: Government Printing Office, 1930), 339–343.

9. Alan Brinkley, *Voices of Protest: Huey Long, Father Coughlin, and the Great Depression* (New York: Vintage, 1983); "Text of the Lundeen Bill," *New York Times*, March 9, 1935, 8.

10. Steven Bret Burg, "The Gray Crusade: The Townsend Movement, Old Age Politics, and the Development of Social Security" (PhD diss., University of Wisconsin–Madison, 1999), 62–67.

11. Edwin Amenta, *When Movements Matter: The Townsend Plan and the Rise of Social Security* (Princeton, NJ: Princeton University Press, 2008), 37.

12. Amenta, *When Movements Matter*, 116; "Negro Townsend Club to Be Organized," *Omaha Guide*, January 21, 1939, 4.

13. Burg, "The Gray Crusade," 220–221; US Census, 1940, vol. 1, www .census.gov/library/publications/1942/dec/population-vol-1.html, 1165; "Negro Townsend Club Play to Be Held at School," *Stockton Evening and Sunday Record*, March 27, 1936, 15.

14. Edwin Amenta thinks that some version of the Townsend Plan actually could have worked, in some ways better than Social Security. Amenta, *When Movements Matter*, 91.

15. I. N. Love, "The Needs and Rights of Old Age," *Journal of the American Medical Association* 29, no. 21 (November 20, 1897): 1033–1039.

16. "Chelan Man Spends $82 First Day in Novel Test of Townsend Plan," *New York Times*, January 19, 1937, 25.

17. Edward Bellamy, *Looking Backward* (Bedford, MA: Applewood Books, 2000), chap. 21 on youth, chap. 18 on old age; Burg, "The Gray Crusade," 73 on Townsend and Bellamy.

18. These quotations taken from Amenta, *When Movements Matter*, 44.

19. Linda Gordon, *Pitied but Not Entitled: Single Mothers and the History of Welfare 1890–1935* (Cambridge, MA: Harvard University Press, 1998), 160; the sociologist Abraham Epstein loathed both the Fraternal Order of Eagles and the Townsend movement. See also Arthur Altmeyer, *The Formative Years of Social Security* (Madison: University of Wisconsin Press, 1966), esp. 32–33; Edwin Witte, *The Development of the Social Security Act* (Madison: University of Wisconsin Press, 1962), 85–86.

20. Lee Welling Squier, *Old Age Dependency in the United States: A Complete Survey* (New York: Macmillan, 1912); Abraham Epstein, *Facing Old Age: A Study of Old Age Dependency in the United States and Old Age Pensions* (New York: Knopf, 1922); John Lewis Gillin, *Poverty and Dependency* (New York: Century Co., 1925 [1921]), 18–20. It is sometimes argued that Social Security was meant to address unemployment by shrinking the labor force. This may be true, but the evidence is scant; the Committee on Economic Security did not mention it in their lengthy report to the president.

21. Both quoted in Gabriel Winant, "The Natural Profits of Their Years of Labor: Mass Production, Family, and the Politics of Old Age," *Radical History Review* 139 (2021): 84.

22. *Old Age Security Progress* (New York: American Association for Old Age Security, 1930), 2, 6–7. For a similar argument made the following year, see J. Prentice Murphy, "Dependency in Old Age," *Annals of the American Academy of Political and Social Science* 154 (March 1931): 39. For anecdotal reports on this, see Ruth Ray, "Studying the 'Burden' of Age: The Work of the Hannan Archival Research Group," in *Nobody's Burden: Lessons from the Great Depression on the*

Struggle for Old-Age Security, ed. Ruth Ray (Lanham, MD: Lexington Books, 2011).

23. *Report of the Committee on Economic Security*; Committee on Economic Security, *Social Security in America* (Washington, DC: Social Security Board, 1937), 137–138.

24. Cybelle Fox, *Three Worlds of Relief: Race, Immigration, and the American Welfare State from the Progressive Era to the New Deal* (Princeton, NJ: Princeton University Press, 2012); Gregori Galofré-Vilà, Martin McKee, and David Stucker, "Quantifying the Mortality Impact of the 1935 Old-Age Assistance," *European Review of Economic History* 26 (2022): 62–77; "Discussion," in *The Care of the Aged*, ed. Isaac Rubinow (Chicago: University of Chicago Press, 1930), 51.

25. Abraham Epstein, "Our Social Security Act," *Harper's*, December 1, 1935, 55–67.

26. Mary Poole, *The Segregated Origins of Social Security* (Chapel Hill: University of North Carolina Press, 2006).

27. Gordon, *Pitied but Not Entitled*, chap. 4; Alice Kessler-Harris, *In Pursuit of Equity: Women, Men, and the Quest for Economic Citizenship in Twentieth-Century America* (New York: Oxford University Press, 2001), chaps. 2–3 on gender and Social Security generally, 137 for this quotation; Lenore E. Bixby, "Women and Social Security in the United States," *Social Security Bulletin* (September 1972): 3–11, here 4, 9.

28. Poole, *The Segregated Origins of Social Security*, 25; Epstein, "Our Social Security Act," 60–61.

29. "Social Security Act Registration Complicated by Puzzling Queries," *Atlanta Constitution*, December 6, 1936, 8A; Robert Quillen, "Social Security," *Atlanta Constitution*, July 9, 1945, 6; John M. Blair, "Of Social Security," *Washington Post*, March 26, 1939, B6; Michael E. Schiltz, *Public Attitudes Toward Social Security, 1935–1965* (Washington, DC: US Social Security Administration, 1970), 82–87.

30. On the congressional politics of the era, see above all Ira Katznelson, *Fear Itself: The New Deal and the Origins of Our Time* (New York: W. W. Norton, 2013); Dorcas Hardy, "Don't Rely Strictly on Social Security," *Chicago Sun-Times*, July 25, 1989, 22; for a more recent example, Amity Shlaes, "Fixing Social Security the FDR Way," *Washington Post*, November 26, 2007, A15; on the New Deal and capitalism, David Kennedy, *Freedom from Fear: The American People in Depression and War, 1929–1945* (New York: Oxford University Press, 1999), chap. 12.

31. Franklin Roosevelt, "Governor's Annual Message," January 7, 1931, in *Department Reports of the State of New York*, vol. 40 (Albany: J. B. Lyon, 1931), 4; Edwin Witte, "America's Old Age Problem," Committee on Economic Security Staff Report (1935), www.ssa.gov/history/reports/ces/ces2witte1.html.

32. Barbara Nachtrieb Armstrong, *Insuring the Essentials* (New York:

Macmillan, 1932), 436–437; Committee on Economic Security, *Social Security in America*, 137; Sheldon Garon, *Beyond Our Means: Why America Spends While the World Saves* (Princeton, NJ: Princeton University Press, 2012), 240–241.

33. Schiltz, *Public Attitudes*, 57.

CHAPTER 3: MEDICARE AND THE INDEPENDENT SENIOR CITIZEN

1. Ronald Kotulak, "Slow Start for Medicare," *Chicago Tribune*, July 2, 1966, 1–2.

2. Bill Bird, "Naperville Woman Country's First Medicare Recipient," *Chicago Tribune*, July 2, 2016, www.chicagotribune.com/suburbs/naperville-sun /ct-nvs-naperville-edward-medicare-anniversary-st-0703-20160701-story.html; *The Budget of the United States Government: Fiscal Year 1970* (Washington, DC: US Government Printing Office, 1969), 27. For projections on all of this, see "Status of the Social Security and Medicare Programs: A Summary of the 2023 Annual Reports," Social Security Administration, accessed February 13, 2024, www.ssa.gov/oact/trsum/.

3. Jason Roe, "From the Impoverished to the Entitled: The Experience and Meaning of Old Age in America Since the 1950s" (PhD diss., University of Kansas, 2012), 35.

4. This paragraph is based on Google Ngrams for those phrases as of July 14, 2023.

5. US Department of Health, Education and Welfare, *Opportunities for Older Americans: A Guide for Senior Citizens Month May 1964* (1964), 3, 5–6.

6. Gabriel Winant, *The Next Shift: The Fall of Industry and the Rise of Health Care in Rust Belt America* (Cambridge, MA: Harvard University Press, 2021), esp. chap. 4.

7. Marvin Sussman, "The Isolated Nuclear Family: Fact or Fiction," *Social Problems* 6 (1958–1959): 333–339; Steven Ruggles, "The Decline of Intergenerational Coresidence in the United States, 1850 to 1900," *American Sociological Review* 72 (2007): fig. 1; Mitra Toossi, "A Century of Change: The U.S. Labor Force, 1950–2050," *Monthly Labor Review* 125 (2002): table 4; US Census Bureau, *Subject Report: Employment Status and Work Experience* (September 1963), 16, www.census.gov/library/publications/1963/dec/population-pc-2-6a .html.

8. "Ratio of Covered Workers to Beneficiaries, 1940–2013," Social Security Administration, accessed March 15, 2024, www.ssa.gov/history/ratios.html; Lenore E. Epstein, "The Aged in the Population in 1960 and Their Income Sources," *Social Security Bulletin* (July 1961): table 6; Andrea Louise Campbell, *How Policies Make Citizens: Senior Political Activism and the American Welfare State* (Princeton, NJ: Princeton University Press, 2005), 18; 1945 number from

Alfred M. Skolnik, "Private Pension Plans, 1950–74," *Social Security Bulletin* (June 1976): 4; 1975 number from US Department of Labor, *Private Pension Plan Bulletin: Historical Tables and Graphs, 1975–2020* (October 2022), 5, www.dol .gov/sites/dolgov/files/ebsa/researchers/statistics/retirement-bulletins/private -pension-plan-bulletin-historical-tables-and-graphs.pdf. For an excellent analysis of postwar pension politics and the ways in which they signaled a defeat for labor, see Michael McCarthy, *Dismantling Solidarity: Capitalist Politics and American Pensions Since the New Deal* (Ithaca, NY: Cornell University Press, 2017).

9. On median incomes, Reynolds Farley and Albert Hermalin, "The 1960s: A Decade of Progress for Blacks?" *Demography* 9 (1972): 356; on benefits, Gayle B. Thompson, "Blacks and Social Security Benefits: Trends, 1960–1973," *Social Security Bulletin* (April 1975): tables 1 and 4 (collated with US Census Bureau, *Supplemental Report on Age* [September 1961], table on p. 2, www.census.gov /library/publications/1961/dec/pc-s1-11.html; by "beneficiaries" here, I mean old-age insurance beneficiaries, not including disability or survivors' benefits); Gayle Thompson, "Black-White Differences in Private Pensions: Findings from the Retirement History Study," *Social Security Bulletin* 42 (1979): table 1; Shirlene Gray, "Old-Age Assistance Recipients in 1965," *Welfare in Review* 7 (1969): 11.

10. Stephen Vider, *The Queerness of Home: Gender, Sexuality, and the Politics of Domesticity After World War II* (Chicago: University of Chicago Press, 2021); Amanda H. Littauer, "Sexual Minorities at the Apex of Heteronormativity (1940s–65)," in *Routledge History of Queer America*, ed. Don Romesburg (New York: Routledge, 2018), 67–81.

11. Elaine Tyler May opens her classic *Homeward Bound: American Families in the Cold War Era*, rev. ed. (New York: Basic Books, 2017), with a discussion of bomb shelters and the family; Betty Carrollton, "Grandma's Pantry Can Save Lives," *Atlanta Constitution*, November 7, 1955, 18.

12. Belle Beard, "Are the Aged Ex-Family?," *Social Forces* 27 (1948): 274–280, here 275; Willard Waller, *The Family: A Dynamic Interpretation*, rev. Reuben Hill (New York: Dryden Press, 1951), 9 ("ideal"), 17 (phases), 447 ("psychological").

13. Talcott Parsons and Robert F. Bales, *Family, Socialization and Interaction Process* (New York: Free Press, 1955), 9; Norman W. Bell and Ezra F. Vogel, "Toward a Framework for Functional Analysis of Family Behavior," in *A Modern Introduction to the Family*, ed. Bell and Vogel (New York: Free Press, 1960), 6; David Riesman (with Nathan Glazer and Reuel Denney), *The Lonely Crowd* (New Haven, CT: Yale University Press, 1950), 57.

14. Kathleen Otis, "Everything Old Is New Again: A Social and Cultural History of Life on the Retirement Frontier, 1950–2000" (PhD diss., University of North Carolina at Chapel Hill, 2008), 191–193; Hermann Vollmer,

"The Grandmother: A Problem in Child-Rearing," *American Journal of Orthopsychiatry* 7 (1937): 378–382.

15. Ernst Rappaport, "The Grandparent Syndrome," *Psychoanalytic Quarterly* 27 (1958): 518–538.

16. Laura Curran, "The Psychology of Poverty: Professional Social Work and Aid to Dependent Children in Postwar America, 1946–63," *Social Service Review* 76 (2002): 365–386; Margaret B. Ryder, "Case Work with the Aged Parent and His Adult Children," *The Family* 26 (1945): 243–250, 243; Bertha Borden, "The Role of Grandparents in Children's Behavior Problems," dissertation abstract, *Smith College Studies in Social Work* 17 (1946): 115–116, 116; William Posner, "Casework with the Aged: Developments and Trends," in *Social Work Education for Better Services to the Aging* (New York: Council on Social Work Education, 1958), 1–14, 3.

17. Nancy McVittie and Timothy Shary, *Fade to Gray: Aging in American Cinema* (Austin: University of Texas Press, 2016), chaps. 2–3.

18. Robert Launer, review of *Aging and the Economy, American Sociological Review* 29 (1964): 629.

19. "Ford Foundation Support for National Committee on the Aging," *Social Service Review* 31 (1957): 92. On the rise of gerontology as a research paradigm, the indispensable source remains W. Andrew Achenbaum, *Crossing Frontiers: Gerontology Emerges as a Science* (New York: Cambridge University Press, 1995).

20. Lawrence Frank, "Gerontology," *Journal of Gerontology* 1 (January 1946): 1–12, here 3, 4.

21. Swartz quoted in Dale C. Larson, "Full Circle and More: Working with the Older Age Group," *Journal of Rehabilitation* 26 (1960): 15–22, here 15. In his preface to the study on normal aging, Erdman Palmore strikes the precise notes that Frank did: the study, he explained, sought to distinguish "normal and inevitable processes of aging from those which may accompany aging simply because of accident, stress, maladjustment, or disuse." Palmore, "Preface," in *Normal Aging I: Reports from the Duke Longitudinal Studies, 1955–1969*, ed. E. Palmore (Durham, NC: Duke University Press, 1970), vii.

22. Stella Walthal Patterson, *Dear Mad'm* (New York: W. W. Norton, 1956), 7–8.

23. Arnold Rose, "Group Consciousness Among the Aging," in *Older People and Their Social World: The Sub-Culture of the Aging*, ed. Arnold Rose and Warren Peterson (Philadelphia: F. A. Davis, 1965), 19–36; Senate Committee on Labor and Public Welfare, *Background Studies Prepared by State Committees for the White House Conference on Aging, Part V* (Washington, DC: Government Printing Office, 1960), 2827–2831.

24. Loyal V. Norman, "Stay Young While Growing Old," *Senior Citizen,* June 1956, 15–16.

25. Shirley Coleman Lombard, "A Clubhouse for Senior Citizens," *Senior Citizen*, July 1956, 9–11; Dwight D. Eisenhower, "Memorandum Concerning Establishment and Functions of the Federal Council on Aging," April 3, 1956, American Presidency Project, www.presidency.ucsb.edu /documents/memorandum-concerning-establishment-and-functions-the -federal-council-aging.

26. "We're Pioneering in the Peace Corps," *Harvest Years*, August 1962, 4–9; President's Council on Aging, *A Guide to Community Action* (May 1966), 7, 13–14.

27. On dementia, David C. Wilson, "The Pathology of Senility," *American Journal of Psychiatry* 111 (1955): 902–906; "take the stand" from Ewald Busse, "Psychoneurotic Reactions and Defense Mechanisms in the Aged," in *Normal Aging I*, ed. Palmore, 88; "societal frame" from Leonard Breen, "Aging and Productivity," in *Older People and the Industrial Community: A Report of the 1957 Spring Meeting* (New York: National Committee on the Aging of the National Social Welfare Assembly, 1957), 6; *Hearings Before the Subcommittee on Federal, State, and Community Services of the Special Committee on Aging, Part 4—Saginaw, MI*, March 2, 1964 (Washington, DC: Government Printing Office, 1964), 320.

28. Russell Lynes, "The Pressures of Leisure," *Modern Maturity*, December 1959–January 1960, 46; Barnett C. Keisling, "Disneyland," *Modern Maturity*, October–November 1958, 6–7.

29. Dorothy Heyman and Frances Jeffers, "Study of the Relative Influences of Race and Socio-Economic Status upon the Activities and Attitudes of a Southern Aged Population," *Journal of Gerontology* 19 (1964): 225–229; "Senior Citizens in the News," *Senior Citizen*, January 1955, 45; Eugene P. Bertin, "Politics Is Fundamentally Sound," *Senior Citizen*, July 1956, 8. The issues of *Harvest Years* analyzed here are from October, November, and December 1965. For the images of nonwhite people, see Ellen Hoffman, "Vista: Part II," *Harvest Years*, October 1965, 35; Ellen Hoffman, "Vista: Part III," *Harvest Years*, December 1965, 13.

30. Reginald Johnson, "Memorandum" on the 1961 WHCOA, January 29, 1961, National Urban League Archives, Box II, Folder D26, Library of Congress, Washington, DC; "Atlanta, New Orleans Bar Negroes in Golden Age Club," *Atlanta Journal and Constitution*, June 10, 1962, 10.

31. Mary Elizabeth Brown, "An Analysis of Recent Employment Histories of Old Age Assistance Recipients in Philadelphia" (master's thesis, University of Southern California, 1951), 51–52; Palmore, ed., *Normal Aging I*, 28, 31, 80–83.

32. I. M. Richardson and R. D. Weir, "Age and Disability," *Journal of Gerontology* 1, no. 4 (December 1961): 185–190; Clark Tibbitts, "The Conference on Aging," *Social Security Bulletin* (October 1950): 16 (revaluate), 17 (opinion), 18 (effort), 19 (adjustment).

33. *The 1961 White House Conference on Aging: Basic Policy Statements and*

Recommendations (Washington, DC: Government Printing Office, 1961), 111 (achievement), 3–4 (rights/obligations).

34. *1961 White House Conference on Aging*, 47.

35. Mollie Orshansky, "Counting the Poor: Another Look at the Poverty Profile," *Social Security Bulletin* (January 1965): 17.

36. On OAA and race, Frank Hammer, "Recipients of Old-Age Assistance: Personal and Social Characteristics," *Social Security Bulletin* 20, no. 4 (April 1, 1957): 4, 6; for the Southern study, Ruth Lindquist and Lora P. Wilkie, "Needs of Persons 60 Years of Age and Over," NC Board of Public Welfare, November 1950, State Archives of North Carolina (Outer Banks), Record 33SER-96, iii, 8–10, 13–14.

37. Paul Starr, *The Social Transformation of American Medicine* (New York: Basic Books, 1982), 313; Rosemary A. Stevens, "Health Care in the Early 1960s," *Health Care Finance Review* 18 (1996): 11–22, covers this period well.

38. *For All the Rest of Your Life*, video, 1963, www.youtube.com/watch?v =7WY29lD2STU; John F. Kennedy, "Address at a New York Rally in Support of the President's Program of Medical Care for the Aged," May 20, 1962, American Presidency Project, www.presidency.ucsb.edu/documents/address-new-york-rally -support-the-presidents-program-medical-care-for-the-aged.

39. Sung Won Kang, "The Political Economy of Social Security Expansion: From 1935 to 1983" (PhD diss., Rutgers University, 2006), 147. On voting, "Vote Tallies for Passage of Medicare in 1965," Social Security Administration, accessed March 24, 2024, www.ssa.gov/history/tally65.html.

40. Diane Rowland and Barbara Lyons, "Medicare, Medicaid, and the Elderly Poor," *Health Care Finance Review* 18 (1996): fig. 8.

41. *1961 White House Conference on Aging*, sec. 10.

42. Amy Finkelstein and Robin McKnight, "What Did Medicare Do? The Initial Impact of Medicare on Mortality and Out of Pocket Medical Spending," *Journal of Public Economics* 92 (2007): 1644–1668; Benjamin D. Sommers and Donald Oellerich, "The Poverty-Reducing Effect of Medicaid," *Journal of Health Economics* 32 (2013): 816–832.

43. David Barton Smith, *The Power to Heal: Civil Rights, Medicare, and the Struggle to Transform America's Health Care System* (Nashville, TN: Vanderbilt University Press, 2016).

CHAPTER 4: THE INVENTION OF RETIREMENT

1. Lorraine Bennet, "Preparation for Golden Years," Los Angeles View, *Los Angeles Times*, August 27, 1975, 1, 10.

2. US Census Bureau, *Educational Attainment* (November 1970), table C, www.census.gov/content/dam/Census/library/publications/1970/demo/p20-207 .pdf; retirement rates from Frank B. Hobbs with Bonnie L. Damon, *65+ in the United States* (Washington, DC: Government Printing Office, 1996), table 4-2;

women's marital status from US Census Bureau, *Subject Report: Marital Status* (December 1972), 5, www.census.gov/library/publications/1972/dec/pc-2-4c.html.

3. Claudia Goldin, "America's Graduation from High School: The Evolution and Spread of Secondary Schooling in the Twentieth Century," *Journal of Economic History* 58 (1998): 348.

4. Michael S. Katz, *A History of Compulsory Education Laws* (Bloomington, IN: Phi Delta Kappa Educational Foundation, 1976), 21–24; Margaret S. Gordon, "The Older Worker and Retirement Policies," *Monthly Labor Review* 83 (1960): 580; James Schulz, *The Economics of Aging*, 4th ed. (Auburn, MA: Dover House, 1988), 77.

5. *Educational Attainment*, table B.

6. Daniel T. Gianturco et al., "The Elderly Driver and Ex-Driver," in *Normal Aging II*, ed. Erdman Palmore (Durham, NC: Duke University Press, 1974): 174; Ross A. McFarland et al., "On the Driving of Automobiles by Older People," *Journal of Gerontology* 19 (1964): 190; "Senior Citizens Play Important Role," *Johnson City Press*, June 24, 1970, 10; Rixie Hunter, "Too Old to Drive?" *Winston-Salem Sentinel*, January 28, 1963, 1; Virginia Baird, "Tour by Senior Citizens Termed Huge Success," *Lansing State Journal*, September 15, 1960, 43.

7. On high school dropout rates, "Digest of Education Statistics," table 219.70, National Center for Education Statistics, November 2018, https://nces.ed.gov/programs/digest/d18/tables/dt18_219.70.asp; Eugene Friedman and Robert Havighurst, *The Meaning of Work and Retirement* (Chicago: University of Chicago Press, 1954), chaps. 3 and 4; Philip Ash, "Pre-Retirement Counseling," *The Gerontologist* 6 (1966): 98.

8. Edward Bortz, "Retirement Neurosis," *Senior Citizen*, July 1955, 13; "Mandatory Retirement Under Fire," *Atlanta Constitution*, May 18, 1957, 15; Clark Tibbitts, "Retirement Problems in American Society," *American Journal of Sociology* 59 (1954): 305.

9. For Youngstown, Earl Zarbin, "Retirement Communities," *Arizona Days and Ways*, January 26, 1964, 7–11; Michele Gaspar, "Retirement Communities Growing," *Chicago Tribune*, March 6, 1977, sec. 12, p. 2A; Charles Longino, "The Retirement Community," in *Aging in America: Readings in Social Gerontology*, 2nd ed., ed. Cary Kart and Barbara Bamard (Sherman Oaks, CA: Alfred Publishing Co, 1981), 368–399.

10. Irving Rosow, *Social Integration of the Aged* (New York: Macmillan, 1967), 294; Margaret A. Perkinson, "Alternate Roles for the Elderly: An Example from a Midwestern Retirement Community," *Human Organization* 39, no. 3 (Fall 1980): 219–220 for a literature review.

11. "Senior Citizens Valentine Dance," *New York Amsterdam News*, February 17, 1973, B5.

12. Ray Kovitz, "Pros, Cons of Adults-Only Life Styles," *Los Angeles Times*, May 4, 1986, 1. The indispensable source for all of this is Judith Trolander, *From*

Sun Cities to the Villages: A History of Active Adult, Age-Restricted Communities (Gainesville: University Press of Florida, 2011).

13. "Huge Globe Will Mark Entranceway of Project," *Los Angeles Times*, August 6, 1961, I1; "Leisure World: New Retirement Concept," *Los Angeles Herald-Examiner*, September 23, 1962, E8; M. J. West, "This and That," *Leisure World*, June 25, 1964.

14. "Leisure World: New Retirement Concept."

15. "Parade at Leisure World," KTTV-TV typescript, folder: clippings 1327, Seal Beach Leisure World Historical Society and Museum, accessed February 14, 2024, https://sealbeachleisureworldhistory.org/documents.html. Photos in the same folder, reproduced from *Orange County Evening News*, November 11, 1964.

16. *Only Four Kinds of People Live at Leisure World*, 1971 promotional brochure, 14. This brochure, among many other documents, has been collected by the Seal Beach Leisure World Historical Society and Museum, https://drive.google.com/drive/folders/1gq0b7x3HugnvzxS6GFlGz1PEqDusDgXO. Frieda Bergen to William Brangham, November 5, 1962, collected in the pamphlet *What Our Residents Say About Leisure World*, Seal Beach Leisure World Historical Society and Museum, https://drive.google.com/drive/folders/19kFshwUSEMYQGWVR5A8tXg5pFnZ2oKnS.

17. Bill Paul, "Not Enough to Do? Consider Retirement at an Activity Home," *Wall Street Journal*, June 10, 1977, 1.

18. Lisa McGirr, *Suburban Warriors: The Origins of the New American Right*, rev. ed. (Princeton, NJ: Princeton University Press, 2015), 40–41; Trolander, *From Sun Cities to the Villages*, chap. 3 on Cortese.

19. *Rossmoor Leisure World: A New Way of Life*, 1961 promotional brochure, 6, Seal Beach Leisure World Historical Society and Museum, https://drive.google.com/drive/folders/1gq0b7x3HugnvzxS6GFlGz1PEqDusDgXO.

20. *Rossmoor Leisure World: A New Way of Life*, 21 ("country club city"); Jerry Jacobs, *Fun City: An Ethnographic Study of a Retirement Community* (New York: Holt, Rinehart, and Winston, 1974), 45; for Miami demographics, Kathleen Otis, "Everything Old Is New Again: A Social and Cultural History of Life on the Retirement Frontier, 1950–2000" (PhD diss., University of North Carolina at Chapel Hill, 2008), 145.

21. "LW Scores Hit with U.N.," *National Golden Rain News*, February 5, 1964, 1, 4.

22. On rates of moving, *Social and Economic Characteristics of the Older Population: 1974* (Washington, DC: Government Printing Office, 1974), table 14; on age and state, US Census Bureau, *Supplementary Report: 1970 Population of Voting Age for States* (August 1973), table 2, www.census.gov/library/publications/1971/dec/pc-s1-3.html.

23. Albert Chevan, "Homeownership in the Older Population," *Research on Aging* 9 (1987): fig. 1.

24. Committee on an Aging Society, *America's Aging: The Social and Built Environment in an Older Society* (Washington, DC: National Academy Press, 1988), 8–9; 137 for housing deficiencies.

25. Interview between William Harrell Harlan and "Grozik," July 1949, Robert Havighurst Papers, Box 175, Folder 7, University of Chicago.

26. Mollie Lucker, "Some Aspects of Adjustment of the Retired Workingman in a UAW Drop-In-Center" (MA thesis, Wayne State University, 1957), 11; Skender Selman, "The Use of Creative Dramatics in Social Group Work Programming with Senior Citizens" (MA thesis, Wayne State University, 1962), 14–15.

27. For an interesting look at the earliest senior center, see Susan Kubie and Gertrude Landau, *Group Work with the Aged* (New York: International Universities Press, 1953).

28. Biographical information about Madar from James W. J. Robinson, "Strikes and Strikeouts: Building an Anti-racist, Anti-fascist Working Class Sports Culture from Below in the United States, 1918–1950" (PhD diss., Northeastern University, 2020); this quotation from p. 122.

29. Robinson, "Strikes and Strikeouts," 153, 156–160.

30. Resolution quoted in Francis J. Coyle, "Report on AFL-CIO Conference on Centers," in *First National Conference of Senior Centers*, ed. Ella Lindey (Washington, DC: National Council on the Aging, 1965): 33; *You and Your Retirement: Discussion Guide* (Older and Retired Workers Department of UAW and AFL-CIO, 1958), course 522.

31. For the 1968 number, Richard Korn, *A Union and Its Retired Workers: A Case Study of the UAW* (Ithaca, NY: Cornell University Press, 1976), 34; Olga Madar, "Recreation in the UAW," *American Federationist* 64, no. 11 (November 1957): 15–16; Eugene Zack, "Retired Workers Enjoy Learning," *American Federationist* 65, no. 5 (May 1958): 18–19.

32. On funding, Korn, *A Union and Its Retired Workers*, 34; "Open 20-Room Center for Headquarters for the Aged," *Chicago Defender*, May 4, 1957, 5; Mabel Kingston Green, "Senior Centers May Add 10 Years to Your Life," *Chicago Tribune*, December 12, 1965, H4; "Senior Center Told to Pare Its Membership," *Los Angeles Times*, December 22, 1960, F12; on the directory, National Institute of Senior Centers, "Seminar on Programming" (held in Airlie, VA, December 1973), Robert J. Havighurst Papers, Box 176, Folder 22; on 1974 sociability, National Council on Aging, *The Myth and Reality of Aging in America* (Washington, DC, 1975), 174–191.

33. From materials in Ellen Winston Archive, various dates, Box 11, Folder 4, University of North Carolina Greensboro; Ronald Smith, "A Study of Programs for the Aging in a Selected Number of Seventh-Day Adventist Churches (Black) in the Delaware Valley" (PhD diss., Howard University, 1980), 42–44.

34. Olga Madar, "The Growing Challenge of Leisure," *Free Labour World*, March 1968, 16.

35. Frances M. Carp, "A Senior Center in Public Housing for the Elderly," *The Gerontologist* 16 (1976): 244.

36. William Pollak, "Utilization of Alternative Care Settings by the Elderly," in *Community Planning for an Aging Society*, ed. M. P. Lawton et al. (New York: McGraw-Hill, 1977), 117.

37. *Trends in Long-Term Care: Hearings Before the Senate Special Committee on Aging*, October 10, 1973 (Washington, DC: Government Printing Office, 1975), 2914–2919.

38. Pollak, "Utilization of Alternative Care Settings by the Elderly," 117; Bruce Vladeck, *Unloving Care: The Nursing Home Tragedy* (New York: Basic Books, 1980), 3; *Reauthorizations of the Older Americans Act, 1981: Hearings Before the Subcommittee on Human Services of the House Select Committee on Aging*, vol. 2, October 15, 1980 (Washington, DC: Government Printing Office, 1980), 25–26.

39. Leonard E. Gotteman and Norman C. Bourestom, "Why Nursing Homes Do What They Do," *The Gerontologist* (December 1974): 502–503.

40. Richard Ratzan, "On Tying Knots," *Journal of the American Medical Association* 244 (1980): 2615–2616; Mark Beers et al., "Psychoactive Medication Use in Intermediate-Care Facility Residents," *Journal of the American Medical Association* 260, no. 20 (November 25, 1988): 3016–3020.

41. Vladeck, *Unloving Care*, 16; US Census Bureau, *1950 Census of Population, Advance Report* (October 31, 1952), www2.census.gov/library/publications /decennial/1950/pc-14/pc-14-05.pdf; US Census Bureau, *General Population Characteristics, 1980* (May 1983), 1–12, www2.census.gov/prod2/decennial /documents/1980/1980censusofpopu8011u_bw.pdf.

42. Ellen Winston, "Social Problems of the Aged," *Social Forces* 26 (1947): 59–60; *A Unit of Learning About Homemaker–Home Health Aide Service: Teacher's Source Book* (New York: National Council for Homemaker Services, 1968), 7.

43. Eileen Boris and Jennifer Klein, *Caring for America: Home Health Workers in the Shadow of the Welfare State* (New York: Oxford University Press, 2012), 50; North Carolina State Board of Public Welfare, *Homemaker Services for the Aged in North Carolina*, Information Bulletin No. 30 (n.d. [1960]), 1, 8–9.

44. Winston's response in *A Survey of Major Problems and Solutions in the Field of the Aged and the Aging: A Compilation of Survey Responses by the Committee on Labor and Public Welfare, US Senate* (Washington, DC: Government Printing Office, 1959), 336; Margaret Hickey, "Later Years Need Not Be Lonely," *Ladies' Home Journal*, October 1958, 35.

45. Annie May Pemberton, "Returning Senile Patients to the Community," *Public Welfare News* (1954): 6.

46. Ellen Winston to Arthur Flemming, August 14, 1970, Ellen Winston Archive, Box 13, Folder 3.

47. Vladeck, *Unloving Care*, 43–44.

48. Vladeck, *Unloving Care*, chap. 3.

49. Gotteman and Bourestom, "Why Nursing Homes Do What They Do," 502. For a cogent analysis of this dynamic, see Carroll Estes and Charlene Harrington, "Fiscal Crisis, Deinstitutionalization, and the Elderly," *American Behavioral Scientist* 24 (1981): 811–826.

50. For more, see "The Nursing Home Scandal," *Newsweek*, February 3, 1975, 23.

51. Ash, "Pre-Retirement Counseling"; Nathan W. Shock, "Age with a Future," *The Gerontologist* 8 (1968): 150.

52. Michael V. Leonesio et al., "The Increasing Labor Force Participation of Older Workers and Its Effect on the Income of the Aged," *Social Security Bulletin* 72 (2012): 61.

CHAPTER 5: BLACK POWER, BLACK AGING

1. Lauren Jae Gutterman, "'Caring for Our Own': The Founding of Senior Action in a Gay Environment, 1977–1985," *Radical History Review* 139 (2021): 178–199.

2. To my knowledge, the only extant publication about Jackson is a short chapter in Delores P. Aldridge, *Imagine a World: Pioneering Black Women Sociologists* (Lanham, MD: University Press of America, 2008), 1–6. There has been, though, a wealth of research on Black gerontology and Black aging on which this chapter will draw, most notably Leslie Pollard, *Complaint to the Lord: Historical Perspectives on the African American Elderly* (Selinsgrove, PA: Susquehanna University Press, 1996).

3. Jacquelyne Jackson, "Goals and Techniques in Three Negro Civil-Rights Organizations in Alabama" (PhD diss., Ohio State University, 1960), 95.

4. Hendry D. Sheldon, *The Older Population of the United States* (New York: John Wiley and Sons, 1958); Oliver Keller and Clyde Vedder, "The Crimes That Old Persons Commit," *The Gerontologist* 8 (1968): 49; Leonard D. Cain, "Aging and the Character of Our Times," *The Gerontologist* 8 (1968): 256.

5. Various documents from this 1946 campaign can be found in National Urban League (NUL) Archives, Box VI, Folder A78, Library of Congress, Washington, DC.

6. Only one study to my knowledge was based on systematic research: Edith M. Alexander et al., *A Study of the Needs of the Negro Aged in New York City*, a May 1946 report made by the Federation of Protestant Welfare Agencies. See also T. Lynn Smith, "The Changing Number and Distribution of the Aged Negro Population of the United States," *Phylon* 18 (1957): 339–354; Walter M. Beattie Jr., "The Aging Negro: Some Implications for Social Welfare Services,"

Phylon 21 (1960): 131–135; Thomas Talley and Jerome Kaplan, "The Negro Aged," *Newsletter of the Gerontological Society*, December 1956, 4, 6. Hobart Jackson and Jeweldean Jones, *Double Jeopardy: The Older Negro in America Today* (National Urban League, 1964), 1, NUL Archives, Box II, Folder E21, for details about its composition. Notably, the pamphlet preceded by five years the more famous essay by Frances Beal that is normally associated with "double jeopardy" and intersectionality.

7. "Dr. Jacquelyne Jackson to Speak at Clark College," *Atlanta Daily World*, March 28, 1974, 11; on Jackson at Duke, see Melody Gao, "Growing Old in the New South: Race and the Center for Aging at Duke University, 1955–1990" (undergraduate thesis, Duke University, 2023), chap. 2; Jacquelyne Jackson, "The Blacklands of Gerontology," *International Journal of Aging and Development* 2 (1971): 157.

8. On lifespans, *Vital Statistics of the United States: Life Tables*, vol. 2, sec. 6 (Hyattsville, MD: US Department of Health and Human Services, 1984), table D; US Census Bureau, *General Population Characteristics, 1980* (May 1983), tables 43 (Black population) and 47–48 (Asian/Indigenous/Hispanic populations), www2 .census.gov/prod2/decennial/documents/1980/1980censusofpopu8011u_bw.pdf.

9. Donald Snyder, "Elderly Poor: Effects of Public Transfers," *Journal of Minority Aging* 4 (1979): 111; Christine Ross, Sheldon Danzier, and Eugene Smolensky, "The Level and Trend of Poverty in the United States, 1939–1979," *Demography* 24 (1987): 591.

10. On the South, US Census Bureau, *General Population Characteristics, 1980*, table 53; on Social Security, Hobart Jackson, "The Black Elderly: Jeopardized by Race and Neglect," *Geriatrician* 27 (1972): 39; on pensions, Gayle Thompson, "Black-White Differences in Private Pensions: Findings from the Retirement History Study," *Social Security Bulletin* 42 (1979): table 1.

11. Andrew Billingsley, *Black Families in White America* (Englewood Cliffs, NJ: Prentice-Hall, 1968), 78; John Nowlin, "Geriatric Health Status: Influence of Race and Economic Status," *Journal of Minority Aging* 4 (1979): 94; Brian Gratton, "Familism Among the Black and Mexican-American Elderly: Myth or Reality?," *Journal of Aging Studies* 1 (1987): 19–32.

12. Willa Granger, "Eldercare at the Margins: Keeping Up to Code at the Stephen Smith Home," *Pennsylvania Magazine of History and Biography* 145 (2021): 318; on St. Louis, Albert F. Wessen, "Some Sociological Characteristics of Long-Term Care," *The Gerontologist* 4, 2 (June 1964): 11; on Louisiana, Jackson and Jones, *Double Jeopardy*, 16; for Louisiana demographics at this time, Alvin L. Bertrand, *Louisiana's Human Resources*, Louisiana State University, Department of Rural Sociology, Bulletin 548 (November 1961), 14.

13. Jacob Gordon, "Use of Aging Services by Elderly Blacks in Douglas County, Kansas," *Journal of Minority Aging* 4 (1979): 88–92; on the minstrel show, Susan Kubie and Gertrude Landau, *Group Work with the Aged* (New

York: International Universities Press, 1953), 124; on senior center convenience, National Council on Aging, *The Myth and Reality of Aging in America* (Washington, DC, 1975), 183; on Tennessee, Jeanne M. Thune, "Racial Attitudes of Older Adults," *The Gerontologist* 7 (1967): 181.

14. Jacquelyne Jackson, "Aging Black Families and Federal Policies: Some Critical Issues," *Journal of Minority Aging* 5 (1979): 167; "Edwin Towers Senior Center," n.d. (c. 1970), North Carolina State Archives, ORC.17.F.18, Civil Rights File, Division of Aging, Raleigh, NC; Louise Saunders to Mr. W. R. Collins, December 30, 1969, in "Cumberland Coordinating Council," North Carolina State Archives, ORC.17.F.18, Civil Rights File, Division of Aging.

15. Gaynor Maddox, "Meals on Wheels," *San Antonio Express*, June 17, 1971, 23; for "get on a bus," Barbara Cowan, "The Black Elderly Experience," p. 2, in NUL Archives, Box III-96, Folder 1; for Meals on Wheels Study, "Methodology of the Project on Portable Meals to the Residences of the Aged and the Chronically Ill," *American Journal of Public Health* 55 (1965): 74; for Baltimore, Carla Jensen, "Meals on Wheels: A Boon for the Shut-In," *Prevention*, August 1973, 95.

16. Elisabeth Kübler-Ross, *On Death and Dying* (New York: Scribner, 2014 [1969]); for an early analysis, see Bruce J. Neubauer and Carol Lee Hamilton, "Racial Differences in Attitudes Toward Hospice Care," *Hospice Journal* 6 (1990): 37–48.

17. National Tribal Chairmen's Association, *Summary Report of the National Indian Conference on Aging* (Phoenix: National Indian Conference on Aging, 1976), 33; Duran Bell, Patricia Kasschau, and Gail Zellman, *Delivering Services to Elderly Members of Minority Groups: A Critical Review of the Literature* (Rand Report R-1862-HEW, April 1976), 44.

18. Melvin D. Briscoe, "Conspiracy Charged After Racial Fight in Denver," *Chicago Daily Defender*, October 19 1968, 9.

19. Jacquelyne Johnson Jackson, "Aged Negroes: Their Cultural Departures from Statistical Stereotypes and Rural-Urban Differences," *The Gerontologist* 10 (1970): 140, 142.

20. Jacquelyne Jackson, "Social Gerontology and the Negro: A Review," *The Gerontologist* 7 (1967): 175; Jacquelyne Jackson, "Social Stratification of Aged Blacks and Implications for Training Professionals," in *Proceedings of "Black Aged in the Future,"* December 15 and 16, 1972, San Juan, PR (Durham, NC: Duke University Press, 1973), 127 for "rampant," 114 for "mind-sets" and "gain control."

21. Jackson, "Aged Negroes," 141.

22. *Trends in Long-Term Care: Hearings Before the Subcommittee on Long-Term Care, Senate Special Committee on Aging*, August 10, 1972 (Washington, DC: Government Printing Office, 1972), 2454–2455.

23. On Jackson, see Pollard, *Complaint to the Lord*, chap. 7; Hobart

Jackson, "National Goals and Priorities in the Social Welfare of the Aging," *The Gerontologist* (1971): 88.

24. H. Jackson, "The Black Elderly."

25. *Evaluation of Administration on Aging and Conduct of White House Conference on Aging: Senate Committee on Aging*, March 29, 1971 (Washington, DC: Government Printing Office, 1971), 139.

26. Senate Committee on Aging, "The Multiple Hazards of Age and Race," working paper (Washington, DC: Government Printing Office, 1971), 35.

27. Hobart Jackson, "National Caucus on the Black Aged: A Progress Report," *Aging and Human Development* 2 (1971): 228–229.

28. H. Jackson, "National Caucus on the Black Aged," 229; H. Jackson, "The Black Elderly," 45; "Elderly Negroes Present Demands," *New York Times*, November 14, 1971, 35.

29. *1971 White House Conference on Aging: A Report to the Delegates* (Washington, DC: Government Printing Office, 1971), v; "Reports of the Special Concerns Sessions: The Aging and Aged Blacks," *1971 White House Conference on Aging*, 3; Jacquelyne Jackson, "NCBA, Black Aged and Politics," *Annals of the American Academy of Political and Social Science* 415 (1974): 141.

30. "Aging and Aged Blacks," 3–4, 8–9.

31. National Tribal Chairmen's Association, *Summary Report*, 9, 15.

32. J. Finton Speller to Hobart Jackson, November 7, 1974, Hobart Jackson Archive, Box 1, Folder 4, Amistad Research Center, Tulane University, New Orleans, LA.

33. A copy of that report can be found in NUL Archives, Box III-90, Folder 2; on collaborations, "The NUL's New Thrust in Advocacy," 1975, NUL Archive, Box III-98, Folder 1.

34. Jackson to Barbara Cowan, May 20, 1975, and May 23, 1975, in NUL Archive, Box III-98, Folder 8.

35. Jacquelyne Jackson, "Editorial," *Journal of Minority Aging* 3 (1978–1979): 3 (for funding; the articles mentioned are also in this volume).

36. *Old, Black and Alive*, video, National Center on Black Aging, 1974, dir. Frank Cantor, https://vimeo.com/151824005, at 9:56.

37. *Old, Black and Alive*, at 19:00.

38. For its continued usage, see "Instructional Strategies," Stanford Medicine Department of Ethnogeriatrics, September 2010, https://geriatrics.stanford.edu/ethnomed/african_american/instructional_strategies.html.

39. "'Miss Jane' Ratings," *Washington Post*, February 2, 1974, B7.

40. *The Autobiography of Miss Jane Pittman*, dir. John Korty (CBS, 1974), at 1:39.

41. José Cuellar and John Weeks, *Minority Elderly Americans: A Prototype for Area Agencies on Aging* (San Diego, CA: Allied Home Health Association, 1980), 25 (income), 29 (health), 33 (nutrition).

42. Jacquelyne Jackson, "Race, National Origin, Ethnicity, and Aging," in *Handbook of Aging and the Social Sciences*, 2nd ed., ed. Robert Binstock and Ethel Shanas (New York: Van Nostrand Reinhold Company, 1985), 286. Kimberlé Crenshaw, "Mapping the Margins: Intersectionality, Identity Politics, and Violence Against Women of Color," *Stanford Law Review* 43 (1991): 1241–1299 is the classic text on intersectionality; age is referenced only in passing, and likely refers more to young people than to old ones (as at footnote 9).

43. Michelle M. Doty et al., *How Discrimination in Health Care Affects Older Americans* (Commonwealth Fund, April 21, 2022), www.commonwealth fund.org/publications/issue-briefs/2022/apr/how-discrimination-in-health -care-affects-older-americans; Jan Mutchler et al., "Precarious Aging: The Spatial Context of Racial and Ethnic Disparities in Economic Security," *Generations*, Summer 2021, https://generations.asaging.org/racial-and-ethnic-disparities -economic-security.

44. Jackson, "Race, National Origin, Ethnicity, and Aging," 284.

CHAPTER 6: THE END OF THE FUTURE

1. *1961 White House Conference on Aging Chart Book: Aging with a Future* (Washington, DC: Federal Council of Aging, 1961); Nathan W. Shock, "Age with a Future," *The Gerontologist* 8 (1968): 147–152.

2. For one overview of changes in other countries, see Ito Peng and Sue Yeandle, "Eldercare Policies in East Asia and Europe," Discussion Paper, UN Women, 2017, www.unwomen.org/sites/default/files/Headquarters/Attachments /Sections/Library/Publications/2017/Discussion-paper-Eldercare-policies -in-East-Asia-and-Europe-en.pdf; on the stagnation of Social Security politics, see James Chappel, "The Frozen Politics of Social Security," *Boston Review*, February 2023, www.bostonreview.net/articles/the-frozen-politics-of-social -security/ and the books reviewed there; on Medicare, Theodore R. Marmor and Kip Sullivan, "Medicare at 50: Why Medicare-for-All Did Not Take Place," *Yale Journal of Health Policy, Law and Ethics* 15 (2015): 141–184.

3. See Edward R. Roybal Papers, Collection 107, Box 469, Folder 15, Chicano Studies Research Center, University of California, Los Angeles, for some examples of Roybal's constituent service dealing with everyday issues of older people.

4. National Retired Teachers Association and American Association of Retired Persons, *The 1971 White House Conference on Aging: The End of a Beginning?* (1971).

5. *Toward a National Policy of Aging: Proceedings of the 1971 White House Conference on Aging* (Washington, DC: US Government Printing Office, 1971), vol. 1, 46 (minority delegates), 57 (inequities).

6. Richard Nixon, "Special Message to the Congress on Older Americans," March 23, 1972, American Presidency Project, www.presidency.ucsb.edu

/documents/special-message-the-congress-older-americans; *Toward a National Policy of Aging*, vol. 1, 75 and 52–143 for all the delegate recommendations and addresses in the Open Forum, esp. 64–65.

7. Booker Griffin, "White House Conference on Aging Begins," *Los Angeles Sentinel*, December 2, 1971, A7.

8. All available in *1971 White House Conference on Aging: A Report to the Delegates* (Washington, DC: Government Printing Office, 1971).

9. *Harold and Maude*, dir. Hal Ashby (Paramount Pictures, 1971).

10. *Bunny O'Hare*, dir. Gerd Oswald (American International Pictures, 1971), at 1:30.

11. *Kotch*, dir. Jack Lemmon (ABC Pictures, 1971), at 0:24, 1:52.

12. *Social Security: Universal or Selective?*, video, 1971, AEI Archives, www .youtube.com/watch?v=gr-_nRnMh2E.

13. For one example of 1950s skepticism, "It's Our Opinion," *Fort Lauderdale News*, August 8, 1953, 4.

14. For one example, Milton Friedman, "The Goldwater View of Economics," *New York Times Magazine*, October 11, 1964, 35, 133–137.

15. For an insightful chapter on George W. Bush's efforts to skirt this problem, see R. Douglas Arnold, *Fixing Social Security: The Politics of Reform in a Polarized Age* (Princeton, NJ: Princeton University Press, 2022), chap. 11.

16. James M. Buchanan, *Public Finance in Democratic Process: Fiscal Institutions and Individual Choice* (Chapel Hill: University of North Carolina Press, 1967), chap. 10; on Buchanan more generally, Nancy MacLean, *Democracy in Chains: The Deep History of the Radical Right's Stealth Plan for America* (New York: Viking, 2017); Martin Feldstein, "Social Security, Induced Retirement, and Aggregate Capital Accumulation," *Journal of Political Economy* 82 (1974): 922.

17. "The Commission on the Social Security 'Notch' Issue," Social Security Administration, accessed March 15, 2024, www.ssa.gov/history/notchfile1.html.

18. Rita Ricardo-Campbell, *Social Security: Promise and Reality* (Palo Alto, CA: Hoover Institution Press, 1977), based on her participation and dissenting comments as one of the few conservative members of Nixon's 1974 Advisory Council on Social Security, for which see *Reports of the Advisory Council on Social Security* (Washington, DC: Social Security Administration, 1975), 93–102; Murray Rothbard, *For a New Liberty: The Libertarian Manifesto*, 2nd ed. (Auburn, AL: Mises Institute, 1978), 398–399; Peter J. Ferrara, *Social Security: The Inherent Contradiction* (San Francisco, CA: Cato Institute, 1980).

19. William A. Rusher, "The Social Security Ripoff," *Human Events*, May 18, 1974, 12; M. Stanton Evans, "Dark Horses," *National Review*, December 9, 1977, 1447; M. Stanton Evans, "Social Security Obligations Soaring Out of Sight," *Human Events*, January 29, 1977, 17; "Insecure Security," *Christianity Today*, July 28, 1972, 23–24.

20. "Social Security: Promising Too Much to Too Many?," *U.S. News*

& *World Report*, July 15, 1974, 26, 28. For more sober analyses from the same period, see Robert S. Kaplan, *Financial Crisis in the Social Security System*, Domestic Affairs Study 47 (AEI, June 1976); Alicia H. Munnell, *The Future of Social Security* (Washington, DC: Brookings Institution, 1977).

21. Howard J. Ruff, *How to Prosper During the Coming Bad Years* (New York: Times Books, 1979), 51–58 on Social Security; this quotation from 52.

22. Richard W. Stevenson, "For Bush, a Long Embrace of Social Security," *New York Times*, February 27, 2005, A1.

23. "Americans Losing Confidence in Social Security, Poll Shows," *Atlanta Constitution*, March 1, 1979, 6A; Sally R. Sherman, "Public Attitudes Toward Social Security," *Social Security Bulletin* 52 (1989): 5.

24. *Social Security: Universal or Selective?* at 8:00.

25. The authoritative account is now Nelson Lichtenstein and Judith Stern, *A Fabulous Failure: The Clinton Presidency and the Transformation of American Capitalism* (Princeton, NJ: Princeton University Press, 2023).

26. Stuart Butler and Peter Germanis, "Achieving a 'Leninist' Strategy," *Cato Journal* 3, 2 (Fall 1983): 547–558; Martha Derthick, *Policymaking for Social Security* (Washington, DC: Brookings Institution, 1979).

27. Natalie Shure, "How Medicare Was Won," *The Nation*, August 6, 2018, www.thenation.com/article/archive/how-medicare-was-won/; for membership statistics, Hutton's opening testimony in *Older Americans Act Amendments of 1968: Hearings Before the Select Subcommittee on Education*, July 15–16, 1968 (Washington, DC: Government Printing Office, 1968), 94.

28. See NCSC, *A National Police for Older Americans: Response to Their Special Needs* (Washington, DC: NCSC, 1975), 2, for a snapshot of seven top leaders, all white men.

29. By 1993, the vast bulk of NCSC's funding came from the federal government, as reported in Tony Snow, "All the Reform Money Can Buy," *USA Today*, August 15, 1994, 11A; "Senior AIDES Serve Local Needs," *ETA Interchange* 7, 2 (February 1981): 7; on ombudsman, NCSC, *A National Police for Older Americans*, 29; Sharon Conway, "HUD to Finance Housing Complex for Elderly," *Washington Post*, September 14, 1978, MD3.

30. *The Gray Panthers Manual*, compiled by Harriet L. Peretz (Philadelphia: Gray Panthers, 1978), 36–58; Roger Sanjek, *Gray Panthers* (Philadelphia: University of Pennsylvania Press, 2009), 233–234.

31. Interview in *Maggie Kuhn on Aging*, ed. Dieter Hessel (Philadelphia: Westminster, 1977), 80.

32. Amanda Ciafone, "The Gray Panthers Are Watching: Gray Women's Media Activism in the 1970s and 80s," *Feminist Media Studies* 21 (2021): 265–280.

33. *Gray Panthers Manual*, 11–12; Maya C. Sandler, "Negotiating Care: The East Bay Gray Panthers and the Over 60 Health Clinic," *Radical History Review* 129 (2021): 166–177.

34. "Gray Panthers: Aiming at New Targets," *U.S. News & World Report*, January 24, 1977, 79; "Gray Panthers Win Medicaid Guideline Dispute in Court," *American Journal of Nursing* 119, no. 1 (February 1979): 204.

35. Diane Lade, "Gray Panthers," *Sun Sentinel* (Fort Lauderdale, FL), January 16, 1989, 3D.

36. Theda Skocpol, *Diminished Democracy* (New York: Oxford University Press, 2004).

37. Donella H. Meadows et al., *The Limits to Growth* (New York: Universe Books, 1972), 120.

38. Robert Havighurst, "Successful Aging," *The Gerontologist* 1, no. 1 (1961): 8; latter quotation from Robert Havighurst, "Public Policy Related to Aging," May 1977, p. 12, in Havighurst Papers, Box 175, Folder 22, University of Chicago. See also "Human Behavior and Development in a Modernized Equilibrium Society," August 1975, Havighurst Papers, Box 173, Folder 6.

39. Bernice Neugarten, "The Future and the Young-Old," *The Gerontologist* 5, 1, part II (1975): 4; Robert Havighurst, "The Future Aged: The Use of Time and Money," *The Gerontologist* 15, 1, part II (1975): 15.

40. Wallace Stegner, *The Spectator Bird* (New York: Penguin, 1976), 116.

41. Edward D. Berkowitz and Larry Dewitt, *The Other Welfare: Supplemental Security Income and U.S. Social Policy* (Ithaca, NY: Cornell University Press, 2013), chaps. 4 and 5.

42. David Heer et al., "The Cluttered Nest: Evidence That Young Adults Are More Likely to Live at Home Now Than in the Recent Past," *Sociology and Social Research* 69 (1985): 436–441.

43. *All in the Family*, season 4, episode 3, "Edith Finds an Old Man," dir. Bob LaHendro and John Rich, aired September 29, 1973.

44. *Sanford and Son*, season 2, episode 21, "Home Sweet Home for the Aged," dir. Peter Baldwin, aired February 16, 1973; *Three's Company*, season 4, episode 7, "Old Folks at Home," dir. Dave Powers, aired October 30, 1979; *Taxi*, season 3, episode 14, "Louie's Mother," dir. James Burrows, aired March 26, 1981.

45. *Chico and the Man*, season 1, episode 21, "Louie's Retirement," dir. James Komack, aired March 7, 1975.

46. *The Amusement Park*, dir. George Romero (Yellow Veil Pictures, 1975).

47. *Going in Style*, dir. Martin Brest (Warner Bros., 1979).

48. Gene Siskel, "'Going in Style' Gives Aging a Bad Name Beautifully," *Chicago Tribune*, December 26, 1979, 64.

49. *A Guide to the 1981 White House Conference on Aging* (Washington, DC: US Department of Education, 1980), 11–13 (this was prepared in the last days of Carter's presidency). See also the remarkable statement from Jerry Waldie, one of the main planners of the event under Carter, in *Oversight on 1981 White House Conference on Aging: Hearing Before the Select Committee*

on Aging, US House of Representatives (Washington, DC: Government Printing Office, 1982), 2–7.

50. Martha Derthick and Steven M. Teles, "Riding the Third Rail: Social Security Reform," in *The Reagan Presidency: Pragmatic Conservatism and Its Legacies*, ed. W. Elliot Brownlee and Hugh Davis Graham (Lawrence: University Press of Kansas, 2003), 182–208.

51. *Final Report: The 1981 White House Conference on Aging*, vol. 2 (Washington, DC, 1982), 107; Caroline E. Rymph, *Republican Women: Feminism and Conservatism from Suffrage Through the Rise of the New Right* (Chapel Hill: University of North Carolina Press, 2006), 217, 291; *Final Report*, 5.

52. *Social Security Financing Issues: Hearings Before Social Security Subcommittee of House Ways and Means Committee*, February and March 1981 (Washington, DC: Government Printing Office, 1981), 451–452; *Final Report*, 74–75. On opposition, see Lawrence Meyer, "Reagan Tells Conference Delegates He's Not an 'Enemy' of the Aging," *Washington Post*, December 2, 1981, A16.

53. *The Politicization of the 1981 White House Conference on Aging: A Report Presented by the Chairman of the Select Committee on Aging, US House of Representatives* (Washington, DC: Government Printing Office, 1984), viii (favorable/adversaries), 16 (pin); *Oversight on 1981 White House Conference on Aging*, 95, 33.

54. *Oversight on 1981 White House Conference on Aging*, 21.

CHAPTER 7: AARP NATION

1. Despite its size and influence, there is a paucity of literature on the AARP, and almost nothing by a historian. The best treatment so far is Christine L. Day, *AARP: America's Largest Internet Group and Its Impact* (Denver: Praeger, 2017).

2. Day, *AARP*, 9–13; Lani Luciano and Eric Schurenberg, "The Empire Called AARP," *Money*, October 1988, 128.

3. "Leader's Plea: Keep Retired People Busy," *Fresno Bee*, May 24, 1965, 36; for one example of many critiques of the term "senior citizen," see David Steinberg, "Senior Citizen Label Confining, Obsolete," *Sun Sentinel* (Fort Lauderdale, FL), December 8, 1986, 3D. Google Ngram for "senior citizens" performed on September 15, 2023.

4. *The Age Discrimination Study: A Report of the United States Commission on Civil Rights* (Washington, DC: Government Printing Office, 1977); letter quoted in *Gray Panther Media Guide* (Philadelphia, PA: Gray Panthers, 1983), 13; Jason Roe, "From the Impoverished to the Entitled: The Experience and Meaning of Old Age in America Since the 1950s" (PhD diss., University of Kansas, 2012), 39; "Maxine: The Birth of the Ageist Birthday Card," Age-Friendly Vibes, November 1, 2021, https://agefriendlyvibes.com/blogs/news/maxine-the -birth-of-the-ageist-birthday-card.

5. For size of age cohorts, see US Census Bureau, *General Population*

Characteristics, 1980 (May 1983), table 43, www2.census.gov/prod2/decennial /documents/1980/1980censusofpopu8011u_bw.pdf; on the AARP and age cohorts, John R. Logan, Russell Ward, and Glenna Spitze, "As Old as You Feel: Age Identity in Middle and Later Life," *Social Forces* 71 (1992): 451–467; Luciano and Schurenberg, "The Empire Called AARP," 131.

6. The classic analysis is Nancy Fraser, "From Redistribution to Recognition? Dilemmas of Justice in a 'Post-Socialist' Age," *New Left Review* 212 (1995): 68–91. See also Serena Mayeri, *Reasoning from Race: Feminism, Law, and the Civil Rights Revolution* (Cambridge, MA: Harvard University Press, 2011).

7. "Educator Wins Honor," *Los Angeles Times*, February 27, 1936, A2; Ethel Percy Andrus, "The Development of an Educational Program for the High-School Girl" (PhD diss., University of Southern California, 1930), 392; Ethel P. Andrus, "General Procedure at Abraham Lincoln High School, Los Angeles," *Junior-Senior High School Clearing House* 9, no. 6 (February 1935): 335.

8. Quoted in Hubert Pryor, "Her Secret," *Modern Maturity*, February-March, 1968, 6; *Hearings Before the House Ways and Means Committee on General Revision of the Internal Revenue Code*, August 1952 (Washington, DC: Government Printing Office, 1953), 1941; Cyril F. Brickfield, "Independence vs. Over-Protection," *Modern Maturity*, October-November 1968, 39.

9. *Hearings Before the House Ways and Means Committee on Health Services for the Aged Under the Social Security Insurance System*, July-August 1961 (Washington, DC: Government Printing Office, 1953), 741–743.

10. *Dynamic Maturity* (pamphlet), WorldsFairPhotos.com, accessed July 2022, www.worldsfairphotos.com/nywf64/booklets/dynamic-maturity.pdf.

11. For AARP numbers in 1968, see Henry Pratt, "Old Age Associations in National Politics," *Annals of the American Academy of Political and Social Science* 415 (1974): 112; for NCSC numbers at the same time, see Hutton's opening testimony in *Hearings Before the Select Subcommittee on Education on Older Americans Act Amendments of 1968*, July 15–16, 1968 (Washington, DC: Government Printing Office, 1968), 94.

12. W. Andrew Achenbaum, *Robert N. Butler, MD: Visionary of Healthy Aging* (New York: Columbia University Press, 2013), 27; Robert N. Butler et al., "Self-Perceived Changes in Community-Resident Aged," *Archives of General Psychiatry* 4 (1961): 501–508; Robert N. Butler, "The Life Review: An Interpretation of Reminiscence in the Aged," *Psychiatry* 26 (1963): 65–76.

13. Carl Bernstein, "Age and Race Fears Seen in Housing Opposition," *Washington Post*, March 7, 1969, A6. This analysis is pursued further in the more famous Robert Butler, "Age-Ism: Another Form of Bigotry," *The Gerontologist* 9 (1969): 243–246.

14. Ben W. Gilbert, "Regency Decision Now a Test Case," *Washington Post*, April 20, 1969, 40. These kinds of housing projects were reasonably common in the early 1970s, and press reports outside Chevy Chase do not mention the

same outcry. See, for instance, James Dilts, "Ground Broken for North Avenue Housing for Elderly," *Baltimore Sun*, June 23, 1971, A12.

15. Ossofsky quoted in David Hackett Fischer, "Books Considered," *New Republic*, December 2, 1978, 31; Erdman B. Palmore and Kenneth Manton, "Ageism Compared to Racism and Sexism," *Journal of Gerontology* 28 (1973): 363–369; David Hackett Fischer, *Growing Old in America* (New York: Oxford University Press, 1977), 211.

16. Bernice L. Neugarten, "Age Groups in American Society and the Rise of the Young-Old," *Annals of the American Academy of Political and Social Science* 415 (1974): 197; Matilda White Riley and John Riley, "The Lives of Older People and Changing Social Roles," *Annals of the American Academy of Political and Social Science* 503 (1989): 14–28.

17. Jack Levin and William Levin, *Ageism: Prejudice and Discrimination Against the Elderly* (Belmont, CA: Wadsworth, 1980), 87 (the main study to advance the theory was Donald Cowgill and Lowell Holmes, eds., *Aging and Modernization* [New York: Meredith, 1972]); David Hackett Fischer, "Putting Our Heads to the 'Problem' of Old Age," *New York Times*, May 19, 1977, 27.

18. For a review of the literature on ageism and culture at the time, see Margo Sorgman and Marilou Sorensen, "Ageism: A Course of Study," *Theory into Practice* 23 (1984): 117–123; *The Myth and Reality of Aging in America* (Washington, DC: National Council on Aging, 1975); Frank H. Nuessel Jr., "The Language of Ageism," *The Gerontologist* 22 (1982): 273–276; Thomas Hopkins, "A Conceptual Framework for Understanding the Three 'Isms,'" *Journal of Education for Social Work* 16 (1980): 63–70.

19. Frank Trippett, "Looking Askance at Ageism," *Time*, March 24, 1980, 88–89; "DP Managers Deny Ageism," *Computerworld*, December 6, 1981, 1; Isabella Lyle, "An Open Letter to Feminists on Ageism," *Off Our Backs* 15, no. 11 (December 1985): 16; Linda Delloff, "Combating Ageism: Agenda for the '80s," *Christian Century*, January 1, 1980, 1116–1118.

20. For a membership list, *Hearing Before Senate Committee on Labor and Human Resources on Legislation to Extend the Older Americans Act*, March 17, 1981 (Washington, DC: Government Printing Office, 1981), 112–113; Henry J. Pratt, "The 'Gray Lobby' Revisited," *National Forum* 62, 4 (Fall 1982): 31–33.

21. *Hearings Before the Appropriations Committee of the House of Representatives on "Downsizing Government and Setting Priorities of Federal Programs," Part 2*, January 12, 1995 (Washington, DC: Government Printing Office, 1996), 126.

22. Theda Skocpol, *Diminished Democracy* (New York: Oxford University Press, 2004), 127.

23. Luciano and Schurenberg, "The Empire Called AARP," 131; advertisement, *Weekly World News*, February 3, 1981, 14.

24. Luciano and Schurenberg, "The Empire Called AARP," 133.

25. Mark Brown, "For $5, Aging Gets Miracles," *Chicago Sun-Times*, May 15, 1988, 12; Luciano and Schurenberg, "The Empire Called AARP," 137.

26. Nancy Brower, "Florida, the Beautiful," *Modern Maturity*, January-March 1972, 34, 41.

27. *Hearings Before the Subcommittee on Problems of the Aged and Aging: Senate Committee on Labor and Public Welfare, on National Organizations in the Field of Aging*, August 1959 (Washington, DC: Government Printing Office, 1959), 71.

28. "The 50 and Over Do-It-Yourself Kit," *National Geographic*, October 1986, 1.

29. William Davis, "Nothing Retiring About These Travelers," *Boston Globe*, January 13, 1980, 1.

30. Nora Lockwood, "For the Elderly, Preservation of Capital Is a Primary Goal," *Providence Journal*, May 4, 1986, F-05.

31. Ira Teinowitz, "'Modern Maturity' Wins Top Spot in Circulation," *Advertising Age*, August 22, 1988, 12; "Tips Worth Considering," *Modern Maturity*, February-March 1968, 69.

32. *To Amend the Older Americans Act of 1965: Hearings Before the Select Subcommittee on Education, Committee on Education and Labor, US House of Representatives*, September-November 1971, part I (Washington, DC: Government Printing Office, 1972), 119; Roe, "From the Impoverished to the Entitled," 69.

33. Luciano and Schurenberg, "The Empire Called AARP," 140.

34. *To Amend the Older Americans Act of 1965*, 129–130.

35. Lauren Selden, letter to the editor, *American Bar Association Journal* 65, no. 2 (February 1979): 168; *Retirement Age Policies: Hearings Before the House Select Committee on Aging*, March 1977, part II (Washington, DC: Government Printing Office, 1977), 2–4; *Age Discrimination and the FAA Age 60 Rule: Hearings Before the House Select Committee on Aging*, October 1985 (Washington, DC: Government Printing Office, 1986), 26.

36. Cyril Brickfield to Wilbur Cohen, October 14, 1982, Robert J. Havighurst Papers, Box 171, Folder 17, University of Chicago.

37. Peter H. Schuck, "The Graying of Civil Rights Law: The Age Discrimination Act of 1975," *Yale Law Journal* 89 (1979): 27–93.

38. Jean Dietz, "Older Workers Make Case for Un-Retirement," *Boston Globe*, December 16, 1987, 95.

39. *The Black Elderly in Poverty: Hearings Before the House Select Committee on Aging*, September 27, 1985 (Washington, DC: Government Printing Office, 1986), 56 (collating with membership numbers in Day, *AARP*, 44); Hubert Pryer, "People Who Quit Life," *Modern Maturity*, April-May 1968, 6; "What to Do in a Riot," *Modern Maturity*, June-July 1968, 14.

40. Irma Hunt, "Remember Patriotism?," *Modern Maturity*, June-July 1972,

19; Hazel Andrews, "Memories of a Country Christmas," *Modern Maturity*, July-August 1971, 9–11; Earl Chapin, "When Radio Was a Miracle," *Modern Maturity*, October-November 1970, 68; Hubert Pryor, "Older Americans CAN Help," *Modern Maturity*, June-July 1968, 6; Irma Hunt, "A Conversation with Roy Wilkins," *Modern Maturity*, May 1972, 61.

41. Jill Day-Foley, "The Door's Open, Come On In," *Michigan Chronicle*, April 30, 1988, 5A; Al Cole, "Diversity Revisited," *Modern Maturity*, August 1993, 10; "Minority Outreach Produces New San Diego Chapter," *Modern Maturity*, December 1993–January 1994, 7; "Edwin Towers Senior Center," n.d. (c. 1970), North Carolina State Archives, ORC.17.F.18, Civil Rights File, Division of Aging, Raleigh, NC.

42. Douglas Nelson, "Old Age and Public Policy," *National Forum* 62 (1982): 27–30.

43. Luciano and Schurenberg, "The Empire Called AARP," 143; Steve Marshall, "AARP Doesn't Endorse Plan," *USA Today*, February 24, 1994, 5A.

CHAPTER 8: AGING BODIES, GOLDEN GIRLS

1. "Shelve the Geritol for Senior Olympics," *Atlanta Constitution*, January 25, 1980, A7B; "EOA to Host 1980 Senior Olympics," *Atlanta Daily World*, January 25, 1980, 5; "Wheelchair Whoopee," *Tacoma News Tribune*, August 26, 1970, 37.

2. Kenneth Marshall, "The USNSO Story," *U.S. National Senior Olympics Program Magazine*, June 1987, 26 (and p. 22 of the same volume for the list of sponsors, and p. 5 for Reagan's welcome note).

3. Demmie Stathoplos, "Silver Threads Among the Gold (Medals)," *Sports Illustrated*, July 3, 1989, 38, 40, 41; Scott Donaton, "Senior Olympics Offer Marketers Forceful Finish," *Advertising Age*, June 19, 1989, 72.

4. Google Ngram, conducted January 2024.

5. Eugene Friedman and Robert Havighurst, *The Meaning of Work and Retirement* (Chicago: University of Chicago Press, 1954), 129–130.

6. *The Golden Girls*, season 1, episode 1, "The Engagement," dir. Jay Sandrich, aired September 14, 1985, at 11:00.

7. For membership numbers, "Laurie Shields, Co-Founded Older Women's League," *Sun Sentinel* (Fort Lauderdale, FL), March 5, 1989, 6B; on health care for divorced women, "Older Women's League Helps Widowed, Divorced," *Times-Press* (Streator, IL), June 24, 1986, sec. 2, 17. In general, see Kathleen Kautzer, "Moving Against the Stream: An Organizational Study of the Older Women's League" (PhD diss., Brandeis University, 1988).

8. *The Golden Girls*, season 1, episode 9, "Blanche and the Younger Man," dir. Jim Drake, aired November 16, 1985. For another example of "old lady" as a slur, see *The Golden Girls*, season 3, episode 2, "One for the Money," dir. Terry Hughes, aired September 26, 1987, at 15:00.

9. Paula Doress-Worters and Diana Laskin Siegal, in cooperation with the Boston Women's Health Book Collective, *Ourselves, Growing Older: Women Aging with Knowledge and Power* (New York: Simon and Schuster, 1987), 4.

10. "Show Case" 1, 1, September 9, 1980, Lincoln Senior Center, in Robert Havighurst Papers, Box 188, Folder 12, University of Chicago; Sharon R. Kaufman, *The Ageless Self: Sources of Meaning in Late Life* (Madison: University of Wisconsin Press, 1986), 5.

11. David Bouchier, "The Golden Years," *Globe and Mail*, August 15, 1990, A11; Linda Barrett Osborne, "Summer Schools for Senior Citizens," *Washington Post*, April 21, 1985, ER6; William Smart, "Sponsored Social Events Help Senior Citizens Ease Back into Dating," *Seattle Times*, October 13, 1986, J5.

12. Alfred C. Kinsey, Wardell B. Pomeroy, and Clyde E. Martin, *Sexual Behavior in the Human Male* (Bloomington: Indiana University Press, 1948), 218–263, on the decline of sexual activity in older men. The companion volume on women briefly mentions the persistence of sexual desire and activity into older age. Alfred C. Kinsey et al., *Sexual Behavior in the Human Female* (Bloomington: Indiana University Press, 1953), 353.

13. For an overview of the early wave, see Kate Ludeman, "The Sexuality of the Older Person: Review of the Literature," *The Gerontologist* 21 (1981): 203–208; Arnold Arluke, Jack Levin, and John Suchwalko, "Sexuality and Romance in Advice Books for the Elderly," *The Gerontologist* 24 (1984): 415–419; Ruth Westheimer, "Adjust Schedules for Lovemaking," *Chicago Sun-Times*, April 1, 1987, 48.

14. Doress-Worters and Siegal et al., *Ourselves, Growing Older*, chap. 7; Arno Karlen, "Appreciating the Sexual You," *Modern Maturity*, April 1992, 53.

15. Sophia is less commonly involved in this sort of banter, but see *The Golden Girls*, season 6, episode 10, "Girls Just Wanna Have Fun Before They Die," dir. Matthew Diamond, aired November 24, 1990; for the orgasm talk, see season 1, episode 22, "Job Hunting," dir. Paul Bogart, aired March 8, 1986, at 20:00; *The Golden Girls*, season 1, episode 3, "Rose the Prude," dir. Jim Drake, aired September 28, 1985.

16. Ken Dychtwald and Joe Flower, *Age Wave: The Challenges and Opportunities of an Aging America* (New York: St Martin's Press, 1989), xiii; Ken Dychtwald, *Radical Curiosity: One Man's Search for Cosmic Magic and a Purposeful Life* (Los Angeles: Unnamed Press, 2021), 136.

17. Ken Dychtwald, "Sex Shouldn't Be a Dirty Word for Older People," *Chicago Sun-Times*, July 2, 1989, 35; Dychtwald and Flower, *Age Wave*, 2 (mates), 3 (retire), 235 (matrix), 262 (housing).

18. Barbara Macdonald, "Do You Remember Me?" *Sinister Wisdom* 10 (Summer 1979): 9–15, here 14; Joan Nestle, "Surviving and More: An Interview with Mabel Hampton," *Sinister Wisdom* 10 (Summer 1979): 19–24. I really do recommend that readers take a look at this amazing issue; it's available,

as of June 2023, at http://sinisterwisdom.org/sites/default/files/Sinister%20 Wisdom%2010.pdf. Feminist and lesbian writings on old age from this period were collected in Barbara Macdonald and Cynthia Rich, *Look Me in the Eye: Old Women, Aging, and Ageism* (San Francisco: Spinsters Ink, 1983); Richard A. Friend, "Gayging: Adjustment and the Older Gay Male," *Alternative Lifestyles* 3 (1980): 234 (competence); for a literature review, see Karen I. Fredriksen-Goldsen and Anna Muraco, "Aging and Sexual Orientation: A 25-Year Review of the Literature," *Research on Aging* 32 (2010): 372–413; the landmark study was Raymond Berger, *Gay and Gray: The Older Homosexual Man* (Urbana: University of Illinois Press, 1982).

19. Karlen, "Appreciating the Sexual You," 53; Louis Peitzman, "Why Gay Men Still Love 'The Golden Girls,'" *Buzzfeed*, March 10, 2014, www.buzzfeed .com/louispeitzman/why-gay-men-still-love-the-golden-girls; *The Golden Girls*, season 2, episode 25, "Isn't It Romantic?," dir. Terry Hughes, aired November 8, 1986; *The Golden Girls*, season 5, episode 19, "72 Hours," dir. Terry Hughes, aired February 17, 1990, at 16:00.

20. *The Golden Girls*, season 1, episode 10, "The Heart Attack," dir. Jim Drake, aired November 23, 1985, at 4:00; *The Golden Girls*, season 6, episode 2, "Once in St Olaf," dir. Matthew Diamond, aired September 29, 1990.

21. *The Golden Girls*, season 5, episode 1, "Sick and Tired: Part 1," dir. Terry Hughes, September 23, 1989, at 7:00 (fine), 14:00 (cruise/color), 17:00 (crazy); *The Golden Girls*, season 5, episode 2, "Sick and Tired: Part 2," dir. Terry Hughes, aired September 30, 1989, at 21:00.

22. On this episode and the long history of "hysterical" women in the clinic, see Amanda Stayton and Bridget Keown, "*Golden Girls*, Chronic Fatigue Syndrome, and the Legacies of Hysteria," *Nursing Clio*, September 25, 2018, https:// nursingclio.org/2018/09/25/golden-girls-chronic-fatigue-syndrome-and-the-legacies -of-hysteria/; Doress-Worters and Siegal et al., *Ourselves, Growing Older*, 216.

23. Eileen Berg, "Senior Citizens Care Most About Health Needs, Poll Finds," *American Medical News*, August 17, 1990, 10; *Los Angeles Times* letter reproduced as appendix A in Robert L. Kane et al., *Geriatrics in the United States: Manpower Projections and Training Considerations* (RAND Report R-2543- HJK, May 1980); *House of God* quoted in Louise Aronson, *Elderhood: Redefining Aging, Transforming Medicine, Reimagining Life* (New York: Bloomsbury, 2019), 44; Sharon R. Kaufman, "Old Age, Disease, and the Discourse on Risk: Geriatric Assessment in U.S. Health Care," *Medical Anthropology Quarterly* 8 (1994): 430–447; Michele Greene et al., "Ageism in the Medical Encounter," *Language and Communication* 6 (1986): 113–124.

24. Kane et al., *Geriatrics in the United States*, 14–15 for stats; see also *Training Physicians to Care for Older Americans: Progress, Obstacles, and Future Directions* (Washington, DC: National Academies Press, 1994); *Rising Health*

Care Costs and the Elderly: Hearings Before the Select Committee on Aging, House of Representatives, January 20, 1984 (Washington, DC: Government Printing Office, 1984).

25. On the decline of medical authority and the rise of managed care, see Mark Schlesinger, "A Loss of Faith: The Sources of Reduced Political Legitimacy for the American Medical Profession," *Milbank Quarterly* 80 (2002): 185–235.

26. Theodore R. Marmor and Kip Sullivan, "Medicare at 50: Why Medicare-for-All Did Not Take Place," *Yale Journal of Health Policy, Law and Ethics* 15 (2015): 141–184; "Gov. Lamm Asserts Elderly, If Very Ill, Have 'Duty to Die,'" *New York Times,* March 29, 1984, A16; Nancy Jecker, "Should We Ration Health Care?" *Journal of Medical Humanities* 10 (1989): 77–90.

27. "The Heart Attack," at 18:00.

28. Doress-Worters and Siegal et al., *Ourselves, Growing Older,* 4.

29. Edna Bell-Pearson, "Sitting Pretty," *American Fitness* 12 (1994): 42. The focus on fitness was not restricted to older people, of course. Danielle Freedman, *Let's Get Physical: How Women Discovered Exercise and Reshaped the World* (New York: Putnam, 2022).

30. Ian Ledgerwood, "Report on Retirement 'Cities,'" *Modern Maturity,* August-September 1969, 21–23; Paula Patyk, "The Right Spa for You," *50 Plus,* March 1984, 60–65; Len Albin, "The Pied Piper of Health," *50 Plus,* March 1984, 28–35; ad for Timex Healthcheck, back cover of same issue; Diane Eicher, "Better Body Mechanics," *Modern Maturity,* February 1991, 68–71, 84; "But Don't Toss Your Gym Shoes," *Modern Maturity,* February 1991, 88; John Wood, "Staying Well," *Modern Maturity,* April 1988, 83.

31. Bell-Pearson, "Sitting Pretty" (referring to the in-person version).

32. Dychtwald and Flower, *Age Wave,* xvi (disregard), 78–79 (rationing), 124 (fitness); see also Ken Dychtwald, ed., *Wellness and Health Promotion for the Elderly* (Rockville, MD: Aspen, 1986), foreword by Robert Butler; Dychtwald, *Radical Curiosity,* 124 (conscious), 127 (1986 founding), 133–137 (CBS/Time/Alliance).

33. James Fries, "Aging, Natural Death, and the Compression of Morbidity," *New England Journal of Medicine* 303, no. 3 (July 17, 1980): 130.

34. Rita Ricardo-Campbell, *The Economics and Politics of Health* (Chapel Hill: University of North Carolina Press, 1982), 71; Donald M. Vickery and James F. Fries, *Take Care of Yourself: A Consumer's Guide to Medical Care* (Reading, MA: Addison-Wesley, 1978), 1, 5, 10 (charts).

35. Author's interview with John Rowe by telephone, July 4, 2022.

36. John Rowe and Robert Kahn, *Successful Aging* (New York: Random House, 1998), 37; Kenneth Minaker and John Rowe, "Health and Disease Among the Oldest Old: A Clinical Perspective," *Milbank Memorial Fund Quarterly* 62 (1985): 322–323; Elizabeth Sanger, "Mount Sinai Names New President,"

Newsday, July 3, 1988, 19; Jim Montague, "How One New York Hospital Is Moving to Head Managed Care Off at the Pass," *Hospitals and Health Networks* 70 (1996): 22–23; Elisabeth Bumiller, "Doctor for a Ruptured Hospital Merger Deal," *New York Times*, March 11, 1990, 2; Laura B. Benko, "Rowe to the Rescue," *Modern Healthcare* 30 (September 11, 2000): 14.

37. Sarah Lamb, ed., *Successful Aging as a Contemporary Obsession: Global Perspectives* (New Brunswick, NJ: Rutgers University Press, 2017); Peter Conrad, *The Medicalization of Society: On the Transformation of Human Conditions into Treatable Disorders* (Baltimore, MD: Johns Hopkins University Press, 2007), 142.

38. Jane Bryant Quinn, "Medicare Choices Get Complicated," *Times Union* (Albany, NY), October 5, 1988, C8.

39. Sharon M. Willcox et al., "Inappropriate Drug Prescribing for the Community-Dwelling Elderly," *JAMA* 272 (1994): 293; Christina Charlesworth et al., "Polypharmacy Among Adults Aged 65 Years and Older in the United States: 1988–2010," *Journal of Gerontology, Series A* 70 (2015): 989.

40. Conrad, *Medicalization of Society*, chap. 2, 42; Leonore Tiefer, "The Medicalization of Impotence: Normalizing Phallocentrism," *Gender and Society* 8 (1994): 363–377.

41. On women's response to Viagra, see Meika Loe, *The Rise of Viagra: How the Little Blue Pill Changed Sex in America* (New York: NYU Press, 2004), 111–113; for this quotation, see letters to the editor, *Modern Maturity*, August 1992, 12.

42. Mark Schlesinger, "Medicare and the Social Transformations of American Elders," in *Medicare and Medicaid at 50: America's Entitlement Programs in the Age of Affordable Care*, ed. Alan B. Cohen et al. (New York: Oxford University Press, 2015), 139; for the 1975 number, *Medicare Gaps and Limitations: Hearing Before the Subcommittee on Health and Long-Term Care of the House Select Committee on Aging*, October 18, 1977 (Washington, DC: Government Printing Office, 1977), 45; for the 2016 number, Juliette Cubanski, *How Much Do Medicare Beneficiaries Spend Out of Pocket on Health Care?* (Kaiser Family Foundation Report, November 4, 2019), www.kff.org/medicare/issue-brief/how-much-do-medicare-beneficiaries-spend-out-of-pocket-on-health-care/.

43. Sharon Kaufman, Janet Shim, and Ann Russ, "Revisiting the Biomedicalization of Aging: Clinical Trends and Ethical Challenges," *The Gerontologist* 44 (2004): 732 (characterized), 734 (interviews).

44. "Table V.A4.—Period Life Expectancy," Social Security Administration, 2022, www.ssa.gov/oact/tr/2022/lr5a4.html; Eileen M. Crimmins and Yasuhiko Saito, "Change in the Prevalence of Diseases Among Older Americans: 1984–1994," *Demographic Research* 3 (2000): 1–20; Eileen M. Crimmins and Hiram Beltrán-Sánchez, "Mortality and Morbidity Trends: Is There Compression of Morbidity?," *Journal of Gerontology Series B*, vol. 66 (2011): 75–86.

CHAPTER 9: FROM SECURITY TO RISK

1. Linda Stern, "Start Saving Now to Make Your Children Millionaires," *St. Louis Post-Dispatch*, February 12, 1990, 9. Paul Merriman was also gracious enough to talk about this story with me over the phone on May 10, 2023.

2. Tori G. Roughley, "U.S. News & World Report Survey: Retirement and Inflation," *U.S. News & World Report*, January 9, 2023, www.usnews.com /insurance/life-insurance/retirement-inflation-survey.

3. Stephan F. Gohmann, "Retirement Differences Among the Respondents to the Retirement History Survey," *Journal of Gerontology* 45 (1990): 126.

4. "Case Record: Fannie, Margaret, and Ruth Bauer," *Social Service Review* 12, no. 4 (1938): 651–686.

5. For facts and figures, see US Department of Labor, *Private Pension Plan Bulletin: Historical Tables and Graphs, 1975–2020* (October 2022), www.dol.gov /sites/dolgov/files/ebsa/researchers/statistics/retirement-bulletins/private -pension-plan-bulletin-historical-tables-and-graphs.pdf.

6. Thomas Hungerford et al., "Trends in the Economic Status of the Elderly, 1976–2000," *Social Security Bulletin* 64 (2000), charts 3 and 4, www.ssa.gov /policy/docs/ssb/v64n3/v64n3p12.html.

7. For women in their late fifties, Alicia Munnell, "What Is the Average Retirement Age?," *Society of Actuaries Newsletter*, February 2012, www.soa .org/news-and-publications/newsletters/pension-section-news/2012/february /psn-2012-iss76/what-is-the-average-retirement-age/; for men in the workforce, Wan He et al., *65+ in the United States: 2005*, National Institute on Aging and US Census Bureau (Washington, DC: Government Printing Office, 2005), 83; on early retirement, Selwyn Feinstein, "Early Retirement," *Wall Street Journal*, January 9, 1987, 1; Jonathan Peterson, "The Golden Handshake—or Shove?," *Los Angeles Times*, Orange County ed., June 7, 1985, 1.

8. Samuel H. Preston, "Children and the Elderly: Divergent Paths for America's Dependents," *Demography* 21 (1984): 436; Christine Ross, Sheldon Danzier, and Eugene Smolensky, "The Level and Trend of Poverty in the United States, 1939–1979," *Demography* 24 (1987): 591; Hungerford et al., "Trends in the Economic Status."

9. *The Golden Girls*, season 5, episode 4, "Rose Fights Back," dir. Terry Hughes, aired October 21, 1989, at 2:00, 11:00, 22:00.

10. On bankruptcy, *The Golden Girls*, season 3, episode 10, "The Audit," dir. Terry Hughes, aired November 28, 1987, at 18:00; for the TV set, *The Golden Girls*, season 3, episode 2, "One for the Money," dir. Terry Hughes, aired September 26, 1987; on the purse, Claudia Luther, obituary for Estelle Getty, *Los Angeles Times*, July 23, 2008, www.latimes.com/entertainment/la-me-getty23-2008jul23-story .html; on Social Security, *The Golden Girls*, season 5, episode 15, "Triple Play," dir. Terry Hughes, aired January 27, 1990.

11. Henry Fairlie, "Talkin' 'bout My Generation," *New Republic*, March 28, 1988, 19.

12. Nelson Lichtenstein and Judith Stern, *A Fabulous Failure: The Clinton Presidency and the Transformation of American Capitalism* (Princeton, NJ: Princeton University Press, 2023), 317–325.

13. *Tomorrow's Elderly: Planning for the Baby Boom Generation's Retirement: First Annual Conference of Americans for Generational Equity* (Washington, DC: AGE, 1986); Peter J. Ferrara, ed., *Social Security: Prospects for Real Reform* (Washington, DC: Cato Institute, 1985).

14. Sally Sherman, "Public Attitudes Toward Social Security," *Social Security Bulletin* 52, no. 12 (December 1989): 2–16 for an overview of the data; Dorcas Hardy, "Don't Rely Strictly on Social Security," *Chicago Sun-Times*, July 25, 1989, 22.

15. "Social Security: Invaluable or Outmoded?," *Modern Maturity*, April 1992, 34–46, 84–85; Alan Simpson, "Why We Need Entitlement Reform," *Modern Maturity*, November 1994, 12; Daniel Patrick Moynihan, "The Case Against Entitlement Cuts," *Modern Maturity*, November 1994, 13.

16. Peter Passell, "Pensions or Productivity?," *New York Times*, May 17, 1983, A26. See, for another example, Rich Spencer, "Future May Find Many Without Pension," *Washington Post*, December 25, 1990, A1.

17. The best account of ERISA by far is James Wooten, *The Employee Retirement Income Security Act of 1974: A Political History* (Berkeley: University of California Press, 2004).

18. Michael V. Leonesio et al., "The Increasing Labor Force Participation of Older Workers and Its Effect on the Income of the Aged," *Social Security Bulletin* 72 (2012).

19. "Mandatory Retirement: Position Paper by the Chicago Gray Panthers," n.d. (1980?), in Robert J. Havighurst Papers, Box 176, Folder 17, University of Chicago; Joseph A. Califano Jr., "The Four-Generation Society," *Washington Post*, March 13, 1983, B8.

20. John W. Rowe, "Physiologic Condition and Physical Performance in Older Persons," in *The Promise of Productive Aging: From Biology to Social Policy*, ed. Robert N. Butler et al. (New York: Springer, 1990), 45; Ken Dychtwald and Joe Flower, *Age Wave: The Challenges and Opportunities of an Aging America* (New York: St Martin's Press, 1989), 177; Al Cole, "Demystifying Money Matters," *Modern Maturity*, April 1992, 79.

21. *The Golden Palace*, season 1, episode 1, "The Golden Palace," dir. Terry Hughes, aired September 18, 1992; *Mama's Family*, season 3, episode 16, "Have It Mama's Way," dir. Dave Powers, aired January 24, 1987.

22. Google Ngram on "retirement," performed July 23, 2023; Kristen Gerencher, "What Happened to Retirement Bashes," *Wall Street Journal*, May 7, 2006, 4.

23. G.W., "The End of Retirement," *Cornell Hotel and Restaurant Administration Quarterly* 28, no. 3 (November 1987): 80; Eugene Lehrmann, "Work and Retirement in the '90s," *Modern Maturity*, September 1994, 7.

24. Susan Champlin Taylor, "The End of Retirement," *Modern Maturity*, October 1993, 32–39.

25. Israel Press and Herbert Peterson, "Better Planning for Year-End Taxes," *Journal of Accountancy* 148 (December 1979): 74 for a paragraph on 401(k)s.

26. *Private Pension Plan Bulletin*, 6 for 1990s shift.

27. Thomas Watterson, "Employers Find Something Better Than IRAs for Retirement Savings," *Christian Science Monitor*, April 30, 1982, 11; Jacob Hacker, *The Great Risk Shift: The New Economic Insecurity and the Decline of the American Dream*, rev. ed. (New York: Oxford University Press, 2008), 119.

28. Daniel Cuff, "Do-It-Yourself I.R.A. Plans," *New York Times*, February 13, 1982, sec. 2, p. 32.

29. Merrill Lynch's research is cited frequently in *Contract with America—Savings and Investment: Hearing Before the Ways and Means Committee of the House of Representatives* (Washington, DC: Government Printing Office, 1996). See also Rebecca Cox, "Study Faults Law Curbing IRA Deductions," *American Banker*, May 3, 1989, 1.

30. Don Underwood, "Toward Self-Reliance in Retirement Planning," *Harvard Business Review*, May 1, 1984, 18–20.

31. Don Underwood and Paul B. Brown, *Grow Rich Slowly: The Merrill Lynch Guide to Retirement Planning* (New York: Viking, 1993), xiv (solve), 13 (35 percent), 135 (strangers).

32. Edwin P. Morrow, "The Origin of Financial Planning Professionals," *Financial Services Advisor* 145 (2002): 20; Loren Dunton and Associates, *The Space Age Approach to More Self Discipline* (Littleton, CO: Creative Motivators, 1968); Loren Dunton, *The Vintage Years* (Berkeley, CA: Ten Speed Press, 1978), 4, 25, 29, 92.

33. Dunton, *Vintage Years*, 153; Loren Dunton, "Social Insecurity," *New York Times*, August 16, 1983, A23; Philip N. Gainsborough, "Social Security: It Won't Be Enough," in *Your Book of Financial Planning: The Consumer's Guide to a Better Financial Future*, ed. Loren Dunton (Reston, VA: Reston Publishing, 1983), 28.

34. Helen Huntley, "Sowing the Seeds of Your Retirement," *St. Petersburg Times*, May 11, 1987, 1E.

35. Lawrence Eichler, "How to Milk Your IRA—for All It's Worth," *50 Plus*, January 1986, 66–71; Horace Deets, "Retirement Planning Will Pay Off," *Modern Maturity*, August 1993, 5; E. M. Abramson, "Mastering Your Money," *Modern Maturity*, December 1990, 75, 76, 90.

36. *The Golden Girls*, "The Audit"; Myrna E. DeJesus, "Financial Planning for the Professional Woman," *CPA Journal* 58 (1988): 87; Gretchen Morgenson,

"Inviting the Cat to Take Care of the Canaries," *Forbes*, June 25, 1990, 252–254; "To Read This Summer," *Ms.*, July 1984, 4; "When Can You Cash In?," *Ladies' Home Journal*, September 1984, 50.

37. *The Golden Girls*, "The Audit," at 18:00.

38. T. Rowe Price circulated more than one hundred thousand copies of its version. Jerry Morgan, "A Basic Pre-Retirement Plan," *Newsday*, March 4, 1990, 58; Abramson, "Mastering Your Money," 76.

39. Dorothy A. Brown, "Pensions, Risk, and Race," *Washington and Lee Law Review* 61 (2004): 1529, 1537.

40. Zhe Li and Joseph Dalaker, *Poverty Among the Population Aged 65 and Older* (Congressional Research Service R45791, December 6, 2022), figs. 2 and 9, https://sgp.fas.org/crs/misc/R45791.pdf.

41. Monique Morrissee, Siavash Radpour, and Barbara Schuster, "Chapter 1. Older Workers," *The Older Workers and Retirement Chartbook* (Economic Policy Institute Report, November 16, 2022), www.epi.org/publication/chapter-1-older-workers/; Elissa Chudwin, "Survey: Older Adults Planning to Work in Retirement for Financial Reasons," AARP blog, July 21, 2022, https://blog.aarp.org/fighting-for-you/working-while-retired-survey.

42. Daniel Thompson and Michael D. King, "Income Sources of Older Households: 2017," *Current Population Reports* (US Census Report P70BR-177, February 2022), table 1.

CHAPTER 10: ASSISTED LIVING

1. The clearest treatment of the issue was in *The Golden Girls*, season 6, episode 18, "Older and Wiser," dir. Matthew Diamond, aired February 16, 1991.

2. Andrea Gross, "The Good Daughter," *Ladies' Home Journal*, November 1989, 301–302.

3. Elaine Brody, "Parent Care as a Normative Family Stress," *The Gerontologist* 25 (1985): 21; on the past, Emily K. Abel, *Hearts of Wisdom: American Women Caring for Kin, 1850–1940* (Cambridge, MA: Harvard University Press, 2000); data on the sixty-five-plus and eighty-five-plus population from Wan He et al., *65+ in the United States: 2005*, National Institute on Aging and US Census Bureau (Washington, DC: Government Printing Office, 2005), table 2-1; on surviving parents, Brody, "Parent Care as a Normative Family Stress," 20; on chronic illness, Ernest M. Gruenberg, "The Failures of Success," *Milbank Quarterly* 55 (1977): 3–24; S. Jay Olshansky and Brian A. Ault, "The Fourth Stage of the Epidemiological Transition: The Age of Delayed Degenerative Diseases," *Milbank Quarterly* 64 (1986): 355–393.

4. Bernice Neugarten, "The Future of the Young-Old," *The Gerontologist* 15 (1975): 4–9.

5. US Department of Health, Education, and Welfare (DHEW), *Public Policy and the Frail Elderly: A Staff Report*, DHEW Pub. No. 79-20959 (Washington, DC, 1978), 1 (persons), v (term). Fernando Torres-Gill, a member of the council, wrote

to me that the main impetus for this distinction between the young-old and the old-old was Bernice Neugarten (personal email, June 30, 2023). This is confirmed by Neugarten's prominence in Cleonice Tavani (main author of the 1978 report), "Meeting the Needs of the Oldest Old," *Aging* 291–292 (January/February 1979): 2–7.

6. Robert Katzman, "The Prevalence and Malignancy of Alzheimer's Disease," *Archives of Neurology* 33 (1976): 216–218.

7. Office of Technology Assessment, *Losing a Million Minds: Confronting the Tragedy of Alzheimer's Disease and Other Dementias* (Washington, DC: Government Printing Office, 1987), 3. In fact, Americans were experiencing something of a "dementia bubble" in the 1980s, and dementia rates began declining soon after. Claudia L. Satizabal et al., "Incidence of Dementia over Three Decades in the Framingham Heart Study," *New England Journal of Medicine* 374 (2016): 523–532.

8. Alicia Munnell, "What Is the Average Retirement Age?," *Society of Actuaries Newsletter*, February 2012, www.soa.org/news-and-publications/news letters/pension-section-news/2012/february/psn-2012-iss76/what-is-the-average -retirement-age/; Eileen Boris and Jennifer Klein, *Caring for America: Home Health Workers in the Shadow of the Welfare State* (New York: Oxford University Press, 2012), 159.

9. Susan Eisenhandler, "The Asphalt Identikit: Old Age and the Driver's License," *International Journal of Aging and Development* 30 (1990): 1–14.

10. Darius Lakdawalla and Tomas Philipson, "Aging and the Growth of Long-Term Care" (NBER Working Paper 6980, February 1999), fig. 1, www.nber .org/system/files/working_papers/w6980/w6980.pdf; Joseph Bondar, "Effects of the Social Security Benefit Increase, December 1988," *Social Security Bulletin* 52, 6 (June 1989): 19.

11.Philip Slopane and Lisa Gwyther, "Nursing Homes," *Journal of the American Medical Association* 244 (1980): 1840; Kate Greer, "What's Happening to American Families?" *Better Homes & Gardens*, November 1988, 60; Elaine Brody, *Women in the Middle: Their Parent-Care Years* (New York: Springer, 1990), 236.

12. Committee on the Quality of Care in Nursing Homes, *The National Imperative to Improve Nursing Home Quality* (Washington, DC: National Academies Press, 2022), 26 and throughout; also, a more candid interview with one of that study's authors can be found in Jay Caspian Kang, "Nursing Homes Are in Crisis," *New York Times*, April 14, 2022, www.nytimes.com/2022/04/14 /opinion/nursing-homes-crisis.html; for a kindred analysis from the ground, see Robert Pear, "U.S. Lags on Rules Mandated in 1987 for Nursing Care," *New York Times*, September 17, 1990, A1.

13. Bruce Vladeck, *Unloving Care: The Nursing Home Tragedy* (New York: Basic Books, 1980), 21; Louise Woerner and Karen Casper, "Alzheimer's Care: A Home Health Model," *American Journal of Alzheimer's Disease and Other Dementias* 2 (1987): 26.

14. For an early attempt to canvass the phrase and the field, see Connie J. Evashwick and Lawrence J. Weiss, eds., *Managing the Continuum of Care* (Rockville, MD: Aspen, 1987).

15. The variability across geography was emphasized by Mary Bethel, chair of the North Carolina Coalition on Aging, when Elaijah Lapay and I interviewed her on July 30, 2021; John Grana and Burton Dunlop, *Long-Term Care in Western Europe and Canada: Implications for the United States: An Information Paper Prepared for Senate Committee on Aging* (Washington, DC: U.S. Government Printing Office, 1984); Brahna Trager, "Non-Institutional Long-Term Care in England, France, and Sweden," *Home Health Care Services Quarterly* 5 (1985): 239; DHEW, *Public Policy and the Frail Elderly*, 58; *Home Health Care, Future Policy: Joint Hearing Before Committee on Labor and Human Resources and Special Committee on Aging, US Senate*, November 23, 1980 (Washington, DC: Government Printing Office, 1981), 130, 169.

16. Horace Deets to AARP Membership, May 6, 1988, Edward Roybal Archives, Box 471, Folder 1, UCLA.

17. DHEW, *Public Policy and the Frail Elderly*; Cleonice Tavani, "Briefing for Candidates," *Baltimore Sun*, August 6, 1962, 12; Tavani, "Meeting the Needs of the Oldest Old," 2–7.

18. DHEW, *Public Policy and the Frail Elderly*, 59, 10.

19. DHEW, *Public Policy and the Frail Elderly*, 58, 130.

20. Catherine Foster Alter, "The Changing Structure of Elderly Service Delivery Systems," *The Gerontologist* 28 (1988): 91–98.

21. Nancy A. Miller, Sarah Ramsland, and Charlene Harrington, "Trends and Issues in the Medicaid 1915(c) Waiver Program," *Health Care Financing Review* 20 (1999): 139 for the budgets and state-by-state stats.

22. Jessica Townsend, "On Lok Senior Health Services: San Francisco, California," in Institute of Medicine, Committee on Service Integration, *Health Services Integration: Lessons for the 1980s*, vol. 3 (Washington, DC: National Academy Press, 1982), 144–146. More generally, see Amanda J. Lehning and Michael J. Austin, "On Lok: A Pioneering Long-Term Care Organization for the Elderly (1971–2008)," *Journal of Evidence-Based Social Work* 8 (2011): 1–2, 218–234.

23. Rick T. Zawadski and Marie-Louise Ansak, "Consolidating Community-Based Long-Term Care: Early Returns from the On Lok Demonstration," *The Gerontologist* 23 (1983): 364–369; Townsend, "On Lok Senior Health Services," 147–148.

24. Townsend, "On Lok Senior Health Services," 155; Thomas Bodenheimer, "Long-Term Care for Frail Elderly People: The On Lok Model," *New England Journal of Medicine* 341 (1999): 1324–1328.

25. Marie-Louise Ansak, interviewed by Leah McGarrigle (1996–1997), Regional Oral History Office, Bancroft Library, University of California, Berkeley,

59–62, https://digitalassets.lib.berkeley.edu/roho/ucb/text/ansak_marie-louise
pdf.

26. Mary Lou Budnick, "Community Care Program," *Issues and Events* (newsletter of Chicago Department on Aging and Disability), August 1985, 5–6, in Robert J. Havighurst Papers, Box 173, Folder 2, University of Chicago; Ruth Bennett et al., eds., *Coordinated Service Delivery Systems for the Elderly: New Approaches for Care and Referral in New York State* (New York: Haworth Press, 1984), xiii.

27. *Home Health Care, Future Policy*, 126; Bodenheimer, "Long-Term Care for Frail Elderly People."

28. "Most Can't Afford Nursing," *Orlando Sentinel*, January 23, 1990, A7.

29. Kenneth Harney, "'Assisted Living' Concept Gains as Alternative for Elderly," *Washington Post*, February 25, 1989, 1F.

30. Public Policy Institute (AARP), *Assisted Living in the United States: A New Paradigm for Residential Care for Frail Older Persons?* (Washington, DC: AARP, 1993), preface. On the Klaassens, "Compassion Pays," *Forbes*, February 24, 1997, 86, 90.

31. Roger Ricklefs, "Care for Life: Communities for Aged Offer 'Total Security,'" *Wall Street Journal*, November 25, 1988, 1; Robert Preer, "Assisted Living Comes to Public Housing," *Boston Globe*, June 11, 2000, WKS 1.

32. "Most Can't Afford Nursing"; "The Selling of Fear: Emergency Help for the Elderly," *Consumer Reports*, January 1, 1991, 5; David Abromowitz and Rebecca Plaut, "Assisted Living for Low-Income Seniors," *Journal of Affordable Housing and Community Development Law* 5 (1995): 63–72 (there were exceptions here, and Medicaid could sometimes be used to cover some expenses at some assisted-living facilities, which were in any case vaguely defined); Nancy Stone Hindlian, "Interview with Dorothy Kirsten French," *American Journal of Alzheimer's Care and Research* 2, no. 6 (November 1987): 19.

33. Brody, "Parent Care as a Normative Family Stress," 21; Tish Sommers and Laurie Shields, *Women Take Care: The Consequences of Caregiving in Today's Society* (Gainesville, FL: Triad Publishing, 1987), 92.

34. Erin Greig, "Historical Perspectives of Alzheimer's Disease and Caregiving" (Signature Work Product, Duke Kunshan University, March 2023).

35. Brody, *Women in the Middle*, 35; A. Horowitz, "Sons and Daughters as Caregivers to Older Parents: Differences in Role Performance and Consequences," *The Gerontologist* 25 (1985): 612–617; Jason Karlawish, *The Problem of Alzheimer's: How Science, Culture, and Politics Turned a Rare Disease into a Crisis and What We Can Do About It* (New York: St. Martin's Press, 2021), 120, 122–124, 129–131.

36. "Help for Families and Friends of Alcoholics," *Aging* 361 (Summer 1990): 49.

37. Gross, "Good Daughter," 304.

38. Gross, "Good Daughter," 302; Sommers and Shields, *Women Take Care*, 35, 27.

39. Nancy Mace and Peter Rabins, *The 36-Hour Day* (Baltimore, MD: Johns Hopkins University Press, 1981) (this went through many editions); Steven H. Zarit, Nancy K. Orr, and Judy M. Zarit, *The Hidden Victims of Alzheimer's Disease: Families Under Stress* (New York: NYU Press, 1985), 69; Rosemary Santini and Katherine Barrett, "The Tragedy of Rita Hayworth," *Ladies' Home Journal*, January 1983, 139; Rochelle Distelheim, "Ambushed by Alzheimer's," *Woman's Day*, November 24, 1987, 128.

40. Steven Zarit, Pamela Todd, and Judy Zarit, "Subjective Burden of Husbands and Wives as Caregivers: A Longitudinal Study," *The Gerontologist* 26 (1986): 260–266; Stephen Berman and Meryl Rappaport, "Social Work and Alzheimer's Disease," *Social Work in Health Care* 10 (1985): 68; Sommers and Shields, *Women Take Care*, 33, 28.

41. Marcie Parker et al., "Informal Caregiving: Its Importance in Long-Term Care," *Journal of Home Health Care Practice* 2 (1989): 64; Joan K. Davitt and Sunha Choi, "Tracing the History of Medicare Home Health Care: The Impact of Policy on Benefit Use," *Journal of Sociology and Social Welfare* 35 (2008): 252; Karl Pillemer and David Finkelhor, "The Prevalence of Elder Abuse: A Random Sample Survey," *The Gerontologist* 28 (1988): 55; Jill Lawrence, "No Federal Standards Regulate Home Health Aides," *Washington Post*, April 28, 1987, HE9.

42. Brody, *Women in the Middle*, 230, 247; Zarit, Orr, and Zarit, *Hidden Victims of Alzheimer's Disease*, 4–5.

43. DHEW, *Public Policy and the Frail Elderly*, 34.

44. Melinda Cooper, *Family Values: Between Neoliberalism and the New Social Conservatism* (New York: Zone Books, 2017).

45. Robert Self, *All in the Family: The Realignment of American Democracy Since the 1960s* (New York: Hill and Wang, 2012), 379.

46. Gross, "Good Daughter," 303; Brody, "Parent Care as a Normative Family Stress," 26. I have written elsewhere on the affective logic of neoliberalism, which impacted many other spheres at the same time. James Chappel, "A Servant Heart: How Neoliberalism Came to Be," *Boston Review*, November 2015, www.bostonreview.net/articles/james-chappel-servant-heart-religion-neoliberalism/.

47. John Carmody, "The TV Volume," *Washington Post*, September 22, 1987, D08; *The Golden Girls*, season 3, episode 1, "Old Friends," dir. Terry Hughes, aired September 19, 1987, at 21:00.

48. "Demands of an Aging Population: Family Solutions," *Christianity Today*, May 1980, 12–13; William F. May, "New Ways to Honor Father and Mother," *Christianity Today*, October 5, 1984, 39–44.

49. Laura Katz Olson, *Elder Care Journey: A View from the Front Lines* (Albany, NY: SUNY Press, 2016).

50. Pat Kingcade, "Caring for the Aging," *Miami Herald*, March 22, 1988, 2D; "Meetings," *Boca Raton News*, January 5, 1993, 2E; advertisement for the Atrium, *Boca Raton News*, October 21, 1990, 6G. For the price of the Atrium, Gross, "Good Daughter," 307.

CONCLUSION: MAKE AMERICA OLD AGAIN

1. Em Shrider, "Poverty Rate for the Black Population," US Census Bureau, September 12, 2023, www.census.gov/library/stories/2023/09/black-poverty-rate.html.

2. Astra Taylor, *The Age of Insecurity: Coming Together as Things Fall Apart* (Toronto, ON: House of Anansi Press, 2023).

3. On Medicare's reduction of financial risk, see Silvia Barcellos and Mireille Jacobson, "The Effects of Medicare on Medical Expenditure Risk and Financial Strain," *American Economic Journal: Economic Policy* 7 (2015): 41–70.

4. Christopher J. Cronin and William N. Evans, "Nursing Home Quality, COVID-19 Deaths, and Excess Mortality," *Journal of Health Economics* 82 (2022): fig. A3.

5. "Get the Facts on Economic Security for Seniors," National Council on Aging, June 8, 2023, www.ncoa.org/article/get-the-facts-on-economic-security-for-seniors.

6. Andrea Shalai, "Aging Population to Hit U.S. Population Like a Ton of Bricks," Reuters, July 12, 2021, www.reuters.com/world/us/aging-population-hit-us-economy-like-ton-bricks-us-commerce-secretary-2021-07-12/; C. Eugene Steuerle and Glenn Kramon, "For the Good of the Country, Older Americans Should Work More and Take Less," *New York Times*, October 26, 2023, www.nytimes.com/2023/10/26/opinion/social-security-medicare-aging.html.

7. For a guide to senior mobilization that offers more of a political scientist's perspective than I do here, see Andrea Louise Campbell, *How Policies Make Citizens: Senior Political Activism and the American Welfare State* (Princeton, NJ: Princeton University Press, 2003).

8. Amanda Duarte and Mike Also, "Who You Calling 'Young Lady'?" AARP, February 2, 2018, www.aarp.org/disrupt-aging/stories/ideas/info-2018/ageist-language-glossary.html; Louise Aronson, *Elderhood: Redefining Aging, Transforming Medicine, Reimagining Life* (New York: Bloomsbury, 2019), 71.

9. US Census Bureau, *General Population Characteristics, 1980* (May 1983), table 48, www2.census.gov/prod2/decennial/documents/1980/1980censusofpopu8011u_bw.pdf; Administration for Community Living, *2020 Profile of Hispanic Americans Age 65 and Over* (2021), 3, https://acl.gov/sites/default/files/Profile%20of%20OA/HispanicProfileReport2021.pdf; Thomas Hungerford et al., "Trends in the Economic Status of the Elderly, 1976–2000," *Social Security Bulletin* 64 (2000), chart 2.

10. Reed Abelson and Jordan Rau, "Facing Financial Ruin as Costs Soar

for Elder Care," *New York Times*, November 15, 2023, www.nytimes.com /2023/11/14/health/long-term-care-facilities-costs.html; US Department of Health and Human Services, *2021 Profile of Older Americans* (November 2022), 12, https://acl.gov/sites/default/files/Profile%20of%20OA/2021%20Profile%20of%20 OA/2021ProfileOlderAmericans_508.pdf.

11. Ezekiel J. Emanuel, "Why I Hope to Die at 75," *The Atlantic*, October 2014, 74–81.

12. Eileen Boris and Jennifer Klein, *Caring for America: Home Health Workers in the Shadow of the Welfare State* (New York: Oxford University Press, 2012), 160–161; Kenneth M. Langa et al., "The Explosion in Paid Home Health Care in the 1990s: Who Received the Additional Services?," *Medical Care* 39 (2001): 147–148; Rhacel Parreñas, *Servants of Globalization: Migration and Domestic Work*, 2nd ed. (Palo Alto, CA: Stanford University Press, 2015), chap. 7.

13. John W. Rowe, "The US Eldercare Workforce Is Falling Further Behind," *Nature Aging* 1 (2021): 328; Saif Khairat et al., "U.S. Nursing Home Quality Ratings Associated with COVID-19 Cases and Deaths," *Journal of the American Medical Directors Association* 22 (2021): 2021–2025; David C. Grabowski, Jonathan Gruber, and Brian McGarry, "Immigration, the Long-Term Care Workforce, and Elder Outcomes in the US" (National Bureau of Economic Research, working paper 30960, February 2023), www.nber.org/papers/w30960.

14. Parreñas, *Servants of Globalization*, 180–181.

15. Olga Madar, "The Growing Challenge of Leisure," *Free Labour World*, March 1968, 16–18.

16. Bridgett Ennis, "What Baby Boomers Can Do," *Yale Climate Connections*, June 20, 2023, https://yaleclimateconnections.org/2023/06/what -baby-boomers-can-do-about-climate-change/.

17. D'Vera Cohn et al., "The Demographics of Multigenerational House- holds," Pew Research Center, March 24, 2022, www.pewresearch.org/social -trends/2022/03/24/the-demographics-of-multigenerational-households; Scott Ball and Kathryn Lawler, "The Evolving Promise and Potential of the Granny Flat," *Generations* 44 (2020): 1–8; Evelyn Long, "Why Climate Activists Are Interested in Accessory Dwelling Units," *Environmental Magazine*, January 28, 2021, https://emagazine.com/why-climate-activists-are-interested-in-accessory -dwelling-units/. For an excellent overview of all of this, see Danielle Arigoni, *Climate Resilience for an Aging Nation* (Washington, DC: Island Press, 2023).

18. Julie Kashen, Sarah Jane Glynn, and Amanda Novello, "How COVID-19 Sent Women's Workforce Progress Backward," Center for American Progress, October 30, 2020, www.americanprogress.org/article/covid-19-sent-womens -workforce-progress-backward/.

19. Ai-Jen Poo with Ariane Conrad, *The Age of Dignity: Preparing for the Elder Boom in a Changing America* (New York: New Press, 2015).

INDEX

INDEX

INDEX

INDEX

INDEX

Roosevelt, Franklin D., 42, 46–47, 54, 60–61. *See also* Social Security
Rosow, Irving, 99
Rothbard, Murray, 155
Rowe, John, 220–223, 239
Roybal, Edward, 147, 260
Ruff, Howard, 156
Rusher, William, 155

Sanford and Son (TV show), 168, 169
Saturday Night Live (TV show), 164
SCORE (Service Corps of Retired Executives), 80
segregation, 91, 96
self-care, 201–203, 217–224. *See also* successful aging
Senate Committee on Aging, 167
Senior Action in a Gay Environment, 122
senior centers, 98, 106–111, 128–130
Senior Citizen (magazine), 79–80, 194
"senior citizens," as term, 66–68, 77–79, 178, 285–286
Senior Citizens' Freedom to Work Act, 238
senior citizenship, 80–83
Senior Olympics, 201–203
service, 80–81
Service Corps of Retired Executives (SCORE), 80
Seventh-Day Adventists, 110
sexuality, 210–214, 225–226
Sexually Speaking (radio program), 210–211
Shannon, James, 35
The Shining (film), 141
Shock, Nathan, 146
Simkins v. Moses Cone (1963), 91
Sinclair, Upton, 47, 57
Sinister Wisdom (journal), 213–214
Sit and Be Fit (TV show), 218–219, 220
slave societies, 28–29, 34–35. *See also* enslaved people; National Ex-Slave Mutual Relief, Bounty, and Pension Association
sociability, 109, 190, 191–192. *See also* leisure

Social Security, 43–62. *See also* financial planning; Medicare; older people; pensions
overview, 9
1900–1940 era, 43–62
1900–1975 era, 71, 127, 131–132, 145–147, 152–165
1975–2000 era, 196–197, 199–200, 230–231, 235, 236–237, 245, 249
AARP's views on, 196–197, 236–237
age equality's effect on, 196–197, 199–200
alternatives to in 1930s, 45–57
Black people's participation in, 58, 61–62, 71, 126–127
capacity for evolution of, 61–62
compared to Townsend Plan, 57
conservatives' views of, 155–157, 159, 165, 236–237, 245
criticisms of, 152–164, 235
defined, 44–45
development of, 53–62
distrust of, 156–157, 230
goal of, 54–57
impact of economy on, 155
inclusivity of, 61–62
inequities of, 58–59, 71, 127, 131–132, 231
liberals' views of, 158–164, 235, 237
OAA, 56–57, 60, 85–86
OAI, 57, 60
premise of, 57
privatization of, 165
purpose of, 59–61
reception of, 59
reformation of, 293–294
revenue neutrality of, 44
role in developing a concept of old age, 44
and Roosevelt, 42, 46–47, 54, 60–61
stalling of, 145–147, 155–165
success of, 44, 249, 279–280
support for, 152
and Townsend Plan, 45, 48–53
unsustainability of, 4–5, 235, 236, 283

355

INDEX

James Chappel is the Gilhuly Family Associate Professor of History at Duke University and a senior fellow at the Duke Aging Center. The author of *Catholic Modern*, he has written articles for the *New York Times*, *The Nation*, and the *New Republic*. He lives in Durham, North Carolina.